To Harry, Jean, and Kelvin who provide constant support

~Liz

To Armin, Alan, Betsy, Betty, Bob, Brian, Carol, Carolyn, Catherine, Don D., Don W., Janet, Jay, Judy, Kathy, Kathleen, Ken, James, JimBob, Leslie, Mary, Stephen, Tom and Pam; with whom I have shared special moments, and whose generous gifts of beauty, creativity, dedication, friendship, love, wisdom and support have inspired and sustained me

~Chuck

Contents

Foreword by Dr. John P. Robinson   xi

Preface   xiii

Contributing Authors   xv

Introduction   xvii

CHAPTER   1   *An Introduction to Occupation*   1

Chapter Profile   1
Introduction   2
Reconsidering the Meaning of Occupation   2
How Do You Occupy Your Time?   2
What Occupies You?   6
What Is Your Occupation?   8
Why Are Some People Occupied While Others Are Unoccupied?   16
What Is the History of Occupation?   19
Occupations and Well-Being   22
Chapter Summary   23
References   23

CHAPTER   2   *The Study of Occupation*   29

Chapter Profile   29
Introduction   30
Ways of Knowing   30
Methods of Inquiry for the Study of Occupation   34
Understanding Who   38
Understanding What   38
Understanding When   40

Understanding Where   41
Understanding How   42
Understanding Why   43
Chapter Summary   44
References   44
Endnotes 46

CHAPTER   3 *What Is Occupation? Interdisciplinary Perspectives on Defining and Classifying Human Activity   47*

Chapter Profile   47
Introduction   48
Occupation in Occupational Therapy and Occupational Science   49
Occupation in the Social Sciences   53
Occupation in Government Statistics   55
Chapter Summary   59
References   59
Endnotes   60

CHAPTER   4 *What Do People Do?   63*

Chapter Profile   63
Introduction   64
The Structure of Daily Occupations   64
Conceptualizing What People Do   65
Factors Influencing What People Do   70
Why Study What People Do?   74
How Do We Find Out What People Do?   75
What Do People Do?   77
Chapter Summary   87
References   88

CHAPTER   5 *Occupational Development   91*

Chapter Profile   91
Introduction   92
An Occupational Perspective on Development   93
Interactionism: A Framework for Occupational Development   96
Chapter Summary   115
References   115
Endnotes   119

CHAPTER 6 *Occupation and Identity: Becoming Who We Are Through What We Do* **121**

Chapter Profile   121
Introduction   122
What Motivates Human Occupation?   122
Motivational Factors   123
Maslow's Theory of Needs   126
Goals: External Influences That Shape the Self   127
Achievement Motivation   129
Motivation and Personality   130
Holland's Theory of Vocational Choice   131
Leisure, Occupational Choice, and Identity   131
Flow   133
Occupation and Identity: An Integration of Ideas   133
Chapter Summary   137
References   138

CHAPTER 7 *The Occupational Nature of Communities*   **141**

Chapter Profile   141
Introduction   142
What Makes Communities Inherently Social and Occupational?
    Experiencing Shared Occupations   142
How and Why Did Group Living in Communities Develop?
    Evolutionary Highlights in Developing the Occupational
    Nature of Communities   148
How and Why Do Occupations Determine a Community's Potential to
    Flounder or Flourish?   154
Chapter Summary   167
References   167

CHAPTER 8 *Occupations and Places*   **173**

Chapter Profile   173
Introduction   174
Understanding Place   174
Occupations as Experiences in Places   180
How Places Influence Occupation   182
Places as Environments for Learning and Play   184
How Occupations Influence Places   186

Place, Occupations, and Well-Being   191
Chapter Summary   193
References   194

CHAPTER   9 *Occupations as a Means for Individual and Group Participation in Life*   **197**

Chapter Profile   197
Introduction   197
Fundamental Ideas of Participation in Occupation   198
Beliefs About Occupational Participation   200
Individual Participation in Occupation   206
Community Participation in Occupation   210
Challenges and Opportunities   212
Community Animation   217
Chapter Summary   217
References   218

CHAPTER   10 *When People Cannot Participate: Occupational Deprivation*   **221**

Chapter Profile   221
Introduction   221
Defining Occupational Deprivation   222
Five Illustrations of Occupational Deprivation   223
Disability and Occupational Deprivation   236
Chapter Summary   239
References   239
Suggested Readings   241

CHAPTER   11 *Occupational Justice*   **243**

Chapter Profile   243
Introduction   244
Defining Occupational Justice: Early Considerations   244
Social Justice   246
An Exploratory Theory of Occupational Justice   248
Distinctions Between Occupational and Social Justice   262
Using Stories to Consider an Exploratory Theory of Occupational
    Justice   262

Chapter Summary   267
References   268
Endnotes   273

Glossary   275

Index   281

Foreword

Dr. John P. Robinson
Department of Sociology
Americans' Use of Time Project
University of Maryland
College Park, MD, USA

John P. Robinson, a professor of sociology, directs the Americans' Use of Time Project at the University of Maryland. His areas of specialization include social science methodology, attitude and behavior measurement, social change, and the impact of mass communication and other home technology. He received his doctoral degree in mathematical and social psychology from the University of Michigan.

Dr. Robinson founded and directed the Survey Research Center at the University of Maryland and the Communication Research Center at Cleveland State University. He has been responsible for conducting trend studies of how Americans spend time (with primary support from the National Science Foundation) as well as Americans' participation in the arts for the National Endowment for the Arts.

He is the senior author of *Time for Life, Measures of Personality and Social Psychological Attitudes, The Rhythm of Everyday Life, The Main Source, Polls Apart,* and *How Americans Use Time.* He has published more than 100 articles in journals and books and is a contributing editor to *American Demographics* magazine, in which he has published more than 25 articles related to social trends and the use of time. His most recent articles in scholarly journals are "Children's Use of Time, Family Composition and the Acquisition of Social Capital" in the *Journal of Marriage and the Family* (with Suzanne Bianchi), "The Overestimated Workweek" in the *Monthly Labor Review* (with Ann Bostrom), "Measuring Hours of Paid Work" in the *Bulletin of Labor Statistics* (with Jonathan Gershuny), and "Of Time, Activity and Consumer Behavior" in the *Journal of Business Research* (with Franco Nicosia).

Preface

There is an old story about people describing an elephant, one by touching a leg, one by sitting on the elephant, one by feeling it blow through its large trunk, and so on. Each person has a different understanding of the elephant. Their collected descriptions describe the strength, gentleness, and force of the elephant from different perspectives. To fully understand the elephant, it is necessary to collect many perspectives and to present them as parts of a profile.

Now, consider the English word *occupation*. No doubt many images come to mind. In contemplating this book, our goal was to provide a variety of ways for people to consider how humans occupy their time, dedicate their energy, realize their sense of personhood, and organize their societies. Occupations can be considered in economic terms, in social terms, as expressions of personality, or as "doings" that influence health and well-being.

Historically, the literature of human occupation has focused on particular perspectives. There have been books on time use, books on leisure and work, books on occupational hazards and safety, and books on occupational medicine and occupational therapy, among others. But no book has previously invited authors from a range of disciplines and backgrounds to explore what people do, and why, how, where, with whom, and to what consequences these everyday occupations collectively define, organize, and influence our lives. This book takes the view that occupations include all meaningful acts that collectively define and give meaning to daily living.

In his book *Acts of Meaning*, Jerome Bruner has written that people understand their lives through stories. He then points out that these stories are constructed from the acts that are central to everyday human occupations. In this book, the acts that comprise and give meaning to lives are explored in all their complexity, providing awareness that this is a topic that is large and complex like an elephant. We are delighted that the many talented contributors were willing to share their different points of view in this volume. Our hope is that, collectively, their views of occupation will help readers from many diverse areas gain a broader and enriched perspective of occupations, both as a means of social classification and as a powerful array of experiences shaping everyday life in both obvious and subtle ways.

We present you with a book that examines what people do in their everyday worlds. We invite you to consider the various forces that shape the world of occupations and to reflect on how those experiences shape individuals and communities in the world. As you consider the writings in this book, we invite you to explore individual ideas in more detail through focused readings found through examination of the supporting literature for each chapter and to visit the companion web site for additional opportunities to explore topics. We then challenge you to consider your own occupations and to reflect on how they can be used to shape the meaning of your life story and how occupations might be organized in your culture or community.

This is the first editorial collaboration between two people who share a passion for learning about occupations in everyday life. Through this book, we invite you to join us in an engaging and enlightening occupational pursuit. We are indebted to John Robinson, a pioneer in the study of time use related to human occupation, for his contribution to this volume. We acknowledge with appreciation the work of Linda Buxell, Mark Cohen, Charles Hayden, Melissa Kerrian, and Judy Wolf, who made the occupation of editing this book an enjoyable and memorable chapter in our own life stories.

Charles Christiansen
Galveston, TX, USA

Elizabeth Townsend
Halifax, Nova Scotia, Canada

Contributing Authors

**Robert K. Bing, Ed.D., OTR (Ret.),
FAOTA,** Professor and Dean Emeritus
School of Allied Health Sciences,
University of Texas Medical Branch,
Galveston, Texas, United States

**Charles H. Christiansen, Ed.D., OTR,
OT(C), FAOTA,**
Dean and George T. Bryan
    Distinguished Professor,
School of Allied Health Sciences,
University of Texas Medical Branch,
Galveston, Texas, United States

**Jane A. Davis, Ph.D. (candidate), M.S.c,
OT Reg. (ONT.), OT(C), OTR
Sessional Instructor,**
Department of Occupational Therapy,
University of Toronto,
Toronto, Ontario, Canada

Toby Ballou Hamilton, Ph.D., OTR/L,
Assistant Professor and Program
    Director,
Department of Rehabilitation Science,
Occupational Therapy Program,
College of Allied Health,
University of Oklahoma Health
    Sciences Center,
Oklahoma City, Oklahoma, United
    States

Andrew S. Harvey, Ph.D.,
Professor of Economics, Director,
Time Use Research Program,
Saint Mary's University,
Halifax, Nova Scotia, Canada

Jennifer Jarman, Ph.D.,
Associate Professor,
Sociology and Social Anthropology
    Department,
Dalhousie University,
Halifax, Nova Scotia, Canada

Jennifer E. Landry, M.Sc., OT(C),
Assistant Professor,
School of Occupational Therapy,
Dalhousie University,
Halifax, Nova Scotia, Canada

Wendy Pentland, Ph.D., OT(C),
Associate Professor,
School of Rehabilitation
    Therapy,
Faculty of Health Sciences,
Queen's University,
Kingston, Ontario, Canada

**Helene J. Polatajko, Ph.D., OT Reg.
(Ont.), OT(C), FCAOT,**
Professor and Chair,
Department of Occupational
    Therapy,
Faculty of Medicine,
University of Toronto,
Toronto, Ontario, Canada

**Janice Miller Polgar, Ph.D., OT. Reg.
(Ont.),**
Associate Professor,
School of Occupational Therapy,
Elborn College,
University of Western Ontario,
London, Ontario, Canada

Elizabeth Townsend, Ph.D., OT(C),
   O.T. Reg. (N. S.), FCAOT,
Professor and Director,
School of Occupational Therapy,
Dalhousie University,
Halifax, Nova Scotia, Canada

Gail Whiteford, Ph. D.
Professor and Head,
School of Community Health,
Charles Sturt University,
Albury, Australia

Ann Wilcock, Ph.D.,
Professor of Occupational Sciences and
Therapy, Deakin University, Geelong,
Victoria, Australia

Reviewers

Kathy P. Bradley, Ed.D.
Chair, Occupational Therapy Department,
Medical College of Georgia, Augusta, Georgia

Barbara Rom, OTR/L
Program Director, Occupational Therapy Assistant Program
Green River Community College, Auburn, Washington

Amy Solomon, OTR
Denver Technical College, Denver, Colorado

Introduction

Dr. John P. Robinson
Department of Sociology
Americans' Use of Time Project
University of Maryland
College Park, MD, USA

In this comprehensive new compilation, Charles Christiansen and Elizabeth Townsend have taken on an important but difficult challenge in the emerging field of occupational studies. Their challenge is to outline and identify the multitude of theories, findings, and factors that affect the quality of peoples' occupational lives. In this effort they have enlisted a panel of noted experts across 10 areas of occupational studies to lay out the issues, concerns, and methods that arise in such an endeavor.

The result is a rich and diverse collection of literature reviews documenting the necessary paradigms and concepts that are relevant to the approaches covered. To appreciate the book's organization, I have found it useful to group its contents in terms of the rough outline shown in Figure 1. After the introductory Chapter 1, Chapters 2 through 4 deal mainly with the basic methodological and measurement issues that are available to study occupations, Chapters 5 and 6 with aspects of the *person* in relation to occupation, Chapters 7 and 8 with aspects of the person's larger occupational and social *environment*, and Chapters 9 through 11 with the implications and results of that interaction.

In the study of occupation in Chapter 2, Polatajko first distinguishes the four basic ways of knowing about occupations—authority, intuition, reasoned reflection, and empirical/scientific—and the contrasting traditions of the naturalistic/qualitative and positivitistic/quantitative approaches to achieving the latter *scientific* understanding. With their varying reliance on overall methods such as observation or surveys, each method can be applied to answer the *who, what, when, where, how,* and *why* questions that arise in understanding what persons do as part of their occupation. In Chapter 3, Jarman contrasts three main definitional approaches that have been developed to classify the universe of (usually paid) occupations into categories. Of particular value in Jarman's chapter is her description of the philosophies and assumptions (patients recover more quickly if engaged in some occupation, where examples of occupation vary from driving a car to the "scaffolded play" incorporated

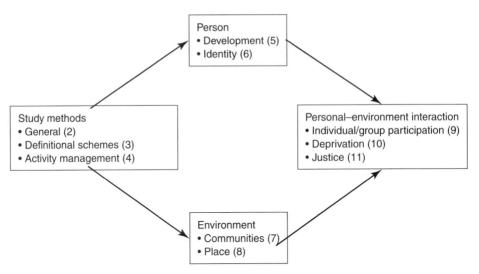

FIGURE 1 An outline of book chapters and topic coverage.

into a parent's gardening activity) that distinguish the interests of occupational therapists from the interests (like mine) of social scientists and government statisticians. Harvey and Pentland in Chapter 4 complete the review of research methods by examining the activity classifications that have been developed in time-diary studies that examine all of a person's daily activities, not just paid work. For reasons to be described, this methodological material (particularly that of Chapter 4) is discussed in more detail later in this Introduction.

The next two chapters of this volume deal with two aspects of the individual person, first in terms of their personal development (Chapter 5) and second in terms of their resulting overall identity (Chapter 6). In Chapter 5, Davis and Polatajko suggest grouping occupations on the basis of things people do across their lifelong process of personal development (1) to care for themselves, (2) to care for their family and others, and (3) to enjoy themselves. Of the four scientific approaches that they identify to describe how individuals develop, the authors clearly find the *interactionist* approach most compelling, the approach that emphasizes multiple patterns of determinants from both personal and environmental sources continuously across the person's life-age stages; optimal occupational situations occurring when there is a proper ("just right") fit of persons with their environments, consistent primarily with the theories of Kurt Lewin. Christiansen in Chapter 6 relies more on the theories of George Herbert Mead, Abraham Maslow, David McClelland, Mihalyi Czikszentmihalyi, and J. L. Holland to describe the complex motivational and goal factors that underlie an individual's identity, again emphasizing the importance of a proper fit of persons with their occupational environments.

The next two chapters then deal with specifics about the larger environment in which different persons must function, namely, their immediate community

(Chapter 7) and their larger sense of place (Chapter 8). In Chapter 7, Christiansen and Townsend describe community factors that influence and are influenced by occupation, with heavy emphasis on game-theoretic considerations; again the fit of persons and communities in producing both social and economic capital is a central component. Chapter 8 by Hamilton goes on to describe how specific aspects of places (like windows, terrain, and symbols) affect occupation through socially constructed meanings and signs that stand for something else, with particular emphasis on the importance of home-like elements and the changes in place brought on by new technology.

As implied in Figure 1, Chapters 9 through 11 can then be seen as examining the intersection or interaction of these person concerns and these environmental concerns in further detail. Chapter 9 at the outset states that occupation is "as essential to health as breathing" and that it requires an active use of the mind rather than just the body. Here, Polgar and Landry use several illustrations to show how occupations enable people to shape their identity, meet goals, develop skills, and more generally create meaning in their lives. Chapters 10 and 11 conclude by examining more dynamic issues that arise in these interactions. Whiteford in Chapter 10 illustrates the five main situations in which individuals are somehow "deprived" from participating properly in an occupation: geographic isolation, unsatisfactory employment, incarceration, gender stereotyping, and refugee status. Chapter 11 more generally examines whether larger standards of occupational "justice" can be brought to bear in the context of real-life occupational discrepancies, such as those vividly illustrated in the contrasting life stories of four individuals. Townsend and Wilcock argue that occupational justice moves beyond today's "social justice" standards in its greater focus on individuals (than groups), in its concern for diversity, and in its focus on quality-of-life issues.

I outline these chapter contents to highlight, first, the great diversity of concepts and goals covered in this volume and the many issues that may be overlooked or underappreciated in my remaining opening remarks, and, second, how much of the material in the book is beyond the purview of empirical social science at this stage of its development (for example, the lack of validated measures of person–environment fit or of occupational deprivation). By laying out the complexity of the terrain involved, however, Christiansen and Townsend have made it possible for themselves and other researchers to begin the important task of prioritizing the main empirical issues from among those they have identified. How then will it be possible to use these diverse theories and observations to provide a more integrated basis for drawing scientific as well as policy conclusions about differences in occupation or occupational justice?

This is a question on which we get little help from social scientists, who have mainly contented themselves with originating new conceptual schemes and theories, rather than integrating and articulating them, as practitioners in the field of occupational therapy must do on a daily basis. Thus over the years, I have been involved in projects that have attempted to apply to specific people what appear to be straightforward, insightful, and reasonable theoretical models of human behavior, such as Reisman's inner-vs.-other directed personality or Maslow's needs hierarchy, only to find real people defying categorization or explanation in terms of these simple models. Rather, most of my own research has begun with the more purely descriptive quantitative data in time diaries in the hope that they can lead to the important organizing principles in people's daily lives.

Thus, my first focus is on the familiar material in Chapter 4, which perhaps for that reason seems the chapter that is most empirically well defined and developed as represented by the only data tables in the book that are generated for national probability samples (meaning that they can be generalized to the population as a whole). Moreover, the diary data come not just from Canada but from six other Western countries as well, providing a most useful basis for a comparative study of activity and occupation.

Indeed, occupational researchers will soon have comparable time-diary data from more than 10 other countries as part of a common effort now under way by Eurostat (an agency in Europe established to coordinate statistical data across countries) to collect parallel standardized data from as many European countries as possible. Considerable care has been taken in the Eurostat project to ensure common diary data from each country and from a well-designed sample, usually chosen by the central statistical agency in each country. Note also that such comparable diary data from representative samples in 12 countries (Canada and Australia not included) were collected in 1965 as part of the Multinational Time Budget Research Project, and that the interested student of occupation can find more than 300 pages of even more detailed tables of daily time varying across the 12 countries in Szalai (1972)(1); these can be used to embellish conclusions from the nine data tables illustrated in Chapter 4.

Perhaps the greatest weakness of these time-diary data for the study of persons and occupations, however, is that they have usually been collected for only 1 or 2 days from each respondent in the study. The illustration in Table 1 of the diary day reported by one respondent in our studies does vividly depict the occupational overload of one contemporary mother. However, this one day is hardly a sufficient base for generalizing about her larger lifestyle or quality of life—the concern of most of the other authors and chapters in this volume. One weekday out of the 25,000+ days in a typical person's life, then, is too brief to be considered representative of that person.

At the same time, the data tables in Chapter 4 (as in Szalai, 1972) do sociologically represent a solid sample of *person-days* of persons in a particular demographic category, such as working mothers in a particular society, and they also provide analysts with an invaluable yardstick for individual assessment. Thus, they can be used to assess whether individual respondents who might be asked to keep a diary for a week or a month are demonstrating occupational behaviors that are typical or atypical for people in that situation in that society.

With regard to the place issues discussed in Chapter 8, for example, such aggregate diary data have been used to identify unique behavioral/occupational choices in different countries, with U.S. citizens spending more time at religious services and French and German citizens more time eating meals and sleeping. Indeed, these distinctive patterns often reflect simple geographical proximities, with Canada and U.S. diary activities generally resembling each other more than French and German, or Eastern European, activity patterns (Robinson and Godbey 1997) (2), (Converse 1972) (3).

TABLE 1   *Sample of Completed Time Diary*

Female, Cook, Age 40, Married with 2 children; Friday—12/3/65					
What Did You Do?	**Time Began**	**Time Ended**	**Where?**	**With Whom?**	**Doing Anything Else?**
Watch TV	12:00	12:15	Home	—	No
Went after daughter at work	12:15	12:30	Transit	Daughter	No
Got ready for bed	12:30	12:50	Home	—	No
Sleep	12:50	4:00	Home	—	No
Got up—made lunches for husband and son and also breakfast	4:00	4:43	Home	—	No
Got ready for work	4:30	4:55	Transit	—	No
Left for work (car)	4:55	5:00	Transit	—	No
Work	5:00	8:00	Restaurant	Employees	No
Coffee break	8:00	8:15	Restaurant	Friend	Talked
Work	8:15	12:00	Restaurant	Employees	No
Ate lunch	12:00	12:15	Restaurant	Employees	Talked
Work	12:15	1:30	Restaurant	Employees	No
Off work—drove home	1:30	1:35	Transit	—	No
Visited with neighbor	1:35	2:00	Yard	Neighbor	Talked
Went after daughter at school	5:15	5:45	Transit	Daughter	No
Took shower	5:45	6:00	Home	—	No
Made supper	6:00	6:25	Home	—	No
Ate supper	7:15	8:00	Home	Family	Talked
Did dishes	8:00	8:30	Home	Daughter	Talked
Washed clothes	8:30	9:00	Home	—	No
Sat down and watched TV	9:00	10:15	Home	Family	No
Went after daughter at work	10:15	10:30	Transit	Daughter	No
Got ready for bed	10:30	10:45	Home	—	No
Went to bed; sleep	10:45	12:00	Home	—	No

In Chapter 4, Harvey and Pentland are further able to use their diary analytic experiences to offer useful operational distinctions in the study of occupation—such as the distinction between tasks, activities, and occupations; or between necessary, contracted, committed, and free-time occupations; or between a person's "projects" that entail division-of-labor vs. work sharing; or between the occupational motivations of physiological, personal, killing time, and social meaning; or between capability and authority vs. coupling constraints on occupational behavior. The authors further point to how the basic data collected by the diary method can be used to arrive at statistically generalizable measures of how time use varies across different segments of the population *in* various locations, *with* various social partners (including time alone), *doing things for* various persons, using various technologies, and involved in various psychological states.

In this latter connection, Harvey and Pentland briefly note an aspect of time usage that provides one important basis for a deeper policy understanding, appreciation, or meaning of the hours devoted to different activities or occupations. That aspect is the *enjoyment* that participants derive from engaging in these activities/occupations. This bears on many issues raised in Chapters 10 and 11, since the analysts of diary data per se have almost no basis for assessing whether time spent on one activity is preferable or superior to time spent on another activity. How concerned should the analyst be if time spent on meals or watching TV is higher for one individual than another? One convenient measuring rod then is how the individuals themselves rate the enjoyment from that activity.

Table 2 summarizes some rough evidence from U.S. diary data in this regard, and that evidence often challenges certain common assumptions about people's choices of activities/occupations, such as the lack of enjoyment from work or the unimportance of sleep. The data come from ratings of all diary activities respondents reported in the 1985 U.S. national time-diary study. Respondents were asked to rate the enjoyment of each activity reported in their diary on a scale from 0 (dislike a great deal) to 10 (like a great deal). The data in Table 2 represent the average ratings for each activity on that 0–10 scale. [It is important to note that the Table 2 ratings differ from ratings respondents gave when asked about the activity *in general;* for example, respondents rate work higher (and TV lower) in general than in the diary, indicating that respondents may overlook distasteful work episodes or satisfactory TV programs when giving ratings to activities in general.]

First, while free-time activities were rated higher in enjoyment than non-free-time activities as expected, there were several important exceptions. The "non-free-time" social interactions with children (rated on average 8.7 on the 0–10 scale) and during work breaks (8.2) in the diary were rated higher than TV (7.8), hobbies (7.5), or phone conversations (7.2). The same was true for the *personal care* activities of sleeping (8.5) and eating meals out (8.2). Work (7.0) was also rated lower than both of these free-time and non-free-time activities, but it was far from at the bottom of the scale. That was reserved for the housework chores of cleaning and laundry (4.8), paying bills and household business (5.1), medical visits (4.7), and trips to car repair shops (4.5). Contrary to expectations (and for ratings in general), women rated these latter activities as unenjoyable as men did.

At the same time, however, few respondents reported these activities on the disliked side of the scale, and far fewer still rated them at points 0, 1, 2, or 3 at the extreme bottom end of the scale. Thus, most people rated participating in their routine daily activities as a generally positive experience. An outside analyst may not find these activities to be particularly profound or significant, but it is important to find that these cross-sections of respondents themselves got through their days in a positive frame of mind. In other words, when people find themselves in activities or occupations that they rate negatively, that can be taken as a sign of noteworthy deprivation.

With enjoyment data such as that listed in Table 2, then, time diaries are able to provide answers to five of the six questions raised by Polatajko in Chapter 2. These are the five journalistic questions of *who, what, when, where,* and *why*—the latter being answered in hedonistic terms; that is, people engage in activities because they enjoy them. Indeed, activity enjoyment ratings were found to be one of the major predic-

TABLE 2   *Ratings of Various Activities on Enjoyment Scale (1985 Diaries)*

Enjoyment Value	Work/House Activities	Personal/ Shopping Activities	Organization/ Education Activities	Free-Time Activities
−10.0	(LIKE A GREAT DEAL)			
−9.0		Sex		Play sports
−8.0	Talk/read to kids	Hug and kiss		Bars/lounges
	Talk with family	Sleep	Church	Attend movies
		Meals away		Relax
				Read paper
				TV
−7.0	Meal at home	Trips	Meetings	Recreational trip
	Baby care	Meal	Social trips	Radio/hobbies
	Paid work	Bath		Phone calls
	Second job	Mall, shopping		
−6.0	Cook	Help adults	Classes	
	Child care	Dress		
	Work commute			
	Unpaid work			
−5.0	Home repair	Grocery shop		
	Pay bills	Banking, business	Home	
	Yard work			
−4.0	Clean house	Doctor, dentist		
	Laundry	Car repair shop		
	Child health			
−3.0				
−2.0				
−1.0				
−0.0	(DISLIKE A GREAT DEAL)			

Source: Americans' Use of Time Project.

tive factors of time spent in an activity (Robinson and Godbey, 1997, Chap. 17) (2); this was not just true in the static one-time survey context, but across a 3-month panel study. In other words, there is a strong tendency for people to choose and engage in activities that they enjoy. While that does not involve a complete explanation of the *why* factor, it does indicate that attitudes toward an activity can be highly predictive of later behavior. The relatively high enjoyment ratings of work in Table 2 also support Polatajko's conclusions from both surveys and depth studies of people's fundamental attachment to work—and rather counter much of Terkel's (4) and others' writings about the alienation and negative feelings attached to work in general.

In our first time-diary study in 1965, respondents were asked the enjoyment question in a more open-ended way: *What parts of the (diary) day did you enjoy most?* and then *What parts of the day did you enjoy least?* we obtained results that supported both points of view. In this sample of mainly employed people aged 18–64, work was rated as the part of the day enjoyed most *and* the part of the day enjoyed least. These results together with those described just above make it clear that assumptions about workers simply putting time in at work to "pay the bills" need to be seriously questioned.

At the same time, another great weakness of present time-diary data is their treatment of work as a "black box." If respondents say they are working in their diary accounts, no further questions are asked about whether that work time involved socializing, daydreaming, or other non-work activities at their place of work. Moreover, few respondents voluntarily note such nonwork periods during the diary work hours (or even work or meal breaks), and even casual observation of workers in public work settings indicate that non-work periods occur; if they did not occur, material for and public appreciation of comic strips such as *Dilbert* would be far less in evidence. This distinction between varying levels of involvement at work is further reflected in the anecdotal evidence from "efficiency studies" that indicate that managers spend less than 15% of their work time actually managing, and the more recent study of Hochschild (1997) (5) in which she observed workers spending more time at work simply to avoid the unpleasant activities that awaited them at home. The latter, of course, represents one example of a phenomenon popularly known as "face time," that is, time workers spend at work simply to impress their employers and not to do needed or meaningful work.

Such contrasting examples point to the need for careful ethnographic studies of the major occupation in most people's lives, time spent at paid work. Several observational studies (like Hochschild's) of single individual companies or factories have been conducted to provide useful anecdotal evidence, but how much conclusions from these studies can be generalized to the workforce as a whole will not be known until something like the method of "representative ethnography" described later is employed.

One recurrent major question about the relevance of diary activity data for the study of occupations in this volume concerns how much activity can be said to relate to "occupation." At the beginning of Chapter 1, Christiansen and Townsend argue that occupations are "more than activity" in their sense of purpose and meaning, yet describe "occupying time" as the classic concern in describing a 25-year-old's occupation. Several authors point out how even sleep fits the criteria for an occupation in terms of purposefulness and meaning. In Chapter 2, Polatajko answers "always" to the question *When do people engage in occupation?*, including presumably the time Terry Waite spent in solitary confinement for more than 4 years. One simple next exercise for the study of occupations, then, might be to achieve more consensus on the distinction between activity and occupation, in particular, in designing diary studies to meet the needs of occupational scientists and therapists.

Most authors in this volume point to the useful and unique insights that emerge from anthropological or in-depth observational studies, and it is clear that this is the main drawback in making inferences from strictly quantitative surveys like the diary studies. These insights take on the most relevance for scientists when they come from comparative studies across contrasting individuals or groups, rather than being isolated anecdotes or hypothetical examples. In this regard, I conclude with three notable examples of serious research attempts to enhance the value of "qualitative" data in the scientific research literature.

First are the studies of "personology," a term coined in the 1930s by Harvard psychologist Henry Murray (6) to describe studies of "single, complex, lived lives over time, from a variety of angles." Researchers in this tradition contrast themselves with conventional psychologists in their analysis of the whole person, rather than the short-term behavior examined in most surveys and experiments, which are invariably detached from the lives in which these behaviors are observed. Personologists ask *Where is the person in personality research?* if one does not study lives as lived, particularly using the technique of psychobiographies.

One particularly illuminating example of this personological approach is provided in the 1958 book *Opinions and Personality* by Smith, Bruner, and White (7). The authors were three Harvard psychologists following in the Murray tradition, who enlisted anthropologists and Harvard researchers from other social science disciplines in the late 1940s. The Harvard group studied only 10 "ordinary" men, all from the Boston area and, while trying to pick a cross-section sample, ended up with a group with an average IQ of 120 (that is, in the top 3% of the population). However, even in this group of men, each of which they intensively interviewed for more than 10 hours, they found little evidence of abstract reasoning in how these 10 men formed their opinions on Russia and the Soviet Union. The men's strategies (of what in the present context might be considered as the occupation of arriving at public opinion) consisted largely of casual evaluation of stray, scattered bits of information gained from often unreliable or unsophisticated sources, such as fellow workers, mass media entertainment, or popular stereotypes. One of their most intriguing insights, however, emerged when each of these 10 individuals was given a "stress test," in which their views were extensively challenged by scholars who could be considered experts in the field of international affairs. Even after this experience, however, the men continued to hold to their original views, ones that they had a hard time defending on logical grounds. New research following this tradition might find that decisions on occupational choices are made on much the same ad hoc conceptual basis.

Another conclusion that emerged from their study was that although it was possible to reliably place these 10 men on a scale from pro-Russian to anti-Russian, the reasoning and paths used to arrive at these positions were so diverse that the scale was of little practical value in understanding the dynamics of public opinion about Russia and how it might change in varying circumstances. An important major recommendation that emerged from the in-depth study was that the most appropriate of the many ways to understand how people felt about a topic was to let them talk about the issue in their own words, and then to ask follow-up questions. The great value of this study, however, was that a *variety* of individuals was interviewed by a *variety* of researchers with a *common* focus. The same sort of exercise of having the various authors in this volume examine the same set of "ordinary" lives in terms of the varied occupations they would encounter could help to integrate and prioritize a research agenda for the field.

A more integrative conceptual/measurement approach that could prove useful in such an exercise was that pioneered by sociologist Robert Havighurst (1958) (8), published about the same time as the Harvard study more than 40 years ago. The Havighurst approach also involved lengthy interviews, but they were focused on much more personal issues than foreign affairs, particularly the individual's investments in the major "roles" of their lives. These roles included worker, spouse, parent, friend, and citizen. The investment ratings were derived from ratings from transcripts of the ways respondents described how they went about fulfilling their role obligations and

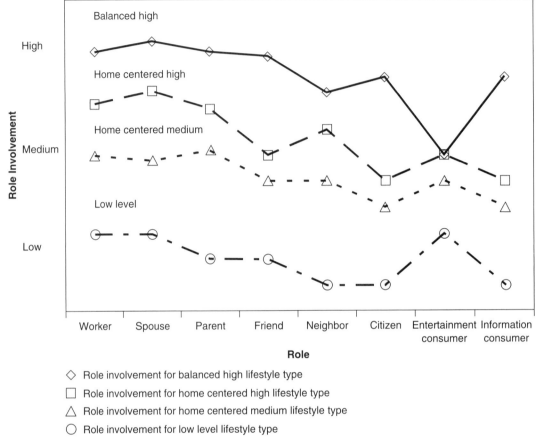

FIGURE 2   Adaptation of Havighurst lifestyle typology

relations in each of these major role settings in their lives. Thus a respondent who was able to describe his ambitious work challenges and how he wrestled to overcome them in considerable detail and with clear dedication and effort was rated as "highly involved" in the role of worker, in contrast to a worker who indicated that he was simply going through the motions, with minimal concern about or devotion to his work duties; such a worker was rated at the low end of the scale.

Roles may not capture the same concepts as occupations, but they come closer than activities, and it is hard to imagine much in an occupation that does not involve some perspective of role. Authors in this volume might wish to substitute a listing of occupations to ask their respondents about rather than roles, but the profiles of lifestyle types generated in the Havighurst study provide a provocative model that warrants replication and extension. Although the four "types" shown in Figure 2 are artificially updated to incorporate new roles generated by today's information technologies, they do capture the type of important larger lifestyle types that Havighurst identified.

The top, balanced-high group in the Figure 2 typology represents respondents who are highly involved in almost all of the roles in which they are involved, perhaps reflected as a form of "life gusto." They seem obviously motivated and positively engaged in all their life roles, with the exception of entertainment media consumer. These are people who probably not only show considerable initiative and enterprise at work, but also in their roles of spouse and parent at home, while at the same maintaining a variety of close friendships, following events closely in the mass media, and being active in their neighborhood and community. Balanced-high people might often be considered "opinion leaders" or self-actualizers in their interactions with others.

In contrast, the next two types show lower and somewhat less universal levels of involvement and initiative, with their lives and life concerns centered mainly around the home. Their lives in both cases are maximally involved in the roles of "spouse" and "parent," with work, friendships, and community being less central. One might expect that their attachment to entertainment media might be above that of the first type, however. In contrast, there is the fourth type, who is minimally involved in all roles in life or perhaps is trying to maximize only one aspect through engagement in hobbies or making money in a dissatisfying job. In his study of Kansas City in the 1950s, Havighurst (8) found about one-sixth of respondents in types 1, 2, and 4, and about half in type 3.

Again, the purpose of Figure 2 is to offer ideas about focused studies that are suggested by the rich variety of concepts and examples cited in the various chapters in this volume. These are important studies that have been largely neglected by social scientists, but that do productively combine features of qualitative and quantitative research of interest to authors of this volume.

As noted earlier, both of these studies can be seen as early examples of a field of "representative ethnography," suggested as needed in the field of public opinion and communication research some 20 years ago in Robinson and Meadow (1982) (9). The approach would take advantage of the rich insights afforded by ethnography and observation on the one hand, by marrying it with the great feature of population generalizability provided by probability sampling on the other. Social scientists in the qualitative tradition have developed the skills to do careful in-depth interviewing from such fields as anthropology and clinical psychology, while those who are more quantitatively oriented have learned enough from their survey experience to draw accurate conclusions from smaller and smaller samples. Survey researchers can call on the talents of professional interviewers who continue to do personal in-home interviews, after decades of experience persuading 70% to 90% of otherwise shy and reluctant respondents to participate in public opinion and demographic studies, and to do so while enjoying learning about the lives of the people they interview. A reading of the "thumbnail sketches" written up by these interviewers provide insights into public opinion not possible otherwise.

While a fully national application of representative ethnography has yet to be carried out, a pilot study application was carried out in 2001 with a sample of 23 Internet users in the Philadelphia area (10). Two interviewing supervisors with more than 30 years of combined interviewing experience were given eight random and scattered addresses in the area and told to locate three Internet users starting at that address and take every third address to the right of that random address, until three Internet users from each area were interviewed. Each interview schedule began with open-end questions about the respondents' favorite free-time activities and TV programs and their reasons for liking them, followed by closed and open questions about Internet use and examples of what that usage meant to them. Upon completion of the interview, one interviewer combined her material into a thumbnail sketch about her interaction with the respondent, relying both on her written notes and on a tape-recording of the interview. Largely based on these sketches, supplemented with staff editing of their interview notes, a somewhat standardized user profile was developed for each respondent. These profiles are illustrated in the three shorthand sketches in Boxes 1, 2, and 3.

As in the Harvard study of public opinion, it was difficult to describe the variety of user Internet usage styles in simple terms. However, if one contrasts the three respondents, Mark, Ernest, and Charles (fictitious names) described in Boxes 1, 2, and 3, respectively, one sees some clear and important distinctions in the occupation of "Internet user" across people. Each of the three has invested considerable time and energy to take full advantage of this new technology, but for dramatically different goals or motivations. For Mark (Box 1), who is something of an Internet evangelist in terms of incorporating the technology into his lifestyle, the technology combines many features that enhance his many and intense life interests—a source of perpetual graduate study, a resource to enhance the lives of the disadvantaged he helps in his work, a limitless source of connections to pursue his broad range of interests, and a way to keep in touch with his many friends who live thousands of miles away. In contrast, Ernest and Charles have also made time-consuming investments in the technology but for narrower purposes of personal enjoyment, like listening to music. Charles uses the Internet to keep up with music, movies, and sports and to maintain contact with more than 100 friends and relatives, and Ernest uses it almost solely to build up his library of jazz music. These are three intense Internet users who take notably different approaches and have different goals for this new information technology.

The point here is that for a relatively small research investment one can take advantage of the techniques of representative ethnography and personology to advance the study of occupations. It can provide more examples of actual contemporary lives to give tomorrow's students of occupations more specific material to relate to and debate. What could become more concrete from such an exercise are the ways in which internal personal needs and external environmental factors come into play in the choice and style of dealing with occupations. Such an exercise could also give researchers more of a hands-on appreciation of the variety of occupations across and within people. Also emerging from these profiles would be a richer appreciation of the range and depth of occupational deprivations and of the steps that might be needed for better realization of occupational justice in both developed and less developed societies.

BOX 1

Mark is a 50-year-old white male who lives with his male domestic partner in the row home they own in Center City Philadelphia. His neighborhood consists of townhouses and apartment buildings, about half of which are rental properties and half are owner occupied. Income levels range from upper to middle. The residents are mostly white, mostly young professionals, with some older/retired persons and some students.

Mark has a master's degree in applied behavioral science and counseling psychology, with an additional year of schooling to be certified in psychiatric rehabilitation. He is the supervisor of an adult literacy program at a mental health center, where he has worked for the past 12 years. He describes his job as that of teacher, trainer, supervisor, and coach. Mark works about 38 hours each week at the center, and spends an additional 4 hours each week working at home.

Free Time: In his free time Mark's favorite activity is reading or, as he says, carrying on his "love affair with the printed word." Although his reading materials in bookcases covering every wall, every table, and much of the floor in the room where we sat reflect his wide interests, Mark says he has a particularly strong interest in Jewish studies—theology and philosophy. He says "I probably would have become a rabbi if I'd come from a more traditional religious background."

Mark's next favorite free-time activity is listening to and performing music. He plays piano, sings and directs a choir at work, and he and his partner go to the orchestra and theater as often as their incomes will allow. Travel is another passion of both Mark and his partner, whose connections in the travel industry allow them to be able to afford frequent trips in the United States and abroad.

Mark enjoys these activities which he sees as part of the "good life." He refers to the importance of his undergraduate liberal arts education, and says he is a proponent of educational philosopher Paolo Freire, commenting that "Development of and exposure to things like these gives you skills for living. They make my life meaningful, keep me challenged, and keep me interested in adult education."

E-Mail/Internet: Mark says that he has no family connections, but does have about 120 friends with whom he stays in contact at least once a year. He explained that, in addition to having many local friends, he has large groups of friends in the Pacific Northwest—his home for 30 years—and in England, where his partner attended school and lived for a number of years.

Mark says that his contacts have "definitely widened" since he began using e-mail and as more and more other people have started using e-mail. The listserves in which he participates are particularly responsible for increasing the number of his contacts.

The first time he used the Internet in 1994, at the home of a friend, Mark found it "amazing." As soon as he was able to access it at work, he did. About the World Wide Web, Mark says, "I love it. I can get lost in it."

BOX 1   *(Continued)*

Mark spends about 6 hours per week, on average, using the Web at home, and another 3 hours on the Web at work. This time varies, of course. "It depends on what I hear or see. I can spend much more at times." Most often, Mark visits sites he has bookmarked, but he often follows links from his original site or links sent to him by someone. "I love links! I get some of the best information from links. They help me to expand the information on a subject I'm already interested in, give me other views of the same topic or related ones. That's how I get lost in the Web, and lose track of time."

The three main web sites Mark uses are those for PBS, C-Span, and the Jewish Theological Seminary. The first two he uses as references for his classroom teaching, for curriculum and lesson planning on "literature, social and cultural studies, history, public affairs, current events—everything." The third site is used for Mark's personal Torah study and other religious information.

Mark feels that using the Web has changed his life a great deal. "How could it not, to have this world of information right at my fingertips? Without moving to New York, where else could I have such access to the world, the world of thought, philosophy, etc. I can take a class [online] at Jewish Theological Seminary, at Harvard School of Divinity, wherever I want to, or participate in discussions on all sorts of topics with people from all over the world. Without the Internet I'd still access this information, but I have much easier access to it now—faster, better and cheaper. It's incredible."

Expanding on the idea of access, and inspired to project beyond his own Internet usage: "The world of the future is going to be about who has access to tools. My poor students, mentally handicapped and impoverished, I'm doing my best to provide access and interest to them." He recalled the book *Ecotopia,* about a fictitious "hippie socialist republic," in which there were learning centers on every block and technology wasn't a negative thing. "A lot can be done with imagination to take technology to more people—computer refurbishing programs, build-a-computer programs. There's so much potential. If we think out of the box, there's no limit to what we can do."

BOX 2

Ernest is a 38-year-old married African-American male with two children who works as a cook for about 40 hours a week. He is a high school graduate living in a moderately sized, single-family home with his wife and two mixed-race children. He has been employed in the restaurant business for his entire life and is currently employed full time in a luxury hotel. Ernest's wife is also employed full time, giving them an annual household income of approximately $75,000.

Ernest's home is located in a subdivision in a township in New Jersey, and has approximately 250 to 300 homes built in the mid to late 1980s. The exteriors of the homes appear well maintained and the majority of the lawns are well groomed. Many children are playing in the neighborhood yards, including Ernest's children. The neighborhood appears middle class and racially integrated.

Free Time: Ernest's major free time and TV interests include watching sports on ESPN and watching reruns of *All in the Family* and *Columbo*. He also enjoys cooking at home, as an extension of what he does at work.

Internet: Ernest uses the Internet for pleasure only via Verizon online at home with no use at work or other locations. He reports no e-mail, chat room, or instant messaging usage at all, having about 10 friends that he talks to personally rather than by phone or mail. Ernest's web interests include music, sports, cooking, and downloading jazz music from free-access web sites.

Ernest seems to have learned whatever he knows about computers and the Internet on a trial-and-error basis. He does not seem particularly computer savvy, yet he owns a top-of-the-line Gateway PC with every conceivable optional piece of equipment, which he installed on his own. Very animated when talking about music, he seems to use infinite patience to pursue anything related to the music, managing to teach himself everything he needs to know to access the music. He simply knows what works for him, primarily typing in web site names.

BOX 3

Charles is a 27-year-old, single white male who lives alone in a duplex he rents in a racially integrated, working class to lower middle class neighborhood in northwest Philadelphia known as Overbrook. Charles has a master's degree in political science and is working toward his doctorate. He is employed full time as high school history teacher in the Philadelphia public school system. He uses the Internet in this job primarily for e-mail.

Free Time: In his free time, Charles golfs, plays softball, shoots pool, and plays Sony PlayStation games. He does all of these activities with friends well enough to belong to a few leagues. He enjoys golf because he finds it "particularly (mentally) challenging; it always forces you to try to do better." His favorite television shows include *Simpsons* ("it's well written, humorous, and satirical), *Seinfeld* reruns, and *Law and Order.*

Charles reports a large social network including approximately 100 people. He reports staying in contact with almost all of them on a regular basis by using e-mail and the telephone and by seeing them socially. Currently he writes no letters or cards and reports never having been much of a writer. However, e-mail has greatly increased both the number of his contacts and the quality of his contacts. "It's easier to use than regular mail. It's faster. You can send it quicker. You don't have to worry about postage. It's something you could do during the normal course of your day. You get a quicker response for questions that you have."

Charles also uses instant messaging frequently and enjoys it because "it's very fast and gives you the impression that you're actually talking to your friend."

Internet: Charles has two computers at home, which are connected to the Internet via a high-speed DSL modem. He also uses computers at work. Charles estimates that he uses the computer for e-mail about 12 hours per week. In an average day he sends about 14 personal one-to-one messages. Charles visits chat rooms and bulletin boards for about 1 hour per week. He primarily goes to bulletin boards to trade live music shows with other users. He's learned that "There're a lot of people interested in the same things I am."

Charles spends approximately 30 hours per week on various web sites, almost all of which are related to music, movies, or sports. His three most frequently accessed web sites are musiccity.com (MP3s and movies I like to watch and listen to for free), *philadelphonic.com* (a bulletin board trading live shows), and *live365.com* (Internet radio stations). He no longer purchases any CDs or movies; he instead downloads them free from the Internet. Last week, Charles became "particularly happy or excited" because he "found the D encryption code for DIVX movies and it unscrambles the encryption so now I can download DVD quality movies and watch them on my PC for free."

Charles seemed very knowledgeable regarding both software and hardware issues. His system includes some of the most expensive and up-to-date technology, which he has assembled by himself. He seems to utilize the Internet almost solely for entertainment purposes, including social e-mail, obtaining music and movies, and checking on sports scores. Although he is pursuing his doctorate and is a teacher, he made almost no mention of research or other educational usage of the Internet.

Clearly, the study of occupations is a dynamic and complex area. As the scope of this volume suggests and this introduction has attempted to illustrate, the role of occupations in person's lives and in society can be better understood through greater interdisciplinary research involving time use studies, interviews, observational analyses, and other strategies, making use of the Internet and other emerging technologies as illustrated above. Perhaps future editions of this volume will document such advances in research and the evolution of theories of occupation that can be harnessed to the benefit of individuals and the groups in which they live.

REFERENCES

1. Szalai, A., Converse, P. E., Feldheim, P., Scheuch, E. K., & Stone, P. J. (Eds.). (1972). *The use of time: Daily activities of urban and suburban populations in twelve countries.* The Hague: Mouton.
2. Robinson, J. P., & Godbey, G. (1997). *Time for life: The surprising ways americans use their time.* Pennsylvania: Pennsylvania State University Press.
3. Converse, P. E. Country differences in time use. In Szalai et al. (Eds.). *The use of time: Daily activities of urban and suburban populations in twelve countries.* The Hague: Mouton.
4. Terkel, S. (1972). *Working.* New York: Random House.
5. Hochschild, A. (1997). *The time bind: When work becomes home and home becomes work.* Metropolitan Books.
6. Murray, H. A. (1938). *Explorations in personality: A clinical and experimental study of fifty men of college age.* New York: Oxford University Press.
7. Smith, M. B., Bruner, J. S., & White, R. W. (1956). *Opinions and personality.* New York: Wiley.
8. Havighurst, R. J. (1972). The nature and value of meaningful free-time activity. In R. W. Kleemeier (Ed.). *Aging and leisure.* New York: Oxford Univ. Press.
9. Robinson, J. P., & Meadow, R. (1982). *Polls apart.* Cabin John, MD: Seven Locks Press.
10. Neustadtl, Alan, Robinson, John P., & Kestnbaum, Meyer. (2002). Doing social science research online. In Barry Wellman and Caroline Haythornthwaite (Eds). *The internet and everyday life,* Oxford, UK and New York: Basil Blackwell.

For reference to website:

Robinson, J. P., Meyer Kestnbaum, & Alan Neustadtl. (2001). An online data web site for internet research. *American Behavioral Scientist, 45* (November 2001): 565–582.

Additionally, to view the webuser profiles visit the following link:

www.webuse.umd.edu/webuser_profiles.htm

CHAPTER 1

An Introduction to Occupation

Charles Christiansen and Elizabeth Townsend
(with contributions from Robert K. Bing)

KEY WORDS

Embedded occupations
Folk taxonomy
Habit
Human occupations
Narrative
Occupation
Occupational classification

Occupational habits
Occupational routines
Occupational science
Occupations
Routine
Taxonomy

CHAPTER PROFILE

In this chapter, the term *occupation* is defined broadly in order to provide a platform for the scope of ideas in the book. Questions regarding occupations are posed that enable us to explore concepts regarding how occupations have been defined and classified in the past. This study of human occupation reveals broad types of human endeavor that have implications for behavior, development, social interaction, well-being, and society. Factors influencing occupational engagement are then briefly explored, and a brief history of occupations through the ages is summarized. The chapter closes with a review of ideas related to human occupation.

www.prenhall.com/christiansen
The Internet provides an exciting means for interacting with this textbook and for enhancing your understanding of humans' experiences with occupations and the organization of occupations in society. Use the address above to access the free, interactive companion web site created specifically to accompany this book. Here you will find an array of self-study material designed to help you gain a richer understanding of the concepts presented in this chapter.

INTRODUCTION

Occupation is derived from the Latin word *occupatio,* meaning "to occupy or to seize." To be occupied is to use and even seize control of time and space (or place) as a person engages in a recognizable life endeavor. Terms such as *activity* and *task* are *not* synonymous with occupation (1, 2). In the simplest definition, occupations are more than activities or tasks. Occupations are invested with a sense of purpose, meaning, vocation, cultural significance, and political power through which some occupations are paid because of their economic value, while others are not, and participation in some occupations is rewarded with greater pay to some than to others.

RECONSIDERING THE MEANING OF OCCUPATION

Humans have occupied their lives with the goal-directed pursuits necessary for their existence and well-being since the dawning of time. Histories are accounts and chronicles of the individual and collective occupations of people over time. The study of history is itself an occupation. Yet, occupation has only recently become a topic of study in and of itself. Occupation is so much a part of our daily human existence that it has escaped attention.

This chapter addresses a series of important questions that serve as a framework for reconsidering occupation at the opening of the 21st century:

1. How do you occupy your time?
2. What occupies you?
3. What is your occupation?
4. Why are some people occupied while others are unoccupied?
5. What is the history of occupation?

HOW DO YOU OCCUPY YOUR TIME?

How do you occupy your time? is such a classic question that it is asked repeatedly in ordinary conversation to discover what people do. The answer may include paid work, but the question invites a far more extensive exploration of occupation in relation to time, that illusive yet defining feature of human existence. Implied in the question is an interest in how time is used in particular places or through particular routines and habits. The simple question *How do you occupy your time?* actually requires a complex consideration of occupation with reference to daily routines and habits in relation to both time and place.

Consider this scene: It is one o'clock in the afternoon on a pleasant Monday in March. Main Street is bustling with people enjoying themselves (Figure 1-1). Some are moving quickly with a given destination in mind, perhaps in a hurry to get back to jobs after their lunch breaks. Others are watching children play, carrying shopping bags, walking dogs, or simply strolling two by two and enjoying conversation. On a corner, a musician strums a guitar behind an open instrument case. On the edge of town are farmers selling local produce. Warehouse managers are storing

FIGURE 1-1   Occupations surround us.
(PhotoLink/Getty Images)

produce for shipping to other communities. Builders are completing roadwork and children are entering school buses for an afternoon outing.

This scene may occur in any town or city in the world. People are engaged in doing many occupations. Although it is not especially remarkable, it offers an entry point for answering the question *How do you occupy your time?* Observation of such a scene is a good way to raise awareness about the vast range of occupations that comprise daily life, as well as the ways in which occupation is related to time and space (or place).

Now imagine an experiment in which a participant embeds a tiny video camera with a transmitter in a lapel pin to be worn continuously during waking hours for one month. In reviewing the many hours of video that result, you, the observer, might be interested in what the person did, where the person spent time, and how much time the person spent doing various occupations. A quantitative, statistical analysis of this information could answer the question *How do you occupy yourself?* During your quantitative analysis, you find that the 25-year-old participant whose month-long video you are analyzing spent 73 hours on the telephone, either at home or at various locations, using a cell or mobile telephone. Being a university student, the participant also spent 80 hours reading and studying, again at various locations, 80 hours in class, and 80 hours at a part-time job in a clothing store. Another 90 hours were devoted to eating, 20 hours to shopping, 15 hours to housework, 60 hours to dressing and grooming, and 65 hours to socializing with friends during the 30-day experiment. Another 45 hours were devoted to driving from one location to another. Nearly 200 hours were spent sleeping.

As Polatajko highlights in Chapter 2, the quantitative study of occupation can provide important information. Here, you might categorize what the participant did into *occupational categories* as in the response to the question *What is your occupation?*

posed later in this chapter. To answer *How do you occupy your time?*, you would calculate how much time was spent in various occupational categories. An increasingly sophisticated statistical analysis could correlate the use of time in particular places or the allocation of time to particular routines and habits. In other words, the simple question *How do you occupy your time?* invites a wealth of exploration about occupation, time, and space.

Our reference to human occupation in this book includes more than engagement in work. Everyday lives reflect participation in a broad range of pursuits (2). As Jarman notes in Chapter 3, the categorization of occupation in sociology and government has focused on defining duties and pay structures for those who occupy some of their time in paid work. Harvey and Pentland (Chapter 4) draw on time use studies to display how multiple purposes for occupying time are categorized internationally. The various ways in which place is integrally linked to time are described by Hamilton, who considers occupation in relation to places that may be built and natural environments (Chapter 8).

A simple starting place for understanding occupation is to list the variety of **occupations** that comprise everyday life—for an individual, a family, a community, or an organization. Discussion and analysis can then be undertaken to consider the complexity of occupation in relation to time and space since it is not actually easy to list or classify occupations based on what a person is doing. For example, the professional tennis player does not experience nor perceive tennis in the same way as the amateur athlete who plays for fun and fitness. Similarly, some people sew or play the piano for relaxation, whereas for others, these same occupations constitute necessary paid work or employment.

Discussion could consider the further complexity associated with the simultaneous participation in more than one occupation. It is not unusual for occupations to be "nested" or **embedded** within other occupations (3) so that it is difficult to determine precisely how time is divided among various occupations (Figure 1-2). Picture someone traveling and at the same time talking on a cell phone or working on a portable computer; or someone planning the building of a new shed while also monitoring children at play; or someone playing a musical instrument while also conducting a group of musicians.

Additionally, consider how occupations occur as **habits** or **routines.** Habits are relatively automatic, repetitive patterns of human behavior (4). Some, but not all habitual behaviors, are occupations. For example, chewing a pencil or biting your nails may be habitual actions, but they fail to qualify as occupations. On the other hand, driving a certain route to work or getting coffee first thing in the morning could be considered habitual occupations (5). Routines have been defined as "habitual, repeatable and predictable ways of acting" (6). Clark offers that routines provide a structure that serves to organize and maintain individual lives (5).

Many people, if asked, would identify habits and routines as an important influence in their individual pattern of time use (Figure 1-3). Despite their importance, until recently, most research on repetitive behaviors has focused on recurring patterns of behavior that are destructive, antisocial, or unhealthy. These include physical addictions (e.g., smoking, alcoholism, or drug use) and psychological addictions, such as gambling, eating, or excessive engagement or preoccupation, for instance, with computer games.

FIGURE 1-2   Nested or embedded occupations occur when people do more than one thing simultaneously.
(Doug Menuez/Getty Images)

FIGURE 1-3   Much of daily life involves habits and routines.
(Ryan McVay/Getty Images)

A more recent approach has viewed habit from the standpoint of its neurological foundations, suggesting that habits, or patterns of time use, can range along a continuum (7). This view proposes that certain habits and routines may be necessary for well-being, whereas other states, such as not having life structure or being dominated by excessive repetitive behavior, are not adaptive and thus not conducive to health and well-being (7).

The idea that some **occupational routines** are useful may seem contrary to prevailing views that focus on their negative consequences. Habits and routines can be useful when they support human behavior or thought by enabling attention or energy to be directed toward thoughts or actions where they best serve the interests of the individual. Inasmuch as routine and necessary behaviors do not require focused attention, they conserve energy and attention to enable quick responses to unexpected contingencies (8).

Researcher John Bargh, among others, has devoted a career to studying automaticity, which refers to behaviors that are done frequently and become automatic, requiring little direct attention or intention (9). Although these automatic skills can preserve attention and energy for other requirements, they can also be problematic, since they may lead to errors, such as getting off an elevator on the wrong floor when the door opens, driving without paying close attention, or avoiding social interactions that could be helpful (10). Bargh believes that automaticity is more pervasive than we may think in influencing our behavioral decisions, and thus may have significant implications for philosophical issues such as free will and the nature and purpose of consciousness (11).

Much more study on habits, routines, and automatic behaviors is necessary before definitive conclusions can be drawn about the role of repetitive patterns of occupation in everyday life. Conventional wisdom holds that some patterns of behavior may be more healthful, adaptational, or balanced than others, leading to greater health or happiness. In the absence of conclusive research, however, it is difficult to claim that one lifestyle is better than another for specific groups of people (2, 12).

Humans actually know from personal experience that the whole of everyday life is comprised of occupations, and time, space, and habitual routines are important to understand in relation to occupation. We have implicit, general knowledge that existence is comprised of occupations, that humans are occupational beings, that time and space are defining characteristics of occupations, and that the organization of societies determines how, when, and where humans occupy themselves. What can be done to make this knowledge more explicit and to deepen understanding of how people occupy themselves? Is this just common sense? If so, how could this *common* sense be made more explicit to recognize and to organize the richness of human experience in different ways?

WHAT OCCUPIES YOU?

The question *What occupies you?* sounds similar to the question *How do you occupy yourself?* Here the question *What occupies you?* is raised to consider qualitative aspects of occupation—to ask *why* people engage in occupations. Suppose for a moment that the experiment described earlier invites the participant to supplement the video record of occupations by keeping a diary to explain *why* the participant is engaging in particular occupations in the times and places noted.

Qualitative analysis of the diary reveals that the participant spent 73 hours on the telephone with a partner. The *why* recorded was that the partner was so jealous of the participant's success at the university that frequent calls were required to reassure that partner that the relationship was still important. Moreover, the 15 hours of housework were undertaken because the participant valued spending only a half hour per day to keep the barest minimum of order at home. In contrast, approximately 2 hours per day were devoted to dressing and grooming and even more to socializing with friends, these being highly valued occupations to this young university student.

This brief suggestion for a qualitative study of occupations could address questions about the relationships between occupational choice and the identity humans generate by selecting and participating in particular occupations, as outlined by Christiansen (Chapter 6). There is a growing sentiment among social and developmental psychologists that a person's sense of self emerges largely as a result of what he or she experiences on a daily basis and over time (13, 14, 15). Some researchers suggest that goals are fashioned around imagined selves, to the extent that occupations are chosen with an aim toward becoming a particular kind of person (e.g., rich, popular, or skillful) or to avoid the unpleasant outcome of becoming impoverished, unpopular, or clumsy, thus risking or encountering social rejection (16). Clearly, fashions and trends in modern society tend to support the idea that self-expression and identity building are important factors in the selection of occupations and, by extension, how time is used.

Questions about human development could also be embedded in asking *why* time is used in particular ways. Drawing on the discussion of occupational development by Davis and Polatajko (Chapter 5), the example here could offer insights into the occupational development of a university student. If the earlier experiment involved a number of university students, contrasted, for instance, with the time use of retired seniors, and if participants from various cultural and social groups were included, the results would provide insights about the changing choices and opportunities for occupations across the life span under various cultural and social conditions. The study could be refined even more to consider differences in occupational development and occupational participation associated with gender, sexual orientation, social class, race, or disability as noted by Polgar and Landry (Chapter 9).

The diary could also be analyzed to consider the meanings of the occupations recorded. Occupations are complex because the meanings associated with different occupations have social as well as individual significance.

In everyday life, occupations provide the context for interaction with others. Christiansen and Townsend highlight the community context in Chapter 7. Human interactions create social meaning. Rituals and ceremonies, such as weddings and funerals, are occupations that have widely understood meanings within cultures. Other experiences have shared meanings but are likely to represent opportunities for engendering personal meaning.

Consider the meaning of a camping trip. Planning such an outing engenders certain expectations about the kind of clothing that one will wear, the kind of food that one will eat, and the kinds of occupations in which one will participate. The conveniences of modern times have made the camping experience symbolize self-reliance and an opportunity to get in touch with the natural surroundings so often absent in the built environment. But the experiences encountered during the camping trip often go beyond these shared meanings and may be intensely individual. A person may always remember the first fish caught, the first bear seen in the wild, or the stories told around the campfire that provided a rare opportunity to gain insight into life's problems or that provided an occasion to share a special experience with a close friend or relative.

Occupations Create Meaning

One dimension of meaning-making in occupations is spiritual in nature. Some occupations, such as listening to music or appreciating art and design, can be viewed as spiritual if they touch the human spirit. Another spiritual dimension of occupations involves contemplation to make sense of the larger purpose of life. Contemplation of one's occupations over time may contribute to a sense of satisfaction about life and the emergence of a satisfactory identity. The very term *contemplate* derives from the Latin words referring to that which takes place within a temple. Thus, the sense of a larger purpose may for some be related to beliefs that one's occupations are guided by powers beyond the individual—whether those greater powers are viewed as fate, chance, mystical practices, or divine influence. Typically, people understand the meaning of their lives by considering their occupations as part of their life stories. It seems that occupations gain meaning over time by becoming part of an individual's unfolding autobiography, or personal **narrative** (17, 18).

The question *What occupies you?* also sparks reflection and introspection about *why* people engage in particular occupations. To explore this question, one might also ask *Why do you choose to be occupied as you do? What motivates you to select some occupations and not others? Why are you interested in particular occupations?* or *What occupations give your life meaning?* If occupation is more than a job—if identity, development, meaning, and possibly other facets of human existence are intricately linked to occupation—what knowledge already exists and what else needs to be known? It is true that jobs and paid work may contribute to identity, development, and meaning for some people at some times in their lives. But how do humans use the multiplicity of daily occupations to create a life for themselves, as well as, to create the policies and other structures that determine what humans can and even want to do?

WHAT IS YOUR OCCUPATION?

When people are casually asked *What is your occupation?* or the previous question, *How do you occupy yourself?*, they generally use what is known as a *folk taxonomy* to describe different types of occupations. Typical folk taxonomy descriptors are *I work as a plumber; I am taking time off; I'm home with the children now; I'm retired; I don't do much of anything; I'm just a homemaker.* This folk system is used to describe occupations and to convey the ways in which certain occupations are valued. For instance, feminists such as Germaine Greer (19) and Betty Frieden (20) have pointed out how home-making is such a socially devalued occupation that those for whom this is their primary occupation are not only unpaid but viewed as lesser contributors to society, being *just* homemakers. The folk taxonomies of everyday language also lack the level of detail or precision that would be necessary for rigorous analysis. For example, someone may casually describe themselves as being occupied in *eating junk food.* This folk category uses the value-laden term *junk,* which suggests that their food is less than healthy. A more careful analysis would possibly describe this as being occupied in *eating popularized food* such as hamburgers and pizza. These are foods that have healthful aspects (inclusion of meat and cheese proteins, carbohydrates in bread or pizza dough, and vegetable products in the condiments) as well as unhealthful aspects (high salt and fat content and possibly unhealthy additives).

In contrast to this commonsense, folk manner of describing occupations, occupational scientists and others are developing **taxonomies,** sometimes referred to as **occupational classifications** or **occupational categories,** to group objects or events according to like characteristics. The development of taxonomies is complex and not without problems, but the grouping of occupations enables comparisons and other analyses of particular occupational categories, populations, cultures, or topics of interest (21).

Human occupations can be classified or grouped in many different ways. One approach is to organize occupations according to their purpose or goal. In this approach, clusters of occupations can be identified based on their intended outcome. For example, grocery shopping, taking out the garbage, cleaning the house, and doing laundry may all be considered chores by some individuals in some cultural contexts. Their common purpose may be to maintain the living environment. Similarly, dressing, bathing, and grooming may all be directed toward personal care of the self.

Occupational classifications can be both useful and problematic, given cultural and individual differences in naming occupations and their purposes. Nevertheless, a range of occupations not limited to paid work but described in everyday language may include several categories, including those designated as housework, leisure, recreation, play, study (including apprenticeship and training), sleep and rest, relaxation, sports, travel, retirement, and personal care. These categories have been used by professionals as well as by lay people in describing how humans use time (22, 23, 24).

Unfortunately, these descriptors are general rather than specific and can be further defined with specific subtypes of categories describing occupational pursuits. For example, the category of work can be subdivided into literally hundreds of specific paid and unpaid, formally recognized vocations, ranging from airline pilot to zoologist. As Jarman notes in Chapter 3, occupational classifications of paid work have been developed for use by researchers and policy developers, including sociologists and government workers.

One study by Graham et al. attempted to identify categories of purposeful behavior based on the goals described by the subjects being studied (25). This study led to the identification of 18 goal categories, many of which emphasized the social nature of occupations (Table 1-1). These goal situations were studied further and

TABLE 1-1 *Social Goal Categories*

Be accepted by others.
Convey information to others.
Help look after other persons.
Be in control of the situation.
Have fun.
Reduce own anxiety.
Maintain self-respect or self-esteem.
Identify financial prospects.
Attain physical well-being.
Meet hunger or thirst needs.
Engage in sexual activity.
Perform competently.
Make a favorable impression.
Seek help, advice, reassurance.
Persuade someone to do something.
Obtain information, learn something new, solve problems.
Engage in pleasant social activity.
Make new friends, develop relationships.

Source: Social Goal Categories, J.A. Graham, M. Argyle, and A. Furnham. 1980. © John Wiley & Sons Limited. Reproduced with permission.

reduced to just three categories: *interpersonal goals, self-achievement goals,* and *pleasure-seeking goals.*

Occupations can also be classified according to what is done, where they are done, when they are done, and how they are accomplished. As Hamilton emphasizes in chapter 8, geographers and architects are interested in understanding the places or locations in which occupations are performed, and how these influence **occupational habits** or particular kinds of occupational behavior. For example, eating and sleeping (and most occupations devoted to care of the self) are necessary for survival and health. They are classified then as obligatory. On the other hand, free time gives us the opportunity to choose what we will do at our discretion—to select occupations that bring pleasure or satisfaction. Harvey and Pentland extend this to four categories of occupations: necessary, contracted, committed, and free time (Chapter 4).

As noted above, occupational classification is problematic. What is work for one may be leisure for another. Play may be unknown in some cultures; rather, work and play may be intermingled into the rhythm of everyday life. Occupations are not often discrete actions because multiple occupations are often embedded, or nested, occurring simultaneously in the same time and space. Folk taxonomies to describe what people do are often nonspecific but may also be far richer in portraying everyday experience. Psychological, social, and economic forces may determine what people *can* do rather than what they would *like* to do with their time. The political nature of occupations means that some occupations are officially recognized for pay while others are not, or some people are paid more for the same occupations than are others. Nevertheless, the question *What is your occupation?* is so prevalent in daily life that it is important to consider common ways in which occupations are classified. The international time use classification illustrates some of what is already known about occupations classified as paid work, play, leisure, care of self, household and life maintenance, and sleep.

Paid Work

Most of the effort in developing systematic classifications of occupations has been done in the area of paid work. Occupations that produce goods and services are necessary for economic strength. Nations, therefore, have had a strong economic incentive to study, understand, and support information about work-related occupations—that is, jobs.

An example of a frequent method for classifying jobs is known as the *behavioral requirements approach.* For example, Fine developed a classification that examines vocational occupations on the basis of the objects (things), information (data), and people required for the job. Using these three categories, jobs can be described according to the degree of complexity of skill required as the worker encounters things, data, or people in the job. This approach formed the basis for developing the classification system in the *Dictionary of Occupational Titles,* which for many years was used in the United States for classifying types of paid work or vocations (26, 27).

Most countries around the world have developed similar classifications of paid occupations (28), such as Canada's National Occupational Classification (29) and Britain's National Vocational Qualifications System (30). Jarman (Chapter 3) highlights the interests of sociology and governments in developing these economically oriented classifications of occupations.

A related approach to classification of occupations is known as the *ability requirements approach.* In this approach, tasks are described based on the abilities required of the performer, such as reasoning, strength, or vision. Early work by Fleishman (31) identified 52 abilities that could be used to describe and classify different worker roles. These abilities still serve as a basis for classifying jobs in the United States. The current system for organizing information about job categories in the United States is called O*NET. This online system, operated by the Department of Labor, relies on a combination of abilities, task requirements, and other factors to differentiate among jobs and to provide easily accessible information to employers and workers (32). Similar systems are in place in other western industrialized nations, as shown in Table 1-2.

Play

The inclusion of play as an occupational category is of interest particularly in studying child development (see Chapter 5), but also in considering the relationships between occupation and health, well-being, quality of life, and justice (see Chapters 10 and 11). Play is one of the primary occupations of childhood. It is often described as self-motivated or chosen, pleasurable, and important from a developmental perspective since play offers abundant opportunities for learning. Because it is self-chosen and pleasurable, *play* is also a term often used to describe the nonwork occupations of adults. Parham (33) and Takata (34) have each observed that play can be described best as a behavioral style or attitude. For this reason, periods of work may be interspersed with playful moments.

TABLE 1-2   *Selected Occupational Classification Systems*

Name	Brief Description
Australian Standard Classification of Occupations (ASCO)	Contains 1,079 occupations classified according to skill level (e.g., skilled vs. semiskilled) and the work performed. Administered by the Bureau of Statistics. Uses information from a standard set of descriptors called job content factors (JCFs) to classify and report data about occupations.
International Standard Classification of Occupations (ISCO)	This system is being developed and maintained by the European Union. Occupations are clustered based on the duties performed. Information reported includes a brief (one-paragraph) description of the duties and a listing of the education level generally required. These provide the basis for a hierarchical system that contains 10, 28, 116, and 390 titles at each respective level of the hierarchy.
National Occupational Classification (NOC) (Canada)	This system classifies occupations using two main criteria: skill type and skill level. There are 10 major categories of skill type ranging from management to manufacturing and processing. Under skill level, there are four categories, including university degree, college, technical school or apprenticeship training, high school completion and on-the-job training, and short demonstration training or no formal educational requirements. Using the skill type and level matrix, more than 900 profiles have been developed for 522 unit groups. Each is provided with ratings and descriptor scales in several areas using the updated 2001 classification.
National Vocational Qualifications System (Great Britain)	Based on the competences required in particular occupations, NVQs are made up of a number of units which set out industry-defined standards of occupational competence. These describe the skills and knowledge people need to be able to perform effectively at work. Eleven major sectors of industry/commerce are identified, and each sector contains five levels of competencies, which range from general foundational skills to skills required in senior management positions.

Dutch historian Johan Huizinga (35) expressed the notion of play as an attitude and behavioral style, rather than a specific type of occupation. In his 1938 book, *Homo Ludens,* Huizinga traced the evolution of play from preindustrial times. Huizinga noted that play comes from an attitude of finding and sharing joy in the requirements of everyday life, so that even seemingly serious events can reveal playful elements. He lamented that, in the modern age, the fundamental nature of play was being commercialized into sport and entertainment that lacked the community-based and cultural values of play viewed as important in earlier times.

Most approaches to describing play have emerged from theorists interested in how play influences social, physical, and cognitive developments during childhood (Figure 1-4). Influenced by Jean Piaget (36) and others, these approaches describe play as intrinsically motivated and active, noting that play focuses on process rather than outcome.

FIGURE 1-4 Play is an important occupation for development during youth and provides physical, psychological, and social benefits.
(EyeWire Collection/Getty Images)

Behavioral scientists have proposed various play classifications. For younger children, play is classified according to its social dimensions, beginning with solitary play and progressing to types of cooperative play with others. Another approach to classifying play focuses on its processes, including functional play, which consists of simple repetitive movements, to more advanced types of play involving creativity, imagination, and the use of rules. Typically, types of play in children correspond to particular stages of development, since they require different levels of cognitive, physical, and social skills (37).

Leisure

Leisure has been defined as an occupational classification, as discretionary time, and as a state of mind (38, 39). Freedom of choice in participation and not having a particular goal other than enjoyment seem to be the defining characteristics of leisure (40). This "state of mind philosophy" dates back to the Greek philosophers Aristotle and Plato, who viewed leisure in terms of its opportunity for expression and self-development.

Stebbins (41) has identified two broad categories of leisure, which he has termed *casual leisure* and *serious leisure*. Casual leisure seems to be derived from occupations that are pleasurable, of short duration, intrinsically rewarding, and require no special training for enjoyment. In contrast, serious leisure includes amateurism, hobbyist pursuits, self-development, and volunteering.

Serious leisure can be identified by these characteristics: significant personal effort (including acquisition of knowledge, training, or skill) perseverance, lasting benefit, strong feelings of identification, and a set of beliefs and subculture (41).

FIGURE 1-5 Fishing is a popular form of casual leisure for young and old alike. (EyeWire Collection/Getty Images)

Fandom and hobbies are two subsets of serious leisure. Fandom pertains to those serious leisure occupations surrounding media (radio, television, and movies), personalities, sports, science fiction, and musicians. Hobbies include engaging in various kinds of crafts (such as sewing or carpentry, collecting, model-making). Stebbins (42) has also identified liberal arts hobbies as a type of serious leisure, which he describes as a fervent pursuit of knowledge for its own sake during free time. Although other types of serious leisure may require study, the pursuit of knowledge in those cases is secondary to participation in the activity. In liberal arts hobbies, the acquisition of knowledge is the primary goal (42).

According to more recent theories, leisure participation fulfills important psychological needs. Recent attempts to classify specific leisure occupations have focused on the personality types attracted to them or on the psychological needs they meet. For example, research (43) has matched leisure preferences to six personality types from John Holland's theory. More recently, a taxonomy of leisure based on need gratification has been proposed (44). This classification has 11 clusters of leisure pursuits that fulfill identified needs and was based on analysis of 82 leisure occupations that were ranked by nearly 4,000 subjects (44). These needs include agency, novelty, belongingness, service, sensual enjoyment, cognitive stimulation, self-expression, creativity, competition, vicarious competition, and relaxation.

Leisure participation has economic as well as personal and social implications (Figure 1-5). Historically, wealth and the time available for leisure were related (45). As industrialized nations developed, more leisure time became available for the working classes. In contemporary western nations, the time available for leisure activities seems to be declining (46).

Care of Self

Occupations classified as care of self include eating, dressing, bathing, personal hygiene, and other occupations that are generally considered to be physiologically necessary for survival or health. Often included in this category are health-related occupations, such as self-medication, blood pressure monitoring, or managing insulin or dietary requirements. In some time use studies, this category of occupation is referred to as *primary activities.*

Household and Life Maintenance

Household and life maintenance are the instrumental occupations required for everyday living, such as housework, laundry, shopping, cooking, and related chores. These are sometimes referred to in time use studies as *secondary activities.* Parenting and caregiving for older family members or those who are ill or disabled would fall into this general category of unpaid, maintenance-related work. Studies have shown that these daily occupations consume an average of between 15% and 20% of waking hours for working adults. Time requirements for persons with disabilities are typically greater.

Although household and life maintenance occupations are a fundamental requirement for survival and well-being, they also provide the foundation for social life. Much socialization centers around maintaining the living space and community, and an adequate presentation of self (47) is a requirement for social acceptance and communal living (48).

Sleep

Despite the fact that humans spend nearly one-third of their lives sleeping, scientists have known little about sleep until the past two decades. To name sleep as an occupation is itself controversial because occupations are usually equated with action. Nevertheless, sleep requires actions to prepare for sleep (making beds, engaging in relaxation routines) or to create a sleep environment (closing curtains, shutting out noise, arranging for a suitable sleeping surface whether sleeping on a mattress indoors or camping on a mat outdoors). Most people as well as scientists now understand that sleep is essential to good health, that all mammals, not only humans, require it, and that disturbed sleep leads to difficulties during wakefulness (49).

A full understanding of bodily processes during sleep is not yet known. We do know that sleep consists of five phases, and that the body cycles through these phases several times each night. Each cycle includes a stage of deep (delta) sleep, and culminates in a paradoxical condition in which the eyes move rapidly and the brain shows high electrical activity. This is known as REM or rapid eye movement sleep. During this REM stage, lasting 20 to 30 minutes, the body has no control over muscles of the posture and extremities, even though respiration and heart rate have increased substantially. It is during REM sleep that dreams occur.

Some evidence exists to suggest that stressors during the day can affect REM sleep (50, 51). Certain compounds found in foods or pharmaceuticals can disrupt sleep patterns and diminish the restfulness of sleep (52). Significant numbers of people are affected by various sleep disorders, such as insomnia, narcolepsy, and sleep apnea. Because some of these disorders are quite disabling, the amount of scientific attention devoted to understanding the occupation of sleep is increasing.

Because dreaming is associated with REM sleep, questions are also being asked about the relationship that dreams may have with wakened states (53). Some have speculated that dreaming reflects unconscious mental processes, while others speculate that sleep serves as a respite from the need to process environmental information. Sleep seems to be related to restoration of the body, immune function, energy conservation, memory function, temperature regulation, and general development (54).

What is your occupation? is such a commonplace question, but like the other questions raised in this chapter, there are many answers and many complexities. The question opens the floodgates of occupational classification and the categorization of occupations. General categories, such as paid work and leisure seem straightforward, but much remains to be known about these and other occupations. Moreover, the categorization is itself controversial because each category has cultural implications, and occupations are rarely easily and simply assigned to one category. Because occupations are more than activities and tasks, the answer to *What is your occupation?* requires more than the naming and listing of action. Implied in the question is a request to distinguish the purpose of some occupations in relation to others, for instance, to reply with reference to paid or unpaid occupations. Cultural and social conditions will determine whether the answer raises issues of power, as in stating that your occupation is parenting, for which there is strong social value, but little economic value. There is a growing understanding, both in literature and in the general population, that people need to include more than paid work in everyday life. What else do we need to know so that responses to the question *What is your occupation?* are more informed?

WHY ARE SOME PEOPLE OCCUPIED WHILE OTHERS ARE UNOCCUPIED?

The occupations people choose influence their lifestyles, their comfort, their productivity, their social relationships, and, indeed, their health and well-being.

That is, if you examine a typical week, you are likely to see a consistent pattern for what is done over time. These patterns are influenced by biological factors, by psychological factors, and by social or environmental factors. Typically, these three types of influence interact to explain how time is used. Consider some examples of these influences on daily occupation and time use.

Biological Factors

Biological influences on time use include age, physical status, and chronobiology, or bodily rhythms. Clearly, as people age, their typical use of time changes over their life spans. Most infants spend a great deal of time sleeping. In young adulthood, the amount of time spent in sleep often decreases.

Physical status may change time use because it imposes extra demands on the time required to perform different occupations. People with chronic diseases, for example, may have diminished strength or energy, which in turn influences their ability to engage in different occupations.

Our bodies also influence time use through natural rhythms of attention and activity that are influenced by hormones through the endocrine system. A special field of biology, called *chronobiology,* focuses on these influences. Daily patterns of activity may be influenced by circadian rhythms. The term *circadian* is from the Latin words *circa,* meaning "around," and *dia* meaning "day." A 24-hour day constitutes a *round* of activity. Scientists are just now beginning to understand the roles of hormones and how they influence our attention and engagement in activity over time. This understanding helps us to find ways to cope with situations where our required activities are not aligned with our bodily rhythms. Most people know about jet lag, which occurs when travelers cross many time zones. The disruption that sometimes occurs following such travel is called *circadian desynchronization.* This disruption of internal biological clocks can also occur as a result of shift work and can be of limited duration or longer term. Common symptoms include sleep loss, fatigue, diminished performance, loss of appetite, nervous tension, and a feeling of malaise or ill health.

Biological clocks inside humans depend on everyday events in the environment to "set" themselves. Exposure to light, having meals, and other routines or patterns of social activity are now known to be important to daily occupational rhythms. The study of human occupation often shows the connection between internal and external influences (such as social factors) on occupational selection and time use (55).

Psychological Factors

As we mature, our preferences and beliefs begin to take shape within a unique personality that influences our choices and everyday behavior. Personality type may influence our career choice as working adults, as well as our preferences for how leisure time is spent (56). Our values and beliefs, along with our characteristic tendencies to view and interpret the world (sometimes called *cognitive style*), strongly influence our choices of occupations. These preferences include not only what we choose to do, but also where and with whom we choose to spend our time. Current theories of occupational choice emphasize psychological factors, such as personality and self-identity, as important influences on occupational time use and lifestyle patterns.

Environmental and Social Factors

The environment influences what we do. Physical factors include natural conditions, such as the weather; landscape and the built environment; and the availability of objects such as tools, furniture, and equipment necessary to undertake certain activities. To cite some obvious examples, ice skating is a limited occupation near the equator, and water sports are impractical in the Sahara desert. Near the Arctic, long durations of daylight or darkness can influence occupational cycles. Similarly, differences in the built environment can influence transportation occupations. Traveling by water taxis is common in Venice, whereas traveling by street taxis and subways is more practical in London.

Sometimes, the physical characteristics of landscape and objects invite particular occupations. For example, because of their design, chairs and other smooth horizontal objects invite sitting. Substances and surfaces that can be shaped or manipulated invite touch. Handles invite grabbing. These characteristics of objects and designs were named *affordances* by Gibson, the father of ecological psychology (57). Affordances are environmental properties that both induce and support goal-directed behavior (58).

Another factor that influences engagement in occupations in industrialized societies is the availability of raw materials, finished goods, and services. The supply of objects and tools necessary for some occupations can influence our ability to engage in certain occupations. Thus, without the basketball, the schoolyard game cannot take place. Without parts, repair technicians cannot get on with their work. Without building materials and tools, the construction business comes to a standstill; restaurants and supermarkets depend on regular delivery of fresh produce. Most types of work, play, and leisure depend on the availability of some type of products or services.

In the industrialized world, people are increasingly finding that a key factor influencing occupation is the availability of energy. Without electricity, natural gas, or refined petroleum products, transportation services, businesses, and other aspects of daily existence (and, therefore, occupations) are constrained. Clearly, the availability of objects, manufactured goods, and services is tied to our everyday lives. This connection between occupations and commerce helps to explain why economists are interested in studying human occupations as a means for understanding how people produce or consume goods and services. Thus, people are not only citizens of states or nations; they also constitute a valuable resource known as human capital. This capital has value, however, only because of human occupations—the occupations related to producing or consuming goods or services.

Because humans are social beings, we live in groups and both influence and are influenced by other people and by the policies, laws, media, and other conditions that determine what is possible or even thinkable. According to established theories (59, 60), groups of people, whether they are families, cultures, or societies, create, resist, or act within rules, customs, and traditions. Social expectations, whether they are formal (such as policies and laws) or informal (such as traditions or customs), greatly influence our patterns of daily occupations. Social groups influence our beliefs about the world, about right and wrong, and about life in general. This influence occurs through teaching and experience. Beliefs, in turn, greatly influence our occupational choices and patterns of time use. When people choose lifestyles that are different from societal norms, their behavior may produce social change or may be classified as deviant (61). Many categories of resistance or deviance result in lifestyle patterns that are unique to certain groups, sometimes called *subcultures*.

Flowing from social norms and expectations are the regulations that societies put in place to coordinate and control what people can and, indeed, want to do in the everyday world (62). We know implicitly that what we do is determined by what is allowable and accepted. But we are often unaware of what forces determine our daily occupations. Theories of social norms and deviance address this issue of what is allowable and accepted from the point of view of values and beliefs. However, the more directly powerful, practical forces that define norms and deviance in society are policies, legislation, and market forces. For instance, employment policies, occupational classifications, and market forces determine what occupations receive financial rewards and what occupations are considered private and unpaid (63). Consider the regulation of occupations in hunting and gathering societies. Likely such communities have very few written policies, but the economy and understood policies are that all males participate in gathering food, while all females and children participate in preparing food. The national policies that govern what such communities can do may define these people as unemployed, since their gross annual income is minimal. As unemployed people, they may not be eligible for national health insurance or for national pensions for seniors, even though they have engaged in meaningful occupations and "worked" all their lives. Contrast the regulation of hunting and gathering occupations with that of occupations in the global telecommunications industry. The occupations are subject to a huge, interconnected, written, but often taken-for-granted network of policies, laws, and financial regulation. Anyone who has invested in telecommunications or has worked in this field will know that the occupations that use video display terminals (VDTs), for example, are highly regulated as a component of international telecommunications. Salaries are low and repetitive motion injuries are high for heavy VDT users, who are primarily women in office occupations, such as secretarial work (64, 65, 66). Hence, the often taken-for-granted control of occupations is not always direct, but rather has a filter-down impact that is invisible and connected with world events and major, powerful forces that shape everyday life.

Social factors, whether they be traditions, expectations, or regulating policies, interact with biological factors to influence patterns of time use across the life span. During childhood, greater periods are spent in exploration and play, which are vital for learning and physical maturation. Typical patterns exist for students, for working adults, and for retired people. Many retired people have greater periods of discretionary time available to them than they did when they were employed. Certainly, some people are different, but general patterns of time use can be found that characterize different stages of life. These vary somewhat across cultures (67).

The availability of free time and how it is used is a topic of interest to social scientists from many fields. The amount of time apportioned toward leisure, paid work, and unpaid work has social, political, and economic implications. After several decades in which the amount of discretionary time for working class individuals steadily increased, there is evidence that these trends may have reversed so that the time available for relaxation and leisure may be diminishing (46).

WHAT IS THE HISTORY OF OCCUPATION?[1]

An understanding of occupations today is better achieved if a person has an appreciation for what people did during previous eras. Archaeologists and anthropologists agree that from the dawn of time, humans' primary purpose was to survive. As early humans developed language and intellect, adaptation to the forces of nature required a division of labor. In very early times men were the foragers and gatherers and women, being child-bearers, were the preservers and fashioners of materials for eating and bartering. The basic occupations at this time included agriculture, the making of essential tools, and the creation of pottery, textiles, and basketry (68).

While an in-depth exploration of the history of work and leisure could easily fill volumes, a review of everyday occupations through the ages and how these influenced (and were influenced by) the cultures and attitudes of the time provides a useful context in which to view the present. History illustrates how work and play have long coexisted and been jointly influenced by cultures and environments. Examples highlight European and North American trends, largely within the Christian world.

In later centuries, the Greeks were among the first advanced culture to appreciate a distinction between work and leisure (69). Work was seen as the gods' curse on humankind. The Greek word for "work" was *ponos*, meaning a sense of a heavy burdensome task, downright drudgery. Within this culture, however, division of labor was based on status within the culture. There was little dignity or value in work, other than as a means for avoiding hunger and death, or for reaching prosperity and the opportunity for leisure. Slaves, peasants, and craftspeople did the work of gathering and preserving raw materials and of fashioning goods. A middle class was made up of merchants, who did the bartering. The nobility and priests became the upper class, whose work was to indulge in the pleasurable occupations of life, such as teaching, discovering, thinking, or composing music. At this time, leisure became one of the foundations of Western culture. The English word *school* is derived from the Greek word *skole* for the place where education and teaching occur (69).

Three prominent Greek philosophers provided classical insights regarding work and the pursuit of the thoughtful life (70). Socrates was known to frequent the shops of Athens, observing artisans at work, doing what he thought were nonessential tasks. Aristotle, on the other hand, believed that well-being did not come from the pursuit of pleasure (hedonism); rather, it came from the meditative life (leisure). Late in his writings, Plato, declared that life must be lived as play, playing certain games and making sacrifices. In this manner a person could gain favor with the gods and provide a defense against enemies (71).

The Roman philosophers also held views about occupation (72). Cicero, the great orator and philosopher, claimed there were but two worthy occupations: agriculture and business, especially if the latter led one to an honorable and stately retirement into the quiet of the countryside. The Hebrews also held an admiration for work and the meditative life. The Talmud states that labor is a holy occupation and even if one does not need to work to survive, he or she must nevertheless labor, for idleness results in an early death (73).

Alfred the Great (849–899 A.D.), king of Wessex, established the right of freeborn Englishmen to the three-eights division of the day into work, rest, and leisure. During this same time various festivals emerged, particularly to recognize sacred or seasonal events. Consecrations, sacrifices, sacred dances and contests, and performances all were occupations for celebrating a festival (35). During the period from 350 to 800 A.D., people returned to a simpler life (74); yet, the class stratification remained as peasant, merchant, and nobleman. In the early 16th century, Martin Luther believed that work and serving God were synonymous and one was expected to do the best job possible, thereby earning dignity. One was called to one's work since all daily occupations were divinely inspired (75).

In the 17th century, a Frenchman, John Calvin, whose writings have had a significant impact on Western cultures, added to the prevailing beliefs by declaring there was no room for idleness, luxury, or any activity that softened the soul (76). Meditation was not acceptable because Calvin believed that God was not in the habit of revealing "himself" to humans through thinking. A person was expected to extract the greatest good from work, including a profit. Successful work would result in wealth, which was to be used to care for those less fortunate. This link between work and wealth became known as the Protestant work ethic.

The Agrarian Age (c.1800–1880) brought the tools necessary to produce the goods required by the world. Because most occupations were seasonal, the worker could control periods of leisure and rest. This ended with the onset of the Industrial Revolution, beginning in the middle of the 18th century and lasting for 100 years. Time took over as the key to nearly all daily occupations. One no longer worked at home in what had often come to be thought of as "cottage industries." The worker left home to work in large buildings, with large numbers of individuals, often accomplishing the same occupations alongside one another. Machinery replaced tools as the focus of labor. Compensation was determined by someone other than the worker and was based on the clock, usually displayed prominently in the workplace. This was the beginning of paid occupations in the industrialized world.

During the Industrial Revolution, leisure occupations departed from the home and became centered in the community. Many factory owners assumed responsibility for their workers' play time. An example was the community established in the 1880's by the Pullman Company, south of Chicago. The town was carefully laid out to include a wide variety of parks and structures for the pleasure of all members of the workers' family. Despite this, considerable unrest resulted, and strikes often occurred over wages and the adequacy and control of leisure time (62, 63).

During the Great Depression of the 1930s, the U.S. government assisted with numerous occupational programs, including the WPA, or Works Progress Administration (77). As one WPA enrollee said after just 3 weeks on the job: "Now I can look my children straight in the eyes. I've gained my self-respect. It's different now" (64, p. 812). Allied nations rallied behind the war effort. Yet, time was taken for leisure occupations. Movie attendance set new records. Attending nightclubs and sporting events, taking vacations, and being entertained at home, such as listening to the radio, reading paperbacks, and playing various parlor games, became popular leisure occupations (78).

The present era, sometimes known as the Postindustrial or Information Age, was described by Ferguson as a social transformation resulting from personal transformation—change from the inside out (79). Naisbitt claimed that Western society was reluctantly leaving behind the Industrial Age and entering the Information Age, where the new wealth was in know-how (80). In the current era, with the universal two-income family, leisure occupations have undergone a drastic change. Cross says a stressed leisure class now exists along with great inequities between men and women (81). Women in the workplace return home to care for children and housework. They are

FIGURE 1-6 Occupations can have significant implications for personal health and happiness. (Steve Mason/Getty Images)

frequently denied the after-work leisure time enjoyed by many men. Cross speculates that home-based entertainment, such as rented movies and high-quality sound systems, are used as convenient substitutes for other forms of leisure, but probably fall short of giving the satisfaction that other more involved options might offer (81).

We can speculate about how attitudes toward work and leisure occupations are influenced by cultures. We can ask why many people are feeling less satisfied with their work and leisure than in the past. Or we can consider how the Information Age might influence the types and locations of occupations in the future. A better approach is to study occupations systematically, taking a broad look at the many dimensions that influence everyday human pursuits. Durant stated it well when he observed: "The present is the past rolled up for action, and the past is the present unrolled for understanding" (82, p. viii).

OCCUPATIONS AND WELL-BEING

A growing body of literature is showing that lifestyle and occupational choices influence both physical and psychological well-being (Figure 1-6). The field of health promotion has for years recognized that most diseases and injuries are preventable, and that lifestyle choices such as regular exercise, nutrition, adequate sleep, and avoidance of stress, tobacco, and excessive alcohol use can improve health and increase the life span (83). What is important in modern health systems, critics argue, is attention to social, environmental, and behavioral issues that enable people to make responsible lifestyle choices (84).

Research now supports these claims. Behavioral scientists interested in how individual differences, personality, and lifestyle factors influence well-being have shown that engagement in occupations can influence happiness and life satisfaction (85, 86). So-called "person–environment" or ecological models of adaptation suggest that people thrive when their personalities and needs are matched with environments or situations that enable them to remain engaged, interested, and challenged (87, 88).

CHAPTER SUMMARY

To rethink occupation is to recognize the richness and complexity of occupation. The task of defining occupation is not simply a matter of translating the Latin word *occupare*. Nor can occupation be fully understood by listing categories of paid occupations. When Roman poet and philosopher Horace offered the admonition *carpe diem*, meaning "seize the day," he was suggesting something far more than merely passing time or existing. In rethinking occupation, we can surmise that Horace was recommending that people live life to the fullest by learning about and making full use of occupation as the fabric for experiencing and structuring everyday life.

In the preceding pages, the complexity of human occupation was described. It has been shown that occupations reflect time use according to both individual and cultural characteristics, and that biological, ecological, and psychological factors influence our occupational choices.

Approaches to identifying categories of occupational pursuit were described. We noted that international time use studies provide useful information on human productivity and social trends. These studies are helping to provide a beginning taxonomy for describing and classifying human occupations. Although classification will remain problematic given different individual, cultural, policy, and economic perspectives. Some categories of occupations, including paid work, leisure, sleep, basic self-care, and household work, were introduced and described. Each of these areas of human endeavor has implications for health and well-being.

As an area of interest and study, human occupation cuts a broad swath across the social and behavioral sciences, yet only recently has emerged as an occupational interdisciplinary science. Occupation appears to be fundamental to human existence and to the organization of societies. An *Introduction to Occupation* is only a beginning.

REFERENCES

1. Nelson, D. L. (1988). Occupation: Form and performance. *American Journal of Occupational Therapy, 42*(10), 633–641.
2. Christiansen, C., Clark, F. A., Kielhofner, G., & Rogers, J. (1995). Position paper: Occupation. *American Journal of Occupational Therapy, 49*(10), 1015–1018.
3. Bateson, M. C. (1996). Enfolded activity and the concept of occupation. In R. Zemke & F. Clark (Ed.), *Occupational science: The evolving discipline*. Philadelpia: F. A. Davis.
4. Camic, C. (1986). The matter of habit. *American Journal of Sociology, 91*, 1039–1087.
5. Clark, F. A. (2000). The concepts of habit and routine: A preliminary theoretical synthesis. *The Occupational Therapy Journal of Research, 20*(Supplement 1), 123S–138S.

6. Corbin, J. M. (1999). The role of habits in everyday life. In *A synthesis of knowledge regarding the concept of habit.* Pacific Grove, CA: American Occupational Therapy Foundation.

7. Dunn, W. W. (2000). Habit: What's the brain got to do with it? *The Occupational Therapy Journal of Research, 20*(Supplement 1), 2S–5S.

8. Young, M. (1998). *The metronomic society.* Cambridge, MA: Harvard University Press.

9. Bargh, J. A. (1997). The automaticity of everyday life. In R. S. Wyer (Ed.), *Advances in social cognition.* Mahwah, NJ: Lawrence Erlbaum.

10. Bargh, J. A., Chen, M., & Burrows, L. (1996). Automaticity of social behavior: Direct effects of trait construct and stereotype priming on action. *Journal of Personality and Social Psychology, 71,* 230–244.

11. Bargh, J. A., & Chartrand, T. L. (1999). The unbearable automaticity of being. *American Psychologist, 54,* 462–479.

12. Christiansen, C. (1993). Three perspectives on balance in occupation. In F. Clark, R. Zemke (Ed.), *Occupational science: Selections from the symposia.* Philadelphia: F. A. Davis.

13. Erikson, E. H. (1982). *The life cycle completed.* New York: Norton.

14. Christiansen, C. (1999). Occupation as identity. Competence, coherence and the creation of meaning. *American Journal of Occupational Therapy, 53*(6), 547–558.

15. Bateson, M. C. (1990). *Composing a life.* New York: Penguin.

16. Markus, H., & Nurius, P. (1986). Possible selves. *American Psychologist, 41,* 954–969.

17. Bruner, J. (1990). *Acts of meaning.* Cambridge, MA: Harvard University Press.

18. McAdams, D. P. (1993). *The stories we live by: Personal myths and the making of the self.* New York: Guilford Press.

19. Greer, G. (2000). *The whole woman.* New York: Anchor Books.

20. Frieden, B. (1963). *The feminine mystique.* New York: W. W. Norton.

21. Christiansen, C. (1992). *The study and classification of occupation.* In N. Gillette (Ed.), *AOTF research colloquium.* Houston: American Occupational Therapy Foundation.

22. American Occupational Therapy Association. (1994). Uniform terminology for occupational therapy (3rd ed.). *American Journal of Occupational Therapy, 48*(11), 1047–1054.

23. Canadian Association of Occupational Therapists. (1991). *Occupational therapy guidelines for client centred practice.* Toronto: CAOT Publications.

24. Hagedorn, R. (1992). *Occupational therapy: Foundations for practice.* Edinburgh: Churchill Livinsgstone.

25. Graham, J. A., Argyle, M., & Furnham, A. (1980). The goal structure of situations. *European Journal of Social Psychology, 10,* 345–366.

26. Fine, S. A. (1988). Functional job analysis. In S. Gael (Ed.), *The job analysis handbook for business, industry, government* (pp. 1019–1035). New York: Wiley.

27. Fine, S. A. (1955). A structure of worker functions. *Personnel and Guidance Journal, 34*(October), 66–73.

28. Hoffman, E. (1991). *Mapping the world of work: An international review of the use and gathering of occupational information.* Washington, DC: Bureau of Labor Statistics.

29. *National occupational classification.* (2001). Ottawa, Canada: Human Resources Development Canada.

30. Elias, P. (1996). *A review of the standard occupational classification.* Coventry: Institute for Employment Research, University of Warwick.

31. Fleishman, E. A., & Quaintance, M. K. (1984). *Taxonomies of Human Performance: The Description of Human Tasks.* Orlando: Academic Press.

32. Peterson, N., Mumford, M., Borman, W., Jeanneret, P., Fleishman, E., & Levin, K. (1997). *O*NET final technical report* (Vols. 1–3). Salt Lake City, UT: National Center for O*NET Development, U.S. Department of Labor.
33. Parham, L. D. (1996). Perspectives on play. In R. Zemke, F. Clark (Ed.), *Occupational science: The emerging discipline* (pp. 71–88). Philadelphia: F. A. Davis.
34. Takata, N. (1971). The play milieu—a preliminary proposal. *American Journal of Occupational Therapy, 23,* 314–318.
35. Huizinga, J. (1964). *Homo ludens: A study of the play element in culture* (4th ed.). Boston: Beacon.
36. Piaget, J. (1969). *The psychology of the child.* New York: Basic Books.
37. Bergen, D. (1988). *Play as a medium for learning.* Portsmouth, NH: Heinemann.
38. Gunter, B. G., Stanley, J., & St. Clair, R. (1985). Theoretical issues in leisure study. In: B. G. Gunter & R. St. Clair (Eds.), *Transitions to leisure: Conceptual and human issues* (pp. 35–51). Lanham, MD: University Press of America.
39. Witt, P. A., & Goodale, T. (1992). Stress, leisure and the family. *Recreation Research Review, 9*(3), 28–32.
40. Iso-Ahola, S. E. (1979). Basic dimensions of definitions of leisure. *Journal of Leisure Research, 11,* 28–39.
41. Stebbins, R. A. (1997). Casual leisure: A conceptual statement. *Leisure Studies, 16,* 17–25.
42. Stebbins, R. A. (1994). The liberal arts hobbies: A neglected subtype of serious leisure. *Leisure and Society, 17*(1), 173–186.
43. Holmberg, K., Rosen, D., & Holland, J. L. (1990). *The leisure activities finder.* Odessa, FL: Psychological Assessment Resources.
44. Tinsley, H. E., & Eldridge, B. D. (1995). Psychological benefis of leisure participation: A taxonomy of leisure activities based on their need gratifying properties. *Journal of Counseling Psychology, 42*(2), 123–132.
45. Veblen, T. (1899). *A theory of the leisure class: An economic study of institutions.* New York: Macmillan.
46. Sullivan, O. G. (2001). Cross national changes in time-use. *British Journal of Sociology, 52*(1), 331–348.
47. Goffman, I. (1963). *Stigma: Notes on the management of a spoiled identity.* Englewood Cliffs, NJ: Prentice Hall.
48. Christiansen, C. H. (2000). The social importance of self-care intervention. In C. H. Christiansen (Ed.), *Ways of living: Self-care strategies for special needs* (pp. 1–12). Bethesda, MD: American Occupational Therapy Association.
49. Aronoff, M. S. (1991). *Sleep and its secrets: The river of crystal light.* Los Angeles: Insight Books.
50. Horne, J. A. M. A. S. (1985). Sleep and sleepiness following a behaviourally 'active' day. *Ergonomics, 28,* 567–575.
51. Meguro, K., Ueda, M., Yamaguchi, T., Sekita, Y., Yamazaki, H., Oikawa, Y., et al. (1990). Disturbance in daily sleep/wake patterns in patients with cognitive impairment and decreased daily activity. *Journal of the American Geriatrics Society, 38*(11), 1176–1182.
52. Minors, D. S., Rabbitt, P. M. A., Worthington, H., & Waterhouse, J. M. (1989). Variation in meals and sleep-activity patterns in aged subjects; its relevance to circadian rhythm studies. In *Chronobiology International* (pp. 139–146). Oxford: Pergamon Press.
53. Siegel, J. M. (1994). Brainstem mechanisms generating REM sleep. In M. K. Kryger, W. C. Dement (Eds.), *Principles and practice of sleep medicine* (2nd ed., pp. 125–144). New York: W. B. Saunders.
54. Hobson, J. (1995). *Sleep.* New York: Scientific American Library.

55. Halberg, F. (1994). *Introduction to chronobiology.* Minneapolis: Medtronic.

56. Furnham, A. (1981). Personality and activity preference. *British Journal of Social Psychology, 20*(1), 57–68.

57. Gibson, J. J. (1979). *The ecological approach to vision perception.* Boston: Houghlin-Mifflin.

58. Shaw, R. E., Kugler, P. N., & Kinsella-Shaw, M. M. (1990). Reciprocities of intentional systems. In R. Warren, A. H. Wertheim (Ed.), *Perception and control of self motion* (pp. 579–619). Hillsdale, NJ: Lawrence Erlbaum.

59. Cooley, C. H. (1902). *Human nature and the social order.* New York: Charles Scribner's.

60. Mead, G. H. (1934). *Mind, self and society.* Chicago: University of Chicago Press.

61. Goode, E. (1996). *Social deviance.* Boston: Allyn & Bacon.

62. Smith, D. E. (1987). *The everyday world as problematic: A feminist sociology.* Toronto: The University of Toronto Press.

63. Townsend, E. (1997). Occupation: Potential for personal and social transformation. *Journal of Occupational Science, 4*(1), 18–26.

64. Houtman, I. L. D., Bongers, P. M., Smulders, P. G. W., & Kompier, M. A. J. (1994). Psychosocial stressors at work and musculoskeletal problems. *Scandinavian Journal of Work, Environment and Health, 20,* 139–145.

65. Landisbergis, P., Schnall, P. L., Dietz, D. I., Warren, K., Pickering, T. G., & Schwartz, J. E. (1998). Job strain and health behaviors: Results of a prospective study. *American Journal of Health Promotion, 12,* 237–245.

66. Tittiranonda, P., Burastero, S., & Rempel, D. (1999). Risk factors for musculoskeletal disorders among computer users. *Occupational Medicine, 14,* 17–34.

67. Szalai, A. (Ed.). (1972). *The use of time.* The Hague, Netherlands: Mouton.

68. Stringer, C., & Gamble, C. (1993). *In search of neanderthals: Solving the puzzle of modern human origins.* New York: Thames and Hudson.

69. Pieper, J. (1963). *Leisure: The basis of culture.* New York: New American Library.

70. Warner, R. (1958). *The Greek philosophers.* New York: Mentor.

71. Brunschwig, J., & Lloyd, G. E. R. (Ed.). (2000). *Greek thought: A guide to classical knowledge.* Cambridge, MA: Harvard Univesity Press.

72. Cicero, M. T. (1960). *Cicero: Selected works.* London: Viking (Penguin-Putnam).

73. Rappapport, S. (1910). *Tales and maxims from the Talmud.* London: George Routledge's Sons.

74. Dark, K. (2000). *Britain and the end of the Roman empire.* Stroud, United Kingdom: Tempus Publishing.

75. Lindberg, C. (Ed.). (1999). *The European reformations sourcebook.* Oxford: Blackwell.

76. McGrath, A. E. (1990). *A life of John Calvin: A study in shaping the Western culture.* Oxford: Blackwell.

77. Leuchtenburg, W. (1963). *Franklin D. Roosevelt and the new deal.* New York: Harper & Row.

78. Jeffries, J. W. (1996). *Wartime America: The World War II home front.* Chicago: Ivan R. Dee.

79. Ferguson, M. (1980). *The acquarian conspiracy: Personal and social transformation in the 1980s.* Los Angeles: J. P. Tarcher.

80. Naisbitt, J. (1982). *Megatrends: Ten new directions transforming our lives.* New York: Warner Books.

81. Cross, G. (1990). *A social history of leisure since 1600.* State College, PA: Venture Publishing.

82. Durant, W. (1957). *The story of civilization: Part VI: The reformation.* New York: Simon & Schuster.

83. McKeown, T. (1976). *The role of medicine, dream, mirage or nemesis?* London: Nuffield Provincial Hospital Trust.

84. Callahan, D. (1998). *False hope.* New York: Simon & Schuster.

85. Christiansen, C., Backman, C., Little, B. R., & Nguyen, A. (1999). Occupations and subjective well-being: A study of personal projects. *American Journal of Occupational Therapy, 53*(1), 91–100.

86. Diener, (2000). Subjective well-being: The science of happiness and a proposal for a national index. *American Psychologist, 55*(1), 34–43.

87. Csikszentmihalyi, M. (1990). *Flow—The psychology of optimal experience.* New York: Harper and Row.

88. Christiansen, C. H., Little, B. R., & Backman, C. (1998). Personal projects: A useful approach to the study of occupation. *American Journal of Occupational Therapy, 52*(6), 439–446.

Endnote

1. This section was authored by Dr. Robert K. Bing.

CHAPTER 2

The Study of Occupation

H. J. Polatajko

It is neither wealth nor splendour, but tranquillity
and occupation which give happiness.

Thomas Jefferson

KEY WORDS

Epistemology

Metacognition

Methods of inquiry

Multivariate

Naturalistic paradigm

Occupationology

Occupations

Occupational science

Paradigm

Positivistic paradigm

Qualitative research

Reductionistic

CHAPTER PROFILE

This is a "how-to" chapter. The reader will learn how to learn about occupation, that is, how to become a student of occupation. Some would describe this as learning to be a scientist who specializes in studying occupation, sometimes described as an occupationologist or occupational scientist. A range of formal and informal methods for studying occupation will be introduced. The chapter offers a point of entry to the world of scholarly inquiry about occupation. First, the chapter will discuss what it means *to understand* occupation. Six questions form a template to unravel the mysteries of occupation and current methods of inquiry.

www.prenhall.com/christiansen

The Internet provides an exciting means for interacting with this textbook and for enhancing your understanding of humans' experiences with occupations and the organization of occupations in society. Use the address above to access the free, interactive companion web site created specifically to accompany this book. Here you will find an array of self-study material designed to help you gain a richer understanding of the concepts presented in this chapter.

INTRODUCTION

We each engage in numerous **occupations** every day. We see the people around us engage in occupations and we see occupations portrayed in print, on television, and at the movies. As a result, each of us has a great deal of familiarity and personal experience with occupation. So, it would be easy to conclude that we understand occupation, that we are all occupational experts. But are we? Do we know, for example, whether children in Papua, New Guinea, are occupied in playing the same games as children in Atlanta, Georgia? Whether Michael Jordan would have been as successful if he had chosen the occupation of hockey rather than basketball? Whether the Canadian hockey player Wayne Gretzky did, in fact, *choose* the occupation of hockey? Do we know what makes a gifted musician or a great surgeon? Can we tell which child will grow up to be the prime minister of Canada, president of the United States of America, or a leader in the United Nations? Do we know which occupations a community will determine are worth developing when that community's primary occupations of livelihood—for example, a steel mill—become obsolete?

Our personal experiences are very important in helping us develop an understanding of occupation, but are they sufficient? An understanding of occupation cannot be gained from direct experience alone. Constructing an understanding of occupation requires careful examination of the context of the doing, the perspective of the doer, and the framework of the knower. The process of examination always starts with a question. Six basic questions about occupation are asked in this chapter to help bring about an understanding of this phenomenon. These same questions guide journalists in their investigative reporting: *Who?*, *What?*, *When?*, *Where?*, *How?*, and *Why?*

Each of the six questions leads us to various **methods of inquiry.** The methods of investigative journalism, like personal experience and observation, can be applied to the study of occupation and can tell us a fair amount about it. However, no *one* method of inquiry is sufficient. Occupation is such a complicated, **multivariate** phenomenon that understanding it requires a multifaceted approach. Methods, ranging from stories to statistics and drawn from both qualitative and quantitative methods of inquiry, are needed. The chapters in this book illustrate many methods of inquiry associated with our six basic questions. These questions provide a template for inquiry (1) that can be used for understanding occupation in response to inquiries about who, what, when, where, how, and why. To explain and demonstrate the process, an overview of possible methods of inquiry will be presented along with at least one example for each of the six questions.

WAYS OF KNOWING

Understanding the Who, What, When, Where, How, and Why of Occupation

To understand . . . to perceive the meaning or explanation of, grasp the idea of, or comprehend: to be thoroughly acquainted with or familiar with. (2)

How people go about understanding something depends on what it is they want to know and how well they want to know it. If we want to know someone's name, we

TABLE 2-1   *Female vs. Male Ways of Knowing*

Female Epistemological Perspectives	Male Epistemological Perspectives
Silence—The self is experienced as mindless and voiceless, subject to external authority. **Received knowledge**—The self is conceived of as capable of receiving, even reproducing, knowledge from the all-knowing external authority. **Subjective knowledge**—Truth and knowledge are conceived of as personal, private and subjectively known or intuited. **Procedural knowledge**—The processes of learning and applying of objective procedures for obtaining and communicating knowledge are values and actively cultivated. **Constructed knowledge**—All knowledge is viewed as contextual; The self is seen as a creator of knowledge and both subjective and objective strategies for knowing are valued.	**Basic duality**—The world is viewed in polarities: right/wrong, black/white, we/they, good/bad; everything is knowable; the learner is dependent on external authority to hand down truth. **Multiplicity**—It is realized that there is diversity of opinion and a multiplicity of perspectives in some areas; faith in absolute authority is shaken. **Relativism subordinate**—Opinion alone is recognized as inadequate; evidence and support that can stand up to scrutiny are required; an analytical, evaluative approach is actively cultivated. **Relativism**—Truth is understood to be relative; the meaning of an event is understood to depend on the context of the event and the framework of the knower; relativism is seen to pervade all aspects of life.

Source: As described by Belensky and colleagues [Gathered from Belensky, et al., (5)]

might ask him or her. If we want to know how we can hear the answer, we can read a book on the human auditory system. If we want to know more than a person's name, that is, if we want to get to know a person, we might spend time with that person in order to observe and learn about his or her everyday routines and interests. If we want to truly understand our best friend, we might do all of the above, and more.

Researchers tell us that how we go about understanding something depends not only on what we want to understand, but also on who we are: our age and education (3), our social and economic advantage, and our perspective on the nature of the world (4). Our understanding is also influenced by whether we are male or female (5).

Shared learning and deeper understanding require representational thought, built on reflection, abstraction, and an exchange of ideas. Once an exchange of ideas occurs, any number of ways of knowing can be adopted. William Perry, in his classic work *Forms of Intellectual and Ethical Development in the College Years* (6) described a scheme for representing the various ways of understanding. He called these ways of knowing *epistemological positions*. Later, Belenky and her colleagues (5) among others, argued that women and men, although similar, approached understanding in different ways (see Table 2-1). The simplest way of knowing involves personal experience and direct observation of the actual, the concrete, and the specific in the present. Belenky and her colleagues (5) noted that personal experience and observation were the ways of knowing used by the youngest and most disadvantaged women in their study. They referred to this way

of knowing, this epistemological perspective, as *Silence* to denote the total sub-
missiveness of disadvantaged women to authority. This approach provides for a
very rudimentary understanding of the here and now but does not allow for any
understanding of the past or the future, for any reflection, or for any shared learning (see Table 2-1).

Taken together, the work of Perry and Belenky's research teams provides a
comprehensive description of four modes of understanding, four **epistemologies.**
In the first mode, knowledge may be accepted from authorities at face value and
without question; truth is viewed as essentially dichotomous—black or white. In the
second approach, authority is not considered absolute, because a variety of perspectives or opinions are recognized. Truth is viewed as subjective, personal, and intuitive. This second way of knowing is similar to the prevalent reliance on intuition
that preceded scientific thought and is considered central to many Eastern philosophies. A third way of knowing is to recognize that neither knowledge from authority nor intuitive knowledge are adequate ways of knowing. Instead, only knowledge
that is gained from reasoned reflection or based on support and evidence and subject to formal analysis and evaluation is viewed as dependable. In this third mode of
understanding, truth is viewed critically—that is, it is subject to verification. The
fourth way of knowing is to recognize knowledge as constructed and changing, subject to the situation and the perspective of the knower. In this fourth approach,
truth is recognized as relative and is thus viewed critically. Included in these perspectives of knowledge is the full range of methods for understanding, extending
from the informal methods of the individual knower to the formal methods of dis-
ciplined inquiry used by recognized researchers.

Disciplinary Ways of Knowing

Disciplines, formed by groups of like-minded individuals concerned with understanding particular phenomena, are similar to individuals in that they have particular ways of knowing (7, 8). The modes of inquiry used by a specific discipline have
to do with the nature of the phenomena of interest, as well as the epistemological
perspectives of the members of the discipline (9). Put more simply, each discipline
adopts a way of understanding, a mode of inquiry, that is appropriate to the people
who make up the discipline and the nature of what is to be understood (3, 4, 7, 8).

Disciplinary ways of knowing, referred to as disciplinary **paradigms,** although
specific to a discipline, are not necessarily unique to that discipline. A number of
disciplines have adopted similar ways of knowing; for example, chemistry, physics,
engineering, and psychology have all adopted the experimental method as a primary mode of inquiry. In addition, disciplines may adopt several ways of knowing.
For example, sociology uses experimentation, survey, field study, and nonreactive
study as its preferred ways of understanding phenomena (10).

Disciplinary paradigms are not static or fixed. Rather, they change as understanding of phenomena evolves (8, 11). Change may also be prompted by a need to
gain deeper understanding, as has happened in psychology (12–14). Because of the
changing nature of inquiry among disciplines, a large and ever-growing range exists

of "how-to" literature on inquiry—a literature that covers a broad and varied range of methods in a number of disciplines.

Paradigms for Inquiry

Disciplinary paradigms have tended to emanate from one of two major epistemological perspectives. The first perspective is called the **naturalistic paradigm** and is also referred to as **qualitative research.** The second perspective is the **positivistic paradigm,** which is also referred to as the quantitative, experimental-type, or **reductionistic** approach (7, 8, 10, 15, 16, 17, 18). A third perspective, critical social science, is not included in this chapter.

The **naturalistic paradigm** is based on the assumption that the world is made up of multiple, overlapping realities that are subjectively experienced, socially constructed, complex, and constantly changing. The role of the qualitative researcher is to come to an in-depth understanding of these realities and how they are constructed. Qualitative researchers immerse themselves, often over a long period, into the natural settings and lives of groups being studied in order to gain an understanding of and to interpret their experiences and perspectives. The **qualitative research** process is understood to be a subjective one with the researcher being the main instrument of data collection.

The positivistic paradigm is based on the assumption that the world is made up of observable, measurable facts. In this approach, the role of the quantitative researcher is to uncover these facts and to discern laws that govern the relationship between cause and effect by conducting carefully planned studies that control as many variables as necessary. The ultimate goal of quantitative research is to explain and predict and, to this end, research is expected to be objective, unbiased, and logical (4, 12, 15–18).

With the advent of modern science in the Western world, the predominant Western perspective on understanding became firmly based in positivism. Until relatively recently, naturalistic perspectives were viewed as suspect or inadequate and thus were devalued (4, 7, 14). The growth of modern science produced a literature on methods of inquiry that was almost exclusively quantitative. However, this is rapidly changing. A number of disciplines are beginning to realize the limitations of reductionistic methods of inquiry and the potential contributions of naturalistic methods to a complete understanding of their phenomena of interest. More and more the merits of employing these two paradigms for understanding the same phenomenon, used simultaneously or in stages, are being recognized (4, 7, 12, 14, 15, 19). As a result, an excellent literature on methods for both paradigms of inquiry has emerged. Let us look at the different ways in which these two paradigms can help us to understand occupation.

Paradigms for the Study of Occupation

Interest in occupation, as a phenomenon worthy of study in its own right, is relatively new. Although many excellent studies can be found that inform us about occupation, for example, *Working,* the documentary masterpiece by Terkel (20), or *The Historical Meanings of Work,* a collection of scholarly essays edited by Joyce (21), these emanate from a variety of disciplines. No one discipline has claimed the study of occupation as a central domain of concern and, hence, no paradigm of inquiry has been identified for the study of occupation.

It has been suggested that a new discipline, dedicated to the study of occupation, is needed (22) and, indeed, some scholars, most notably Elizabeth Yerxa and her colleagues (23), have advocated for the development of a new **occupational science.** They have argued that this new science[1] ought to be a basic science, one that could support such professions as architecture, career counselling, environmental engineering, industrial psychology, kinesiology, leisure studies, and occupational therapy. Yerxa and her colleagues (23) have proposed that occupational science needs to define appropriate paradigms of inquiry. They have suggested disciplinary paradigms and research methods of inquiry that hold particular promise for the study of occupation, in particular, methods based in naturalistic inquiry. Notwithstanding the efforts of these and other scholars, no well-established discipline devoted to the study of occupation exists as yet. Consequently, there is no established disciplinary paradigm of inquiry and no accumulated literature detailing methods for the study of occupation.

The study of occupation remains in its infancy, so understanding is rudimentary. Further, there has been little open discussion of the methods of inquiry that are most appropriate to the study of occupation. Indeed, in the absence of a well-established discipline, no obvious forum exists for such a discussion. It is the opinion of this author that it is still far too early to adopt a particular epistemological perspective or a paradigm of inquiry for the study of occupation. It is proposed, therefore, that all basic questions of inquiry be asked. That is, who, what, when, where, how, and why seem to be appropriate questions to begin our study; and all methods of inquiry, particularly naturalistic and positivistic, should be considered as potentially useful.

METHODS OF INQUIRY FOR THE STUDY OF OCCUPATION

An understanding of occupation can come from three primary sources: personal experience, existing data sources, and new investigations. Our direct experience of engaging in occupations is very important in helping us to understand occupation, but our own experience is insufficient. Constructing an understanding of occupation requires careful examination of the phenomenon in its entirety, including the context of the doing, the perspective of the doer, and the framework of the knower. This examination must be built not only on personal experiences but also on formal methods of systematic inquiry.

What follows is a first attempt at explaining the formal methods of inquiry for the study of occupation, referred to here as occupationology,[2] and other places in this volume as occupational science. The methods selected are those that are consistent with meeting the aims of any program of disciplinary inquiry, that is, to *describe* and *explain*, with a view toward predicting and controlling.[3] The methods identified are by no means novel. They have been drawn from the literature of a number of disciplines concerned with the study of humans and societies. Richard's (24) observations about his own work apply aptly to these methods: "A few of the separate items are original. One does not expect novel cards when playing a traditional game; it is the hand which matters" (19, p. 1).

The scale of the literature on methods of inquiry is such that it is far beyond the scope of a single chapter to present all available methods, let alone describe them in any detail. The intent here is to be illustrative rather than exhaustive. Other authors in this book offer additional illustrations. For instance, Jarman (Chapter 3) refers to the positivistic inquiries used by governments to examine occupational classifications, and Whiteford (Chapter 10) cites the narratives of those who experience occupational deprivation. An overview of the more common methods of inquiry is provided here. The purpose is to supply sufficient information on methods of inquiry to afford the reader a point of entry into this vast literature. The reader is directed to the cited sources for in-depth explanations of the methods and for a broader, more comprehensive listing of available methods. These sources should be considered as a starting point for identifying all methods of inquiry that may be useful in understanding occupation.

Methods of inquiry into occupation should have the same basic structure as any other inquiry: question, design, data collection, data analysis, data interpretation, and conclusion. Questions, designs, and data collection methods will be discussed here because these steps set an inquiry into motion. In the sections that follow, care has been taken to identify common methods from both the naturalistic and the positivistic paradigms. This has been achieved by surveying recent texts addressing both perspectives in related disciplines, in particular: education, social and behavioural sciences (4, 7, 10, 16, 18, 19, 25), health sciences (8, 9, 17), and psychology (12–15, 26).

The Question

The first step of any process of inquiry is the formulation of a question. Our understanding of occupation is so rudimentary that all of the questions of basic inquiry are appropriate to ask. We can ask both the descriptive questions (who, what, when, and where) and the explanatory questions (how and why). The specific question will depend on the aspect of occupation that is of interest to the knower and the paradigm of inquiry. Table 2-2 gives some examples of specific questions that could—and should—be asked about occupation.

Design and Data Collection Methods

The design and data collection methods[4] reviewed here emanate from the two major paradigms of formal inquiry addressed here. Once a question has been formulated, the next step is to carry out a literature search to determine if the question has already been answered. Knowing what is already recorded also helps to refine a research question. Then one chooses a design that is consistent with the question and the paradigm of inquiry. Once the design is set, the actual data collection methods are chosen.

Many designs and data collection methods are available to answer questions about occupation. The more common ones are summarized in Table 2-3. The classification appearing in Table 2-3 is an amalgam of a number of different classifications,[5] not that of any particular author: The classification for quantitative designs is essentially that presented in (19) and (9); the classification for qualitative designs is

TABLE 2-2   *Six Questions of Basic Inquiry and Possible Subquestions Applied to Human Occupation*

Purpose	Question	Subquestions
Describe	**Who** engages in occupations?	Do all people engage in occupations?
		Do age, gender, race, religion, ethnicity, ability, health, or socioeconomic status affect occupational engagement?
		Did early humans engage in occupations?
	What occupations are there?	Are there patterns of occupations, i.e., are there occupational profiles?
		Do occupational profiles differ among individuals, groups systematically?
		Do the differences in occupational profiles reflect individual or group differences?
	When do people engage in occupations?	Are occupations engaged in at any time of day, week, year, or life?
		Are there daily, weekly, seasonally, yearly or life patterns of occupational engagement?
		Have the occupational profiles of humans changed over time?
	Where do people engage in occupations?	Are all/any occupations universal or are they environmentally specific?
		Are some environments more conducive to occupational engagement than others?
		Are specific occupations done in specific places?
Explain	**How** are occupations performed?	How are occupations created/learned?
		How does the process of occupational engagement happen?
		What skills are required to perform occupations?
		How do personal or environmental resources influence occupational performance?
	Why do people engage in occupations?	What meanings are ascribed to occupations?
		Do people ascribe the same meanings to all occupations?
		Why do people choose particular occupations and not others?
		Why do some people seem to need to be occupied all the time and others not?

that presented in (16). The particular design elements that appear in Table 2-3 were chosen not only because they are commonly used but also because (1) they fit well with the constructs of description and explanation; (2) they eliminate like terms having different meanings, or (3) their meaning is logically intuitive.

Table 2-3 also provides a listing of the more common methods of data collection for both paradigms. Design and methods of data collection have been distinguished for two reasons: (1) *Clarity;* frequently there is no distinction made between design and methods of data collection, resulting in confusion in the meaning of terms (e.g., an observational study versus observation as a means of data collection; and (2) to make it obvious that some methods of data collection (i.e., observation and interview) span the quantitative/qualitative divide (15).

The more common designs for the quantitative paradigm are descriptive and experimental (9, 19). In *descriptive studies* information is gathered for the purpose of

TABLE 2-3 *Common Research Methods in the Quantitative and Qualitative Paradigms*

Quantitative	Qualitative
Study Designs	**Study Designs**
Descriptive studies (aka correlational, observational, survey)	Ethnography (observational)
	Case study
Experimental studies (including quasi-experimental, true experimental)	Phenomenology
	Grounded theory
Methods of Data Collection	**Methods of Data Collection**
(Passive) observation	(Participant) observation
Interview	Interview
Questionnaire	Document and record collection,
Measurement	Audiovisual materials
Instrumentation	
Document and record collection,	
Audiovisual materials	

Source: This classification is an amalgam of classifications presented by Banister et al. (4), Breakwell, et al. (12), Clark-Carter (15), Creswell (16), DePoy and Gitlin (17), Glaser & Strauss (18), Glesne and Peshkin (19), Lincoln and Guba (25), and Pedhazur and Shmelkin (26).

documenting the nature and meaning of the phenomenon at a specific point in time; describing how it changes over time; and exploring relationships among phenomena. In descriptive studies, no assignment of subjects or control of variables occurs. In *experimental studies* hypotheses regarding cause and effect are tested by the manipulation of certain variables and the control of others. In true experimental studies, assignment of subjects is random; in quasi-experimental studies, it is not.

The more common designs for the qualitative paradigm are ethnography, case study, phenomenology, and grounded theory (4, 16). In *ethnographic studies,* through a process of long-term immersion, a researcher gathers information, primarily by participant observation and interview, about the attitudes, beliefs, and behaviors of a group of people or a culture for the purpose of understanding the forces that shape those behaviors and feelings. In *case studies,* the researcher uses a variety of data collection methods, over a sustained period of time, for the purposes of understanding a particular activity or phenomenon. In *phenomenological studies,* through a process of extensive and prolonged engagement, using observations and interviews, the experience and meaning of individuals' lived realities are examined. In *grounded theory studies,* the researcher, using multiple stages of data collection, collects, codes, and analyzes observational and interview data until the data being collected become redundant. Through a process of constant comparison of data, relevant categories and their relationship are identified and theoretical constructs are formulated.

Several designs can be used to answer any particular question. In addition, the same design can be used to answer a number of the questions. The designs corresponding to basic questions about occupation are discussed next and examples are given.

UNDERSTANDING WHO

It hardly seems necessary to ask the question *Who engages in occupations?* Experience tells us that everyone we know, everyone we see around us, everyone we see in the media, everyone we hear about and everyone we read about—whether in the present or past—engages in occupations. Further, the answer to this question seems to be well established in the historical, anthropological, social, and psychological literature; that is, all people, regardless of the variables that typically distinguish groups, engage in occupations because occupations are what people do.

Yet there are individuals who do not engage in occupations—or do so only sparingly. Indeed, there likely have been times, perhaps brief, when you, the reader, did not engage in occupations. Nevertheless, it is self-evident that most humans engage in occupations most of the time under most circumstances.

What warrants investigation, then, is the exception; that is, who does *not* engage in occupation? General qualitative methods of inquiry, such as ethnographies, are more likely to lend themselves to finding the exception. Quantitative inquiry, if used to study both the rule and the exceptions, may also be useful. Examination of existing data can also be informative, for example, documents or records describing individuals or groups of individuals, biographies, and autobiographies.

A good example of an autobiographical account detailing an individual's nonengagement in occupation is *Terry Waite Taken on Trust* (27). Terry Waite was held in solitary confinement in Beirut by terrorists for 1,763 days. During most of that time he was left with nothing to do. His environment afforded him nothing to do for the greater part of most days. This remarkable man created his own, albeit unorthodox, occupations. That is to say, he wrote his autobiography entirely in his head throughout the duration of his captivity. What becomes blatantly evident from this book is that nonengagement in occupation is difficult to induce. The mind seeks to occupy itself if environmental stimulation is absent. Further, severely limited engagement is so difficult to bear that individuals create environmental support, and they resume more occupations or more meaningful occupations as environmental support increases. In other words, when one is considering a person doing an occupation (the who), what they are doing along with when and where they are doing it must also be considered. These issues constitute the *what, when,* and *where* questions of occupation that must be addressed in order to establish a contextual storyline.

UNDERSTANDING WHAT

Personal experience tells us that there are a tremendous number of occupations—possibly too many to count. One merely needs to look in the do-it-yourself sections of bookstores, or in the hobbies or careers sections, to see how many occupations there are. Also, numerous sources, whether in the popular literature, the arts, or the historical, anthropological, social, and psychological literature, give accounts of the various occupations of various people.

Moreover the naming of occupations is such a cultural act that a list of occupations in one cultural context would differ greatly from a list in another cultural context. Understanding occupations, then, requires that we listen to and observe what people are doing or contemplating in the context of their lives. The study of occupational repertoires and profiles can be dealt with in a number of ways including case studies or descriptive studies. Ethnographies provide detailed profiles of individuals or communities, and surveys generate profiles of large groups.

National census databases are excellent sources of survey data on large groups. As Jarman notes in this volume (Chapter 3), virtually every country has a national agency that routinely collects demographic, socioeconomic, and social information about the paid occupations of its population. The U.S. Census Bureau provides statistics on a large variety of topics that include information on what people do. In the area of labor and employment alone, the Census Bureau provides information on the demographics of the labor force, commuting to work, occupation, industry, and class of worker. It also provides links to statistics from more than 100 U.S. federal agencies. Under the Canadian Statistics Act, Statistics Canada is required to collect and publish statistical information on virtually every aspect of the nation's society and economy. Originally the census was just a simple population count, but today Statistics Canada collects and distributes information from a variety of surveys, offering a rich source of information on the occupations of Canadians. Two types of surveys are routinely used. The first involves population surveys (census) in which every possible respondent is approached. The second features sample surveys that gather data from representative groups of the population. Both types use various survey designs. For instance, a repeated survey design consists of a series of separate cross-sectional surveys. Longitudinal or panel surveys collect information on the same individuals at different points in time. A national census is a repeated survey that employs both census taking and sampling techniques.

Although a census provides a good overview of a nation's occupations, it does not provide a detailed breakdown on occupational patterns. However, a number of other population surveys are available that provide detailed information about occupational or activity patterns. The American and the Canadian General Social Surveys (GSS) monitor changes in the health and activity of Americans and Canadians. These surveys provide rich data on what people do in a huge range of occupations.

To use the Canadian population survey as an example, a repeated telephone survey is conducted approximately every 5 years and includes questions on education, paid work, unpaid work, personal care, physical activities, socializing, passive leisure such as watching television and reading, sports, and other entertainment. This survey also asks about activity limitations. The Canadian GSS is collected from a representative sample of residents 15 years of age and over who reside in Canada. It is noteworthy that the GSS survey refers to *activities,* which this book would define broadly as occupations. Consider what can be learned about a broad range of occupations from a GSS survey. Findings indicate that, aside from personal care, the most common occupations encompass tasks around the home, with 90% of the people participating in household work and related occupations for an average of 3.6 hours a day. Women spend an average of 1.5 hours more each day on housework than do men. Seventy-seven percent of the population over the age of 15 watches television for an average of 3 hours a day ranging from a low of 2.3 hours per day for females age 25–34 to a high of 4.3 hours per day for males over 65 (28). In Chapter 4, Harvey and Pentland illustrate how the GSS can be used to understand what people do. One can surmise that future national surveys may eventually collect data on a wide range of occupations, rather than activities, in order to understand how Canadians organize their occupations into routines, meaningful vocations, community building, or paid work.

What becomes evident from existing data on human occupation is that humans have always engaged in a tremendous variety of occupations and that occupations differ among individuals, groups, cultures, and nations. Yet there are also patterns of occupations that are commonly experienced as humans' occupational repertoires and profiles attest. Furthermore, it seems clear that understanding the *what* of occupation also requires an understanding of the *who, when,* and *where* of occupation.

UNDERSTANDING WHEN

Our personal experience clearly suggests an answer to the question *When do people engage in occupations?* The answer is *Always.* Some might answer that occupations occur only during humans' waking hours, depending on whether or not they consider sleep an occupation. Yet sleep is planned, is goal directed, and is more active (both physically and mentally) than most people think. Indeed, those who have travelled with children in the back seat of a long car ride know that people always want to be doing something. Interesting questions about *when* include these: *When do people not engage in occupations? Which people engage in which occupations at what times? For how long?* Understanding *when* is a matter of understanding how occupations and time are related. Occupations occur in the context of time. By asking when, we will understand how humans create occupational patterns across the day, week, month, year, life, and, indeed, across history.

We can understand when occupations occur by looking at popular literature and, for instance, literature in the arts, history, anthropology, sociology, health, and psychology. The work on circadian rhythms offers fascinating insights into the daily patterns of human occupation. The expression of the circadian rhythm through activity (29) reveals typical patterns of daily occupations (Figure 2-1). The literature on human development also offers notable insights, into the patterns of human occupation across the life span (see also Chapter 5). Moreover, historical analyses of activity patterns provide glimpses into how people's occupations have changed throughout history (30, 31).

A number of methods of inquiry can be used to study when occupations occur through patterns of occupational engagement. Virtually all qualitative designs can be used to record and reflect on occupational patterns. Within the methods of inquiry, time and motion studies are of particular use based either on self-report data or observational data.

A good example of a self-report time log is the study conducted by Herrmann, who collected data from a group of 20 single adolescent mothers (32). Herrmann described their daily activities to learn about role conflicts between their maternal and adolescent roles. She asked the young women to keep a time log on which they chronicled all of their activities over a period of 4 days, ascribing them to either the mothering or adolescent role and noting their level of satisfaction with the particular activity. The data from the time log showed that these young women spent the majority of their time (78%) doing adolescent activities, leaving much of the child

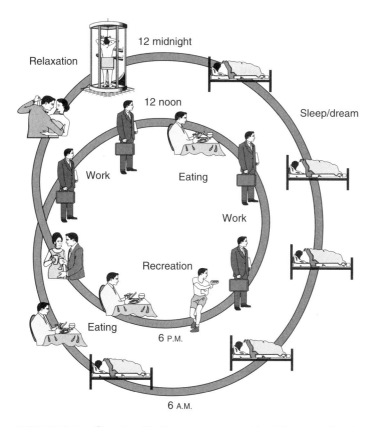

FIGURE 2-1   Circadian Rhythms are expressed in daily occupational patterns.

care to others. Herrmann points out that, unexpectedly, this pattern did not differ over weekdays, when the women were in school, and on weekends.

Herrmann's findings (32) show that the individual does not determine occupational patterns alone, but rather in concert with the environment. With little change in occupational patterns from weekday to weekend, it seems that occupational patterns are not only affected by time but also by the environment in which these patterns occur. Once again, occupation cannot be understood by asking a single question, such as *When do occupations occur?* The challenge of understanding *when* occupations occur is linked with questions about *who, what,* and *where.*

UNDERSTANDING WHERE

Personal experience, popular literature, and the arts all tell us that occupations happen everywhere—even in those environments where there are attempts to prevent occupational engagement, as Terry Waite experienced in captivity. A more interesting question to ask, therefore, is *What impact does location or geography have on occupational engagement?*

There are several ways of understanding the impact of location or geography on occupations. Qualitative and quantitative methods are all appropriate for studying the impact of location on occupation. Fields as diverse as human geography, industrial psychology, architecture, sociology of community, urban planning, and community development all provide information on the interaction between occupations and environments. A rich and colorful source of data on the effects of location and geography on occupations, now and in the past, is the journal *National Geographic,* published in the United States. A browse through issues of *National Geographic* shows that occupations occur everywhere, including under the ocean and on the moon. Some occupations occur all around the world, such as infant care, but are done differently in different places (as described by Hamilton in Chapter 8), whereas others occur only in specific places, such as surfing.

Schisler, who was interested in examining the impact of environmental change on occupational engagement, carried out an ethnographic study of Burundian refugees in Southwestern Ontario, Canada (33). Schisler spent more than a year interacting with and participating in the Burundian refugee community. She spent 17 months as an informal participant observer in this community and one academic term conducting formal participant observations. She also conducted in-depth interviews with 8 of 18 adult members of this community and did individualized member checks with 6 of these individuals. Using the constant comparison method of data analysis, Schisler found that all participants experienced dramatic changes in their occupations as a result of the physical, social, cultural, and economic differences between Burundi in Africa and Southwestern Ontario in Canada. Of particular interest was the finding that the changes in occupation resulting from the environmental changes affected the people themselves and they too changed. In other words, *where* people engage in occupations affects *when* and *what* they do, which in turn affects *who* they are. How does this happen?

UNDERSTANDING HOW

Whereas the who, what, when, and where of occupation are beginning to be well understood, relatively little is known about *how* people perform occupations. Personal experience can only inform us very superficially about the *how* of occupations. Much of the process of occupational performance is not readily observable or knowable; that is, only relatively gross movements involved in the performance of a particular occupation can be observed and only processes that reach **metacognition** can be reported. A more in-depth understanding of how occupations are performed requires careful examination of the relevant components of persons and elements of the environment. Quantitative methods of inquiry, often involving specialized instrumentation in an experimental design, are useful for an in-depth understanding of many of the processes involved in occupational performance. Many examples of such studies exist, especially in the ergonomic, medical, movement science, occupational therapy, psychology, and social science literature.

Smyth and Mason (34) carried out an experimental study to investigate differences in the role of vision and proprioception in a positional, aiming task between normal children and children with a developmental coordination disorder (DCD). The two groups of right-handed children (73 with DCD and 73 control children, matched on age, sex, and verbal ability) were asked to move their hand under a tabletop into alignment with a target on top of the table. The position of the target was made known to the children by vision, proprioception (their body's sense of where their arms and hands were), or both. Accuracy of performance over 24 trials was measured in millimeters along the horizontal (x) and vertical (y) axes. Results indicated that, with proprioception alone, errors were made to the outside of the targets; that the control children tended to favor proprioceptive input, whereas children with DCD tended to favor visual input—but only with their left hand. The authors concluded that detailed error analysis in aiming tasks provided information about target representation that cannot be gleaned from less specific measurement strategies. This study provides experimental evidence of the impact of person and occupational factors on performance and demonstrates the usefulness of controlled studies in understanding how occupations are performed. Many more studies of this type, investigating all aspects of performance, are necessary before we can truly understand how occupations are performed.

UNDERSTANDING WHY

The final, and perhaps most difficult question to be asked in this chapter about occupations is *Why*? There is a general belief, supported by the media, that the basic reason for occupational engagement is survival. In other words, we work because we have to, meaning that we do what we do because it, directly or indirectly, provides us with food and shelter. The implicit notion is that other occupations, such as eating, sleeping, resting, or bathing and grooming, support the main task of work for survival.

Personal experience tells us that there are endless examples of occupational engagement that negate, or at least bring into serious question, this basic survival premise. For example, the survival premise does not explain why people who do not have to work do so, why very young children engage in occupations, or why people do what they do even without pay. In particular, the basic survival premise does not explain why people do things that put them at serious risk of survival.

All available methods of inquiry need to be used to uncover the *why* of occupation and new methods need to be developed. The American GSS (35) provides an example of how surveys can be used to look at work values and the meaning of work. Specifically, in the 1973–1996 GSS this question was asked: "If you were to get enough money to live as comfortably as you would like for the rest of your life, would you continue to work or would you stop working?"[6] The work referred to earlier by Terkel and that by Joyce provide evidence that a phenomenological study—designed specifically to uncover the meanings people ascribe to their work experiences—is particularly useful in learning to understand why people perform the work-related occupations they undertake.

A smaller scale study that was similar to that of Terkel was carried out by Rudman et al. (36). In-depth interviews were carried out with 12 community-dwelling, well elderly persons to discover their perspectives on the role and importance of occupations in their lives. The informants were chosen to allow for maximum variation. After an initial analysis of transcripts using a constant comparative method, two member checking group sessions were held. The results of these discussions were incorporated into the analyses, again using the constant comparative method. The emergent themes indicated that occupations were a means of expressing and managing personal identity, a means of staying connected to people associated with their past, present, and future, and a means of organizing time. More importantly, engagement in occupations contributed to the sense of well-being of the seniors, to their continued existence, and to the quality of that existence. As one informant put it:

> Most people have a job and that's the only thing, one job all their lives. And the trouble with them is that when they retire, they don't know what the hell to do with themselves. In 2 years, they usually get sick and die. (36, p. 643)

CHAPTER SUMMARY

Understanding occupation, that is, *truly* understanding the who, what, when, where, how, and why of occupation is a complex task, requiring many methods of inquiry. This chapter illustrated how to learn about occupation. A range of formal and informal methods of inquiry was discussed to open points of entry into the world of scholarly inquiry in occupation. The six questions used to frame this chapter provide guideposts on the road to greater understanding of occupation. Readers are encouraged to participate now in unravelling the mysteries of occupation.

REFERENCES

1. Ferguson, D. L., & Patten, J. (1979). *Journalism today: An introduction*. Skokie, IL: National Textbook.
2. *International Webster New Encyclopedic Dictionary of the English Language & Library of Useful Knowledge*. (1972). New York: Tabor House.
3. Kolb, D. A. (1981). Learning styles and disciplinary differences. In A. W. Chickering and associates (Eds.), *The modern American college: Responding to the new realities of diverse students and a changing society* (pp. 232–255). Washington, DC: Jossey-Bass.
4. Glesne, C., & Peshkin, A. (1992). *Becoming qualitative researchers: An introduction*. White Plains, NY: Longman.
5. Belenky, M. F., Clinchy, B. M., Goldberger, N. R., & Tarule, J. M. (1986). *Women's ways of knowing: The development of self, voice, and mind*. New York: Basic Books.
6. Perry, W. G., Jr. (1970). *Forms of intellectual and ethical development in the college years: A scheme*. Toronto, ON: Holt, Rhinehart and Winston.
7. Drew, C. J., Hardman, M. L., & Weaver Hart, A. (1996). *Designing and conducting research: Inquiry in education and social science* (2nd ed.). Toronto, ON: Allyn and Bacon.
8. Neutens, J. J., & Rubinson, L. (1997). *Research techniques for the health sciences* (2nd ed.). Boston: Allyn and Bacon.

9. Portney, L. G., & Watkins, M. P. (1993). *Foundations of clinical research: Applications to practice.* Norwalk, CT: Appleton and Lange.
10. Jackson, W. (1999). *Methods: Doing social research* (2nd ed.). Scarborough, ON: Prentice Hall Allyn Bacon Canada.
11. Kuhn, T. S. (1970). *The structure of scientific revolutions* (2nd ed.). Chicago: University of Chicago Press.
12. Banister, P., Burman, E., Parker, I., Taylor, M., & Tindall, C. (1994). *Qualitative methods in psychology: A research guide.* Philadelphia: Open University Press.
13. Haworth, J. (Ed.). (1996). *Psychological research: Innovative methods and strategies.* (pp. 2–14). New York: Routledge.
14. Hayes, N. (Ed.). (1997). *Doing qualitative analysis in psychology.* Hove, England: Psychology Press.
15. Clark-Carter, D. (1997). *Doing quantitative psychological research: From design to report.* Hove, England: Psychology Press.
16. Creswell, J. W. (1994). *Research design: Qualitative and quantitative approaches.* Thousand Oaks, CA: Sage.
17. DePoy, E., & Gitlin, L. N. (1994). *Introduction to research: Multiple strategies for health and human services.* St. Louis, MO: Mosby.
18. Lincoln, Y. S., & Guba, E. G. (1985). *Naturalistic inquiry.* Thousand Oaks, CA: Sage.
19. Pedhazur, E. J., & Schmelkin, L. P. (1991). *Measurement, design, and analysis: An integrated approach.* Hillsdale, NJ: Lawrence Erlbaum.
20. Terkel, S. (1975). *Working.* New York: Avon Books.
21. Joyce, P. (Ed.). (1989). *The historical meanings of work.* New York: Cambridge University Press.
22. Csikszentmihalyi, M. (1990). Foreword. In J. A. Johnson & E. J. Yerxa (Eds.), *Occupational science: The foundation for new models of practice* (pp. xv–xvii). New York: The Haworth Press.
23. Yerxa, E. J., Clark, F., Frank, G., Jackson, J., Parham, D., Pierce, D., Stein, C., & Zemke, R. (1990). An introduction to occupational science: A foundation for occupational therapy in the 21st century. In J. A. Johnson & E. J. Yerxa (Eds.), *Occupational science: The foundation for new models of practice* (pp. 2–17). New York: The Haworth Press.
24. Richards, I. A. (1926). *Principles of literary criticism* (2nd ed.). London: Routledge & Kegan Paul.
25. Glaser, B. G., & Strauss, A. L. (1968). *The discovery of grounded theory: Strategies for qualitative research.* Chicago: Aline.
26. Breakwell, G. M., Hammond, S., & Fife-Schaw, C. (Eds.). (1995). *Research methods in psychology.* Thousand Oaks, CA: Sage.
27. Waite, T. (1993). *Terry Waite taken on trust.* Toronto: Doubleday Canada.
28. Statistics Canada. (1999). *General social survey: Overview of the time use of Canadians in 1998* (Catalogue No. 12F0080XIE). Ottawa: Minister of Industry.
29. Fincher, J. (1984). *The brain: Mystery of mind and matter.* Toronto, ON: Torstar Books.
30. Davis, J. A., Polatajko, H. J., & Ruud, C. A. (2002). Children's occupations in context: The Influence of History. *Journal of Occupational Science, 9*(2), 54–64.
31. Wilcock, A. A. (1998). *An occupational perspective of health.* Thorofare, NJ: Slack Inc.
32. Herrmann, C. (1990). A descriptive study of daily activities and role conflict in single adolescent mothers. In J. A. Johnson & E. J. Yerxa (Eds.), *Occupational science: The foundation for new models of practice* (pp. 53–68). New York: The Haworth Press.

33. Schisler, A. M. C., & Polatajko, H. J. (2002). The Individual as mediator of the Person-Occupation-Environment Interaction: Learning from the experiences of refugees. *Journal of Occupational Science, 9*(2), 82–92.
34. Smyth, M. M., & Mason, U. C. (1998). Direction of response in aiming to visual and proprioceptive targets in children with and without developmental coordination disorder. *Human Movement Science, 17,* 515–539.
35. National Research Council. (1999). *The changing nature of work: Implications for occupational analysis.* Washington, DC: National Academy Press.
36. Rudman, D. L., Cook, J. V., & Polatajko, H. (1997). Understanding the potential of occupation: A qualitative exploration of seniors' perspective on activity. *American Journal of Occupational Therapy, 51*(8), 640–650.
37. Johnson, J. A., & Yerxa, E. J. (Eds.). (1990). *Occupational science: The foundation for new models of practice.* New York: The Haworth Press.
38. Polatajko, H. J. (1992). Muriel Driver lecture. Naming and framing occupational therapy: A lecture dedicated to the life of Nancy B. *Canadian Journal of Occupational Therapy, 59*(4), 189–200.

Endnotes

[1] Johnson, Yerxa and her colleagues (37) have called the new science *occupational science.* Polatajko (38) has suggested that the study of occupation ought to be referred to as *occupationology.*

[2] Polatajko (38) uses the term *occupationology* to preclude the *a priori* presumptions inherent in the term *science.* The classic view of science is of inquiries that are conducted in a number of set stages starting with a hypothesis [Popper, 1972, as cited by Clark-Carter (15)], thereby excluding qualitative inquiries.

[3] Clark-Carter (15) suggests that, for psychology, *control* is understood to mean intervene for the purposes of improving human life. In the case of occupational therapy, control is understood in the collaborative sense to mean "enable" for the purposes of prompting, facilitating, or otherwise enabling people to generate insights or opportunities to choose their occupations.

[4] Note, some confusion exists in the literature about the use of the terms *method* and *design.* As used here, the term *method,* used in conjunction with the phrase *of inquiry* (i.e., *method of inquiry,*) refers to all aspects of a study including the paradigm to be used, the design, and the specific data collection methods and procedures, analysis, and interpretation. The term *design* refers to the overall structure and plan of a study that emanates from the paradigm of inquiry and the question and determines the specific procedures and data collection methods to be adhered to in conducting the study. The term *method,* used either alone or in conjunction with the phrases *of data collection, analysis,* and *interpretation,* refers to the specifics of data collection, analysis, and interpretation, respectively.

[5] A number of ways can be used to classify designs. Some are based on purpose; others are based on data collection strategies or analytical strategies; many are based on a mixed model of naming (15, 26). There is no agreement on the best classification, nor is there any agreement on the terminology used to name what are essentially the same designs, for example, the terms *nonexperimental, correlational, survey* and (passive) *observational* have all been used to refer to the same designs (19).

[6] Most Americans indicated that they would continue to work. The numbers range from a low of 65% in 1974 and a high of 77% in 1980. The most recent results (1996) indicate that 68% would continue to work.

What is Occupation? Interdisciplinary Perspectives on Defining and Classifying Human Activity

Jennifer Jarman

KEY WORDS

Division of Labor
Gendered
Interdependence
International Standard Classification of
    Occupations (ISCO)

Social Class
Suboccupation

CHAPTER PROFILE

The purpose of this chapter is to challenge taken-for-granted ideas about occupations by examining three different ways in which human activities in occupation are related to the way in which *occupation* has been defined. Presented here are the perspectives of three communities with interests in occupation: (1) occupational therapy and occupational science, (2) social science, and (3) governmental departments that create and track statistics on the occupations associated with the workforce. All three communities, even the government community of statisticians, have struggled with the work/nonwork division, though feminists have argued, that a focus on formal labor force occupations ignores much of the activity performed by women (1).

www.prenhall.com/christiansen

The Internet provides an exciting means for interacting with this textbook and for enhancing your understanding of humans' experiences with occupations and the organization of occupations in society. Use the address above to access the free, interactive companion web site created specifically to accompany this book. Here you will find an array of self-study material designed to help you gain a richer understanding of the concepts presented in this chapter.

Additionally, the chapter explores what is at stake in these debates over broadening versus narrowing and what consequences the different meanings have for our understanding of the social world and important issues pertaining to it. Let us be clear that it is not that any one definition or classification of occupation is better than any other, but that different criteria are used in order to define and classify occupation for different purposes. Most readers may come across this term in several different contexts, so it is important to understand these reasons and different definitions in order to communicate effectively across disciplinary and professional boundaries without confusion.

INTRODUCTION[1]

People's occupations are such a basic part of our social world and culture that even very young children are well acquainted with their existence. Children's rhymes are full of references to a variety of occupations:

> Rub-a-dub dub, three men in a tub,
> The butcher, the baker, the candle-stick maker,
> They all jumped out of a rotten potato.

Mother Goose Nursery Rhymes

> Cobbler, cobbler, mend my shoe
> Get it done by half past two.
> Half past two is much too late!
> Get it done by half past eight.

Mother Goose Nursery Rhymes

Children's songs are similarly full of references:

> Oh, who are the people in your neighborhood?
> In your neighborhood?
> In your neighborhood?
> Say, who are the people in your neighborhood?
> The people that you meet each day?

> Oh, the postman always brings the mail
> Through rain or snow or sleet or hail
> I'll work and work the whole day through
> To get your letters safe to you

> 'Cause a postman is a person in your neighborhood
> In your neighborhood
> He's in your neighborhood
> A postman is a person in your neighborhood
> A person that you meet each day

[and so on through verses involving the fireman, the baker, the teacher, the barber, the bus driver, the dentist, the doctor (female Muppet), the grocer, the shoemaker, the cleaner and the trash collector] Originally sung by Bob McGrath and the Anything Muppets Sesame Street, written by Jeffrey Moss.

These rhymes and songs introduce a child to a variety of work occupations and tell them a little bit about what a person in such an occupation does on a day-to-day basis. All of these rhymes and songs suggest that occupation is most often viewed as intrinsically about work; however, this book will challenge readers to consider the many ways in which humans are occupied, including ways that go beyond work.

If a 5-year-old knows about occupations through nursery rhymes, you may be asking yourselves why we need an entire chapter devoted to the question of *What is occupation?* The answer is that the 5-year-old may have a straightforward answer to the question on a simple level. As a social scientist, I would argue that occupations are actually complex concepts that have different usages in different contexts. Defining the concept *occupation* is a complex task in all of these contexts. It is even complex and controversial to define occupation as a "concept" versus a "phenomenon" or maybe a "process" or an "interaction" involving humans in their environments.

OCCUPATION IN OCCUPATIONAL THERAPY AND OCCUPATIONAL SCIENCE

Occupational therapy grew from age-old beliefs that being occupied helps people to learn to look after themselves. It seems that being occupied in a variety of ways makes people actually experience educational, health, social, and other benefits. In fact, occupational therapy took its name both from its interest in occupation and its use of occupations to advance health and well-being in everyday life and education, and became a profession in the early part of the 20th century. Occupational therapists drew on an idea that is fairly old—the idea that people regain their health more quickly if they are involved in some kind of activity. H. E. Sigerist noted that "our brain slips into chaos and confusion unless we constantly use it for work that seems worthwhile to us" (2). In 1922, Meyer wrote: "Occupational therapy contends that what people do with their time, their occupation, is crucially important for their well-being. It is a person's occupation that makes life ultimately meaningful" (3). Much 20th-century therapy has developed around the notion of an engagement between an occupational therapist and a medical patient. The aims tend to be to identify occupations that are meaningful and that assist patients to develop their skills to deal with everyday life more successfully despite an illness, disability, or limitations faced by those who are aging.

Occupational therapists work toward a very finely nuanced understanding of what an occupation means with respect to any individual or category of health impairment, disability, or limitation on daily participation. This work can involve complex testing of motor skills, communications/interactions skills, and social psychological aspects of human existence. In the following excerpt, we can see the minuteness of the analysis of human occupation that is entailed. This excerpt is drawn from an analysis of the interaction between an occupational therapist and a woman trying to regain her driving skills after she received a head injury in a car accident. In the excerpt, the woman is driving the car, and the occupational therapist is analyzing her actions.

> . . . Fifteen minutes into the occupation, the patient's car is stationary for 40 seconds at a stop sign marking a major road. The route called for a right turn, but steady traffic moved by at approximately 50 miles per hour. The driver in the car behind her throws up his hands in apparent frustration.
>
> . . . The traffic on the major road confused the patient. She misperceived the speed of oncoming cars, and the glare of the sun on the windshield compounded the problem. The apparent frustration of the man in the car behind her made her feel anxious. When it finally appeared that there was a break in the traffic flow, she overestimated the force necessary to depress the accelerator and underestimated the interval between accelerating and turning.
>
> . . . Initially at the intersection, the patient simply wanted to make a right turn and be on her way. However, the longer she waited at the stop sign, the more she felt torn between wanting to be safe and wanting to escape the discomfort. When she almost lost control of the car, she had a powerful desire to right its course. Then she consciously wanted to learn from her mistake.
>
> . . . At the busy intersection, the patient's occupational performance was marked by 40 seconds of repeated trunk and neck rotation with alternating glances at the rear-view mirror. Suddenly, she made an uncommonly quick move of the right foot from the brake to the accelerator and then plantar flexed her foot with power. Next, she forcefully rotated the steering wheel to the right. Immediately after, she frowned and declared forcefully "I've got to take my time and concentrate on the right thing." A few moments later in a calmer voice, she stated, "That guy behind us has his own problems . . . I had enough to concentrate on." She said further, "You know, I used to avoid situations like this and go only where there are stop lights. That's been the story of my life—avoiding things. (4, pp. 776–777)

In this case, "driving a car" is defined as an occupation. This is further divided into the **suboccupation** of "turning right in a stressful situation." Nelson also breaks the occupation down into "occupational performances,"[2] which include looking at the street map, posture in the driver's seat, the patient's foot push on the foot pedal and accelerator, turning the steering wheel, and speaking. What is noteworthy about the analysis is that the occupational therapist goes beyond observing the physical performances involved in the act of driving (pushing one's foot down, turning one's head a number of times in a particular way) and assesses much of the emotional and decision-making work that is also part of the occupation of driving.

The minute detail in which this occupation of everyday life is considered enhances an understanding of the complexity of human social life. Skills and acts that are taken for granted by most of us are revealed to be complex interplays of many different physical and social skills and processes when seen from the perspective of an ill or injured person by a therapist. Occupation is not just something that is done, nor is it just a category of work. Instead occupation involves a series of thoughts, actions, and interactions in particular places and times. To understand this, the observer must analyze the components of daily human performance.

Although the example just given involved an occupation of a person struggling with medical impairment, this is not the only area of interest expressed by occupational therapists. Loree Primeau is both an occupational therapist and an occupational scientist (the difference will be explained shortly). Her work examines how parents shape the balance between work and play in their interactions with their children in order to understand how these occupations may influence the health and life satisfaction of family members. She analyzes a number of "household" occupations. Let us look at one illustration of her use of the term *occupation*. In this illustration, Brent is the father, Riley is a young son, and Laura is a young daughter.

> Brent picked up a lawn edger, a long-handled, mechanical tool that trims the edge of the lawn. He took it and ran it along the grass at the edge of the driveway. Riley immediately asked, "Can I do it, Daddy? Can I do it?". . . When Brent was finished with it, he gave the lawn edger to Riley who began to edge the lawn along the curb of the street. Brent got the hedge clippers out and began to clip the hedges. . . . After a couple of minutes, Laura got off of her tricycle and went over to Riley. She wanted to try the lawn edger too. Riley reluctantly gave Laura the edger. . . . She tried to imitate Riley, but was having difficulty. When Riley asked for the lawn edger back, Laura gave it to him and then ran over to Brent, asking him to let her do what he was doing. Brent said, "Okay, but I'll have to help you." He put his hands over hers on the hedge clippers and helped her to cut off parts of the hedge. He would point out to her what part they were going to trim, then he would direct her hands over to that spot, and help her clip it. Riley, after watching this, asked for a chance to trim the hedge too. He told his dad that he didn't need help; he knew how to do it. Brent just pointed out the parts for him to trim, and Riley cut them off. (5, pp. 192–193)

This is an example of what Primeau calls *scaffolded play,* meaning that the parents structure an adult occupation so that it involves their children in as independent a manner as possible. Here the elements of the occupation can be seen to be different depending on whose perspective is chosen. Looking at the activities of the parent, the occupation involves both child care and yard work, whereas a focus on the child makes us realize that the occupation involves both play and yard work. Primeau's conclusion is that families organize work and play as patterns of segregation and inclusion. This is an example of children being included in a parent's work occupation. A pattern of segregation would be one in which children were separated when a parent was engaged in a work occupation. For our purposes, we must note that an occupation may contain bundles of activities, and deciding where one occupation leaves off and another begins is a decision for the analyst. We should also note that there might be different levels of analysis, which in this case has been handled by the introduction of the idea of a suboccupation.

The second observation that we can make about the way occupational therapists view occupation is that the profession proceeds with a fairly broad and nonjudgmental way of thinking about what kinds of occupations are meaningful to individuals. Occupational therapists work with people to identify "occupations" that are meaningful to them, and to devise strategies that enable individuals to be able to resume or relearn these occupations, or indeed to learn new occupations in order to live a meaningful life. In so doing, occupational therapists are forced to come to an

understanding of the complexity of the social aspects of what it means to be human—to come to terms with how complicated our everyday lives are in terms of the
ways in which we interact with social, physical, and policy environments. Occupational therapists also consider a wide range of ways in which people occupy their
time. In assessing the occupations of children, for example, an occupational therapist is forced to go beyond the commonsense notion that occupation innately has
something to do with work. The occupations of children may revolve much more
heavily around playing and learning; similarly, the occupations of elderly people
may revolve around maintaining active, involved, and independent lifestyles.

Not surprisingly, occupational therapists consider fundamental questions about
the nature of modern society, because they must consider what type of world they
are helping people to actively negotiate. Indeed, others begin to consider how that
world has produced some of the dysfunctions associated with the occupations that
they analyze. This takes them beyond the individual concerns to communal and societal considerations. Some occupational therapy writers develop a critique of mainstream culture as a result. Not surprisingly, questions concerning the pace and
nature of modern life—its speed, spiritual values or lack thereof, and a concern for
ritual and meaning arise frequently (6, 7).

Such is the importance of occupation in everyday life that an interdisciplinary
research discipline, *occupational science,* was established in the 1980s with the goal of
exploring and understanding the nature and meaning of occupation. If occupations
help maintain health, then it is certainly important to have a good understanding of
how they are constituted. Although occupational therapists have taken a strong lead
in formulating occupational science, researchers from anthropology, economics, geography, political science, sociology, and other fields with concerns for everyday life
have also been drawn to its study. Let's look at a few ways in which occupational scientists have defined occupation:

> Occupations are the ordinary and familiar things that people do every day. This
> simple description reflects, but understates, the multidimensional and complex
> nature of daily occupation. (8, p. 1015)

> Occupation, that is, purposeful activity. . . . Occupation is the mechanism by
> which individuals demonstrate the use of their capacities by achievements of value
> and worth to their society and the world. (2, pp. 17–18)

> . . . [O]ccupation is the active process of everyday living. Occupation comprises
> all the ways in which we occupy ourselves individually and as societies. Everyday life
> proceeds through a myriad of occupations, embedded in time and place, and in the
> cultural and other patterns that organize what we do. Moreover, occupations are
> named, organized, and given value and meaning by each culture. Occupation is
> highly gendered, with household work and parenting typically allocated to women.
> The active process of occupation is a basic human need since it enables humans to
> develop as individuals and members of society. To live is to enfold multiple
> occupations which provide enjoyment, payment, personal identity and more. (9, p. 19)

What do these definitions have in common? They all suggest that occupations
emerge from the routine and everyday aspects of daily living, and they all contain
the same assumption—that everyday living is actually a very complex process. Sev-

eral of the definitions relate occupation to demonstrations of worth and value in society. Furthermore, Townsend informs us that "occupations are not random acts," but rather represent "purposes, goals, meaning and even . . . express personal and cultural ideas of spirituality" (9, pp. 20–21). So occupations are not just any kinds of activities, they have a sense of purpose to them and give meaning. Daily life may comprise "myriads of occupations," but all of these occupations are not necessarily viewed equally. Whereas it was mentioned earlier that occupational therapists tend to be fairly open minded about what constitutes a significant occupation viewed from the perspective of any particular individual, Townsend recognizes that some occupations are more highly valued within a society than others. Finally, she suggests that some occupations are **gendered** in the sense that they tend to be undertaken by one gender or the other.

So far we have examined the concept of occupation as used by occupational therapists and occupational scientists. We have learned that occupations are finely nuanced and are assessed in a lot of detail. Furthermore, we have learned that they may be drawn from activities usually considered to be "work," but that they may also go beyond these boundaries to include "play" occupations, "leisure" occupations, "therapeutic" occupations, or indeed any kind of occupation that is meaningful to the individual and the analyst. Sometimes it is difficult to decide precisely what constitutes the boundary between one occupation and another, so some writers have introduced terminology such as *suboccupation* or *occupational scaffolding* to describe the way in which occupations have components nested within them.

In defining occupations, occupational therapists and scientists are led into a direct assessment of the commonsense notions that we typically have learned through our socialization. It also appears that occupations have a purposful character and are meaningful to those engaged within them. Although they may be meaningful in different ways to individuals, there are broad social understandings that certain occupations are more valued than others. These understandings are derived from the structures of social inequality present in most societies. In contemporary societies, "work" occupations have been more highly valued for a variety of historical, religious and ideological reasons, and many occupational therapists and scientists are currently seeking to challenge their primacy and assert the importance of occupations in other spheres of life (10).

OCCUPATION IN THE SOCIAL SCIENCES

"Occupation" has also been a concept of central concern to social scientists interested in understanding the nature of our contemporary world. One of the most significant early attempts to understand the role of occupations in society was outlined in what has become a classic sociological book, *The Division of Labor in Society* (11). It was written by French sociologist Emile Durkheim (1859–1917), who is commonly regarded as one of the most important founding figures of the discipline of sociology. Durkheim made a distinction between traditional (preindustrial) societies and modern societies, and he based this distinction on the nature of the **division of labor** in society. In his view, earlier societies had a simple division of labor with a limited specialization of functions. Modern societies with modern industrial production systems developed with a fine division of labor. It looked to many 19th century social observers that the old world that they had known was falling apart, and that a major amount of social conflict (revolutions, uprisings, class warfare) was going to be a feature of industrial society. It was an essential part of Durkheim's argument, however, that the finer and finer division of labor that was emerging in modern societies created greater and greater *interdependence* of human beings on one another. In earlier hunting and gathering societies, individuals (or family groups) were relatively self-sufficient. In contemporary societies, where tasks are highly specialized, individuals and even families are very far from being self-sufficient and instead depend on the work of others on a day-to-day basis. It was Durkheim's view that a complex division of labor creates peace because competition between organisms of the same type is reduced:

> In the same city, different occupations can co-exist without being obliged mutually to destroy one another, for they pursue different objects. The soldier seeks military glory, the priest moral authority, the statesman power, the businessman riches, the scholar scientific renown. (11, p. 265)

If we consider what is meant by Durkheim's use of the term *occupation,* we can see that it is somewhat different from the way in which occupational therapists use the term. Durkheim is using the term to refer to what the *Chambers 20th Century Dictionary* terms "one's habitual employment, profession, craft or trade" (12). Virtually all of the examples of occupations that he uses are based on what would now be called the *formal economy.* They refer to situations of paid employment. Presumably the concept still can be considered to contain notions of goal-directed activities that were present in the occupational therapists' definitions. Goals that might be fulfilled by engaging in occupations in the formal economy might include earning wages and benefits, interacting socially with other people, and making a contribution to society.

Just as we noted that occupational therapists introduce ideas that some occupations are valued more highly than others, Durkheim's analysis also introduces this aspect of occupation. Some occupations receive higher pay than others (professional basketball players earn more than kindergarten teachers), some occupations have more social status than others (university professors have more social status than dockworkers), and some occupations have better working conditions than others (secretaries have better working conditions than garbage collectors).

One of Durkheim's primary concerns, and one that many other social scientists after him shared, was that one's occupations should be based on one's talents and capacities and that there should be no obstacles to someone undertaking an occupation for which his[3] or her talents and capacities are fitting. This would constitute injustice in Durkheim's view and would become the basis for conflict in society.

Many other social scientists have picked up Durkheim's themes—the intricate division of labor that characterizes contemporary industrial societies, as well as the relationship of the occupational structure to social inequality and class conflict. Harry Braverman, for example, started a debate about the impact of technology in creating changes in the occupational structure of American society (13). He examined the American economy and argued that over time occupations were becoming less and less skill based and that this skill was being transferred into machines, especially computers. For example, no longer does one need to hire a really accurate and skilled typist because the spell-checker in a word-processing program can quickly correct many of the mistakes. His work is intrinsically about the meaning of the changes associated with the decline of certain occupations and the rise of others, and he argues that with the loss of skill also comes a loss of status and bargaining power over wages for the majority of workers in the labor force.

The gender and racial composition of occupations has also been explored as social scientists ask what kinds of people hold what kinds of occupations and what consequences this has for social inequality. The racial composition of the occupational structure has been studied since the 1950s, with researchers trying to estimate the extent of racial discrimination in labor markets. More recently, the gender composition of occupations has been of interest; in particular, how well women do when entering occupations that are traditionally male (such as steelworker, engine mechanic, and doctor), and how well men do when entering occupations that are traditionally female occupations (nurse, elementary schoolteacher, telephone operator).

Social scientists in many countries have developed scales that measure **social class** or *social advantage*. These scales are based on occupations. These are generally used to investigate levels of social inequality and social difference on a whole range of subjects: health and illness outcomes, voting patterns, wealth and income distribution, housing quality, propensity to obtain higher education, and so on. Examples include Canada's Blishen–McRoberts (14) and Pineo–Porter (15) scales, the United Kingdom's Registrar-General's Scale as well as the Cambridge scale, based on occupational, friendship, and marriage scores (16, 17).

To summarize the way in which social scientists use the concept of occupation, we can see that once again it emerges as a concept of fundamental importance. Occupations tend to have been viewed as arising from the work sphere, but in more recent years the boundaries have begun to be challenged as feminists have stressed the need to consider how women's occupations are defined, whether they are included, and in what detail they are enumerated (18–20). Social scientists have been very interested in how occupational structures change over time and what meanings this has for understanding the evolution of society and broad patterns of social inequality.

OCCUPATION IN GOVERNMENT STATISTICS

So widespread has been the focus on "occupation" as a category for research and government policy making that most governments around the world systematically and regularly collect statistical information about the occupations of the general population in the censuses, in labor force surveys, in general household surveys, and in health surveys. Many different constituencies of people use official statistics: researchers, policy makers, and even the business community. There is wide agreement across nations that "occupation" is of major interest when trying to understand trends in the labor market, health, consumption patterns, voting behavior, and general life advantages.

In the section on occupational therapists and occupational scientists' usage of the term *occupation*, I noted that occupation could be defined by an occupational therapist in terms of a meaningful activity for an individual. When governments are collecting data, however, they go to great lengths to try to ensure that all of the information that has been collected is classified in a way that is uniform from one individual to the next if they give the same information. To ensure this kind of uniformity, national governments develop extensive classification manuals that define how occupations are to be coded so that information from one state or region can be reliably compared to information from another.

These classifications, however, are not arbitrary nor are they set in stone. Underlying any particular classification scheme is a whole set of assumptions that have been debated at length. Look for a moment at a small section of one widely used occupational classification scheme—the **International Standard Classification of Occupations (ISCO),** which was introduced in the year 1988. Some countries have developed their own classification methods that are tailored to the types and detail of occupations found in the labor market and industrial structure of their own country. Creating such systems, however, involves resource allocations that are often not a priority, especially for countries of the Southern Hemisphere. Many countries, therefore, rely on the International Labour Office's scheme. It was designed to be an international standard and to try to include occupations that are relevant in both Northern and Southern contexts, and to be relevant to both industrial economies and agricultural economies. This classification system is organized hierarchically. When analysts just need to work with very general categories, they can use the 10 major groups. If they need more detail, there are 28 sub-major groups (subdivisions of major groups) available. If they need even more detail, there are 113 minor groups (subdivisions of sub-major groups). If they need a fine level of detail, then there are 390 unit groups (subdivisions of minor groups) available. Table 3-1 illustrates how the first major group breaks down into smaller groups.

How does an examination of the ISCO-88 classification deepen our understanding of occupation? As two experts in the development of occupational classification schemes clearly explain:

> ISCO-88 organizes occupations in a hierarchical framework. At the lowest level is the unit of classification, a job, which is defined as a set of tasks or duties designed to be executed by one person. Jobs are grouped into occupations according to the degree of similarity in their constituent tasks and duties. Thus, for example, the following jobs are grouped together in ISCO-88 to form the occupation unit group 3472: Radio, television and other announcers: News announcer, radio announcer; television announcer; disc jockey; media interviewer; newscaster. Although each job may be distinct in terms of the output required from the person who executes the constituent tasks, the jobs are sufficiently similar in terms of the abilities required as inputs into these tasks for them to be regarded as a single occupational unit for statistical purposes. (21)

In this example "occupations" are "sets of tasks or duties performed by a single individual," which are then grouped into occupations according to similarities of task and duty. Peter Elias and Margaret Birch (21) recognize that there may be differences in the tasks of duties from one person to another, but some generalization of content is made in order to distinguish an occupation. While all of this looks very straightforward at first glance, the attempt to develop standardized occupational classification schemes has been rocked by major debates. Earlier, I noted that Townsend made the point that occupations were gendered, and we observed that this gendering was not necessarily neutral in terms of the way in which occupations

TABLE 3-1   *Major Group 1: Legislators, Senior Officials and Managers (Illustration of Detail from Corporate Managers).*

12	**Corporate managers**	
	121 Directors and chief executives	
		1210 Directors and chief executives
	122 Production and operations managers	
		1221 Production and operations managers in agriculture, hunting, forestry and fishing
		1222 Production and operations managers in manufacturing
		1223 Production and operations managers in construction
		1224 Production and operations managers in wholesale and retail trade
		1225 Production and operations managers in restaurants and hotels
		1226 Production and operations managers in transport, storage and communications
		1227 Production and operations managers in business services enterprises
		1228 Production and operations managers in personal care, cleaning and related services
		1229 Production and operations managers not elsewhere classified
	123 Other specialist managers	
		1231 Finance and administration managers
		1232 Personel and industrial relations managers
		1233 Sales and marketing managers
		1234 Advertising and public relations managers
		1235 Supply and distribution managers
		1236 Computing services managers
		1237 Research and development managers
		1239 Other specialist managers not elsewhere classified

Source: Elias, P., & Birch, M. (1994). *A guide for users. Establishment of community-wide statistics.* ISCO-88. Coventry, England, Institute for Employment Research, University of Warwick.

were valued (Box 3-1). Even though the meaning being assigned to the term *occupation* is somewhat different here with respect to its use in government statistics, major controversies have emerged that concern both the nature of gendering (or even sexism) inherent in the way that occupational classification schemes have been constructed and also the relationship of the categories to the more important issues of gendering of the occupational structure in various countries.

Feminist attention has been focused on the existence of some occupations in which there are large numbers of women—clerical worker is a classic example—but the occupations are insufficiently subdivided to capture the range of work that is entailed. Men's work, it is argued, has received far more attention from experts and is far more carefully described and subdivided into a myriad of fine categories. Sylvia Walby has argued that "Workers with such significantly differing amounts of autonomy and authority as a typist in a pool and a managing director's secretary need to be distinguished"[4] (22). Today, certainly far more attention is given to the formal, paid work of women, and those designing classification schemes are generally attentive

BOX 3-1   Gender Issues in Culture and Classification

Japan is one nation that has undergone extensive cultural change during the last fifty years. Historically, the roles of men and women have been influenced by highly prescribed cultural expectations, to the point that nearly one-third of marriages in Japan are prearranged by families. Economics, culture, and communication have changed these practices and others, including more extensive participation by Japanese women in the workforce, who now comprise 40% of all workers. The Japanese government has undertaken extensive policy initiatives and programs to promote gender equity in public employment. Division of labor in the home, however, is more difficult to change. A 1997 survey of married men indicated that over 50% are not inclined to share in housework even if their working spouse earns a higher income. Yet some traditions in Japan, such as expecting wives to manage household finances, provide a degree of autonomy and responsibility that may reduce the attraction of those benefits for employment outside the home. Household work is an important economic role that may be inadequately reflected in economic and occupational classification schemes (23, 24).

FIGURE 3-1   Cultural stereotypes concerning the roles of men and women in the workforce are slowly changing in Japan.
Source: (Ryan McVay/Getty Images)

to trying to capture the complexity of women's work in the same level of detail as that of men's work. Nevertheless, particularly when using older classification schemes, attention must certainly be given to the gendered assumptions inherent in the occupational classifications themselves.

A second area that has experienced much controversy concerns the inclusion or exclusion of certain categories of work from occupational classification schemes. In countries that use self-report categories for census data, for example, some respondents have identified their occupation as "prostitute." Prostitutes certainly perform paid work, and an interesting case can be made concerning the similarity and differences between what some would see as the "oldest occupation on earth" and other occupations with wider social acceptance. "Prostitute" does not, however, generally feature in occupational classification schemes and so responses like this would either be lost or recoded.

There have also been lengthy debates about whether "housewife" is an occupation that should be included in national occupational schemes. Housewives do not tend to get paid in wages, but rather make a contribution to the economic viability of households. Although most would see "housewives" as having much greater social legitimacy than "prostitutes," their relationship to labor markets is not as clear.

An examination of how government statisticians work with the concept of occupation shows that they are less open to "individual" definitions than the occupational therapists and scientists, and more concerned with providing definitions that are stable across large groups of people. In general, the focus is on paid employment, but there are also boundary issues as to what is work and what is not work, as the examples of prostitute and housewife illustrate. Finally, we see that the issue of levels of analysis comes up in this context also. Occupational therapists and scientists struggle with boundary issues in terms of deciding where one occupation leaves off and another begins by introducing terminology such as *occupational scaffolding* or *suboccupation*. The government statisticians do something similar by introducing into classification schemes ideas about major unit groups (large occupational groupings) and minor groupings that are more detailed. Thus we see that in both communities, the concept of nesting occupations within larger occupational groupings has been developed.

CHAPTER SUMMARY

This chapter has presented an analysis of the way in which the concept "occupation" is used in several different communities, that of the occupational therapy and science community and that of the sociology and government statistical office community. It is fair to say that in each community, "occupation" plays a central conceptual role. In the occupational therapy community, occupations were argued to be highly relevant to health and health recovery. In the sociological community and in government statistical bureaus, occupations were assumed to refer to work or trades. The main focus of research was on questions about the relationship of occupation to social advantage. More broadly, the question of whether or not the different traditions of usage in these communities can usefully learn anything from one another about the nature of occupation is a question that has been posed by the editors of this book to the writers of the chapters and to you, the readers. This chapter represents an attempt to address this question from one perspective within sociology.

REFERENCES

1. Waring, M. (1988). *If women counted: A new feminist economics.* San Francisco: Harper & Row.
2. Wilcock, A. A. (1993). A theory of the human need for occupation. *Journal of Occupational Science: Australia, 1*(1), 17–24.
3. Meyer, A. (1922). The philosophy of occupation therapy, *Archives of Occupational Therapy, 1*(1), 1–10.
4. Nelson, D. L. (1996). Therapeutic occupation: A definition. *American Journal of Occupational Therapy, 50*(10), 775–781.

5. Primeau, L. A. (1998). Orchestration of work and play within families. *American Journal of Occupational Therapy, 52,* 188–195.

6. do Rozario, L. (1994). Ritual, meaning and transcendence. The role of occupation in modern life. *Journal of Occupational Science: Australia, 1*(3), 46–53.

7. Howard, B., & Howard, I. R. (1999). Occupation as spiritual activity. *American Journal of Occupational Therapy, 51*(3), 181–185.

8. Christiansen, C., Clark, F., Kielhofner, G., Rogers, I., & Nelson, D. (1995). Position paper: Occupation. *American Journal of Occupational Therapy, 49*(10), 1015–1018.

9. Townsend, E. (1997). Occupation: Potential for personal and social transformation. *Journal of Occupational Science,* 4(1), 18–26.

10. Frank, G. (1992). Opening feminist histories of occupational therapy. *American Journal of Occupational Therapy, 46*(11), 989–999.

11. Durkheim, E. (1964). *The division of labor in society.* New York: The Free Press.

12. Kirkpatrick, E. (Ed.). (1983). *Chambers 20th century dictionary.* Edinburgh: W & R Chambers.

13. Braverman, H. (1975). *Labour and monology capital: The degradation of work in the 20th century.* New York: Monthly Review Press.

14. Blishen, B., McRoberts, H. A. (1976). A revised socioeconomic index for occupations in Canada. *The Canadian Review of Sociology and Anthropology, 13*(1), 71–79.

15. Pineo, P., Porter, J., & McRoberts, H. (1977). The 1971 census and the socioeconomic classification of occupations. *Canadian Review of Sociology and Anthrology, 24*(4), 91–102.

16. Prandy, K. (1990). The revised Cambridge scale of occupations. *Sociology 24*(4), 629–655.

17. Stewart, A., Prandy, K., & Blackburn, R. M. (1980). *Social stratification and occupations.* New York: Holmes and Meier.

18. Litterst, T. (1992). Occupational therapy: The role of ideology in the development of a profession for women. *American Journal of Occupational Therapy, 46*(1), 20–25.

19. Jackson, J. (1998). Is there a place for role theory in occupational science? *Journal of Occupational Science: Australia, 4*(2), 56–65.

20. Jones J. (1992). Therefore be it resolved. *American Journal of Occupational Therapy, 46*(1), 72–77.

21. Elias, P., & Birch, M. (1994). *A Guide for users. Establishment of community-wide statistics.* IS CO-88 (COM). Coventry, England.

22. Walby, S. (1986). Gender, class and statification: Towards a new approach. In R. C. M. Mann (Ed.), *Gender and stratification* (pp. 23–39). Cambridge: Polity Press.

23. Martinez, D. P. (Ed.). (1998). *The worlds of Japanese popular culture: Gender shifting boundaries and global cultures.* Cambridge: Cambridge University Press.

24. Fujimura-Fanselow, K., & Kameda, A. (Eds.). (1995). *Japanese women: New feminist perspectives on the past, present, and future.* New York: The Feminist Press of the City University of New York.

Endnotes

[1] I would like to thank Elizabeth Townsend for her enthusiasm for this topic as well as for her help with locating relevant occupational therapy and occupational science literature. I would also like to thank Tracey Pye for her careful library research.

[2] Nelson defines occupational performance as "The person's voluntary doing in the context of occupational form" (4, p. 777). Occupational form is defined as "The composition of

objective physical and sociocultural circumstances external to the person that influences his or her occupational performance" (p. 776). Occupational form, in this instance, would include the car, the map, the city streets, intense sunshine, the physical presence of the therapist in the front seat, and the therapist's words.

[3] Emile Durkheim was very much a product of the 19th century. His concern really was limited to men's talents and capacities and obstacles to men's mobility in the workplace. Durkheim's views about women's talents and capacities were informed by 19th-century anthropology that suggested that women had smaller brains than men and so on. He did, however, discuss the gender division of labor. Indeed, he saw this as one of the most fundamental divisions of labor on which a society is based.

[4] Note that this criticism is not being leveled at ISCO-88, but at the available British classifications of the time.

4

What Do People Do?

Andrew S. Harvey and Wendy Pentland

There is a way in which the collective knowledge . . . expresses itself,
for the finite individual, through mere daily living . . . a way in
which life itself is sheer knowing.

Sir Laurens Van der Post, *Venture to the Interior* (1, p. 136)

KEY WORDS

Activities
Activity
Behavioral area
Committed occupations
Committed time
Contracted occupations

Contracted time
Free time
Free time occupations
Necessary occupations
Necessary time
Tasks

CHAPTER PROFILE

The understanding of human occupation is facilitated through the use of methods to conveniently describe and differentiate what people do from day to day. This chapter introduces terms and concepts that contribute to a taxonomy of daily time use. It begins with an acknowledgment that the requirements of daily living provide a natural basis for naming and grouping occupations. Recognized in this chapter are characteristics of occupations that provide the basis for four generic categories, and identify social roles and individual projects as other influences on time use and

www.prenhall.com/christiansen

The Internet provides an exciting means for interacting with this textbook and for enhancing your understanding of humans' experiences with occupations and the organization of occupations in society. Use the address above to access the free, interactive companion web site created specifically to accompany this book. Here you will find an array of self-study material designed to help you gain a richer understanding of the concepts presented in this chapter.

means for characterizing occupational pursuit. The chapter concludes with a description of the factors that influence occupational behavior.

INTRODUCTION

We live life one minute, one hour, one day, one week, one month, and one year at a time. . . . The years turn into decades and the decades into generations. At the same time, through memory, the minutes come back, the hours come back, the days come back, and the months, and the years, and the decades. During it all we spend our life doing. Occupation is what we do. It is what we are doing now, what we have done, and what we will do as time flows on. What we do is affected by what time it is on the clock and on the calendar, where we are, who we are with, and myriad of other factors. This chapter introduces a way of looking primarily at what people do in terms of activities and occupations. It suggests ways of conceptualizing them, ways of identifying and measuring them, and finally provides insight into what we have learned from previous studies of daily living.

THE STRUCTURE OF DAILY OCCUPATIONS

Our interest in and ability to choose and engage in a variety of occupations defines us as individuals as we move day by day and year by year through our lives. When we look at what people do, then, we need to look at occupations beyond "work." Through engagement in a variety of occupations, we express ourselves, find meaning in our lives, and adapt to life's challenges. Our "doing" in various occupations is our way of meeting our basic needs (e.g., survival, emotional, self-actualization) and coping with environmental demands (e.g., physical, social/cultural expectations).

Daily life consists of engaging in **tasks** to perform **activities** required by occupations. Each day we perform countless tasks that enable us to carry out activities of living. We sleep, wash, cook, eat, care for a child, work, study, play, talk, socialize, read, reflect, watch TV, listen to the radio, create, and engage in a wide range of other activities that help us fulfill our varied occupations.

Tasks, activities, and occupations are not synonyms, as noted by Christiansen and Townsend in Chapter 1 of this volume. In fact, they represent a hierarchy of undertakings on which daily life is constructed. At the lowest level, tasks are undertaken as a means of accomplishing the activities that comprise an occupation. Hence, one gets out a pan, fills it with water, puts it on the stove, turns on the stove, waits until the water boils, adds eggs and boils them. Simply put, the individual is engaged in the occupation of cooking, or more precisely boiling eggs. There is little ambiguity in what the individual did.

What does the foregoing tell us about the occupational meaning of this of cooking? Actually, it tells us virtually nothing with respect to a broad classification discussed below that distinguishes occupations as necessary, contracted, committed or using free time. The person may be a chef preparing the eggs as part of her paid job. The person may be a father preparing the eggs for his children to meet his family commitment to them. The person may be a hobbyist who in his or her free time decorates eggs. Hence, inherently, tasks and activities are devoid of higher level meaning until they have been put in context. Understanding what people do is important because tasks and activities have both desirable and undesirable effects on the individuals undertaking them and the environment around them.

The nature and structure of occupation is best understood by considering behavior units (activities) and **behavioral areas** (activity groups) (2). An activity is an observable unit of behavior, for an individual, which has observable or determinable temporal beginning and end points (2). One sleeps, reads, talks, shops, buys, makes bread, and eats. Behavioral areas (activity groups) form a broad framework within which activities are organized (2). In essence, behavioral areas reflect occupations.

We may perform activities and occupations one at a time or we may engage in two or three simultaneously. Hence, we may eat, or eat and watch TV, or cook, care for a child, listen to the radio, and wait on hold on the telephone. During our lifetime we have a variety of occupational roles: child, student, spouse, parent, employed worker, unemployed worker, employer, manager, professional, grandparent, retiree, caretaker, or organization member. Often we will be involved in several occupations and occupational roles at a time: child/student, spouse/parent/student/ friend. Our circumstances, beliefs, values, and attitudes are expressed through what we do. The occupations that we do each day and over the course of our lives sustain us; organize our lives; enable us to connect with, adapt to, and have some sense of control in our environment; allow us to express ourselves; and give us our sense of who we are.

Our daily occupations not only define our individual lives; they define our communities and our cultures. In fact, we frequently use "do-ing" based labels to describe whole groups and communities; hunter-gatherers, students, stay-at-home mothers or fathers, teachers, and mountain climbers. Through occupations we create communities (farming, professional associations, backpacking club, choir), and we pass on culture and beliefs from generation to generation through rituals and practices that themselves are made up of occupations. It has often been said "we are what we do." In this sense, knowledge of the occupations that humans choose to do each day reveals what their lives are really like and provides a window on their actual lifestyles and cultures, and indeed, over time, is evidence of social change.

CONCEPTUALIZING WHAT PEOPLE DO

This section outlines four ways of conceptualizing what people do: as occupations, as occupational roles, as life projects, and as meaningful behavior.

Four Types of Occupations

In 1980, Aas (3) observed that in general terms, humans' daily lives are remarkably regular, similar, and systematic. On this basis he proposed that all human use of time, occupational behavior, falls into four categories based on the obligation or constraint inherent in the performance of the occupation. Aas proposed these four categories to be (1) necessary time, (2) contracted time, (3) committed time, and (4) free time. He hypothesized that humans allocate time on a priority basis to the first two categories of necessary time and contracted time, whereas the remaining two categories tend to get whatever time is left over.

Necessary Occupations

Occupations that comprise **necessary time** are those aimed at meeting our basic physiological and self-maintenance needs. These occupations include eating, sleeping, resting, sex and personal care activities related to health, and hygiene such as bathing and grooming. Extensive research internationally reveals that time spent in **necessary occupations** does show some differences, but by and large it is remarkably stable across populations and cultures.

Contracted Occupations

Occupations occurring in **contracted time** are typically those involved in paid productivity or formal education. They are normally governed by an explicit contract extending over long periods including specified obligations relating to start time, finish time, and amount of pay or other reward. Participation in **contracted occupations** is normally in exchange for pay or some type of formal graduation or certification. Contracted time constrains committed and free time and to some extent necessary time. Aas (3) argued that one defining feature of contracted occupations is that they are normally required to be performed outside the home in the workplace, thus they clearly divide up the daily routine of human behavior. However, that was an observation made in the 1980s. With the recent surge in flexible work hours and home and mobile offices, contracted occupations are no longer restricted to an outside single "workplace" and no longer occur in the large discrete blocks that they once did.

Committed Occupations

Occupations engaged in during **committed time** have a work or productivity character, but are typically not remunerated and duration (hours) of work is often diffuse and unspecified. These include household work, meal preparation, shopping, child care, elder care, and home and vehicle maintenance. From an economist's standpoint, **committed occupations** involve nonmarket production. Committed time is unique from contracted and free time in that some people purchase the completion of these tasks as a service by paying others to do these occupations for them.

Free Time Occupations

Free time is the time that is left over after necessary, contracted, and committed occupations are completed. Because necessary time is generally not flexible, free time can be increased in the short term mainly by deferring some of one's committed responsibilities. Free time can be increased in the long term primarily by planning and organizing to reduce contracted time obligations (e.g., reducing work or studies to part time). Aas (3) was careful to distinguish leisure time from free time. He regarded leisure as a qualitative and personally defined experience of self-expression and engagement in satisfying occupations. While free time is indeed leftover time, it does not necessarily consist entirely of leisure. **Free time occupations** can include occupations we feel forced to do to some degree, such as attend a neighborhood social or the office holiday party.

Occupational Roles

What people do can also be viewed in terms of their occupational roles (4). The term *role* refers to a pattern of behavior that involves certain rights and duties that an individual is expected, trained, and often encouraged to perform in a particular social situation. Our roles may be short term such as a soccer game spectator, or of varied duration such as child, parent, or spouse. Role has been defined as "a culturally defined pattern of occupation that reflects particular routines and habits" (5). Any one occupation may be found in a number of roles. For example, parents maintain a household, and they nurture and read to children as part of their committed time. Nurturing and reading to children are also occupations that are typical for teachers, who occupy a role distinct from that of parent.

Our occupational roles influence much of our everyday behavior. Some occupational roles we choose, others are thrust on us, and still others fall somewhere between choice and obligation. Clearly, engagement in occupational roles is dynamic, in that engagement and changes evolve across the life course (6–8). Some roles have powerful culturally prescribed "norms" in terms of whether and when one is expected to adopt them and how one is expected to operationalize the role. Tindale (9) in his research on work, family, and balancing time, discusses how the increase in two-earner families and greater involvement of women in the paid work occupations has altered the timing and age at which women have children. These couples speak in terms of "on times" and "off times" to have children and assume the parent role. This seems similar to the on and off stage behavior described by Erving Goffman in his classic description of roles, *The Presentation of Self in Everyday Life* (10).

Cultural expectations can function as a form of "social clock" for occupational roles and underlie our judgments about what is "normal" and "deviant" in what people do. We use this information in turn to identify and target resources for both individuals and social problems. The messages we get about which roles to adopt and when are often very subtle and can be confusing. Examples include when widows or widowers or teenagers should begin dating or having sex; and, whether or not or when to have children. Whether and when to engage in other roles is much clearer for us, and in fact may even be legislated, such as the age at which children start school or the age of mandatory retirement.

Shifts in the cultural expectations of people's engagement in occupational roles can reflect significant changes in a society and can profoundly impact others' role performance. An increase in women entering the workforce is one example; increased integration and employment of people with disabilities is another example. There has been much research and endless media speculation about the social role impacts of increasing numbers of women in the paid work role and about the impacts this is having on the roles of teachers, children, spouses, and the expectations of employers and employees. Environmental factors also shape and change role performance, which in turn modifies the complexion of society and culture. Witness, for example, the impact of computer technology on the existence and characteristics of certain roles (e.g., assembly-line worker, student, researcher, pilot, stock broker) (11).

The nature of our occupational roles typically varies and evolves over years and decades and may be determined by factors that endure throughout our full lifetime or at least for major portions of it. We generally continue through our lifetime with the sex role with which we were born. But virtually all other roles such as child, student, spouse, parent, employed worker, unemployed worker, employer, manager, and professional are with us for varying periods throughout our lives. We remain a child, sometimes much to our chagrin, as long as we have a parent alive. The duration of time as a spouse or parent revolves, to some extent, around our marital and parental success or failure. Paid work roles revolve around our choices and success in the labor market.

In addition to a number of factors already mentioned, how long individuals occupy certain roles depends on societal customary and legislated time requirements related to study and training, licensing, retirement legislation, and other time-related forces. Custom and legislation vary across occupations, sometimes in paradoxical ways. Hence, judges who can sit on the bench until they are 75 years old have decreed that professors must retire at the age of 65 (12, 13). Furthermore, the demands of many occupations dictate feasible durations of occupancy. For example, professional football players or fire fighters would normally be expected to retire well before the age of 65 because these occupations become too physically demanding for maximum performance.

There is endless variability in how people perform a given role and its inherent occupations. Some roles allow more choice and individual expression than others. Compare, for example, the daughter role or the watercolor artist role with the student or the bank teller role. Variability in role performance is a function of individuals' characteristics, circumstances, and environments. It is this potential for variation that allows humans personal expression and individuality and enables adaptation to life changes and challenges that otherwise might cause a sudden and unwanted role loss. Varying our "doing" allows us to adapt to life circumstances and continue in or adopt roles that are important for our survival and well-being and that of our community. Examples are modifying the way of "doing" the parent role in order to continue as a loving involved parent despite acquiring a significant disability or being separated many miles from one's children due to divorce or an overseas job posting.

The concept of looking at what people do in terms of occupational roles is embedded in all areas of our culture. We speak of taking on a new role, role loss, role balance, and role conflict. It can be argued that it is occupational roles that most profoundly influence what people do each day and, as such, who they are. Occupational behavior, or what people do within selected occupational roles, has received little attention. A review of time budget studies indicates that the major factors affecting daily occupational behavior include day of the week and personal characteristics such as sex, employment status, child responsibility, and the presence of children (14–19). Understanding the occupational behaviors intrinsic to specific roles will help us to identify the positive and negative impacts of role participation and can guide role modification efforts to improve participation and well-being.

Life Projects

Another way of conceptualizing and classifying what it is people do is to focus on the projects in which they engage. Little (20) suggested that at any point in time an individual's occupational behavior is focused on several goals or projects. These life projects dictate what the person does with his or her time. Occupations can be grouped according to the life project with which they are connected. Ellegard (21) looks at projects from the opposite direction. She argues that "when different activities of a particular person are related to each other by aiming at the same goal, they constitute a project" (p. 29).

The project may be relatively small and time limited, such as going to a movie. Or a project may be a major life occupation such as attending college or medical school or having children. In the instance of a smaller project such as attending the theater, the occupations would include arranging for a babysitter; buying tickets; bathing and dressing; executing transportation to the theater by walking, driving or taking a bus or taxi; handling money; attending the show; and returning home. Conversely, on a larger scale, should an individual decide to enter medical school, the contract occupation will have a profound effect on their activities, the decision will prescribe possibly 80% of their activities, context, and occupations during the next 5 to 8 years.

Obviously, we choose some life projects, whereas we do not choose others, such as recovery and learning to live following a traumatic spinal cord injury. Research suggests that increased life satisfaction is associated with spending most of one's time on projects that the individual chooses, values highly, and are within the individual's abilities (22). Other aspects of the life project occupations that have been studied are the *cross impact* or extent to which individuals perceive their various projects to be complementary to or in conflict with each other (22).

Ellegard (21) shows that, within the household, projects can be approached in different ways. Hence, in caring for the household and household members there are at least two different strategies, the *division of labor* strategy and the *work-sharing* strategy (21). Clearly, the activities carried out by household members will be greatly affected by the strategy adopted. More poignantly, in a single-parent household neither strategy is possible, and everything falls on the single parent.

Important factors to consider when examining the impact of life projects on health and well-being are choice and personal control and the impact that individuals' life projects have on their immediate community and society. In particular, understanding behavior in terms of projects can facilitate community and social response to given problems. For example, child care facilities need to be concerned not only with the care of children while they are there, but also with relevant timing and transport needs and demands placed on parents. The concept of life projects is a useful framework for understanding what people do and for assisting people to construct meaningful satisfying lives.

Meaning of Activities and Occupation

An alternative approach to addressing activities and occupation is to view them in terms of what they mean to the actors concerned. Elchardus and Glorieux (23) see meaning as arising from the motivation of the actor to perform the occupation and the criteria used to evaluate performance in it. They identify seven general meanings of time, time devoted to *satisfaction of physiological needs,* for example, medical, hygienic, and dietary; *personal gratification,* that is, time yielding pleasure; *duty,* time spent as an obligation so as to avoid punishment; *instrumental behavior,* time traveling to get to work; *affect/solidarity,* time with others to strengthen relationships; *obligation,* based on one's perception of how he or she should behave; and *killing time,* none of the foregoing. Through analysis Elchardus and Glorieux found that the seven categories could be reduced to four. They found that duty, affect/solidarity, obligation, and instrumentality folded into one factor they called *social meaning* (23, p. 247). Hence, they arrived at four meanings, namely: physiological needs, personal gratification, killing time, and social meaning. In analysis relating these to a variety of occupational coding schemes, they concluded that although such schemes seemed to capture variation in the meaning of activities, the schemes did not allow one to infer motivations, and thus if one wanted to get at meanings it was necessary to do so explicitly.

FACTORS INFLUENCING WHAT PEOPLE DO

Many disciplines and theories of human behavior have begun to recognize and examine the complex interactions between individual characteristics (intrinsic) and the environment (extrinsic) that result in human occupational behavior.

Humans' "doing" influences both individual and community health and wellbeing. To facilitate healthy and satisfying occupational behavior, we must understand those factors that influence "doing." Why humans do what they do is an incredibly complex concept to explain. Simply stating what an individual did, and ignoring context, gives us only a shallow understanding of occupational behavior. The context within which an occupation is performed gives it meaning and provides the basis for assigning it to a specific behavioral area deemed to represent a particular form of behavior. Next we examine three sets of contextual factors that influence and describe what people do: intrinsic factors, extrinsic factors, and contextual factors.

Intrinsic and Extrinsic Factors Influencing Occupational Behavior

One set of forces shaping behavior can be classified as intrinsic and extrinsic factors. These can independently or interactively influence occupational behavior. Intrinsic (to the individual) factors are those that are innate in the individual such as physical/organic factors and psychological traits. Extrinsic factors are external to the individual and include resources (social support, income), the environment (physical, social, political), and cultural influences. Table 4-1 lists some of these factors. Many, although not all, of the intrinsic factors tend to be fixed and more difficult to change. Conversely, factors in the environment can change and evolve or can sometimes be escaped from, eliminated, or modified (24).

TABLE 4-1   *Factors Influencing What People Do*

Factors Intrinsic to the Individual
- Personality/temperament
- Preference
- Skills, abilities, knowledge
- Basic needs (e.g., Maslow)
- Health/chronic illness disability
- Biological rhythms
- Age, gender, socioeconomic status
- Values/attitudes/meaning we give to what we do/spirituality

Factors Extrinsic to the Individual
- *Zeitgebers* (physical and social), etc.
- Tempospatial environment
- Socioeconomic environment and social support
- Cultural environment
- Physical environment
- Circumstance
- Resources (time, money, space)

Source: Drawn from Christiansen and Baum (24).

The World Health Organization (11) has conceptualized an extensive list of environmental factors that influence human behavior. They include social networks, family structure, political systems and government, legal systems, economic organizations, health and social services, educational services, public infrastructure services, community organizations, social rules, values and attitudes, land development, and technology. Extrinsic or environmental factors that influence what we do include *zeitgebers,* which are cues that influence our occupational behavior to the extent that our natural free-running rhythms will resynchronize in response to these *zeitgebers*. Physical *zeitgebers* include daylight, nightfall, and noises. Social *zeitgebers* include mealtimes, bedtime rituals, and start times for work and school.

Circumstance also influences what we do. Things happen to us that we have no or little control over such as disability, death of a spouse, relocation of a family due to one member's job, or nonacceptance at university. Societal circumstances may profoundly affect our occupational behavior such as economic recession or depression, famine, an epidemic, or war.

Dimensions of Occupational Behavior

At any given time an individual must be doing something that can be considered his or her *primary activity* even if it is just resting or reflecting. The term **activity** will be used here to link with current literature, but the discussion is actually about occupations as defined in this book.

Numerous contextual factors facilitate or constrain activities and occupational behavior (4). This section identifies a variety of contextual factors (secondary activities, time, location, with whom and for whom the activity is done, tension, enjoyment, and technology) and contextual constraints (capability, authority, and coupling), which facilitate or impede involvement in "activity" (and occupational behavior).

Secondary activities are activities undertaken simultaneously with a primary activity. Virtually anything can be done along with something else, but typically a relatively few activities account for the major share of the total number identified. Secondary activities take on meaning when we recognize that individuals have multiple senses and generally use them concurrently. An individual can be watching soccer on TV, listening to the better play by play on the radio, and drinking a beer, all with friends. All of these activities—TV viewing, radio listening, drinking and socializing—are concurrent. It makes no sense to try to time slice, allocating one-quarter of the time to each. Unquestionably, it is the mix of activities and contexts that provides life with meaning and richness. So much so, in fact, that often respondents find it difficult to report only one activity at a time.

Time has several dimensions beyond duration. In particular, timing and sequence play an important part in individual behavior. Activities are not randomly distributed. Rather, in a given society, most activities follow a predominant pattern in terms of when they occur and in what order. This is true of various scales of time measurement. Dominant patterns exist on a daily basis too: getting out of bed, work and schooling, meals, and even free time activities. Similarly, there tend to be weekly, monthly, annual, and life course patterns and rhythms (25–27). While any one individual may deviate from such patterns, they cannot easily avoid being affected by them. People who work in the evening have greatly reduced access to cultural events that take place only in the evening. Shopping has to be carried out before meals can be prepared and they must be prepared before they are eaten. Then meal cleanup follows. In fact, a great deal of activity is routine (28). It is argued that the temporal order is a major stabilizing factor in daily living. Hence, any study of activities and occupations cannot ignore temporal dimensions such as timing and sequence.

Location is a fundamental activity dimension. A person may be doing several things simultaneously, with several different people, or working under several motives, but they can only be in one place at a time. Typically, location is defined generically in terms of home, work, restaurant/bar, other public places, or mode of travel. Some studies have captured in which room in the house each activity was undertaken.

Being able to identify work locations is important as a reflection of socialization and community participation (29). Research shows specific activities, that is, occupations, frequently occur in a wide range of locations. For example, although productive work time may be traditionally viewed as all time spent at the paid workplace, teachers' paid productive time invades their home and family life (30, 31).

Time–space diaries have captured not only activities but also the specific geographic location of activities on a one-tenth-kilometer map grid (32). Specific geographic location information is also a significant contextual dimension of activities and occupations and there is an extensive body of literature in this area. It includes study of direction and distance of travel, speed of travel (33, 34), and diurnal patterns of geographic space, for example, the temporospatial rhythm of the city.

With whom, or social contact, is an important contextual dimension of occupational behavior (18, 29). Activity and occupational behavior may be a solitary undertaking, or it may involve family members, friends, work/school colleagues, or various other people. The company we keep can have a significant effect on the nature of our experience.

For example, in Canada in 1992, the workplace provided the major source of time with others. Persons working at the workplace spent more time with persons other than family (about one-half of total time) than individuals working elsewhere (29). Furthermore, individuals working at the workplace only spent about one-half as much of their time with family members compared with persons working only at home (29). Clearly, work arrangements have an impact on social contact time.

For whom an activity is performed provides information for understanding an individual's motivation for performing an activity. It is particularly useful in studies of voluntary activity and instrumental material services in a helping network (35). In Australia, "for whom" information was captured in terms of self, family, friend/neighbor, community, and other (36). One study of teachers provided a broader choice including, as well as the above, various types of students, administration, and the community (31). For whom an activity is done is particularly useful in determining whether it can or should be considered as work.

Tension, time pressure, or stress, often associated by the popular press with concerns about balancing work and family life, have become contemporary issues of interest to occupational researchers. Tension or stress is typically captured by means of a graded scale ranging from no tension to great tension or stress. There is evidence that a "subjective sense of time pressure is grounded in objective reality" with individuals carrying heavier work burdens (paid and unpaid) reporting higher perceived time pressure (37).

Enjoyment or *satisfaction* influences motivation for activities and occupational engagement and is a reflection of the meaningfulness of occupational behavior. Enjoyment is strongly associated with free time or leisure occupations (38). Not only are different activities considered leisure by different people, but the same activity may be leisure at one time and not at another for the same person (39, 40).

Technology, manifest in facilities and equipment, influences occupational behavior at a number of levels. It includes, among other items, household equipment and facilities available, and means of travel, media, and communication technology. Access to such facilities and equipment reduces the time required to do various activities or gives one the ability to do more in the same amount of time. Access to automobiles and cell phones significantly increases an individual's ability to interact with others and their environment. How the technology affects behavior is unclear. It may lead people to spend less time doing laundry or it may lead them to change their clothes more often. A cell phone may lead to less travel or to more. Thus, while there is a relationship between technology and behavior, the nature of the relationship is unclear.

Contextual Constraints Influencing Occupational Behavior

Hagerstrand (41), provides further insight into individual behavior in occupational performance by suggesting that activities are subject to three types of constraints: capability, authority, and coupling constraints.

Capability constraints limit the activities of an individual because of his biological construction and/or the tools he can command (41). Necessary activities such as eating and sleeping are examples of capability constraints. They are subject, most directly, to the forces of circadian rhythms. Variations in such constraints will result from socioeconomic factors such as age, sex, employment status, family status, and income.

Authority constraints refer to the degree of control that exists over something that is considered a control area or domain. Such domains are organized in a hierarchy with smaller ones (for example, Dad's favorite chair) protected only by immediate power or custom, and larger ones (for example, private property and national territory) protected by law and, if necessary, armed force. Store opening hours, work hour legislation, and similar devices represent an exercise of authority over domains that impinge on individual occupational behavior, both obligatory and discretionary. Many such constraints are likely to be reflected in an examination of occupational context.

Coupling constraints "define where, when and for how long the individual has to join other individuals, tools and materials" (41). Thus the concept of coupling constraints adds an additional contextual element: "other individuals" or, more commonly, "social contacts." Ellegard (21), drawing on the time-geographic approach of Hagerstrand, explores behavior in terms of activity purpose, temporal flow of the day, social contact, and geographic context. Her work highlights the fact that projects are manifest in a flow of activities and goal-oriented occupational behavior may not be a continuous act but intermittently undertaken as time flows on.

WHY STUDY WHAT PEOPLE DO?

Try to generate a list of questions about what people do. It is endless because there are so many things to know and so many areas of daily life to consider. This endless list of questions about what people do, about their occupations, has prompted the authors of this book to introduce occupations in a new and creative way. Here are some examples of common yet important questions that ask about occupation. What would your list of questions look like?

Are people working longer hours or is leisure increasing? Is stress related to long hours at work? Is stress the result of trying to do too many things at once? Is the gender division of labor changing? What is a balanced life? Which people are leading balanced lives? What is going to happen to automobile traffic during the next decade? Who teleworks? Is religious involvement increasing or decreasing? What is the value of housework, volunteer work, do it yourself work? What is the real pattern of work hours? Are parents spending more or less time with their children? How much time are people spending on the Internet? Are people becoming couch potatoes? Are retirees becoming more active? What activities are behind the pattern of household energy use? How long do people spend exposed to toxic fumes in traffic or parking garages? Do students work longer hours than regular job holders? Are individuals and families becoming more isolated from others? Who is watching television? When are they watching? Are shopping hours convenient? Are we becoming too dependent on fast food? Do the hours of child care and shopping facilities put undue pressure on workers? Are people time poor? Who is still up at midnight? Are people getting enough sleep? Who are the volunteer workers? Who is taking care of the elderly? This list could go on and on. Likely, you can add to it.

The preceding questions should provide insight into why it is important to study what people do. How people spend their time, the activities and occupations they engage in, is central to each and every question presented. The foregoing questions are important to virtually everyone, including sociologists, child care specialists, economists, environmentalists, psychologists, nutritionists, home economists, sleep researchers, traffic planners, marketing specialists, media specialists, human resources personnel, and rehabilitation professionals who want to understand the lives of those with whom they work.

Planning and policy making, in any endeavor, require knowledge of what *is*. And daily activities or occupations are a major facet of what is. Eastern European countries, lacking a market economy, long looked to time use studies to provide insight into what people did and needed. Western countries, on the other hand, have depended on the market economy to provide the signals for what is wanted and needed. However, it has become increasingly obvious that the market economy is only a part of the real economy, which also includes work done by parents, homemakers, volunteer workers, caregivers, and others. In fact, governments are using time use data to quantify the extent of nonmarket activity. They are quantifying and valuing time spent in activities and occupations in the nonmarket sectors of the economy and society. In short, time use and occupational analyses help people who are planning and policy making.

We have seen that we can conceptualize activities and occupations in a variety of ways. We have also seen that they are contextually dependent and subject to a number of influences and constraints. We have seen that there are many reasons for wanting to know what people do. However, we still have not answered the question *What do people do?* We will address that question after looking at how we learn about what people do. You are encouraged to use Chapter 2 to understand the varieties of ways in which one can study occupation. Here, the focus is on studying time in relation to occupation.

HOW DO WE FIND OUT WHAT PEOPLE DO?

Occupations occur in time, over time, and they occur in sequence. To understand them at any point on the continuum we must observe them in some manner. But how can we do that? Have you every stopped to reflect on what you are doing? Seldom do we reflect on our actions; we just act. Have you ever asked yourself "What am I doing?" or "Why did I do that?" If you have, it is likely because you reached a point where your actions were routine and you suddenly realized you acted without thinking. If we do not know what we are doing, how can we know what someone else is doing? The answer to both questions is the same. We can record and reflect on what we do and on the environment in which our actions occur.

Strategies of recording what we do include keeping a diary, a day planner, or simply jotting things down on a calendar or a Palm™ Pilot. Later, reflecting on what we wrote, we see what we did and hence gain insight into what we were doing: "our occupations." But what would we write? What information would be relevant in understanding what we were doing? Recording our tasks in excruciating detail would be counterproductive. We need to create a line drawing, not a snapshot, by abstracting from a myriad of tasks on any given day to yield a meaningful set of activities carried out within the framework of our occupations and occupational roles.

What we record is only a small part of the complex detail of our daily events. I write in my day planner "11:30 am meet Joe at Lucy's—call first." Obviously, there is much information assumed in that statement. What have I assumed? I know why I am meeting Joe, I know or can find out where Lucy's is and how to get there, and whom to call and the number. I know Lucy's is a restaurant. All this and more is taken for granted as I make my note. When I actually meet Joe at Lucy's, I will have phoned and then traveled by some means to Lucy's. I will be there with Joe. Quite likely I will be eating lunch, and since Joe runs a summer college painting business, I am discussing going to work for him. I finish at 12:30 P.M. What would an observer see? How can you capture the information needed to understand what I am doing?

You could shadow me around, carry a notebook, and record all the things I do and details about them, which is known as *observation* (42, 43). Or you could give me a questionnaire asking me a series of questions known as *stylized questioning* about what I did (44). For example, you might ask "How many hours a week do you work at a paid job?" Both of these approaches would provide some picture of what I was doing. Of course, it would be very costly to follow me around—and you may not see all I do as I see it. Alternatively, you might ask a series of many stylized questions, which, although somewhat informative, fail to capture the stream of what I am doing (my occupational behavior). Additionally, stylized questions tend to yield incomplete and inaccurate recording of a full day's or week's activities.

Fortunately, a proven technique is available that enables you to capture the information you want. *Time use studies* are specifically designed to capture the flow of activities inherent in occupation and the context in which they are carried out. Time use studies are about life, minute by minute, day by day. They are not snapshots, they are line drawings. They provide a skeleton representation of what one does. Using a diary format, an individual records, in sequence, each activity or occupation they engage in, usually 20 to 30 per day, and the context in which that activity or occupation was carried out. Literature to guide an individual in undertaking time use studies exists (19, 45).

To understand more fully what people do, it is necessary to capture in time diaries a variety of dimensions focused on occupations and their contexts. Individuals often engage in multiple occupations at once, giving rise to the need to capture in a diary simultaneous occupations, described in current literature as primary and secondary activities. Additionally, as indicated earlier, a number of contextual dimensions influence activities and occupational behavior. These include location, social contact (with whom), for whom, tension, and technology. A combination of these and other relevant dimensions, depending on the issue of concern, needs to be captured in specific diary studies. Figure 4-1 shows a prototype diary to be completed by an individual. It incorporates several of the dimensions discussed above.

The earliest published accounts of time use studies appear to have been conducted in the early 1900s in the United Kingdom (46) and the United States (47). Then in the 1920s, time use research emerged in Europe in conjunction with early studies of living conditions of the working class in response to pressures generated

FIGURE 4-1   Prototype Time-
Use Diary

What you did from midnight until 9 in the morning

What did you do?	Time began	What else were you doing?	Where?	With Whom?	For Whom?

by industrialization. Household time-allocation studies date from 1915 in the United States (48). These various investigations examined shares of activities such as paid work, housework, personal care, leisure, and so on in the daily, weekly, or yearly time budget of the population. They also examined how time use varied among population groups such as workers, students, and housewives, and the use of leisure time. Most commonly, activity has been captured by stylized questions, asking respondents to estimate how much time they allocated to various activities. However, in view of a number of shortcomings of this approach, since the 1960s time diary studies have flourished, starting with the Multinational Time-Use Study (49).

WHAT DO PEOPLE DO?

Most of us are used to thinking about what we do in terms of how we spend time during the day. The clock (mechanical and biological) and calendar run much of our lives and we are used to scheduling our time. We can talk readily about our experience with time-related concepts such as having enough, too little, and saving or spending time. Consequently, much of what we know about what it is that people do comes from time use studies that have asked large groups of people to recall the activities that occupied their time in a given period, usually a 24-hour day.

As noted earlier, diary studies exist for many countries around the world as well as many population subgroups such as the elderly, women, teachers, and persons with disabilities. Actual activities are recorded, as well as considerable contextual information. Objective information about participation in an activity such as when, where, or with whom it was performed, as well as subjective information such as how the person felt while engaging in the activity, is often captured. The activities reported are then grouped or classified into major areas that generally reflect occupational behavior and can be examined within or across groups or populations and over time.

When examining the time use data presented later in this chapter, the reader should realize two things. First, the data, unless otherwise noted, refer to time spent in primary activities; that is, the main activity the person was doing. Second, the average times presented in the tables are dependent on the prescribed coding definitions used. In coding the information we gain the ability to compare groups and to see differences and changes in behavior over time. These are important for assessing impacts of numerous factors ranging from individual (aging, disability, sex) to environmental (cultural expectations, social programs, poverty, war). However, obviously individuals might not code their activities and occupations in the same way. What is one person's work may be another's leisure, or what feels like leisure to an individual at one time may feel like work at another (39, 40). Depending on the intended use of the information, it is important to recognize that the purpose and meaning that an individual ascribes to his or her occupation will be critical, especially when considering issues such as the relationships between occupational behavior and health and well-being. As noted elsewhere, contextual information is used to help code data as closely as possible to its meaning for respondents.

Time diary data provide a simple way of understanding daily life. Averaged over 1998, male Canadians allocated 4.1 hours per day to paid work, compared with 2.5 hours for females (Table 4-2). The higher average for males came from two forces: those men who worked on any given day spent slightly longer hours than did females at paid work (8.2 compared to 7.1 hours, respectively), and a higher proportion of men than females engaged in paid work on an average day, 49.9% and 35.5%, respectively (Table 4-2). Across the whole population, the only activity taking more time per day than paid work is sleep, at 8.0 and 8.2 hours for males and females, respectively. The average for people who do sleep is the same since virtually everyone participates in sleep each day.

What more is there to life than working and sleeping? There is television, the third largest consumer of daily time for both males and females, averaging 2.4 and 2.0 hours per day, respectively. For men socializing (1.2 hours) and eating meals and other personal activities (1.1 hours each) are next in importance. For women socializing and other personal activities (1.4 hours) and cooking and washing up and eating meals (1.1 hours each) are next.

The remainder of time in a day is allocated over a broad range of activities as individuals fulfill their roles and pursue their occupations. What is particularly interesting to note in Table 4-2 is the small amount of time, overall, that is allocated to paid work, particularly by women. The data clearly reflect the need to view occupation broadly from a population perspective.

Time Use Across Countries

The daily time allocation to necessary, contracted, committed, and free time differs very little among countries. Calculated over all persons and all days of the week and nine different countries or years, contracted hours per day ranged, in eight out of the nine cases, between 3.4 and 4.2 hours per day (Table 4-3). Austria, which registered 4.8 hours, has a very large agricultural component.

This is further evident in major differences in time use that emerge between the sexes in contracted and committed time. Men register between 1.3 more hours in Finland and 3.3 more hours in Austria on contracted time in comparison with women, who register from 1.4 to 3.8 hours more on committed occupations (Table 4-3). However, gender differences in necessary and free time are far smaller between men and women. Women register between 0.1 and 0.6 hours (6 to 36 minutes) more per day on necessary time and men register between 0.2 and 0.8 hours (12 to 48 minutes) more free time per day.

TABLE 4-2 *Allocation of Primary Activity Time and Participation Rates by Sex, Canada, 1998*

	Population		Doers		Participation Rate	
	Male (hours)	Female (hours)	Male (hours)	Female (hours)	Male (%)	Female (%)
Paid work	4.1	2.5	8.2	7.1	49.9	35.5
Activities related to paid work	0.1	0.0	0.7	0.5	9.2	6.4
Travel to/from work	0.4	0.3	0.9	0.8	44.5	31.8
Cooking and washing up	0.4	1.1	0.7	1.3	63.0	85.3
Housekeeping	0.3	1.0	1.5	1.8	21.9	58.7
Maintenance and repair	0.2	0.1	2.7	2.0	9.1	3.6
Other household work	0.4	0.4	1.6	1.1	26.6	33.5
Shopping for goods and services	0.7	0.9	1.8	1.9	38.3	46.7
Child care	0.3	0.6	1.8	2.4	15.7	24.3
Civic and voluntary activity	0.3	0.4	2.0	1.9	17.1	19.3
Education and related activities	0.5	0.6	6.0	6.3	8.7	9.2
Meals (excl. restaurant meals)	1.1	1.1	1.2	1.2	92.0	91.1
Night sleep/essential sleep	8.0	8.2	8.0	8.2	99.8	100.0
Other personal activities	1.1	1.4	1.2	1.4	94.4	96.2
Restaurant meals	0.3	0.3	1.6	1.5	19.5	17.5
Socializing in homes	1.2	1.4	2.5	2.3	49.3	61.0
Other socializing	0.3	0.3	2.7	2.6	12.3	11.9
Watching television	2.4	2.0	3.0	2.7	79.6	75.2
Reading books, newspapers	0.4	0.5	1.3	1.4	30.2	33.7
Other passive leisure	0.1	0.1	1.1	1.1	9.3	8.9
Sports, movies, and other	0.2	0.2	2.6	2.8	6.2	5.8
Active sports	0.6	0.4	2.3	1.7	25.6	22.0
Other active leisure	0.5	0.5	2.4	2.1	21.2	21.8
DAILY TOTAL	24.0	24.0				

Source: Statistics Canada General Social Survey, Cycle 12, 1998.

TABLE 4-3   *Daily Time Allocation, Selected Countries and Years (in hours per day)*

	Hours per day					
	Necessary			**Contracted**		
	Total	**Man**	**Woman**	**Total**	**Man**	**Woman**
USA, 1985	4.0	10.0	10.4	6.2	5.1	3.1
Finland, 1987	4.0	10.5	10.6	6.6	4.7	3.4
Canada, 1992	3.9	9.7	10.3	6.7	5.0	3.0
Germany, 1992	4.2	10.3	10.6	5.5	5.5	3.1
Austria, 1992	4.8	10.5	10.8	4.5	6.6	3.3
Australia, 1992	3.8	10.3	10.4	5.8	5.0	2.6
Australia, 1997	3.7	11.0	11.2	5.3	4.8	2.7
Canada, 1998	4.0	9.7	10.2	6.6	5.0	3.1
France, 1999	3.4	11.9	12.2	4.5	4.2	2.6
	Committed			**Free Time**		
	Total	**Man**	**Woman**	**Total**	**Man**	**Woman**
USA, 1985	3.5	2.4	4.4	10.3	6.4	6.1
Finland, 1987	2.8	2.1	3.5	10.5	6.8	6.5
Canada, 1992	3.3	2.3	4.2	10.0	7.0	6.5
Germany, 1992	3.9	2.6	5.0	10.5	5.7	5.3
Austria, 1992	4.0	2.0	5.8	10.7	4.9	4.1
Australia, 1992	4.0	2.6	5.1	10.4	6.0	5.9
Australia, 1997	4.0	2.8	5.1	11.1	5.5	5.1
Canada, 1998	3.5	2.6	4.2	9.9	6.7	6.5
France, 1999	3.4	2.4	4.4	12.1	4.9	4.2

Source: Calculated from the Multinational Time-use Study (MSTU) datafiles for the selected countries and years.

Time Use Across Sub-Populations

Figure 4-2 presents the time allocations to the four occupational areas for various role groups of the 1998 Canadian population defined in terms of gender (M, F), age (< 25 to 50+), living arrangements (A, alone; PS, partner or spouse; P, parent; LP, lone parent; NF, nonfamily) and child status (C< 5, child under 5; C5+, child 5–14; NC, no child). The groups presented in Figure 4-2 are not exhaustive of all role groups but represent meaningfully sized groups in the sample. Figure 4-2 shows the great variation in occupation across the various defined role groups.

Of the 13 groups presented in the 25–49-year-old age group, all but 4 allocated an average of about 6 or more hours per day (42 hours per week) to contracted (paid) activities (Figure 4-2). The 4 registering fewer hours consisted of female (F) lone parents (LP) with children 5+ years old (C5+); the same group with children

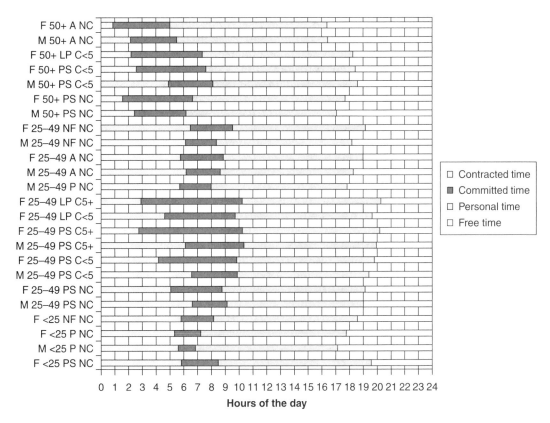

FIGURE 4-2 Time Allocation by Occupation, Canada, 1998.
Source: Harvey, Marshall, and Frederick, 1991.

under 5 years old; females living with partner/spouse (PS) with a child under 5; and same group with no children (NC). While contract time was low for these groups, in general they exhibited the highest combined contracted and committed time, often referred to as *productive time*, registering about 10 hours per day (70 hours per week). Additionally, males age 25–49 living with a spouse/partner and children either under or over 5 years of age registered about 10 hours per day. These same groups, male and female, can be seen to have the least free time, approximately 4 hours per day. In contrast, both males and females, age 50+, living alone (A) with no children (NC), have 7 hours per day (49 hours per week) of free time. In general, there is very little difference across all groups in the time allocated to necessary activities.

A life course perspective for individuals is reflected in Figure 4-2 with economically productive work being less in younger and older ages and more in middle adulthood. This is evident in Figure 4-2 where the subpopulations are ranked bottom to top by age, starting with persons under 25 years of age. In the middle age group, combined contracted time on the job and committed time caring for household and family significantly reduces free time available.

The brief overview just provided of time allocation as a measure of occupation shows a fundamental fact, indeed it could be called a law: The variation in time allocated to different occupations within countries varies more among subpopulations than overall time allocation varies across different countries. The reality of this view emerged in the Multinational Time-Use Study in the mid-1960s (50) and remains true today. Societies appear, at an aggregate level, to have very similar needs and provide similar opportunities with respect to occupational time allocation. However, the burdens and opportunities are differentially distributed within societies. The foregoing also vividly illustrates the extent to which the allocation of time in occupational behavior is affected by at least some of the intrinsic factors identified in Table 4-1.

Table 4-4 presents information that allows you to compare the time use of three specific subpopulations (able-bodied adults, elderly persons, and men with spinal cord injury) in four occupational areas that have frequently been used in occupational research. These areas differ from the four areas identified above in the following ways: Productive time consists of both contracted and committed time as used above, and sleep is included in necessary time in the Aas (3) classification.

Men with spinal cord injury, relative to their general population counterparts, spend much more time on personal care, much less time on productivity, and some time on leisure and sleep (Table 4-4). Across all classifications, elderly persons fall between the other two subpopulation groups. In general, the differences between men with a disability and elderly persons are less when compared to the general population. The findings show clearly that the occupational patterns among the three groups differ. Research is needed to help us understand the implications of the differences, why they exist, and if they should be altered and how.

TABLE 4-4   *Time Allocation to Occupations for Different Populations (in hours per day)*

	Canadian Men	Canadian Elderly (> 65)	Spinal Cord Injured Men
	1992	**1992**	**1995**
Personal care	2.3	3.7	4.7
Productivity	7.7	4.7	3.1
Leisure	6.0	7.2	7.5
Sleep	8.0	8.5	8.7

Source: Pentland, Harvey, & Walles (1999). Time use patterns of men with spinal cord injury. *Journal of Occupational Science. 5*(1): 14–25.

Studies also exist of other subpopulations such as homemakers (51), industrial workers (52), employed mothers (53, 54), and people with disabilities (55, 56) (19) that provide insights into the conduct of time use studies. As well, there are studies of general populations such as those conducted in Canada and Australia (57, 58).

The Context of Doing

Time spent in primary activities or occupations, as shown earlier in Table 4-2, reveals powerful similarities and differences in what people do. But how much time we spend in the various activities and occupations tells us little about the quality of someone's life. It is more the attributes of engagement in the activity or occupation that have a bearing on quality of life, well-being, and health. These include the objective and subjective context, whether we are in a suitable location, whether we are with people we like or don't like, time pressures, personal control (whether we are doing the activity because we want to or have to), the meaning of the activity for us, and whether we have the skills to perform the activity or such advanced skill that we are bored in that occupation (59). It is this contextual information that begins to give us a sense of what occupational engagement is doing for individuals and their society.

Secondary Activity

As previously noted, individuals often engage in concurrent activities in addition to their primary activities. Data from a 1997 Australian time use study provide some insight into this phenomenon (58). It shows that a short but not inconsequential list of activities accounts for most secondary activities. The top five most frequent secondary activities accounted for 80% of all such episodes (Table 4-5). Communication, media, and child-related activities dominate secondary activities. These are important dimensions of daily life and social involvement that are missed if studies do not collect secondary activity data. Some activities can be virtually totally missed if secondary activities are ignored, with minding children and caregiving heading the list of often ignored activities. Minding children was recorded in diary episodes as a secondary activity far more frequently than as a primary activity in the Australian 1997 time use study (60).

Secondary time can be significant. A study of teachers in Nova Scotia, Canada, found that one-fifth of a teacher's paid work time is considered to be a secondary activity, 10.2 hours per week out of a total of 52.4 (31). This interpretation was made by listing as secondary activities such things as grading while supervising students or preparing materials for class while watching TV.

Location

The main location for activities and occupations is the home. In 1998, Canadian females averaged 16.2 hours per day at home while Canadian males averaged 15.3 hours at home (Table 4-6). The second major site of activities and occupations was

TABLE 4-5   *Secondary Activities, Australia, 1997*

	Episodes (N)	**% of Total**	**Cumulative %**
Communication (casual, leisure)	34,238	22.93	22.93
Listening to radio	32,524	21.78	44.70
Minding children	22,848	15.30	60.00
Watching TV	20,710	13.87	73.87
Playing/reading with child	9,101	6.09	79.96
Using audio/visual media	3,557	2.38	82.34
Drinking/nonalcohol	2,414	1.62	83.96
Reading newspaper	2,346	1.57	85.53
Listening to records	1,858	1.24	86.78
Reading (not further defined)	1,458	0.98	87.75
Meal preparation	1,209	0.81	88.56
Eating	1,185	0.79	89.35
Thinking	959	0.64	90.00
Other secondary	14,940	10.00	100.00
Total Secondary	149,347	100.00	100.00
Total Primary Only	256,786		
Total Episodes	406,133		

Source: Calculated from Australian Bureau of Statistics, *Australian Time Use Study,* 1997.

TABLE 4-6   *Average Hours per Day Spent at Various Locations, Canada, 1998*

Location of Activity	**Female**	**Male**
At home	16.2	15.3
At workplace	3.0	3.7
At someone else's home	1.0	1.0
At another place	2.5	2.6
In transit	1.3	1.3
As an automobile driver	0.8	1.0
As a passenger in an automobile	0.3	0.1
Walking	0.1	0.1
Taking bus or other public transit	0.1	0.1

Source: Statistics Canada General Social Survey, 1998.

the workplace, where females averaged 3.0 hours and males 3.7 hours. Both males and females spend 1.3 hours per day in transit and 1.0 hours per day in someone else's home. Hence, although there were very notable differences in the activities and occupations of males and females, the location of behavior is very similar.

With Whom

Excluding sleep and personal care time, Canadian males spend 6.0 hours a day and Canadian females 5.8 hours a day alone (Table 4-7). Female members were more

TABLE 4-7 *Average Hours per Day Spent with Various Other Persons, Canada, 1998*

Social Contacts During Activity	Total	Male	Female
Alone	5.9	6.0	5.8
With household members:			
Spouse or partner	3.1	3.3	2.9
Child(ren) under age 15	1.5	1.1	1.9
Parent(s) or partner(s)-in-law	0.3	0.2	0.3
Other members including children age 15+	0.7	0.6	0.8
With persons outside the household:			
Respondent's child(ren) under age 15	0.1	0.1	0.1
Respondent's child(ren) age 15+	0.2	0.1	0.2
Parent(s) or partner(s)-in-law	0.2	0.2	0.3
Other relative(s)	0.6	0.5	0.7
Friend(s)	1.7	1.8	1.7
Other person(s)	3.1	3.5	2.8
With household members only	4.6	4.3	4.8
With persons outside the household only	5.4	5.6	5.1
Social contact not applicable to activity (includes sleep)	9.0	8.8	9.2

Source: Statistics Canada General Social Survey, 1998.

Figures to be used with caution. The coefficient of variation of the estimate is between 16.6% and 33.3%.

likely than male members to spend time only with household members, 4.8 hours compared with 4.3 hours. Women spend nearly twice as long (1.9 hours compared to 1.1 hours) as men with household children under the age of 15. Males and females spend roughly the same amount of time each day with friends living outside the household (1.8 and 1.7 hours, respectively). Time for which social contact was not considered applicable, namely, sleep and personal care time, plus time spent alone, accounts for about 15 hours per day, 14.9 hours to be exact. There is little difference between females, 15.0 hours, and males, 14.8 hours. In essence, this leaves only about 9.0 hours per day of stated social contact.

The Social Environment

Although it is informative to understand where and with whom activities and occupations are carried out, it can be more meaningful to understand the interaction between these contextual dimensions. A meaningful way to explore the relationship between social contact and location can be cast in terms of social environment (29). The social environment is one's social circle, consisting of those people with whom an individual comes in contact, and social space, the locations occupied by persons. Looked at in this way, Canadians spend about 10% more time alone at home than do individuals in Norway and Sweden, 31.2% compared with 21.9% and 21.2%, respectively (Table 4-8). In contrast, little difference is seen among Canada, Norway, and Sweden in the amount of time spent alone in transit, about a half a percent of

TABLE 4-8 *Social Environment in Selected Countries*

Social circle	Home (%)	Work-place (%)	Community (%)	Transit (%)	Total (%)	Total (minutes)
	Social Space					
Canada 1992						
Alone	31.2	3.1	3.4	3.5	41.2	390.0
Family	19.9	0.4	5.2	2.5	27.9	263.9
Others and multiple	3.8	14.5	11.1	1.4	30.9	291.8
Total	54.8	18.1	19.7	7.4	100.0	945.6
Norway 1990						
Alone	21.9	7.4	3.3	3.2	35.8	345.4
Family	26.1	0.6	6.2	2.6	35.6	343.0
Others and multiple	4.1	13.4	9.4	1.8	28.6	276.0
Total	52.2	21.4	18.9	7.5	100.0	964.5
Sweden 1991						
Alone	21.2	5.2	2.7	3.7	32.7	335.1
Family	26.5	0.4	2.2	1.9	31.0	317.3
Others and multiple	5.8	18.7	9.4	2.3	36.3	371.9
Total	53.5	24.3	14.3	7.9	100.0	1024.4

Source: Harvey and Taylor, 2000 (29).

total time per day. With respect to family time, both Norwegians and Swedes spend a larger proportion of their time at home with their family than do Canadians. In terms of time in the community, both Canadians and Norwegians spend approximately 20% of their time there, whereas in Sweden the figure is less than 15%. The lesson to be learned here it is that different peoples play out their day-to-day lives in somewhat different social environments. As well as understanding why people do certain activities, it is also necessary to understand the context in which they do their activities or occupations.

Technology

Technology plays a role in everyday life in many ways. We can observe in Table 4-6 that in 1998 Canadians spent 1.1 hours per day in a car either as driver or passenger, and only 0.1 hours per day on public transit.

The 1997 Australian time use study provides insight into the use of communications technology (58). Nearly one-half of recorded communication was in person, as illustrated in Table 4-9. Approximately one-fifth of reported communication was written and slightly more than one-fifth was fixed phone. The data reflect relatively little use of computers and an infinitesimal amount of mobile phone use and fax. These numbers could reflect one of two things. On one hand, the use of mobile

TABLE 4-9 *Communications Technology, Australia, 1997*

Mode	Number of Events	Percent
In person	14,866	48.39
Mobile phone	39	0.13
Fixed phone	7,165	23.32
Written	6,486	21.11
Fax	62	0.20
PC	1,816	5.91
Undescribed	286	0.93
Total	30,720	100.00

Source: Calculated from 1997 Australian Time-Use Data, Australian Bureau of Statistics (36).

phone, fax, and other communication means may have been underreported in the diaries. Underreporting is a real possibility because using a mobile phone may often be a very short activity. However, the low numbers could reflect reality in the face of hype. Often, much is made about the length of time spent on the Internet and dealing with e-mail. Such numbers are derived from extremely biased samples in a manner that leaves the impression that a phenomenon is much greater than it is. Which of these is a better explanation is worthy of exploration. Of course, households have far more technological equipment in the form of appliances, tools, entertainment equipment, and more. Far too little research has been carried out to help us understand the strengths and follies of such goods.

CHAPTER SUMMARY

This chapter has discussed a variety of ways of conceptualizing what people do and the factors that influence and characterize human occupational behavior. Measurement of human time use is well developed and applied across numerous disciplines. We have briefly reviewed some of the methods of recording and measuring time use. Each affords us unique information about human doing and will proscribe different approaches to the understanding and assessment and facilitation of health and well-being.

Finally, data were presented and compared on the use of time among various groups and across countries. We have noted that, in reality, paid work accounts for a rather small portion of time on a lifetime basis. This suggests that it is important to view occupation in a broad manner so as to identify and understand all occupations engaged in and how they interrelate in life from one day to a lifetime. We have also noted that activities and occupations vary much more among subpopulations in a given country than they do in total across countries. This suggests that populations as a whole, reflected by the countries, have very similar occupational needs. It further suggests that these needs are met, in each case nationally, by a division of work and responsibility determined by some of the forces identified in this chapter as well as other forces discussed elsewhere in this text. While the chapter has tended to focus on individual human occupation, many of the constructs discussed can be applied to the occupational behavior of communities.

REFERENCES

1. Van der Post, L. (1951). *Journey to the Interior.* New York: Morrow.
2. Harvey, A. S., & Neimi, I. (1994). An international standard activity classication (ISAC): Toward a framework of relevant issues. In *Fifteenth reunion of the International Association for Time Use Research.* Amsterdam: NIMMO.
3. Aas, D. (1980). Designs for large scale time use studies of the 24 hour day. In *It's about time.* Sofia: Institute of Sociology at the Bulgarian Academy of Science.
4. Harvey, A. (1982). Role and context: Shapers of behavior. *Studies of Broadcasting, 18,* 70–92.
5. Canadian Association of Occupational Therapists. (1997). *Enabling occupation: An occupational therapy perspective.* Ottawa: Author.
6. Ickes, W., Knowles, E. S., & Kidd, R. F. (Eds.). (1982). *Personality, roles and social behavior.* New York: Springer-Verlag.
7. Mancuso, J. C., & Sarbin, T. R. (1985). The self-narrative in the enactment of roles. In T. R. Sarbin, K. E. Scheibe (Eds.), *Studies in social identity* (pp. 233–253). New York: Praeger Publishers.
8. Marks, R. R. (1977). Multiple roles and role strain: Some notes on human energy, time and commitment. *American Sociological Review, 39,* 567–568.
9. Tindale, J. (1999). Variance in the meaning of time by family cycle, period, social context, and ethnicity. In W. Pentland, A. S. Harvey, M. P. Lawton, & M. A. McColl (Eds.), *Time use research in the social sciences* (pp. 155–182). New York: Kluwer Academic/Plenum Publishers.
10. Goffman, E. (1959). *The presentation of self in everyday life.* New York: Doubleday.
11. World Health Organization. (2001). *International classification of functioning, disability and health.* In *ICIDH-2.* Geneva: Author.
12. Canada. Supreme Court of Canada. (2001). About the court. In http://www.scc.csc.gc.ca/aboutcart/judges/aboutjusticies_e:html.
13. McKinney, V. (1990). *McKinney v. University of Guelph* (p. D/171). Supreme Court of Canada.
14. Cheek, N. H., & Burch, W. R. (1976). *The social organization of leisure in human society.* New York: Harper and Row.
15. Forbes, W., Singleton, J., & Agavani, N. (1993). Stability of activities across the lifespan. *Activities, Adaptation and Aging, 18*(1), 19–28.
16. Harvey, A. S., Elliot, D. H., & Procos, D. (1977). *Sub-populations relevant to the study of the use of time: A working paper.* Halifax, Nova Scotia: Dalhousie University–Regional and Urban Studies Center.
17. Lounesbury, J. W., & Hoopes, L. L. (1988). Five year stability of leisure activity and motivation factors. *Journal of Leisure Research, 20*(2), 118–134.
18. Schneider, A. (1972). Patterns of social interaction. In A. Szalai (Ed.), *The use of time: Daily activities of urban and suburban populations in twelve countries.* Amsterdam: Mouton & Company.

19. Pentland, W., Harvey, A. S., Lawton, M. P., & McColl, M. A. (Eds.). (1999). *Time use research in the social sciences.* New York: Kluwer Academic/Plenum Publishers.
20. Little, B. R. (1983). Personal projects: A rationale and method for investigation. *Environment and Behavior, 15,* 273–309.
21. Ellegard, K. (1993). Activities in their every-day context: Using individual diary data to set forth the complex pattern of people's activities in their every-day life. In *Time use methodology: Toward consensus.* Rome: Italian National Statistical Institute.
22. Palys, B. R., Palys, T. S., & Little, B. R. (1983). Perceived life satisfaction and the organization of personal project systems. *Journal of Personality and Social Psychology, 44,* 1221–1230.
23. Elchardus, M., & Glorieux, I. (1993). Towards a semantic taxonomy classifying activities on the basis of their meaning. In *Time-use methodology: Toward consensus.* Rome: I. Stat.
24. Christiansen, C., & Baum, C. M. (1997). Person–environment–occupational performance: In C. Christiansen & C. M. Baum (Eds.), *Person–environment occupational performance: A conceptual model for practice* (2nd ed., 47–70). Thorofare, NJ: Slack Inc.
25. Maric, D. (1997). *Adopting working hours to modern needs: The time factor in the new approach to working conditions.* Geneva: International Labour Office.
26. Zuzanek, J., & Smale, B. (1994). Life cycle variations in across-the-week allocation of time to selected daily activities. *Society and Leisure, 15*(2), 559–586.
27. Frederick, J. A. (1995). *As time goes by. . . time use of Canadians. General survey.* Ottawa: Statistics Canada (Housing, Family and Social Division).
28. Cullen, I., & Godson, V. (1975). Urban networks:The structure of activity patterns. *Progress in Planning, 4*(1), 1–96.
29. Harvey, A. S., & Taylor, M. E. (2000). Activity settings and travel behavior. *Transportation, 27,* 53–73.
30. Drago, R. (1999). New estimates of working time for elementary school teachers. *Monthly Labor Review, 4,* 31–40.
31. Harvey, A. S., & Spinney, J. (2000). *Life on and off the job: A time use study of Nova Scotia teachers.* Halifax: St. Mary's University Time Use Research Program.
32. Elliot, D., Harvey, A. S., & Procos, D. (1976). An overview of the Halifax time-budget study. *Society and Leisure, 3,* 145–159.
33. Goodchild, M., & Janelle, D. (1982). Diurnal patterns of social group distributions in a Canadian city. *Economic Geography, 59*(4), 403–425.
34. Janelle, D. G., & Goodchild, M. F. (1983). Transportation indicators of space–time autonomy. *Urban Geography,* No. 4, 4.
35. Blanke, K., & Schafer, D. (1993). What for whom? Experience from the diaries of the pretest of 1991/1992. In *ISTAT time use methodology: Toward consensus.* Rome: Instituto Nationale D. Statistica.
36. Australia Bureau of Statistics. (1988). *Time use survey of Australia: User's guide.* Canberra: Australian Commonwealth Government Printer.
37. Zuzanek, J., Beckers, T., & Peters, P. (1998). The "harried leisure class" revisited: Dutch and Canadian trends in the use of time from the 1770s to the 1990s. *Leisure Studies, 17*(1), 1–19.
38. Robinson, J. P. (1977). *How Americans use time: A social psychological analysis of everyday behavior.* New York: Praeger Publishers.
39. Shaw, S. (1985). The meaning of leisure in everyday life. *Leisure Sciences, 7*(1), 1–23.
40. Sorokin, P., & Berger, C. Q. (1939). *Time budgets of human behavior.* Cambridge, MA: Harvard University Press.

41. Hagerstrand, T. (1970). What about people in regional science? *Papers and Proceedings of The Regional Science Association, 24,* 7–24.
42. Skjoensberg, E. (1989). *Change in an African village: Kefa speaks.* West Hartford, CT: Kumarian Press.
43. Altman, R. M. (1974). Observational study of behavior: Sampling methods. *Behavior, 48,* 227–267.
44. Ho, T. J. (1979). Time costs of child rearing in the rural Phillipines. *Population and Development Review, 5*(4), 643–662.
45. Harvey, A. S., Szalai, A., Elliot, D. H., Stone, P. J., & Clark, S. (1984). *Time budget research: An ISSC workbook in comparative analysis.* New York: Campus Verlag.
46. Pember-Reeves, M. (1913). *Round about a pound a week.* London: Bell.
47. Bevans, G. E. (1913). *How working men spend their spare time.* Unpublished doctoral dissertation, Columbia University.
48. Bailey, I. (1915). A study of management of farm homes. *Journal of Home Economics, 7,* 348.
49. Szalai, A. (Ed.). (1972). *The use of time.* The Hague, Netherlands: Mouton.
50. Converse, P. E. (1972). *The social organization of leisure in human society.* New York: Harper and Row.
51. Walker, E., & Woods, M. E. (1976). *Time use: A measure of household production of family goods and services.* Washington, DC: Center for the Family, American Economics Association.
52. Zuzanek, J. (1980). *Work and leisure in the Soviet Union: A time budget analysis.* New York: Praeger Publishers.
53. Michelson, W. (1985). *From sun to sun: Daily obligations and community structure in the lives of employed women and their families.* Ottawa: Rowman and Allanheld.
54. Robinson, J., & Bianchi, S. (1997). The children's hours. *American Demographics, 19*(12), 22–24.
55. Ujimoto, K. (1987). Organizational activities, cultural factors and well-being of aged Japanese Canadians. In D. E. Gelfand (Ed.), *Ethnic dimensions of aging* (pp. 145–160). New York: Springer.
56. Klumb, P., & Baltes, M. (1999). Time use of old and very old Berliners: Productive and consumptive activities as functions of resources. *Journal of Gerontology, 54B*(5), 271–278.
57. Harvey, A. S., Marshall, K., & Frederick, J. (1991). *Where does time go?* (Catalogue 11-612E, no. 4). Ottawa: Statistics Canada.
58. Marshall, K. & Frederick, J. A. (1997). *How Australians use their time.* (Report 4153.0). Canberra: Commonwealth of Australia, Bureau of Statistics.
59. Csikszentmihali, M., & Larson, R. (1987). Validity and reliability of the experience-sampling method. *Journal of Nervous and Mental Disease, 175*(9), 526–536.
60. Harvey, A. S., Australian Bureau of Statistics. (2000). *Use of context in time use research.* Paper given at Expert Group Meeting on Methods for Conducting Time-Use Surveys, New York, United Nations Secretariat–Statistics Division.

CHAPTER 5

Occupational Development

Jane A. Davis and Helene J. Polatajko

KEY WORDS

Active participation
Continuity theory
Environmentalist viewpoint
Interactionist viewpoint
Mastery
Maturationist viewpoint

Multiple determinicity
Multiple patternicity
Multiple variation
Preformationist viewpoint
Tabula rasa

CHAPTER PROFILE

Watson (1928) assumed that genetic factors place no restrictions on the ways that environmental events can shape the course of a child's development and claimed that by properly organizing the environment he could produce a Mozart, a Babe Ruth, or an Al Capone. (1, p. 8)

In this chapter the reader will be asked to consider whether Watson's perspective has merit. In other words, the reader will be asked to consider the nature and course of occupational development. Human growth and development have been studied for more than a century. Although a variety of domains have been investigated, some including mention of occupation, very little has been written specifically about how humans develop as occupational beings. In this chapter the authors present a framework of occupational development that has been constructed from the existing developmental literature. First the authors present perspectives on occupation and on development. Then a framework for occupational development is

www.prenhall.com/christiansen

The Internet provides an exciting means for interacting with this textbook and for enhancing your understanding of humans' experiences with occupations and the organization of occupations in society. Use the address above to access the free, interactive companion web site created specifically to accompany this book. Here you will find an array of self-study material designed to help you gain a richer understanding of the concepts presented in this chapter.

proposed, including principles of occupational development. Finally, a preliminary discussion of the ages and stages of occupational development across the life span is offered.

INTRODUCTION

The study of human growth and development has been of interest for more than a century. By its very nature, such study is an interdisciplinary enterprise concerned with various aspects of human development. Textbooks on development typically describe changes in a number of areas, for example, changes in growth, such as body size and body shape, and changes in specific behavioral domains, such as the physical, motor, cognitive, language, social, sexual, moral, or personality domains. These domains, however, have relevance to occupational development only as they come together in the performance of daily occupations in various contexts.

Occupation is rarely included among the domains of development, except in the context of career development, where the concept of occupation has a very specific meaning related to economically productive work. Nevertheless, many of the descriptions of development found in the literature are stated in terms of what people do at various ages and stages of life, in other words, in terms of occupation. This can be seen vividly in Shakespeare's profile of the ages and stages of life in *As You Like It*, a romantic comedy written in the late 16th century:

> All the world's a stage
> And all the men and women merely players;
> They have their exits and their entrances;
> And one man in his time plays many parts;
> His acts being seven ages. At first the infant,
> Mewling and puking in the nurse's arms.
> Then the whining school-boy, with his satchel
> And shining morning face, creeping like snail
> Unwillingly to school. And then the lover,
> Sighing like a furnace, with a woeful ballad
> Made to his mistress' eyebrow. Then a soldier,
> Full of strange oaths and bearded like the bard,
> Jealous in honour, sudden and quick in quarrel,
> Seeking the bubble reputation
> Even in the cannon's mouth. And then the justice,
> In fair round belly with good capon lined,
> With eyes severe and beard of formal cut,
> Full of wise saws and modern instances;
> And so he plays his part. The sixth age shifts
> Into the lean and slipper'd pantaloon
> With spectacles on nose and pouch on side,
> His youthful hose, well saved, a world too wide
> For his shrunk shank; and his big manly voice,

Turning again toward childish treble, pipes
And whistles in his sound. Last scene of all,
That ends this strange eventful history,
Is second childishness and mere oblivion,
Sans teeth, sans eyes, sans taste, sans everything.

Shakespeare, Act II, scene vii

If occupation refers to the everyday pursuits that capture people's time and attention, it is possible to construct a framework for occupational development from work already done by developmental theorists. Theories of human development that are consistent with this perspective of occupation can be used to create an integrative model of *occupational* development. The purpose of this chapter is to present such a model from the existing developmental literature. Accordingly, in this chapter, the reader is introduced to a framework of human occupational development, relevant theories, a potential model of development, and a preliminary discussion concerning the ages and stages of occupational development across the life span.

AN OCCUPATIONAL PERSPECTIVE ON DEVELOPMENT

Perspective on Occupation

Humans are essentially occupational beings; they derive meaning in their lives from their occupations. "Doing" is central to human life. As Fidler and Fidler (2) noted, "doing is viewed as enabling the development and integration of the sensory, motor, cognitive, and psychological systems; serving as a socializing agent, and verifying one's efficacy as a competent, contributing member of one's society" (p. 305). Ultimately, "occupation is the crucible in which our identities are formed" (3).

Humans within all cultures engage in a wide variety of occupations, the choices of which are influenced by individuals' innate cognitive, affective, and physical abilities and by the environments in which they live, work, and play. The classification of occupations has taken many forms. One way of approaching classification has been to group occupations by the purpose they serve: (1) things people do to care for themselves; (2) things people do to contribute to their community, family, or culture; and (3) things people do for enjoyment (4, 5). These groupings vary among societies and are affected by cultural characteristics and by personal meaning. For example, a mother may consider cooking to be an activity of daily living, a chef may consider it work, and a child may consider it play.

The specific occupations in which people engage are influenced by their preferences, values, and lifestyles, and by the physical, cultural, social, and institutional environments in which they act. A reciprocal relationship is assumed to exist between the person and the environment, each influencing the other and causing the other to change. To quote Wilcock, ". . . occupation has the potential to change the world or the species and this provides the mechanism for human survival and development which in turn impacts and maintains health and well-being and offers the individual the ability to adapt to their environmental demands" (6, p. 35).

Occupational performance is considered to be "the result of a dynamic, interwoven relationship between person, environment, and occupation over a person's life span . . . " (5, p. 181). Occupational performance is influenced by a person's emotions, physical abilities and skills, and ability to process information. The developmental literature indicates that individual performance in these domains changes and develops across the life span. Because competence is achieved when there is a match between the abilities of the individual, the demands of the occupation, and the supports of the environment (7, 8), a person's ability to engage and master occupations can be presumed to change and develop throughout life.

Perspective on Development

Human development has been of interest since the time of Aristotle, who observed: "What makes men good is held by some to be nature, by others habit or training, by others instruction" (9, p. 975). Since that time, attempts have been made to more fully understand developmental influences. In the 20th century, a concerted effort was made to gain scientific knowledge. Theories and research on human development expanded within a variety of disciplines, including psychology, anthropology, sociology, biology, and history, leading to the formation of a distinct body of knowledge.

Until recently, developmental research has focused almost exclusively on the first 20 years of life. Thus, concepts of development were essentially concepts of "child" development. In the last few decades, however, greater emphasis has been placed on understanding development in adulthood and older age. It is now generally accepted that development is a lifelong process. This perspective includes both the concepts of child development and of adult development and aging (10–13).

Human *development* is a lifelong process of *change*. These two terms, *development* and *change*, are often used interchangeably. Yet, there are significant differences in their meaning. Although "development involves change, . . . not all change is developmental" (14, p. 5). The differences between the two terms involve the notions of (1) reversibility, (2) distinctiveness, (3) length of time, and (4) growth and maturation. For example, the emergence of facial hair in a young man is the result of developmental maturation, while shaving off a beard involves a change that is not developmental, because it is easily reversed, can reoccur, happens within a few minutes, and does not add to what has already happened. As a lifelong process, unlike most changes, development is not easily reversed, is distinct in nature from prior occurrences, occurs over long periods of time, and is influenced by growth and maturation.

Historically, there have been four major perspectives on how development occurs. These four major viewpoints are called **preformationist, maturationist, environmentalist,** and **interactionist.** These perspectives differ by the relative level of importance placed on the concepts of maturational, environmental, and interactional influences on an individual's development. The *preformationist view,* popular from the Middle Ages to the latter part of the 18th century, viewed little children as miniature adults (15) acquiring all their lifetime characteristics at conception, including body shape and personality. *Maturationists* believed that human development was dictated by a person's genes. Therefore, heredity alone was thought to direct the course and nature of a human's development. *Environmentalism* had its origins with John Locke, an English physician and social philosopher from the mid-17th century, who believed that all individuals were born empty of influence (sometimes referred to as **tabula rasa,** which is Latin for "blank slate") and that they developed through their life span due to their different life experiences. This belief holds the view that the environment alone impacts development.

The *interactionist view,* which is of particular relevance to occupational development, holds that individuals are involved in a reciprocal interactive relationship with their environment that ultimately delineates human development across the life span. Individuals bring their genetic makeup, or *genotype,* to this dynamic relationship. Their genotype dictates a certain outward expression of human characteristics, or *phenotype,* within the constraints of their environment, which is thought to play a significant role in an individual's development across the life span. As individuals grow and mature, the nature of this interactive relationship stays the same. However, the phenomena involved may change and build on previous occurrences, making development a cumulative experience. The beginnings of the interactionist perspective on development can be traced back to Aristotle (16).

The strength of the interactionist perspective is that it draws on concepts from both maturationism and environmentalism, influenced by developmental research during the last few decades. Arnold Gesell (17, 18) used the term *maturation* to mean developmental changes that are caused or directed by genes. He believed that children's development unfolds due to the action of the genes and that the environment plays a supportive but limited role in children's development. The concept of maturation holds that development occurs in fixed sequences, as noted in embryonic change in which there is an exact order of biological development. This sequential development continues after birth, with changes from reflexive to controlled movements, in a head to foot (cephalo-caudal) fashion. As infants grow, a similar sequence of gross and fine motor skills development occurs, along with cognitive and perceptual milestones.

Although Gesell believed that genes are the main regulatory mechanism for development, he also believed that individuals are products of their environment. As individuals age, the rates of developmental change increasingly vary as the influence of the environment, including physical, cultural, and social factors, shapes development. Children require positive influences of the social and cultural environments to realize their full potential within society. Gesell and Ilg (18) believed that developmental potential is maximized when socializing forces have a goodness of fit with the unfolding maturation of the individual.

Most researchers currently lean toward an interactionist perspective, having agreed that both genetics and the environment play important roles in development. The unanswered question seems to be *What role does each factor play in the individual's development?* It is currently believed that the influences of the person and the environment act together, making it extremely difficult to determine the unique influences of each on human development. Researchers have attempted to determine how much each factor contributes and have found this question extremely difficult to answer. Consequently, some investigators have shifted their study from *How much?* to *how* genes, the environment, and their interaction influence development (19–23).

INTERACTIONISM: A FRAMEWORK FOR OCCUPATIONAL DEVELOPMENT

> In 1784, K. L. Reinhold wrote (as cited in J. Schmidt (Ed.), 1996), *"The disposition to everything that man can become in the world is the direct work of nature. What man has actually become is the result of all the situations from his cradle onward, through which he had to pass." (24)*

Researchers in occupation believe, as Reinhold did, that occupational performance (5, 25) and occupational competence (7, 8) result from the dynamic interaction between the individual and the environment. Further, the interaction is viewed as bidirectional, meaning that not only does the person respond to change in the environment, but also people adapt the environment to suit their needs. This perspective is similar to the interactionist perspective on development. Thus, it follows that the changes observed in type, meaning, and form of occupations across the life span are expressed as a function of the growth, maturation and experiences of the person in ". . . progressive, mutual accommodation, throughout the life span, between a growing human organism and the changing immediate environments in which it lives . . . " (26, p. 514). These expressions are known within the field of biology as *phenotypes,* which are the observable qualities of a person, or the way he or she appears, feels, or thinks. Kurt Lewin believed that past experiences played an important part in one's development across the life span. By adapting a widely known formula derived from Lewin's field theory (27), which is expressed as $B = f(PE)$, meaning behavior (B) is a function of the person (P) and his or her environment (E), we can characterize occupational development from an interactionist perspective as $OD = f(PoE)$, where o signifies an active process that directs time and attention toward an occupation. It should be noted that occupation is not simply the result of an interaction between a person and environment. Rather occupations result from an intentional and particular behavior by a particular person with particular aspects of the environment.

Principles of Occupational Development

The interactionist perspective on development supports the idea that occupational performance is the result of an interaction between person, environment, and occupation (5, 25). Occupational development is defined as "the gradual change in occupational behaviors over time, resulting from the growth and maturation of the individual in interaction with the environment" (5, p. 40). The interactionist perspective on development provides a way of framing occupational development and identifying the principles that govern the interaction.[1] These principles are continuity, multiple determinicity, and multiple patternicity, and they provide a model of

TABLE 5-1   *Principles of Human Development*

Child/Adolescent Development	Adult Development and Aging	Occupational Development
Active Child	Continuity	**Continuity**
Behavioral reorganization	History and context	**Multiple Determinicity**
Continuity/discontinuity	Mastery	*Person Determinants*
Expanding environments	Multidirectionality	Heredity
Interaction of heredity and environment	Multiple causality	Learning/plasticity
Learning/plasticity	Plasticity	Active participation
Motivation	Trajectories and transitions	*Environment Determinants*
		Physical and social
		Historical and cultural
		Interaction Determinant
		Multiple Patternicity
		Multiple variation
		Changing mastery

occupational development, as shown in Table 5-1. In the sections that follow, each of the three principles is explained.

Continuity

Development is a lifelong process, starting at conception and continuing until death, with no specific age or stage seen as dominant. From personal experience it is clear that the occupations in which individuals engage occur across the life span, yet they vary throughout life. Many of these changes occur in concert with lifelong changes in growth and development. Individual life pathways are comprised of periods of both growth and decline, or occupational transitions, across the life course. Thus, occupational development is a lifelong process involving the "... expansion, culmination and contraction in activities and accomplishments ... " across the life span (28, p. 11). Occupations emerge at various points of the life span with different occupations developing at different rates and involving different skills. **Continuity theory** (29), a theory of continuous adult development, follows this notion of continuous occupational development. This theory allows for adults, as they age, to adapt to changes in their life situations. Atchley (29) found that many older adults maintain consistent activity engagement, or occupational engagement, far into older adulthood: "The key is to conceptualize continuity as the persistence of general patterns rather than as sameness in the details contained within those patterns" (p. 2). Changes in physical, psychosocial, and cognitive readiness and interest lead to occupational changes. Thus, changes in occupations across the life span mirror developmental changes (Figure 5-1). For example, the infant spends much of its waking time grasping at objects, the toddler cruising the furniture, the 4-year-old playing and running, the 10-year-old playing Nintendo ©, the adolescent listening to music, the adult working, and the retiree golfing.

FIGURE 5-1   New occupations can occur at any age.

Multiple Determinicity

The interactionist perspective holds that no single factor (e.g., heredity or environment) determines development. Proponents of this perspective argue that all of these factors are relevant to occupational development and that occupational development is governed by multiple determinants. This is referred to here as the principle of **multiple determinicity.**

The multiple factors that are the determinants of occupational development have some relationship to those of human development (see Table 5-1); however, they also relate to occupational performance and competence. The multiple determinants of occupational development are organized under the headings of person, environment and interaction.

Person Determinants   The three person determinants of occupational development are heredity, learning/plasticity, and active participation.

1. **Heredity:** It was once generally held that individuals were born to their occupations; hence, a son was expected to "follow in his father's footsteps." Historically, in some cultures, last names indicated the work of the family (e.g., Smith for a metalworker, and Cooper for a barrel maker), as though type of work was a result of

genetic predisposition. It is still argued that Mozarts are born, not made. This would suggest widespread belief in the concept that occupational development is governed by the genetic makeup of the individual.

The belief in a heredity predisposition for occupations is now creeping into the career counseling field as witnessed by the popularity of such books as *Do What You Are* (30). In addition, new evidence in support of this perspective is emerging from recent findings drawn from studies of identical twins. Wright (31) discusses the well-publicized findings of twins James Springer and James Lewis, who were reared apart and reunited in 1979 at age 39. The twins were found to have many similarities in personality and in occupations: "both Lewis and Springer enjoyed carpentry and mechanical drawing. . . . Both had worked part time in law enforcement" (31, p. 44). However, this is clearly not true for all twins. There are numerous examples of identical twins, even those reared together, who do not engage in the same occupations, in the same way (32). As Plomin et al. (19) point out, it is now recognized that genes do not "program the unfolding of development" (p. 15), but rather that development is governed by the interaction of genes and environment. Thus, genes influence development but do not control it. Scarr and McCartney (33) suggest that heredity influences the individual's development in two ways, through its expression as phenotypes, and through its direct impact on the choices of environment an individual makes.

2. **Learning/plasticity:** The genetic makeup with which an infant is born endows that infant with abilities, interests, and temperament that influence development and interactions with environments. It "defines what can be learned, when it can be learned, how likely behaviors are to occur, and what is reinforcing" (23, p. 1335). Learning governs the interaction between the person and the environment and regulates the course of development (27). It ". . . is the process by which behavior or the potential for behavior is modified as a result of experience" (27, p. 31). Learning occurs in all aspects of life, involving occupations with social, spiritual, religious, play, work, leisure, and survival purposes. Cultural systems and societal structures are created for the transfer of information to infants and children (34) to allow for development of behaviors that "fit" with societal expectations.

The ability to learn is a function of neural *plasticity,* a neuroscientific term referring to the "ability of the central nervous system to adapt structurally or functionally in response to environmental demands" (35). The degree of change that the central nervous system can undergo is age dependent; that is, the degree of change decreases with increasing age. Learning is thought to occur more readily in early life when plasticity is greatest, and especially the first year of life when the human brain undergoes a fast rate of growth. The human brain triples in size from the time of birth to maturity (36). This growth in brain size is paralleled by an increase in occupational competence.

Humans are totally dependent at birth, incapable of survival without the care of adults. This level of dependence is greater than that of other species and it lasts for a longer period. Yet, at maturity, humans are the most technologically and cognitively advanced species, having acquired a vast myriad of skills. This dramatic change in occupational competence is the result of the interaction between growth, maturation, and learning. Over the life span, as human abilities develop, humans learn to feed themselves, protect themselves from the elements, navigate their environments, explore their world, express their individuality, and be creative. Plasticity allows for this change in the phenotype of the individual, the overt expression of behavior resulting from the interaction of genotype and environment (37). Thus, learning/plasticity is an important determinant of the development of occupational competence.

3. **Active participation:** It is now generally believed that children are active participants in their own development, shaping, controlling, and directing their life course from birth. It is known that children are born, not as a *tabula rasa* as Locke hypothesized, but with many abilities and a distinct temperament (38). The active child, with her innate and unique predispositions, affects the environments in which she interacts, thus acting as an agent in her own development, by selecting the pathways she wishes to follow (12).

Because occupation involves active doing, it follows that occupational development, at all ages, must demand the **active participation** of the individual. In the absence of opportunity for active participation or human agency (e.g., in deprived environments), occupational development is stunted or becomes abnormal. This is tragically evident in the story of Genie (39) who was ". . . locked away in almost total isolation for her entire childhood. . . . At night she was placed in a kind of straitjacket and caged in a crib with wire mesh sides and a cover" (13, p. 160). Not only was Genie's confinement a form of environmental deprivation, but occupational deprivation (see Chapter 10) as well, because "she could only move her hands and feet and had virtually nothing to do every day of her life" (13, p. 178). When she was found at 13 years of age, Genie had none of the typical occupations of her age group. In fact, she did not even have the typical skills of a toddler; she could not stand erect or walk and was not toilet trained. Across the life span, individuals act on their environment and are active in other's environments (21). Active participation remains essential throughout life, as in the later stages of life where it has been shown that engagement in occupation can help maintain capacities and slow down physical and cognitive decline (40).

An individual's motivation toward initiating a behavior, which refers to an individual's "needs, goals and desires that provoke them to action" (27, p. 35), also affects development, by influencing further acquisition of additional behaviors. Without a motive or motivation to develop, stagnation could occur in certain areas of development within an individual, possibly affecting health and well-being. Active participation in an occupation is influenced by the individual's motivation toward engaging in the occupation. The stronger the motivation an individual has for an occupation, the more likely it is that the person will engage in the occupation and acquire the necessary competencies for the occupation to develop. For example, the only thing that young Wayne Gretzky ever wanted to do was skate and play hockey. He started skating at age 2 and by age 5 ". . . he lived on the backyard rink, carrying the puck in and out of pylons made from Javex © bleach containers, or any other plastic jug we could find, working on his skating and puck control. Sometimes you had to argue to get him to come in at night" (41, p. 56).

Environment Determinants   The role of the environment in development has been discussed in the child/adolescent literature under the principles of "expanding environment" and "interaction of heredity and environment," and in the adult development and aging literature under "multiple causality" and "history and context." Embedded in these principles are discussions of the physical, social, cultural, and temporal environments.

    1. **Physical and social:** Humans exist in a physical and social context. Learning from experience gained through interaction with the physical and social environments occurs across the life span, but note that different aspects of learning can occur at different periods of the life span, at different rates, and to varying degrees.

    From birth on, the size of the individual's world is ever increasing. When infants are born, their environment includes what they can see, hear, taste, smell, and touch. Yet, these abilities are limited in infants due to their immaturity at birth. Their interactions with their environments are restricted to the immediate situations, although many environments affect their care. As infants become mobile, they begin to explore their space more broadly. As individuals grow and mature, they are able to interact to a greater extent with more environments that influence their development. In early childhood, as independence increases, children begin to move into their neighborhoods and communities close to home. Once they enter school, they spend increasingly more time away from their home environments at progressively greater distances. For the independent adult, no geographical limitations are placed on the environment in which they operate. They can even fly to the moon.

    Since the discovery of Victor, the "wild boy" of Aveyron, in the 1790s (42), researchers have recognized that the environmental context can significantly alter development. This young boy had spent much of his childhood living in the wild, isolated from society. Victor, at the age of 12, had none of the occupational skills typical of his age group, which is similar to the state of Genie. However, unlike Genie, Victor had not been occupationally deprived and had developed a number of skills that allowed him to survive alone in the wild. He could find food, climb trees, and run at a great speed, although he did so on all fours. These occupations, not typical of childhood at the time, were developed in response to environmental demands. Similar effects of the environment were seen in a study by Elder (43) who examined children of the Great Depression. Elder found that environments deprived as a result of economic limitations had greater implications for middle-class children and their parents than those from the working class. However, there were also many common elements in the changes of individuals' occupations across socioeconomic status. Boys developed a greater role in paid employment and girls had an increased role in household duties and child care, while the mothers left the home to work. Thus, it is clear that the specific occupations people develop are at least, in part, environmentally determined.

    The importance of the environment for occupational development has been repeatedly corroborated by reports from orphanage studies where young children have undergone environmental deprivation. The more recent experiences with children from Romanian orphanages have shown that the detrimental effects of environmental deprivation are reversible to some extent. However, this is dependent on the length of deprivation and the age at which it occurred (44), as well as the child's exposure to toys and attention from care givers (45). This evidence would suggest that the environment interacts with the maturational stage of the child in determining occupational development.

2. **Historical and cultural:** The physical and social environments in which humans live are constructed by their historical and cultural contexts. Although pioneers such as Margaret Mead and Lev Vygotsky (Box 5-1) have made us aware of the importance of society and culture on development (46–48), the extent to which history influences sociocultural development, and hence human development, has been given less consideration. Only recently has the importance of history, or the temporal context, been discussed as having a substantial effect on development (12). Research is now showing how the historical period in which an individual lived, for example, the Industrial Revolution, World War I, the Great Depression, or during the invention of the personal computer, has influenced occupational development (49, 50).

Originally, Bronfenbrenner (26) identified four aspects of the human environment that influence development: *microsystem, mesosystem, exosystem,* and *macrosystem.* More recently, he added a fifth structure to his General Ecological Model, the *chronosystem,* which "encompasses change or consistency over time not only in the characteristics of the person but also of the environment in which that person lives", (51, p. 1646). This system recognizes the importance of examining the influences of environmental changes due to historical developments and their contribution to cultural shifts. Historical and cultural influences on human development are typically widespread and difficult to reverse.

Historical trends and circumstances shape culture and influence the individual's development of values, beliefs, preferences, lifestyles, and skills. "Cultures define what is desirable to be learned, what is to be believed, and how to behave" (23, p. 1335); in other words, cultures shape human occupation (Figure 5-3).

Interaction Determinant   The interactionist perspective brings into focus the notion that the interaction between person and environment is, in itself, a determinant of development. The person and environment ". . . interpenetrate one another in such a complex manner that any attempt to unravel them tends to destroy the natural unity of the whole and to create an artificial distinction between organism and environment" (52, p. 316). The interaction determinant is considered to be so important in the developmental process that it serves as the name for the perspective, as a whole.

The question regarding development is no longer whether the person's genetic makeup or the environment determines its unfolding, rather it is how the interaction occurs and to what extent it plays a role in development. Evidence is being accumulated to suggest that this interaction is not simply additive (19), but operates in complex ways. Scarr and McCartney (33) hypothesized that people make their own environments based on their genetic makeup. Along with this idea, Scarr and Ricciuti (53) proposed the notion of "a good enough environment" (p. 19), which they feel is the "typical" environment available to most children in most cultures. It is proposed that the typical environments in which most children are raised contain many variables that provide the basics for "normal" human development and, therefore, normal development takes place. According to Scarr and Ricciuti, the "good enough environment" provides individuals with environments from which they can choose experiences that "match" their genetic makeup. However, similar to the belief of Gesell (17, 18) outlined previously, Scarr and Ricciuti (53) note that this theory requires that this environment be varied and allow for opportunities that match

Box 5-1   Lev Semenovich Vygotsky

An Interactionist's View of Cognitive Development

Lev Semenovich Vygotsky (1896–1934; Figure 5–2) was a Russian educator who became a psychologist. He was raised in a provincial town in Belorussia and from 1913 to 1917 studied philosophy, history, and law in Moscow. He returned to his birthplace (Gomel') from 1917 to 1924 to teach literature and psychology at several schools and colleges. During this time he also wrote extensively about language, poetry, learning, and drama. Most of Vygotsky's work about language development in children was not translated and published in the Western world until the 1960s, decades

FIGURE 5-2   Lev Semenovich Vygotsky. *Source:* Felicia Martinez/ PhotoEdit George

after his death. Vygotsky gave a paper in 1924 that so impressed those attending that he was invited to join the Moscow Psychological Institute, where he continued his research and writing until his death.

Vygotsky's most well-known work, *Mind in Society* (48), provided two important concepts that continue to influence our understanding of child development. Vygotsky theorized that cognitive development occurs in humans based on the use of language, which provides an internal dialogue from which the mind can interpret the surrounding world. With this view, it seemed clear to him that culture, experience, and a child's interactions with things (objects, events, and particularly people) in the immediate surroundings were instrumental to the child's understanding of the world. Indeed, social processes were at the heart of Vygotsky's understanding of mental development.

Two of his related concepts, in particular, have continued to influence those interested in human development and learning from a practical standpoint. The first is known as the *zone of proximal development.* Vygotsky (48) maintained that the learner follows the teacher's (parent, grandparent, sibling) example and gradually develops the ability to do certain tasks without help or assistance. He called the difference (or space) between what a child or learner can do with help and what he or she can do without guidance the *zone of proximal development.*

This notion led to a second concept that inspired a teaching and training approach now called *scaffolding.* Scaffolding is based on the belief that humans can acquire skills through a step-by-step process that improves their competence by providing means by which an individual can complete a task with gradually decreasing amounts of support as the individual moves toward a goal of independent performance. Vygotsky's developmental concepts seem highly appropriate for understanding occupational development because they emphasize person-environment interactions and opportunities for mastery that take place in everyday situations.

FIGURE 5-3   Occupations shaped by history and culture.
Source: © by Jane A. Davis, 2002.

the individual's genotype; infants and people who are limited in making their own choices about occupations cannot be expected to develop normally.

Scarr and McCartney (33) suggest that if the genotype and environment do not match, the effects of either can be greatly diminished. For example, if a child has innate talent for drawing, it is unlikely to be realized unless the child is exposed to a rich and supportive artistic environment. Hence, as an adult, the engagement in a drawing-related occupation, either for work or leisure, may never be realized. This would suggest the need for a goodness of fit between the individual's genotype and the environment and also demonstrates the importance of individuals engaging in diverse occupations. This seems especially important for children, whose occupational exposure may be under control of the adults in their lives. An example of the impact of occupational exposure on occupational development can be seen in the story of Maryanne, whose parents have a developmental delay (54). Maryanne was not exposed to music or singing until her aunt came to care for her when she was in her mid-teens. She found that she not only had a love of music but that her abilities had a goodness of fit with the musical occupation of singing. She currently sings in a choir and aspires to study music therapy.

This is similar to the concept of a "just right challenge," which proposes that the environment and activity must present the appropriate challenge to be engaging

BOX 5-2   A Word About Gender and Occupational Development

Gender has become a predominant topic in the discussion of health, work, and occupational choice. The impact of one's gender on the occupational development of that individual can be seen throughout cultures. Levinson (57) discusses the concept of gender splitting, "the creation of a rigid division between male and female, masculine and feminine, in human life" (p. 38). He believes that gender splitting occurs in virtually every culture, although the patterning may be different. Levinson states that for years, women's lives have centered around the "domestic sphere." "It has been the key source of their identity, meaningful activity, and satisfaction, as well as dissatisfaction" (p. 39). He feels that there has been a gender revolution occurring that is reducing this gender split. Women are being "impelled, by powerful social forces as well as inner motivations, into the public occupational world. And men are, much more slowly, becoming involved in family life and accepting the entry of women into all sectors of the occupational system" (p. 45).

Although changes have occurred over time with respect to the available occupational pathways through which both men and women can develop, an occupational division does still exist between their self-care, productivity, and leisure occupations. Sports and many business and management occupations are still male dominated, whereas caretaking professions and homemaking activities remain the main occupations of women. The interaction of the individual's gender with the demands of society is seen to impact the occupational development of each individual. As the demands of society are being altered, changes in occupational development are being seen.

(55), to allow "flow," or a feeling of enjoyment (56). Extending this concept into the realm of development, it would seem likely that there needs to be a "just right environment" that matches the individual's genotype, to allow for, and to support each individual's optimal occupational development and occupational competence.

The active child shapes her environment, which enables the interaction of the child's genetic makeup with her environment, hence affecting development throughout life. The ongoing effects of experiences are determined, in part, by the individual's characteristics and her other social, cultural, physical, and institutional environments in which she lives (Box 5-2). Controversy does remain as to whether early or late life experiences have a greater impact on development, because it is believed that the genetic unfolding of different characteristics occurs at different times throughout the life span.

Multiple Patternicity

It is presumed that the patterns of occupational development mirror those of general human development. Two patterns of **multiple patternicity** are suggested: one,

FIGURE 5-4 Multiple variation: occupational similarities at different ages and for different reasons.

multiple variation, characterizing the nature and direction of the patterns of occupational development, and the other, changing **mastery,** characterizing the patterns of proficiency across the life span.

1. **Multiple variation:** The principle of multiple variation is that growth and development is neither smooth nor unidirectional, involving both decline and growth. Different aspects of development show different patterns at different times (Figure 5-4). This is the principle of continuity/discontinuity in the child/adolescent literature. The principles of multidirectionality and trajectories and transitions, in the adult development and aging literature, describe the pattern of gains and losses across the life span. These principles are combined here under the title of multiple variation to denote not only the patterns of growth, development, and decline seen in occupations across the life span, but also the variation in rate, characteristics, quality, quantity, complexity, and specialization involved in the patterns of change.

A life course or pathway is seen as following a trajectory, which is modified by various transitions through life. Trajectories are continuations of development, whereas transitions are periods of change or disruption in the trajectory. Potential occupational transitions or milestones, such as baby's first step, starting kindergarten, the first camping trip away from home, graduating from school, getting the first job, or retiring from a lifelong career, are extremely dependent on individual characteristics. Hence, each individual shows multiple variation in occupational development.

The patterns of occupational development parallel the development of the components that support occupational performance and competence (e.g., elements of cognitive, affective, and physical function). For example, the development of competence in reading is influenced by the child's cognitive and language skill development. Gymnastic prowess is enabled by physical growth and motor development; and accomplishment in team sports requires social development as well as physical and motor skills.

Muir (58) describes four patterns that characterize the development of various attributes, abilities, and skills. These are *continuous,* gradually increasing with age (e.g., height, weight); *step,* increasing in a stop and start manner (e.g., mobility, cognition); *inverted-U shape,* first increasing, then reaching a plateau, and then decreasing (e.g., visual acuity, coordination); and *U shaped,* first decreasing, then being absent, and then increasing, (e.g., the step reflex, auditory localization function). Therefore, occupational development can be continuous, step, inverted-U, and U shaped. It is believed to occur in both continuous and discontinuous patterns.

2. **Changing mastery:** The principle of mastery is taken from the adult development and aging literature where it refers to the observation that levels of proficiency change over the course of development as a result of maturation and experience with a skill.

People are thought to have a natural drive for mastery, which "... requires an individual to integrate his behavior and develop skill in performing certain tasks" (59, p. 92). The concept of mastery is addressed in the child/adolescent literature under the principles of behavioral reorganization and learning/plasticity, that is, the increase in specialization, complexity and integration of behavior, and skill acquisition, respectively. The term *mastery* is preferred here, because it is more congruent with the concept of interactionism, which is central to occupational development. The authors propose that mastery is not static, that it changes across the life span; hence, the phrase *changing mastery.* Changing, rather than increasing, is used to allow for the principle of multiple variation discussed earlier, that is, that change in occupational development is not unidirectional.

The development of mastery begins in infancy, when behaviors are very global in their intent. Crying, for example, is used by infants as a general form of communicating discomfort, hunger, tiredness, or boredom. Behaviors that have an unspecified or global intent, during infancy, such as crying and reaching or grasping, become more specialized and distinct in nature as the child gains control of primitive reflexes and develops voluntary movement patterns. The skills that are typically first developed in infancy appear to be "virtually released" through interaction with the environment and are quickly and easily mastered (60). In comparison, mastery

BOX 5-3   Robert J. Havighurst **Changing Mastery**

After obtaining a Ph.D. in the area of physical chemistry, Havighurst shifted his career focus to the fields of aging and experimental education. In his work, Havighurst defined the principal developmental tasks of six age periods from infancy to later maturity. He felt that schooling was created to enable children to successfully achieve certain developmental tasks constructed by society, so that the children could progress to the next stage of development. Havighurst believed that "nature" provided individuals with the possibilities for the acquisition of occupations, which he called developmental tasks, including walking, talking, reading, and kicking a ball (61). However, possibilities are only realized when learning related to the "occupation" of interest occurs. Havighurst felt that this learning was influenced by the needs of the individual in interaction with the demands of society.

> As the individual grows, he finds himself possessed of new physical and psychological resources. The infant's legs grow larger and stronger, enabling him to walk. The child's nervous system grows more complex, enabling him to reason more subtly and to understand the complexities of subjects such as arithmetic. The individual also finds himself facing new demands and expectations from the society around him. The infant is expected to learn to talk, the child to learn to subtract and divide. (61, p. 5)

Hence, Havighurst felt there were three sources of developmental tasks: (a) physical maturation, (b) sociocultural pressure, and (c) personal values and aspirations (which Havighurst believed emerged from the interaction of organic and environmental forces). In interaction, these three sources affect, to varying degrees, the development of different occupations across the life span, such as walking and reading; the three sources also influence occupational choice, that is, what type of paid work or what leisure occupations one chooses to perform.

of learned skills is dependent on the development of these "prewired" skills and proceeds at a much slower rate. Increasingly, skills are performed to meet specific goals, showing greater usefulness in their intent. For example, as children develop language and other forms of communication skills, their crying becomes more specialized in its form, intention, and usefulness.

Along with the notion of specialization, behaviors also become more complex during development. The discrete features of children's behaviors increase in quantity, and become more refined and skilled, demonstrating a higher quality behavior (Box 5-3). The increased quality is due, in part, to the increased integration of the cognitive, emotional, and physical components of behavior. As children develop, these components show greater interplay. This can be seen in children's increasing sophistication in toy use; for example, banging blocks on a table top in comparison to constructing a fort out of blocks.

Each phase of development across the life span sees the emergence and disappearance of mastery of a variety of occupational skills. The term *mastery* appears in the adult development and aging literature primarily in reference to the level of competency achieved in a career. However, mastery can refer to a high level of skill or proficiency in any everyday occupation. When an individual masters a skill, control and power are achieved over a task or situation. ". . . The instinct to master one's environment . . . has a biological foundation, which is a function of man's attempt to control or change some portion of his environment through the combined use of his intellectual and neurological processes" (59, p. 92).

At birth, babies are totally dependent on caregivers for basic necessities. Through interactions with their developing child, caregivers provide opportunities for learning and adaptation. In infancy, primitive reflexes are reorganized into simple voluntary movement patterns. Preschool children are focused on mastering the foundational skills required for occupational competency in their elementary school years. Throughout adolescence and adulthood, the number of occupations over which mastery is achieved increases as does the quality and complexity of the occupations. In late adulthood, there is no longer a general trend to the mastery of new occupations. Great individual difference is seen, with many individuals taking up new occupations, or hobbies, after retirement, while others reduce the number of occupations in which they engage (14) and still others maintain their old interests and skills, using them for engagement in different forms of similar past occupations (29, 62, 63) (Figure 5-5).

The Ages and Stages of Occupational Development

The ages and stages of human development have been catalogued in various sources and in various ways. Among the best known and most detailed accounts of ages and stages of development is that provided by Gesell (64). Through careful observation and detailed study, Gesell and his colleagues developed detailed behavioral norms of infant and early childhood development that are still applicable today. Many of these descriptions focus on what children do, that is, children's occupations, at various ages and stages (e.g., at 5 years old children skip using feet alternately, copy triangles, dress and undress independently, and play dress-up). Thus, the temptation would be simply to adopt these as descriptions of the ages and stages of occupational development. However, this temptation must be avoided.

Descriptions of human development emanated from a focus on neuromotor development. While they can be seen as indicators of the neuromaturational preparedness of children for various occupational activities at various ages and stages (e.g., skipping at 5 years), the reader should keep in mind that occupational engagement is not solely the result of neuromaturation. Rather, occupational engagement results from the interaction of person, environment, and occupation. It is very possible that in certain cultures, or environments, 5-year-old children, although maturationally prepared to skip, do not skip. As a person ages, maturation is less significant and social and cultural environmental factors are more significant in influencing occupational engagement. Indeed, as Elder (50) has shown,

FIGURE 5-5   Grandmother and granddaughter reading: an example of an intergenerational occupation.

socioeconomic circumstances can influence the occupational development of entire generations throughout their life course.

To date, no one has attempted to replicate Gesell's work with respect to occupational development. Clearly this must occur before the ages and stages of occupational development can be discerned with confidence. Indeed, it may be that because of the interactional nature of occupational development, there are no clear ages and stages, or that there are significant occupational transitions rather than ages and stages. This will undoubtedly be a very important and fruitful area of research for occupational scientists in the future. Nevertheless, there are sources, such as Gesell, that can give us hints at what occupational development could look like, at least in childhood. Using a variety of descriptive sources, a potential profile of early occupational development has been compiled (see Table 5-2). This is a first attempt at outlining the potential ages and stages of the occupational development of children. The reader is cautioned that this profile is in need of empirical validation. It has been limited to early occupational development, because, in the view of the authors, it is only in the early years that a profile involving ages and stages is possible. As individuals age and become more influenced by their environments, a profile that has broad applicability becomes difficult to construct. The profile in Table 5-2 is offered as a point of departure for those interested in examining occupational development across the life span.

TABLE 5-2   *Ages and Stages of Occupational Development*

Age (YRS.)	Stage	Characteristic Occupations	
		Self-Care	**Productivity/Leisure**
0–1	Infancy	■ Opens mouth when spoon with food is present ■ Removes food from spoon with mouth ■ Sucks and chews on crackers ■ Eats solid food ■ Crawls across floor on hands and knees, without stomach touching floor ■ Opens doors that require only pushing and pulling	■ Shows interest in novel objects or new people ■ Reaches for familiar person ■ Picks up small objects with hands, in any way ■ Transfers object from one hand to the other ■ Picks up small objects with thumb and fingers ■ Plays with toys or other objects alone or with others ■ Plays with very simple interaction games with others ■ Uses common household objects for play ■ Shows interest in activities of others ■ Imitates simple adult movements, such as clapping hands or waving good-bye, in response to a model
1–2		■ Drinks from cup of glass unassisted ■ Feeds self with spoon ■ Indicates wet or soiled pants or diaper by pointing, vocalizing, or pulling at diaper ■ Sucks from a straw ■ Feeds self with fork ■ Removes front-opening coat, sweater, or shirt without assistance ■ Walks as primary means of getting around ■ Climbs both in and out of bed or steady adult chair	■ Participates in at least one game or activity with others ■ Rolls ball while sitting ■ Climbs on low play equipment ■ Marks with pencil, crayon, or chalk on appropriate writing surface
2–3	Toddler	■ Feeds self with spoon without spilling ■ Urinates in toilet or potty chair ■ Bathes self with assistance ■ Defecates in toilet or potty chair	■ Imitates a relatively complex task several hours after it was performed by another ■ Engages in elaborate make-believe activities, alone or with others

(continued)

TABLE 5-2   *Continued*

Age (YRS.)	Stage	Characteristic Occupations	
		Self-Care	**Productivity/Leisure**
		■ Asks to use toilet ■ Puts on "pull-up" garments with elastic waistbands ■ Puts possessions away when asked ■ Walks up stairs, putting both feet on each step ■ Walks downstairs, forward, putting both feet on each step ■ Runs smoothly, with changes in speed and direction ■ Opens door by turning and pulling doorknobs	■ Jumps over small objects ■ Screws and unscrews lid of jar ■ Pedals tricycle or other three-wheeled vehicle for at least 6 feet ■ Builds three-dimensional structures, with at least five blocks ■ Opens and closes scissors with one hand
3–4	Early childhood	■ Brushes teeth without assistance ■ Helps with extra chores when asked ■ Washes and dries face without assistance ■ Puts shoes on correct feet without assistance ■ Answers the telephone appropriately ■ Dresses self completely, except for tying shoes ■ Walks down stairs with alternating feet, without assistance	■ Climbs on high play equipment ■ Cuts across a piece of paper with scissors
4–5		■ Summons to the telephone the person receiving a call, or indicates that the person is not available ■ Sets the table with assistance ■ Cares for all toileting needs, without being reminded and without assistance ■ Puts clean clothes away without assistance when asked ■ Cares for nose without assistance ■ Dries self with towel without assistance ■ Fastens all fasteners	■ Completes non-inset puzzle of at least six pieces ■ Draws more than one recognizable form with pencils or crayons ■ Cuts paper along a line with scissors ■ Uses eraser without tearing paper ■ Unlocks key locks ■ Shares toys or possessions without being told to do so ■ Follows rules in simple games without being reminded ■ Follows school or facility rules

5–6	▪ Assists in food preparation requiring mixing and cooking ▪ Ties shoelaces into a bow without assistance ▪ Bathes or showers without assistance	▪ Cuts out complex items with scissors ▪ Catches small ball when thrown from a distance of 10 feet, even if moving is necessary to catch it ▪ Rides bicycle without training wheels, without falling ▪ Follows community rules
6–8	Late childhood	
	▪ Uses fork, spoon, and knife competently ▪ Initiates telephone calls to others ▪ Dresses self completely, including tying shoelaces and fastening all fasteners ▪ Makes own bed when asked ▪ Fastens seat belt in automobile independently ▪ Uses basic tools ▪ Sets table without assistance when asked	▪ Plays more than one board or card game requiring skill and decision making ▪ Makes or buys small gifts for caregiver or family member on major holidays, on own initiative
8–10	▪ Sweeps, mops, or vacuums floor carefully, without assistance, when asked ▪ Orders own complete meal in restaurant ▪ Dresses in anticipation of changes in weather without being reminded. ▪ Tells time by 5-minute segments ▪ Cares for hair without being reminded and without assistance ▪ Uses stove and microwave oven for cooking ▪ Uses household cleaning products appropriately and correctly	▪ Returns borrowed toys, possessions, or money to peers, or returns borrowed books to library ▪ Uses appropriate table manners without being told ▪ Watches television or listens to radio for information about a particular area of interest
11–12	▪ Correctly counts change from a purchase costing more than a dollar ▪ Uses the telephone for all kinds of calls, without assistance ▪ Cares for own fingernails without being reminded and without assistance ▪ Prepares foods that require mixing and cooking, without assistance	▪ Goes to evening school or facility events with friends, when accompanied by an adult ▪ Initiates conversations on topics of particular interest to others

(continued)

TABLE 5-2 *Continued*

Age (YRS.)	Stage	Characteristic Occupations	
		Self-Care	**Productivity/Leisure**
12–15	Adolescence and adulthood	▪ Uses a pay phone ▪ Straightens own room without being asked	▪ Has a hobby ▪ Repays money borrowed from caregiver
16–18 +		▪ Makes own bed and changes bedding routinely ▪ Cleans room other than own regularly, without being asked ▪ Sews buttons, snaps, or hooks on clothes when asked ▪ Budgets for weekly expenses ▪ Manages own money without assistance ▪ Plans and prepares main meal of the day without assistance ▪ Takes complete care of own clothes without being reminded ▪ Budgets for monthly expenses ▪ Sews own hems or makes other alterations without being asked and without assistance ▪ Has checking account and uses it responsibly	▪ Participates in nonschool sports ▪ Watches television or listens to radio for practical, day-to-day information ▪ Holds full-time job responsibly ▪ Earns spending money on a regular basis ▪ Performs routine household repairs and maintenance tasks without being asked

Source: Adapted from Sparrow, S.S., Balla, D. A. & Cicchetti, D.V. (1984) (65).

The primary source for this profile has been the Vineland Adaptive Behavior Scales, which provide descriptors of personal and social behaviors of individuals, from birth to adulthood, in four domains: communication, daily living skills, socialization, and motor skills. The items in the table were selected from the scale on the basis of their relevancy to occupation and must be treated as preliminary, requiring empirical validation.

CHAPTER SUMMARY

The purpose of this chapter was to present the reader with a framework of human occupational development, relevant theories, a model of occupational development, and a discussion of the ages and stages of occupational development across the life span. The authors have presented a framework for occupational development across the life span, taking the perspective that occupation is ". . . everything people do to occupy themselves. . . " (5, p. 181). This perspective was discussed from the concept of the human as an "occupational being" interacting in the environment and requiring engagement in occupation as a mechanism for development across the life span.

The perspective on development outlined a brief history of the views taken in the study of human development, and development was discussed in relation to the term *change* to enable a clearer understanding of the concept. The interactionist perspective on development was proposed as the perspective of choice because it is consistent with the identified perspective on occupation. This concept was used as the basis for the construction of the framework of occupational development.

The interactionist framework of occupational development incorporated the relevant principles found in the child/adolescent development literature, that is, active child, interaction of heredity and environment, behavioral reorganization, continuity/discontinuity, expanding environments, learning/plasticity, and motivation. The interactionist framework drew also from adult development and aging literature, that is, continuity, trajectories and transitions, multidirectionality, plasticity, history and context, multiple causality, and mastery. From these ideas three principles of occupational development from an interactionist perspective were proposed: *continuity, multiple determinicity,* and *multiple patternicity,* creating a model of occupational development. These principles were described in relation to the framework of occupational development and the formula $OD = f(PoE)$. Finally, a discussion about the ages and stages of occupational development was initiated, and the beginning of a potential profile of the ages and stages of early occupational development was provided.

REFERENCES

1. Hetherington, E. M., & Parke, R. D. (1999). *Child psychology: A contemporary viewpoint* (5th ed.). (Rev. ed. by R. D. Parke & V. O. Locke). Toronto, ON: McGraw-Hill College.
2. Fidler, G. S., & Fidler, J. W. (1978). Doing and becoming: Purposeful action and self-actualization. *American Journal of Occupational Therapy, 32*(5), 305–310.
3. Polatajko, H. J. (1998). *A portrait of the occupational human.* Keynote Address at the 12th International Congress of the World Federation of Occupational Therapists, Montreal, Canada.

4. American Occupational Therapy Association (AOTA). (1994). Uniform terminology for occupational therapy - third edition. *American Journal of Occupational Therapy, 48*(11), 1047–1054.

5. Canadian Association of Occupational Therapist (CAOT). (1997). *Enabling occupation: An occupational therapy perspective.* Ottawa, ON: CAOT Publications ACE.

6. Wilcock, A. A. (1998). *An occupational perspective of health.* Thorofare, NJ: Slack Inc.

7. Polatajko, H. J. (1992). Muriel Driver Lecture: Naming and framing occupational therapy: A lecture dedicated to the life of Nancy B. *Canadian Journal of Occupational Therapy, 59*(4), 189–200.

8. Polatajko, H. J. (1994). Dreams, dilemmas, and decisions for occupational therapy practice in a new millennium: A Canadian perspective. *American Journal of Occupational Therapy, 48*(7), 590–594.

9. Morley, C., & Everett, L. D. (1944). *Bartlett's familiar quotations.* New York: Garden City Publishing Co., Inc.

10. Baltes, P. B. (1987). Theoretical propositions of life-span developmental psychology: On the dynamics between growth and decline. *Developmental Psychology, 23*(5), 611–626.

11. Bigner, J. J. (1983). *Human development: A life-span approach.* New York: Macmillan Publishing Co., Inc.

12. Elder, G. H. Jr. (1998). The life course as developmental theory. *Child Development, 69*(1), 1–12.

13. Santrock, J. W. (1999). *Life-span development.* (7th ed.). Toronto, ON: McGraw-Hill College.

14. Papalia, D. E., Camp, C. J., & Feldman, R. D. (1996). *Adult development and aging.* Montreal, PQ: The McGraw-Hill Companies, Inc.

15. Aries, P. (1962). *Centuries of childhood: A social history of family life.* Trans. Robert Baldick. New York: Alfred Knopf.

16. Ekehammar, B. (1974). Interactionism in personality from a historical perspective. *Psychological Bulletin, 81,* 1026–1048.

17. Gesell, A. (1954). The ontogenesis of infant behavior. In L. Carmichael (Ed.), *Manual of child psychology* (2nd ed.). New York: John Wiley. (Original work published 1946)

18. Gesell, A., & Ilg, F. L. (1943). *Infant and child in the culture of today: The guidance of development in home and nursery school.* New York: Harper & Bros.

19. Plomin, R. (1994). *Genetics and experience: The interplay between nature and nurture.* Thousand Oaks, CA: Sage Publications.

20. Plomin, R., DeFries, J. C., McClearn, G. E., & Rutter, M. (1997). *Behavioral genetics.* (3rd ed.). New York: W. H. Freeman.

21. Rutter, M., Dunn, J., Plomin, R., Simonoff, E., Pickles, A., Maughan, B., Ormel, J., Meyer, J., & Eaves, L. (1997). Integrating nature and nurture: Implications of person-environment correlations and interactions for developmental psychopathology. *Development and Psychopathology, 9,* 335–364.

22. Scarr, S. (1992). Developmental theories for the 1990s: Development and individual differences. *Child Development, 63,* 1–19.

23. Scarr, S. (1993). Biological and cultural diversity: The legacy of Darwin for development. *Child Development, 64,* 1333–1353.

24. Schmidt, J. (Ed.). (1996). *What is enlightenment? Eighteenth-century answers and twentieth-century questions* (pp. 65–77). Los Angeles, CA: University of California Press.

25. Christiansen, C. H., & Baum, C. M. (1997). The occupational therapy context: Philosophy-principles-practice. In C. H. Christiansen & C. M. Baum (Eds.), *Enabling function and well-being* (2nd ed, pp. 26–45). Thorofare, NJ: Slack.

26. Bronfenbrenner, U. (1977). Toward an experimental ecology of human development. *American Psychologist, 32,* 513–531.
27. Conger, J. J., & Galambos, N. L. (1997). *Adolescence and youth: Psychological development in a changing world* (5th ed.). Don Mills, ON: Addison-Wesley Educational Publishers.
28. Kimmel, D. C. (1990). *Adulthood and aging.* Toronto, ON: John Wiley.
29. Atchley, R. C. (1999). *Continuity and adaptation in aging: Creating positive experiences.* Baltimore, MD: The Johns Hopkins University Press.
30. Tieger, P. D., & Barron-Tieger, B. (1995). *Do what you are: Discover the perfect career for you through the secrets of personality type* (2nd ed.). Toronto, ON: Little-Brown.
31. Wright, L. (1997). *Twins and what they tell us about who we are.* Toronto, ON: John Wiley.
32. Segal, N. L. (1999). *Entwined lives: Twins and what they tell us about human behavior.* Toronto, ON: Penguin Books.
33. Scarr, S., & McCartney, K. (1983). How people make their own environments: A theory of genotype → environment effects. *Child Development, 54,* 424–435.
34. Newman, P. R., & Newman, B. M. (1997). *Childhood and adolescence.* Pacific Grove, CA: Brooks-Cole.
35. Jacobs, K. (1999). *Quick reference dictionary for occupational therapy* (2nd ed.). Thorofare, NJ: Slack.
36. Leakey, R., & Lewin, R. (1992). *Origins reconsidered: In search of what makes us human.* Toronto, ON: Doubleday.
37. Bogin, B. (1999). *Patterns of human growth* (2nd ed.). New York: Cambridge University Press.
38. Saudino, K. J., & Eaton, W. O. (1991). Infant temperament and genetics: An objective twin study of motor activity level. *Child Development, 62,* 1167–1174.
39. Curtiss, S. (1977). *Genie: A psycholinguistic study of a modern day "wild child".* New York: Academic Press.
40. Schaie, K. W. (1994). The course of adult intellectual development. *American Psychologist, 48*(1), 304–313.
41. Gretzky, W., & Taylor, J. (1984). *Gretzky: From the back yard rink to the Stanley cup.* Toronto, ON: McClelland & Stewart.
42. Itard, J. M. G. (1962). *Wild boy of Aveyron.* New York: Meredith Publishing Co.
43. Elder, G. H. Jr. (1992). The life course. In E. F. Borgatta & M. L. Borgatta (Eds.), *The encyclopedia of sociology.* New York: Macmillan.
44. Rutter, M. & the English and Romanian Adoptees (ERA) study team. (1998). Developmental catch-up, and deficit, following adoption after severe global early privation. *Journal of Child Psychology and Psychiatry, 39*(4), 465–476.
45. Morison, S. J., Ames, E. W., & Chisholm, K. (1995). The development of children adopted from Romanian orphanages. *Merrill-Palmer Quarterly, 41*(4), 411–430.
46. Harkness, S. (1992). Human development in psychological anthropology. In T. Schwartz, G. M. White, & C. A. Lutz (Eds.), *New directions in psychological anthropology* (pp. 102–122). Cambridge: Cambridge University Press.
47. Damon, W. (1989). Introduction: Advances in development research. In W. Damon (Ed.), *Child development today and tomorrow* (pp. 1–13). San Francisco, CA: Jossey-Bass.
48. Vygotsky, L. S. (1978). *Mind in society: The development of higher psychological process* (M. Cole, V. John-Steiner, S. Scribner, & E. Souberman, (Eds.)). Cambridge, MA: Harvard University Press.
49. Davis, J. A., Polatajko, H. J., & Ruud, C. A. (2002). Children's occupations in context: The influence of history. *Journal of Occupational Science, 9*(2), 54–64.

50. Elder, G. H. Jr. (1999). *Children of the great depression: Social change in life experience.* Chicago, IL: University of Chicago Press. (Original work published 1974)

51. Bronfenbrenner, U. (1994). Ecological Models of Human Development. In T. Husen, & T. N. Postlethwaite (Eds.), *The international encyclopedia of education* (2nd ed., pp. 1643–1647). New York: Elsevier Science.

52. Hall, C. S., & Lindzey, G. (1970). *Theories of personality* (2nd ed.). New York: Wiley.

53. Scarr, S., & Ricciuti, A. (1991). What effects do parents have on their children? In L. Okagaki, & R. J. Sternberg (Eds.), *Directors of development: Influences on the development of children's thinking* (pp. 3–23). Hillsdale, NJ: Lawrence Erlbaum.

54. Puchniak, T. (Director). (2000). Is love enough?. In A. Handel (Producer), *Witness.* Ottawa, ON: Canadian Broadcasting Corporation (CBC).

55. Yerxa, E. J., Clark, F., Frank, G., Jackson, J., Parham, D., Pierce, D., Stein, C., & Zemke, R. (1989). An introduction to occupational science: A foundation for occupational therapy in the 21st century. *Occupational Therapy in Health Care, 6*(4), 1–17.

56. Csikszentmihalyi, M. (1975). *Beyond boredom and anxiety.* San Francisco, CA: Jossey-Bass, Inc. Publishers.

57. Levinson, D. J. (1996). *The seasons of a woman's life.* New York: Knopf.

58. Muir, D. (1999). Theories and methods in developmental psychology, In A. Slater, & D. Muir (Eds.), *The Blackwell reader in developmental psychology* (pp. 3–16). Malden, MA: Blackwell Publishers.

59. Osipow, S. H. (1968). *Theories of career development.* New York: Meredith Publishing Co.

60. Bruner, J. S. (1973). Organization of early skilled action. *Child Development, 44,* 1–11.

61. Havighurst, R. J. (1972). *Developmental tasks and education* (3rd ed.). New York: David McKay.

62. Laliberte, D. (1993). *An exploration of the meaning seniors attach to activity.* Unpublished master's thesis. The University of Western Ontario, London, Ontario, Canada.

63. Laliberte-Rudman, D., Cook, J., & Polatajko, H. J. (1997). Understanding the potential of occupation: A qualitative exploration of seniors' perspectives on activity. *American Journal of Occupational Therapy, 51*(8), 640–650.

64. Gesell, A. (1928). *Infancy and Human Growth.* New York: Macmillan.

65. Sparrow, S. S., Balla, D. A., & Cicchetti, D. V. (1984). *Vineland Adaptive Behavior Scales - Interview Edition - Survey Form Manual.* Circle Pines, MN: American Guidance Service.

66. Cole, M., & Cole, S. R. (1996). *The development of children* (3rd ed.). New York: W. H. Freeman.

67. Sroufe, L. A., Cooper, R. G., & DeHart, G. B. (1992). *Child development: Its nature and course* (2nd ed.). Toronto, ON: McGraw-Hill, Inc.

68. Trawick-Smith, J. W. (1997). *Early childhood development: A multicultural perspective.* Toronto, ON: Prentice Hall.

69. Kaufman, S. R. (1986). *The ageless self: Sources of meaning in late life.* Madison, WI: The University of Wisconsin Press.

70. Rutter, M. (1989). Pathways from childhood to adult life. *Journal of Child Psychology and Psychiatry, 30*(1), 23–51.

71. Thomas, J. L. (1992). *Adulthood and aging.* Toronto, ON: Allyn and Bacon.

72. Wheaton, B., & Gotlib, I. H. (1997). Trajectories and turning points over the life course: Concepts and themes. In I. H. Gotlib & B. Wheaton, *Stress and adversity over the life course* (pp. 1–25). New York: Cambridge University Press.

Endnotes

[1] Studies into the nature and course of developmental change have identified a number of principles that govern development. In the literature, these have been identified separately for child and adolescent development, and adult development and older age, the major work having been done in the area of child/adolescent development.

Principles that govern development in child and adolescence that are commonly found in the literature are active child, interaction of heredity and environment, behavioral reorganization, continuity/discontinuity, expanding environments, learning/plasticity, and motivation (1, 27, 34, 66, 67, 68).

Principles governing development in adulthood and older age commonly found in the literature are continuity, trajectories and transitions, multidirectionality, plasticity, history and context, and multiple causality (10, 12, 14, 28, 29, 43, 59, 69–72).

Occupation and Identity: Becoming Who We Are Through What We Do

Charles Christiansen

KEY WORDS

Achievement motivation
Arousal
Attributions
D-needs
Drive theory
Five factor theory
Flow
Homeostasis

Purposive view of motivation
Regulatory motivators
Self-actualization
Self-determination theory
Symbolic interactionism
Traits
Volition

CHAPTER PROFILE

This chapter is about the relationships between daily occupations and a person's personal and social identity. The chapter begins by identifying the motivational factors that impel action toward some purpose. It then reviews various regulatory influences that motivate occupational behavior. Goals are identified as external influences that shape the creation of self.

The chapter continues with a discussion of the relationship between motivation and personality, identifying various theoretical frameworks and models that help to explain occupational choices for work and leisure. A concluding section provides an integration of activities that suggests ways in which people understand their lives and shape their imagined selves through occupational choices.

www.prenhall.com/christiansen

The Internet provides an exciting means for interacting with this textbook and for enhancing your understanding of humans' experiences with occupations and the organization of occupations in society. Use the address above to access the free, interactive companion web site created specifically to accompany this book. Here you will find an array of self-study material designed to help you gain a richer understanding of the concepts presented in this chapter.

INTRODUCTION

It is sometimes claimed that who we are is best understood by knowing what we do. This chapter is about how people form their identities through their daily occupations, beginning in childhood, and extending to the end of life. From birth through death, people engage in a continuous string of occupations that are influenced by internal drives as well as conscious decisions. As newborn babies, they sleep and eat in predictable routines. As people mature, they begin to exhibit more variety in their daily occupations.

Perhaps we would like to think that, as adults, all of our activities are consciously chosen, free of outside influences. Not all of our activities are freely chosen, however. Most people readily acknowledge that they are influenced by habits, and that habits are difficult to change. Thus, many daily activities are routine and predictable. People's lives exhibit regular rhythms and patterns, some of which are influenced by physiological factors and others that are influenced by aspects of the environment.

Yet, it is true that many daily occupations are determined by conscious choice, sometimes known as **volition.** But even these choices are at least partially influenced by genetics, by past experiences, by culture, by regulatory and legal obligations, and by dispositions and values that create tendencies for people to act in certain ways. With each occupational choice, individuals further define who they are, adding to their experiences and creating the meaning they need in order to derive satisfaction from their lives.

This chapter is about the relationship between occupation and identity. The ideas presented here are drawn mainly from social psychology with emphasis on the tradition of symbolic interactionism championed by George Herbert Mead. We understand the relationship between occupation and identity implicitly in the phrase "we are known by what we do." To illustrate why we are known by what we do, the chapter leads the reader through a process of thinking about how experiences shape identities. Four major concepts will be presented, as follows:

1. People are motivated to act by many factors, and their potential to act as humans arises in their motivations, drives, needs, and the external influences that shape those human experiences.
2. Factors that motivate humans include bodily fatigue, pain and arousal, individual goals for purposeful action, individual drive, individual needs, externally driven goals, external influences on goal setting, achievement, personality, vocational choice, needs for leisure, flow, and environmental factors that both afford and press motivation.
3. Participation in occupations influences identity as supported by theories of person–environment fit, such as Maslow's ideas about self-actualization and Deci's self-determination theory.
4. Identity is based in the development of self, the self is a product of motivated acts—experienced as daily occupations and understood as an unfolding life story.

WHAT MOTIVATES HUMAN OCCUPATION?

Given the many choices that they may have, why do people do one thing and not another? When people choose to engage in an occupation, their choice, the length of time they spend doing it, and the vigor or intensity with which they engage in the occupation can be influenced by various conditions. When conditions influence occupations in these ways, they are motivating. *Motivation can be viewed as an explanation for why people are interested in a certain activity and not interested in another. Motivation explains how people gain an identity that is associated with their participation in particular occupations.*

To begin to answer the question of why people choose one occupation over another, a review of current thinking about what motivates human action is necessary. Questions about motivation are at the heart of behavioral science. As scientists have tried to explain individual differences in behavior, it has been necessary to formulate theories of motivation. These theories have identified many types of motivational influences, or factors. Presented here is an occupational perspective of motivation. By looking at motivation in the context of occupations, rather than simply as behaviors, the importance of meaning as a vital aspect of human agency, or occupational engagement, is revealed.

MOTIVATIONAL FACTORS

Behavioral scientists are interested in understanding why people act as they do. Behavioral theories, then, are useful for understanding motivational factors that influence choice and engagement in occupation and how this in turn shapes individual identity.

Two major categories of motivators are particularly pertinent here. They can be illustrated by considering the following common experience. At midnight, Mary decides to pursue the leisure occupation of watching the late movie on television. Despite her interest in the show, she dozes off and falls asleep well before the movie is concluded. She does so because fatigue has overtaken her. In this circumstance, factors other than her intentions and interests have influenced what Mary has done.

In this brief example, two motivational factors are worthy of note. Mary consciously intended to watch a movie, and she intended to complete that goal. This was purposeful behavior. But her fatigue overcame her, and her body's internal mechanisms caused her to sleep. Thus, one type of influence or motivator was purposeful, or *purposive,* and the second was largely unconscious, or *regulatory.*

Regulatory Motivators

Regulatory motivators are often physiological in nature. These types of behavioral influences are based on the principles of **homeostasis.** The word *homeostasis,* coined by the physiologist Walter Cannon in the 1920s, is from the Greek words meaning "to stay the same." Thus, homeostasis pertains to how a body's systems try to maintain those conditions that permit it to thrive. These changes occur in response to conditions from both within and outside of the body (1).

Fatigue is one regulatory mechanism that has a remarkable influence on daily lives. Hunger and pain are also regulatory factors that influence participation in occupations. Fatigue occurs because the body needs energy and must rest regularly in

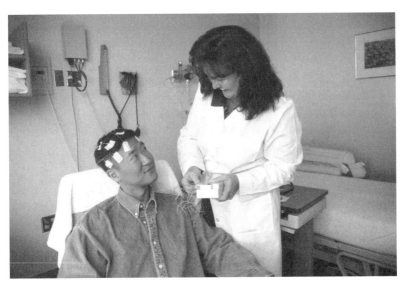

FIGURE 6-1   Electroenephalography measures changes in neuronal activity that can result from autonomic changes.
(Keith Brofsky/Getty Images)

order to restore it. This regulation occurs through a complex system of internal clocks involving the nervous and endocrine systems that provide for a regular cycle of rest and activity. The words *regular cycle* here are important, because they convey an important behavioral influence of regulatory mechanisms. Some regulatory mechanisms can and do influence daily occupational routines.

Pain is another sensation that prompts action to alleviate it. When people act to avoid negative consequences, these behaviors are *aversive.* Individuals avoid using joints or extremities that are injured, and in so doing, avoid pain and enable healing to take place faster. Pain is thus part of an important regulatory mechanism that protects the body and motivates people to participate in occupations in certain ways. That is, people may avoid certain movements or occupations altogether in an attempt to avoid or reduce the pain of movement or exertion.

Another important regulatory influence on daily occupation is **arousal.** Arousal pertains to the state of alertness or activation of an organism. The range of human arousal extends from deep sleep to severe anxiety and emotional agitation. Early theories of arousal (2) emphasized autonomic changes in the body that accompanied certain reactions to drives. Autonomic changes include such things as blood pressure, heart rate, sweating, and increased neuronal activity as measured by electroencephalography (Figure 6-1). When people experience fear (a learned drive), their heart rates may increase, perspiration may increase, and they may feel tense or anxious. In explaining arousal theory, a great deal of attention has been given to the role of the reticular activating system (RAS), a neural structure located in the brainstem, as a source of attention and consciousness. More recent research, however, has shown that other regions of the brain may be equally or more important for arousal than the RAS (3).

The capacity to attend to environmental cues as people participate in occupations varies according to their internal states. Studies have shown that there is an optimal level of arousal (4). That is, an individual's best performance on tasks requires that he be within a certain range of arousal (neither too relaxed nor too excited) (5).

The body seems to know this. If people are bored or disinterested in occupations, they avoid doing them or choose others. These choices help define who they are. Typically, people choose occupations to create optimal interest or attention. Studies of environmental deprivation have confirmed that certain levels of stimulation in the brain are necessary for well-being (6). Similarly, social isolation can become a form of sensory deprivation, resulting in significant psychological distress (7). One might conclude that certain levels of physical and social stimulation are necessary for well-being, and that denial or deprivation of these aspects of everyday living influence people to change their patterns of occupation. Perhaps one reason why people loathe social rejection is that they innately recognize that this will lead to reduced social interaction and the sensory stimulation that goes along with it.

Numerous other examples exist of physiological regulatory mechanisms that influence behavior, each dedicated to the purpose of protecting and preserving the organism from harm to enable its survival. Biology and its several subdisciplines, including ethology and genetics, have provided valuable information in helping to understand regulatory influences that influence choices in daily occupations. The implication is that physiology must not be dismissed as an indirect influence in what people do (and who they are).

Purposeful Motivators

A second approach to understanding motivation focuses on intentional or purposeful action. This approach to understanding motivation focuses on the role of conscious thought (cognition) and is less concerned with physiology and regulatory influences within the body. The **purposive view of motivation** has its roots in philosophy and the behavioral sciences, especially psychology, and emphasizes intentional actions. Intentional actions are by definition goal directed. When people contemplate actions, they try to anticipate the consequences of a given outcome and determine its meaning in terms of their well-being, personal situations, and the probable outcomes of various courses of action.

Although regulatory and purposive-oriented views of motivation are vastly different and originate from clearly distinct traditions of thought, they can each be used to advantage in explaining how participation in various occupations shapes and is also shaped by identity. For example, hunger, a regulatory motivator, may provide the initial motivation to go to the refrigerator (or to a restaurant). Once there, however, the choices of what a person eats may then be influenced more by purposeful motivators, such as a person's perceptions of the benefit or pleasure a given menu choice may bring, as well as its perceived costs (e.g., the weight gain or indigestion that may result!).

Current research in motivation has tended to emphasize the development of purposive theories. However, it is important to appreciate that a full understanding of human motivation requires attention to both regulatory and purposive viewpoints. To go beyond current research, we need to understand how regulatory and purposeful types of motivation support the desire and persistence for participating in occupations.

Drive theory attempts to pick up the threads required to understand influences on occupation and identity. Although drive theory originally came from the ideas of homeostasis and regulatory influences, it has now been expanded to include personality and social psychology. Drive theory has important concepts that are necessary for a basic understanding of motivation (8).

Key terms from drive theory include *need, drive,* and *goal.* Needs can be understood as an individual having either too much or too little of a resource necessary for survival. When needs arise, adaptive behaviors may result, but their occurrence is not certain. For example, the body needs certain vitamins for its survival, but the lack of a critical vitamin seldom results in behavior change.

In contrast, drives *always* lead to adaptive or compensatory behaviors. Drives are similar to needs, and often result from deprivation, such as lack of food or water. However, it is precisely because some conditions of deprivation result in corrective actions and others do not that there is a need for the two related concepts. Behavioral scientists sometimes distinguish between primary and secondary (or learned) drives. This distinction can be used to consider how drives for participation in occupation may influence development.

Hunger, thirst, and pain are sometimes called primary drives in recognition of their biological bases and to emphasize that there is no learning involved in their arousal. Secondary or acquired drives, by contrast, are learned, in that they are based on associations with primary drives. A familiar example of a learned drive is fear. Children are often warned to stay away from dangers, especially hot stoves. When they experience that touching a hot stove results in pain, children may then associate fear with stoves. This is a learned response.

One might ask that if a person is subject to multiple needs and drives at the same time, which would have the greatest influence? One of the best known theories of motivation, developed by Abraham Maslow nearly 50 years ago, attempted to provide an answer to this question.

MASLOW'S THEORY OF NEEDS

Maslow's hierarchy (9) ranks six categories of drives and needs from the most biological to the most psychological (Figure 6-2). Maslow's theory is useful to mention here because it includes both physiological drives and psychological needs, and because it is based on the principle that when a drive or need is met, its value as a motivator is reduced. Maslow's theory accounts for the dynamic or ever-changing nature of motivation. It recognizes that needs, drives, external conditions, and perceptions change continuously in everyday life. As a result, a person may be influenced by a variety of regulatory and purposeful motivational factors throughout a given day. Al-

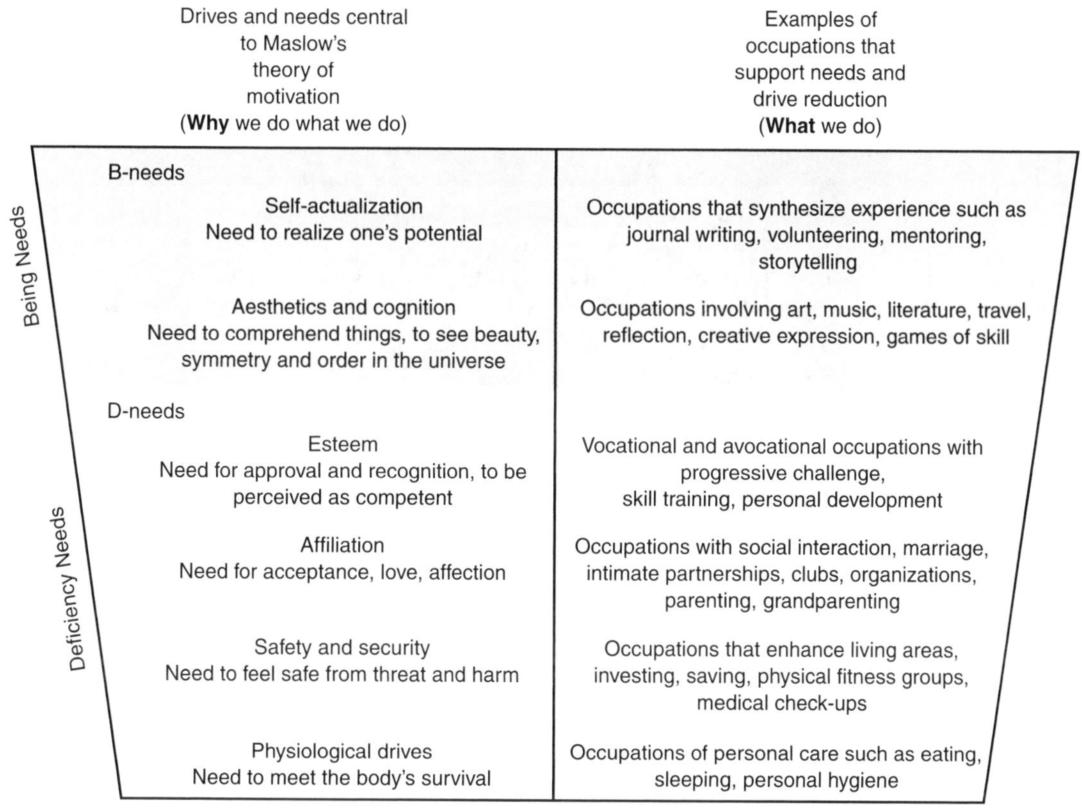

Drives and needs central to Maslow's theory of motivation (**Why** we do what we do)	Examples of occupations that support needs and drive reduction (**What** we do)
B-needs	
Self-actualization Need to realize one's potential	Occupations that synthesize experience such as journal writing, volunteering, mentoring, storytelling
Aesthetics and cognition Need to comprehend things, to see beauty, symmetry and order in the universe	Occupations involving art, music, literature, travel, reflection, creative expression, games of skill
D-needs	
Esteem Need for approval and recognition, to be perceived as competent	Vocational and avocational occupations with progressive challenge, skill training, personal development
Affiliation Need for acceptance, love, affection	Occupations with social interaction, marriage, intimate partnerships, clubs, organizations, parenting, grandparenting
Safety and security Need to feel safe from threat and harm	Occupations that enhance living areas, investing, saving, physical fitness groups, medical check-ups
Physiological drives Need to meet the body's survival	Occupations of personal care such as eating, sleeping, personal hygiene

(*Being Needs* and *Deficiency Needs* labeled on left axis)

FIGURE 6-2   Maslow's theory: Needs and corresponding occupations that help meet them.[1]

though Maslow's theory contains six levels, it also can be described as a two-category theory, because it combines needs met by external as well as internal rewards.

To explain, Maslow's first four levels represent the motivation to respond to unmet needs (**D-needs**). Meeting these needs reduces their potency as motivators. Recall that this is a characteristic of drives. In contrast, aesthetic and self-actualization needs pertain to intrinsic needs to grow and express autonomy, competence, and uniqueness as a person. According to Maslow, addressing these "being needs" becomes self-reinforcing, because they are self-expressive and their strength as motivators increases as the individual participates in them.

GOALS: EXTERNAL INFLUENCES THAT SHAPE THE SELF

Goals represent *external conditions* that influence participation in occupation by reducing primary or secondary drives. Because they serve to reduce drives, goals lose their influence on behavior once they are achieved. For most people, meals are a striking example of how a drive (hunger) is diminished with the participation in a goal activity (eating). The longer we eat, the less interest we have in continuing to do so. This is because the drive is reduced through a very complex system involving the digestive and nervous systems. It should be acknowledged here that eating is a complex goal activity, since it may address multiple needs related to socialization and pleasure.

Recently, psychologists have been interested in studying goals as a way of understanding motivation and individual differences. These studies have permitted some progress to be made in classifying goals (10). The studies show that most goals can be placed into five major categories, including (1) enjoyment, (2) self-assertion (relating to demonstrating one's abilities and skills through influence, competitiveness, or creativity), (3) esteem (goals related to personal growth), (4) interpersonal (fostering rewarding relationships with others), and (5) avoidance of negative affect (reducing anxiety and avoiding stress).

Psychologists have also studied the goals of individuals. Typically, in these studies, people are asked to identify their specific current goal-related projects and then provide details on their feelings and experiences related to these goals. Examples of personal goals might include buying a screwdriver, losing weight, improving a love relationship, learning a language, improving grades, earning a promotion, or taking a trip (10).

Studies have revealed that personal goals range from those representing immediate and practical tasks (eating lunch) to those with longer terms and more enduring personal changes as outcomes (such as becoming a better parent). Personal goals may emerge as a result of challenges or problems, or they may simply represent an interest in self-development. Personal goals tend to differ along three major dimensions: (1) the degree of commitment or investment in the goal, (2) the degree to which the goal is perceived as stressful or challenging, and (3) the anticipated reward or outcome of the goal.

An occupational perspective on drive theory may also generate understanding about the relationship between occupation and identity. Goals, commitment, and challenges in daily occupations determine what people do and, thus, who they are.

When people set goals, several thoughts and emotions, based mainly on past experiences and observations of others, influence them. Important factors in choosing goals include people's expectations of achieving the goal, how they feel about their abilities and skills, and their beliefs about the conditions that influence successful outcomes.

Ajzen, a psychologist at the University of Massachusetts, has proposed a theory of planned or intentional action that summarizes the various factors that influence motivation (11). According to this theory, human action is guided by three kinds of considerations. These include (1) an individual's beliefs about the likely consequences or outcomes of doing something (behavioral beliefs), (2) an individual's beliefs about what other's expect him or her to do in a given situation (normative beliefs), and (3) an individual's beliefs about the presence of factors that may help or hinder performance (control beliefs). As a general rule, if the anticipated consequences of doing something are perceived as favorable, if one believes one is acting as others expect and the goal is important, and if one believes that conditions are favorable for performing the action successfully, the stronger should be the person's intention to perform the behavior in question (12, 13).

Thus, goals are based on the self-perceptions people have of their abilities and skills, their beliefs in why things happen, and their analysis of the challenges represented by a goal. From an occupational perspective, one might say that expectations of success or failure shape people's occupational pursuits and influence how they engage in those occupations and who they do them with, among other things (14).

Successful tennis players, for instance, may be people with high expectancies of success in tennis, and their excellent performance in tennis generates an identity in which they and others agree that they are successful. Their expectancies of success in tennis may actually be derived from strong drives to play tennis combined with physical traits, such as fast reflexes, good vision, pain tolerance, and high concentration. Their purposeful motivators may derive from cultural beliefs that tennis is a great game to play!

Moreover, positive identities are created when people perceive the approval of others. This may come not only from doing what is expected, but from doing it well or competently. Repeatedly getting the approval of others for performing competently creates feelings of effectance, or self-confidence. Robert White proposed in the 1950s that striving for competence was a major motive and that this was influenced through experiences of success (15). Experiences serve to enhance or detract from a person's expectations for future success. If a person experiences success in challenging occupational pursuits, he develops a sense of *self-efficacy*, a perception that he is competent and can perform any particular action successfully (16). Research has shown that people with a sense of self-efficacy do perform better on many tasks, and that this performance is not simply the result of persistence and determination (17).

With reference to occupation and identity, self-confidence grows as effectance in an occupational pursuit develops. The tennis player seeks a state of effectance, a belief in the self as a good tennis player. The social standing associated with being a championship tennis player (or being recognized as outstanding in any occupational endeavor) is motivating because people have a universal need for social approval.

But what about when people fail to accomplish a goal? How do they explain this and how does this influence their participation in the same or different occupations later? To answer this question, attribution theory can prove useful. **Attributions** are the explanations people give to the outcomes of their own behavior or to that of others (18). Abramson and colleagues (19) have shown that if people explain their failure to achieve a goal by blaming it on their own inadequacies and also perceive that they have no control in changing those characteristics, they can develop a pattern of thought known as learned helplessness. When people experience helplessness, they are unlikely to be motivated to work toward resolution of situations that may be viewed as stressful or troublesome because they feel powerless (or helpless) to do anything about it. As might be expected, research has shown a significant relationship between helplessness and depression (20).

ACHIEVEMENT MOTIVATION

In contrast to those who experience helplessness because of their lack of belief in themselves, some people are motivated by a belief in their own capacity to succeed and have a willingness to accept moderate risk for the chance of achieving an important goal successfully. David C. McClelland, a researcher at Harvard, spent 20 years studying this urge to achieve (21). His work showed that people with a high need for achievement like to be challenged but select goals that are within their capability. That is, achievement-motivated people prefer to work on a problem rather than leave the outcome to chance.

Whereas conservative individuals prefer situations in which the risk is small but the gain is more certain, achievement-motivated people prefer a moderate degree of risk. This is because they believe their efforts and abilities will probably influence the outcome. According to McClelland's research, achievement-motivated people often set high personal goals, are more interested in personal goals than external rewards, and constantly seek performance-related feedback. As a result, they are more interested in the outcome than the method. The need for achievement is likely to influence a person's choice of occupations and goals and, of course, their identity. Being achievement oriented is one tendency that, along with others, helps describe a person's personality type. Personality and identity are closely linked, because personality can be described as that unique collection of behavioral tendencies or traits that make people "who they are."

MOTIVATION AND PERSONALITY

Beginning with adolescence, people exhibit relatively stable and predictable tendencies to behave in certain ways. These tendencies to act in particular ways can be analyzed from the standpoint of their underlying motives or needs, and are referred to as **traits.** Because traits are characteristics that individuals change little during adulthood, they can be used to describe, explain, and predict behavior (22).

As research in traits has evolved, the number of different traits that can be used to describe people has varied from a few to as many as 16. Recently, however, support has been growing for the view that five major dimensions, or trait factors, can be used to account for personality differences among individuals. These five dimensions, which make up the **five factor theory,** include surgency/extraversion, agreeableness, conscientiousness, neuroticism, and openness to experience/intellect (Table 6-1) (22).

Clusters of traits can be used to describe particular styles of personality or personality types. Research has shown that people with similar personality types often share

TABLE 6-1   *The Five Factor Theory*

Factor	Corresponding Descriptors
Extraversion	Talkative, open, adventurous, sociable
Agreeableness	Good natured, mild, cooperative
Conscientiousness	Careful, responsible, persevering
Emotional stability	Poised, calm, composed, consistent
Openness to experience	Imaginative, intellectual, polished, artistically sensitive

interests and preferences for various types of daily occupations. These common interests and pursuits have provided the basis for theories of vocational choice and leisure preferences. John Holland developed one prominent example of such theories.

HOLLAND'S THEORY OF VOCATIONAL CHOICE

The theory of vocational choice created by Holland is based on known relationships between personality traits and vocational preferences (23). Six personality types, each having a defined cluster of traits, are defined in the theory. These are depicted in Table 6-2. Holland has proposed that people with particular personality types are at their best when they are in environments that meet the unique needs and interests of their type. Thus, when types are matched with their ideal supportive environments, satisfaction results.

For example, according to the theory, a person with a personality type classified as *social* would prefer vocational environments where there are opportunities to work with other people and be helpful. An environment that emphasizes technical skills and working with equipment might not be satisfying to this type of individual. Holland's theory provides for people to be classified in more than one type according to the strength of the traits they exhibit.

Much research has been done using Holland's theory of vocational choice, and it has shown itself to be quite powerful as a means for relating specific interests and traits to vocational pursuits as well as leisure occupations (24). Because people often define themselves by their work (e.g., "I'm a plumber" or "I'm a lawyer"), it is easy to appreciate the connection between a person's vocation and his/her sense of identity.

LEISURE, OCCUPATIONAL CHOICE, AND IDENTITY

People also often define themselves in terms of their leisure pursuits. When asked what she does in her spare time, a young woman might declare that she is "a golfer" or a "competitive swimmer." Given the vast array of options that people have for using their discretionary time and the considerable industry surrounding leisure activities, it is not surprising that scholars have devoted significant interest toward understanding the factors related to leisure choice. Leisure includes those occupations that create positive feelings and attitudes, are internally motivated, enable one to feel relatively free of constraints, and permit the exercise of perceived competence (25). Current views hold that people engage in leisure pursuits in order to meet needs for self-expression, enjoyment, and mastery.

Research directed at leisure motivation has focused on theories that emphasize internal needs to act and demonstrate competence. Recent research suggests that leisure provides opportunities for meeting needs in 11 major categories: agency, novelty, service, belongingness, sensual enjoyment, cognitive stimulation, self-expression, creativity, competition, vicarious competition, and relaxation (26). Leisure choice may be highly significant in the development of identity because leisure enables people to release themselves from the obligatory and necessary duties of the occupations

TABLE 6-2   *Descriptions of Holland's General Occupational Themes*

Realistic

Robust, rugged, practical, and physically strong; have good motor coordination and skills, usually perceive themselves as mechanically inclined; are direct, stable, natural, and persistent, prefer concrete to abstract problems, like to build things with tools.

Investigative

Strong scientific orientation; usually task oriented, introspective and asocial, prefer to think problems through rather than act them out, have a great need to understand the physical world, enjoy ambiguous tasks; prefer to work independently, have unconventional values and attitudes, are confident of intellectual abilities, describe themselves as analytical, curious, independent, and reserved. Dislike repetitive activities.

Artistic

Prefer free, unstructured situations with opportunity for self-expression; are introspective and social; are creative, especially in artistic and musical media; avoid problems that are highly structured; see themselves as expressive, original, intuitive, creative, introspective, and independent.

Social

Sociable, responsible, humanistic, like to work in groups and enjoy being at the center of the group, have good verbal and interpersonal skills, avoid highly ordered activities, prefer to solve problems through feelings and interpersonal manipulation of others, enjoy activities that involve informing, training, developing, curing, or enlightening others. Perceive themselves as understanding, responsible, idealistic, and helpful.

Enterprising

Have verbal skills suited to selling, dominating, and leading; have a strong drive to attain organizational goals or economic aims, tend to avoid work situations requiring long periods of intellectual effort, have a greater concern than others for power, status, and leadership; see themselves as aggressive, popular, self-confident, cheerful, and sociable. Generally have high energy level.

Conventional

Prefer well-ordered environments and like systematic verbal and numerical activities. Are effective at well-structured tasks; avoid ambiguous situations and problems involving interpersonal relationships; describe themselves as conscientious, efficient, obedient, calm, orderly, and practical; identify with power and value material possessions and status.

Source: Adapted and reproduced by special permission of the publisher, Psychological Assessment Resources, Inc., Odessa, FL 33556, from the Self-Directed Search Assessment Booklet by John L. Holland, Ph.D. Copyright 1970, 1977, 1985, 1990, 1994 by PAR, Inc. Further reproduction is prohibited without permission from PAR, Inc.

of paid work. Leisure choices, as Tinsley noted (26), provide experiences (such as novelty, sensual enjoyment) that may not be provided by paid work and employment. Thus, identity, which typically is defined less significantly by family ties than by what people do, is greatly influenced by work as well as leisure occupations. In leisure, people create and express those elements of their identity that may not be accessible to them in their world of work.

FLOW

Csikszentmihalyi (27), a psychologist at the University of Chicago, has devoted his career to the study of leisure experiences that are particularly engaging. He has proposed a term for peak experiences of human involvement during which the individual becomes so intensely absorbed in an activity that nothing else seems to matter. In these experiences, enjoyment is of such magnitude that people will do it even at great cost. Csikszentmihalyi terms these experiences **flow** and his studies suggest that there are eight components in a flow experience: (1) a clear goal, (2) feedback, (3) challenges that match skills, (4) concentration and focus, (5) control, (6) loss of self-consciousness, (7) transformation of time, and (8) an experience that is pursued for no other purpose or pleasure than engagement itself.

OCCUPATION AND IDENTITY: AN INTEGRATION OF IDEAS

Earlier in this chapter, the notion of human agency and how events influence attitudes and feelings, which then influence behavioral decisions, was described. Regulatory factors and environmental characteristics were also identified as factors that influence these choices.

The theory by Maslow (9) cited earlier identifies a wide range of motivational factors, including both regulatory as well as purposive influences on behavior. Maslow created the theory in an attempt to explain how choices are made in the face of competing motives. He also wanted to make it clear that the intrinsic motivation driven by being fully human (self-actualizing) was the most important motivational influence of all.

Unfortunately, people sometimes develop habit patterns that are maladaptive. An everyday term given for these unhealthy patterns of behavior is *vicious cycle*. A student who feels helpless after failing a test may conclude that he is not a good test taker. Based on this belief, the student feels that additional study is pointless, even though fatigue and not ability was the cause of the poor test score. In such situations, prior experiences, beliefs, personality traits, and new challenges lead to behavioral patterns that are based on incorrect explanations for why events occurred and lowered self-confidence based on poor performance.

If the student feels his math skills are innately poor, he may devote less effort in attending to lectures, taking notes, or studying than is necessary for passing the test. When failure occurs, the experience reinforces the student's self-perception of inadequacy and the vicious cycle continues until one or more of the factors that influence the situation can change: the challenge presented, the student's abilities, the environmental circumstances, or the student's cognitive appraisal of the situation. These elements work together to help explain the level of motivation, the probable outcome of the experience, and the way it is interpreted by the student.

Because people want to feel good about themselves, they learn to select situations and challenges that lead to success and become reinforcing in positive ways. These choices are not always made consciously. Defense mechanisms, such as avoidance or rationalization, can influence occupational behavior in ways that help protect the self-image so we can continue to feel good about ourselves despite setbacks.

Ultimately, motivation is important because it helps us make the choices that lead to the experiences that best express our identities and create a sense of personal satisfaction. Maslow emphasized that we all aspire to achieve persistent states of **self-actualization** but that we encounter difficulties along the way. Maslow wrote (9):

> Human life will never be understood unless its highest aspirations are taken into account. Growth, self-actualization, the striving toward health, the quest for identity and autonomy, the yearning for excellence (and other ways of phrasing the striving "upward") must by now be accepted beyond question as a widespread and perhaps universal human tendency. . . . (p. 306)

Later in his career, Maslow redefined self-actualization so that it represented not a permanent characteristic or trait attained by a few fortunate people, but rather a state of being that could be experienced in defined situations by many people. To attain states of self-actualization, he asserted, people needed to have their deficiency needs met and, therefore, need to be in environmental situations that enable those needs to be met easily. They must also be sufficiently confident to resist the influence of culture, to choose growth over safety, and to overcome the fear of failure and social rejection that they believe failure will bring. In his explanation of self-actualization, Maslow identified several "being" (B) values. These are identified in Table 6-3.

Thus, among other traits, competence, identity, and autonomy are important to self-actualization in Maslow's theory. To become all that they are capable of becoming, people must have a sense that they are expressing their selfhood in ways that are uniquely appropriate to themselves. Maslow wrote that *we do what we are and we are what we do* (28). Although the depth and scope of Maslow's thinking has been masked by simplified descriptions of his hierarchy, his contributions to understanding the complexity of motivation and the importance of choice, identity, and success in human occupation are remarkable. Fortunately, more recent theories of motivation have continued and extended Maslow's thinking, which implicity emphasizes that occupations contribute to identity development, especially when they are performed competently and to the satisfaction of self and others. A good example of a contemporary theory of this type is self-determination theory.

Self-Determination Theory

Edward Deci and Richard Ryan of the University of Rochester have formulated a contemporary needs-based theory that attempts to explain motivation from the

---

TABLE 6-3   *Some Words Maslow Used to Describe His Being or B-Values*

aliveness (process; spontaneity; full-functioning)
beauty (richness; wholeness; perfection; completion)
completion (ending; finality; justice; "it's finished"; fulfillment; *finis* and *telos;* destiny; fate)
effortlessness (ease; lack of strain, grace)
goodness (rightness; desirability; justice; benevolence)
justice (fairness; orderliness; lawfulness; "oughtness")
perfection (necessity; inevitability; suitability; justice)
playfulness (fun; joy; amusement; gaiety; humor)
richness (differentiation, complexity; intricacy)
self-sufficiency (autonomy; independence; separateness)
simplicity (honesty; nakedness; essentiality; structure)
truth; honesty; reality (richness; beauty; completeness)
uniqueness (idiosyncrasy; individuality; novelty non-comparability)
wholeness (unity; integration; order; transcendence tendency to oneness; interconnectedness; simplicity)

Source: Abraham H. Maslow, *Toward a Psychology of Being,* D. Van Nostrand Company, 1968.

standpoint of individuals who seek to develop their identities as competent, autonomous individuals. This theory is called **self-determination theory** (29).

Self-determination theory is based on a view that individuals must fulfill three basic psychological needs in order to function effectively (30). The first is *competence,* or being able to successfully meet environmental demands. The second need is termed *relatedness* and describes the requirement for close relationships with others.

The third basic need, **autonomy,** represents a quality of making individual occupational choices that are integrated with the self and that serve the needs for competence or relatedness. According to self-determination theory, autonomy describes occupations and actions that are done by and for the self. Such behaviors are personally satisfying because they express individuality and help to establish identity (31).

Self-determination theory proposes the idea that success in tasks influences feelings of efficacy and encourages further risk taking and exploration (32). The idea that people must learn to regulate their need-related behaviors in a manner that fosters acceptance and success is fundamental to self-determination theory. A key part of this self-regulation is making appropriate choices. As Deci (33) summarizes it, "without choice, there would be no agency, and no self-regulation" (p. 222).

Self: The Product of Occupational Engagement

I proposed previously (34) that because everyday occupations are named, understood, and engaged in a social world, relationships with others are fundamental to developing identities. I suggest that occupational choices are most often influenced by social and cultural expectations, and that preserving an identity that is acceptable to others and satisfying to oneself represents a fundamental life need. Because

BOX 6-2   George Herbert Mead

One of the most eminent social psychologists to influence thought in the Western world was born in 1863 at South Hadley, Massachusetts, as the son of a Congregationalist pastor. George Herbert Mead (Figure 6-3) studied at Harvard and in Europe, taught at the University of Michigan (1891–1894), and became a professor at the University of Chicago in 1894. He did not publish a great deal, but his lectures, edited posthumously, formed the basis of four books, including *Mind, Self, and Society* (1934), one of the most influential works of the psychological tradition known as symbolic interactionism. This social behavior point of view portrayed the self as developing from a process of communication and interaction with others. Mead was a pragmatist who failed to see a sharp distinction between science and philosophy. He died in 1931.

FIGURE 6-3   George Herbert Mead.
Source: University of Chicago Archive

culture works to influence early choices based on traditions, interests and experiences within the family provide a context that influences later interests and experiences by fostering the development of the knowledge, attitude, and skill necessary for success in a given life course.

My view is based in social psychology and emphasizes the concepts of **symbolic interactionism,** a tradition of thought made popular by George Herbert Mead (35) (Box 6-1). The key postulates underlying symbolic interactionism are that people derive their sense of self mostly through interactions with others and that social acceptance is fundamental to human well-being.

Because identity is a social phenomenon, it is widely accepted that people have multiple identities that often correspond to their various roles and occupations in life. Because of their interactions with others, individuals' multiple selves become "distributed," so that each person's life experiences (and corresponding identity) become part of the story (and identity) of another person. I believe that in adulthood, people understand their lives and identities as unfolding autobiographies, or life stories.

Creating the Self Through the Life Story

The idea that people make sense of their lives (and create their identities) through stories is basic to an area of study described by Sarbin (36) as the "storied nature of human conduct." Jerome Bruner (37) concludes that humans are genetically predisposed to understanding the world through stories, and that much of human action is given meaning through its relevance to the story being lived. Markus (38) carries this idea one step further by suggesting that people are motivated by "possible selves" imagined in the future chapters of a life story, and that avoiding unhappy outcomes can become a powerful influence on choices and behaviors.

Dan McAdams of Northwestern University (39) has studied the important role of the life story in creating a personal sense of unity and purpose in life, or identity. In his research, McAdams has found that when people tell their life stories, they are able to re-create special moments, identify turning points, and reveal ongoing identity issues.

The study of life stories as described by the people who are living them has, not surprisingly, identified power and love as recurring major themes. Two types of "main characters" have been commonplace in the stories analyzed by McAdams: those who are oriented toward love and intimacy (described as communal types) and those who act, think, and feel vigorously (described as agentic types). McAdams (40) is convinced that the meaning contributed by the life story is essential to understanding life experiences and provides a unified identity in the mind of the individual. This sense of identity changes over time, has multiple dimensions, and may or may not be consistent with the identity images viewed by others. However, it is clear from McAdam's research that experiences, life choices, and competence in meeting challenges have an important influence on how life stories are constructed and interpreted. It is important to recognize that experiences, choices, and competence are often embodied in the occupations of daily life.

CHAPTER SUMMARY

In this chapter, the various factors that influence what people do during the course of their lives and how these shape who they are have been considered. In answering the question *What motivates human action?* it has been revealed that people are motivated to act by many factors, and that their potential to act as humans arises in their motivations, drives, needs, and the external influences that shape those human experiences.

Other factors that motivate humans include bodily fatigue, pain and arousal, individual goals for purposeful action, individual drive, individual needs, externally driven goals, external influences on goal setting, achievement, personality, vocational choice, needs for leisure, and flow, which comes from feelings of competence and engagement. A connection was established between the personality traits that people exhibit and their choice of vocational and leisure pursuits.

Participation in occupations influences identity as supported by theories of person–environment fit, such as self-determination theory. Self-determination theory, which highlights agency, competence, and relationships with others as key factors influencing adaptive choices, was offered as an example of a contemporary theory that illustrates how occupational choices create the conditions through which individuals establish identities. This defines their uniqueness and provides a sense of meaning that leads to well-being and satisfaction through doing and being.

Finally, it was observed that identity, as shaped by occupational choices and competent performance, becomes part of an unfolding life story, or autobiography. Life stories permit the integration of events over time, by enabling new goals to be connected to past occupational experiences.

REFERENCES

1. Cannon, W. B. (1927). The James-Lange theory of emotions: A critical examination and an alternative theory. *American Journal of Psychology, 39,* 106–124.
2. Duffy, E. (1934). Emotion: An example of the need for reorientation. *Psychological Review, 41,* 184–198.
3. Steriade, M. (1996). Arousal: Revisiting the reticular activating system. *Science, 272* (5259), 225–226.
4. Eysenck, M N. (1982). *Attention and arousal.* New York: Springer-Verlag.
5. Berlyne, D. E. (1960). *Conflict, arousal and curiosity.* New York: McGraw-Hill.
6. Hebb, D. O. (1955). Drives and the C.N.S. (conceptual nervous system). *Psychological Review, 62,* 243–254.
7. Ray, N., Myers, K., & Rappaport, M. I. (1996). Patient perspectives on restraint and seclusion experiences: A survey of former patients of New York State psychiatric facilities. *Psychiatric Rehabilitation Journal, 20*(1), 11–18.
8. Hull, C. L. (1931). Goal attraction and directing ideas conceived as habit phenomena. *Psychologial Review, 38,* 487–506.
9. Maslow, A. H. (1970). *Motivation and personality.* New York: Harper & Row.
10. Emmons, R. (1997). Motives and life goals. In R. Hogan (Ed.), *Handbook of personality psychology* (pp. 485–512). New York: Academic Press.
11. Ajzen, I. (1992). The theory of planned behavior. *Organizational Behavior and Human Decision Processes, 50,* 179–211.
12. Ajzen, I., & Driver, B. L. (1992). Application of the theory of planned behavior to leisure choice. *Journal of Leisure Research, 24,* 207–224.
13. Doll, J., & Ajzen, I. (1992). Accessibility and stability of predictors in the theory of planned behavior. *Journal of Personality and Social Psychology, 63,* 54–765.
14. Atkinson, J. W. (1964). *An introduction to motivation.* New York: D. Van Nostrand.
15. White, R. W. (1959). Motivation reconsidered: The concept of competence. *American Journal of Occupational Therapy, 66,* 297–333.
16. Bandura, A. (1982). Self efficacy mechanisms in human agency. *American Psychologist, 37,* 122–147.
17. Bandura, A. (1977). Self-efficacy: Toward a unifying theory of behavioral change. *Psychological review, 84,* 191–215.
18. Heider, F. (1958). *The psychology of interpersonal relations.* New York: John Wiley.
19. Abramson, L. Y., Seligman, M. E. P., & Teasdale, J. (1978). Learned helplessness in humans: Critique and reformulation. *Journal of Abnormal Psychology, 87,* 49–74.
20. Seligman, M. E. P., Abramson, L. Y., Semmel, A., & von Bayer, C. (1979). Depressive attributional style. *Journal of Abnormal Psychology, 88,* 242–247.
21. McLelland, D. C. (1985). *Human motivation.* New York: Scott Foresman.

22. Wiggins, J. S. (1997). Personality structure: The return of the big five. In R. Hogan (Ed.), *Handbook of Personality Psychology*. San Diego: Academic Press.

23. Holland, J. L. (1997). *Making of vocational choices: A theory of vocational personalities and work environments* (3rd ed.). Odessa, FL: Psychological Assessment Resources.

24. Gottfredson, G. D. (1999). John L. Holland's contributions to vocational psychology: A review and evaluation. *Journal of Vocational Behavior, 55,* 15–40.

25. Edgington, C. R., Jordan, D. J., Degraaf, D. G., & Edgington, S. R. (1995). *Leisure and life satisfaction: Foundational perspectives*. Dubuque, IA: I. A. Brown & Benchmark Publishers.

26. Tinsley, B. D. (1995). Psychological benefits of leisure participation. A taxonomy of leisure activities based on their need-gratifying properties. *Journal of Counseling Psychology, 42*(2), 123–132.

27. Csikszentmihalyi, M. (1990). *Flow—The psychology of optimal experience*. New York: Harper and Row.

28. Maslow, A. H. (1968). *Toward a psychology of being*. New York: John Wiley.

29. Deci, E. L., & Ryan, R. M. (1985). *Intrinsic motivation and self-determination in human behavior*. New York: Plenum.

30. Deci, E. L., & Ryan, R. (1991). A motivational approach to self: Integration in personality. In R. Dienstbier (Ed.), *Nebraska symposium on motivation, Vol. 38: Perspectives on motivation*. Lincoln: University of Nebraska Press.

31. Ryan, R. M., & Deci, E. L. (2000). Self-determination theory and the facilitation of intrinsic motivation, social development and well-being. *American Psychologist, 55,* 68–78.

32. Sheldon, K. M., Ryan, R. M., & Reis, H. (1996). What makes for a good day? Competence and autonomy in the day and in the person. *Personality and Social Psychology Bulletin, 22,* 1270–1279.

33. Deci, E. L. (1996). *Why we do what we do: Understanding self motivation*. London: Penguin.

34. Christiansen, C. H. (1999). Defining lives: Occupation as identity. An essay on competence, coherence and the creation of meaning. *American Journal of Occupational Therapy, 53* (6), 547–558.

35. Mead, G. H. (1934). *Mind, self and society*. Chicago: University of Chicago Press.

36. Sarbin, T. R., & Allen, V. L. (1968). Role theory. In L. Aronson (Ed.), *Handbook of social psychology*. Reading, MA: Addison-Wesley.

37. Bruner, J. (1990). *Acts of meaning*. Cambridge, MA: Harvard University Press.

38. Markus, H. R. (1986). Possible selves. *American Psychologist, 41,* 954–969.

39. McAdams, D. P. (1993). *The stories we live by: Personal myths and the making of the self*. New York: Guilford Press.

40. McAdams, D. (1992). Unity and purpose in human lives: The emergence of identity as a life story. In R. A. Zucker and A. I. Rabin (et. al) (Eds.) *Personality structure in the life course* (pp. 323–376). New York: Springer-Verlag.

Endnote

[1] It is important to realize that some occupations may meet more than one need or drive at the same time. For example, eating is often a social activity, so it can reduce hunger while simultaneously attending to social needs.

7

The Occupational Nature of Communities

Charles Christiansen and Elizabeth Townsend

KEY WORDS

Adaptation	Game theory
Allee effect	Interdependence
Altruism	Meme
Competition	Memetics
Cooperation	Prisoner's Dilemma
Division of labor	Sense of community
Ecological niche	Social capital
Exaptation	Sociobiology
Free rider problem	Sustainability

CHAPTER PROFILE

This chapter describes the occupational nature of communities from the standpoint of humans as a group-living species. In doing so, it addresses the social factors that contribute to group living and describes the advantages of community occupations in promoting the survival of humans. It proposes that shared or cooperative occupations are a central feature of successful communities and discusses the role of language in the evolution of group living. Specific biological concepts influencing group living, including altruism, ecological niche, cooperation, and competition within species, are also identified. The chapter continues with an examination of factors that contribute to the success of communities, including social sanctions, cultural rituals,

www.prenhall.com/christiansen

The Internet provides an exciting means for interacting with this textbook and for enhancing your understanding of humans' experiences with occupations and the organization of occupations in society. Use the address above to access the free, interactive companion web site created specifically to accompany this book. Here you will find an array of self-study material designed to help you gain a richer understanding of the concepts presented in this chapter.

shared history, art, magic, and religion, volunteerism, work, and sustainable practices. The chapter concludes with a description of communities with occupational characteristics that fail to support success, such as violence and injustices and the absence of trust and shared goodwill or social capital.

INTRODUCTION

As group-living species, humans have evolved occupations that not only contribute to their survival, but also have led to the formation of communities and cultures. In this chapter, we consider the occupational nature of communities by examining the answers to three questions:

1. What makes communities inherently social and occupational?
2. How and why did group living in communities develop?
3. How and why do occupations determine a community's potential to flounder or flourish?

WHAT MAKES COMMUNITIES INHERENTLY SOCIAL AND OCCUPATIONAL? EXPERIENCING SHARED OCCUPATIONS

Human communities consist of groups of people who do things together and individually. People participate collectively through reflection, communication, or action in occupations such as labor, sports, intellectual pursuits, or home building. Bonds that draw and keep people thinking about each other and occupied together may include shared beliefs, shared geography, shared interests, shared experiences, shared traditions, or shared kinship (1).

Communities began historically as geographically and genetically defined groups of people who shared the occupations of survival, such as hunting, gathering, and defense against enemies. Today, without restriction to geographic boundaries or genetically linked clans or tribes, communities having shared interests have arisen, such as communities of musicians around the world or other types of communities that form through shared experiences. Communities have formed because of bonds related to such diverse experiences as old age, disability, ethnicity, race, religion, rural or urban living, or sexual orientation. Clans and tribes are communities that draw on shared geographic history, heritage, and ancestry. These communities are geographically scattered around the world. Many people retain a sense of pride and belonging as members of clans or tribes who may engage in the shared occupations of cultural rituals and artistic expression wherever community members may be.

Alistair MacLeod (2), a Scottish-Canadian writer, wrote an award-winning novel, titled, *No Great Mischief,* about the dilemma of clans being both a source of identity and a trap. His main character Calum, a member of "clan Chalum Ruaidh" of the MacDonald clan, finds himself both nurtured and stuck in his clannish connectedness with Cape Breton Island in Nova Scotia. Clan and occupation are intricately tied. He chances losing his mining job in Ontario to drive for more than 30 hours to participate in the clannish occupation that is his grandfather's wake on Cape Breton Island. Within the clan's strong communities and occupations of this island, language is used to search for connections in conversations that inevitably start with "What's your name?" "What's your father's name?" "What's your mother's father's name?" (p. 28). Family remind each other "always look after your own blood" in finding each other jobs (p. 204). The grandfather who enjoyed his occupations of dancing as well as hard work reveals the essence of strong, nurturing occupation-based and clan-based communities in his frequently uttered statement that ends the book: "All of us are better when we are loved" (p. 283).

Worldwide virtual communities are now connected in the shared occupations of e-mail correspondence, synchronous or asynchronous chat room discussion, and other communication occupations made possible by the Internet and other technologies. There are many kinds of communities, but they have in common social interaction through what they do together—through a wide range of reflective, communicative, and action-based occupations.

The defining features of participation in any of these communities are respect, connectedness, belonging, reciprocity, mutual aid, care for others, and often an altruism to both help and protect one another (3–5). The shared thought, meditation, and action of communities create an interdependence and reciprocal mutual aid in which community members look not only at self-needs but also to the needs of others (6, 7). Consider that the words *community* and *communicate* are from the root word *commune*, which means to share.

Michael Ignatieff, a Canadian historian who describes himself as a citizen of the world, has written about the deep bonds of "blood and belonging" as the basis for the cultural and religious conflicts that have festered for years in the Balkans and other parts of the world (8). His insights emphasize the interdependence and reciprocity of kindness in everyday actions required for people to consider the "needs of strangers" as well as their own needs (9). His recent writings on the Rights Revolution highlight the importance of creating communities where bonds are based on both equality and differences. He indirectly points to shared and individual occupations (decorating ourselves, dressing) in the communities through which we:

> . . . commit ourselves to a special way of thinking about the relationship between human equality and human difference. . . . What we have in common as human beings is the very way we differentiate ourselves—as peoples, as communities, and as individuals. So it is not the naked body we share in common, but the astoundingly different ways in which we decorate, adorn, perfume, and costume our bodies in order to proclaim our identities as men, women, members of this tribe or that community. (10, p. 41)

Belenky and her colleagues (11) attend to the "otherness and silence" of those who are viewed as "different, deficient, unworthy of being full participants in society, their interests subordinated to those in power" (p. 3). Their work focuses on women's and children's occupations in communities, but they have also included in their study groups people of color such as African North Americans. A rather interesting example of collaborative, enabling parenting illustrates the diversity of ways of knowing about as well as doing occupations. The mother's purpose is:

> . . . to engage Alice [daughter] in a shared, mutual activity. Pam [mother] begins by disassembling [the] lego blocks. . . . Pam's conversation is rich with questions followed by full pauses, a pattern that encourages her child to participate as a full partner: "Can we try to make him?" "Is that this part here?" "Can you get it?" Pam provides Alice with guidance, yet does so through questions that draw her daughter into the activity: "Now on the bottom of that we need what?" (11, pp. 149–150)

In other words, the occupational nature of communities is characterized by gender, race, and many other differences in the ways people understand, accomplish, and speak about what they do. From earlier work, we might say that diverse "ways of knowing" (12) produce diverse ways of doing. The struggle for rights to be equal while also respecting difference, as described by Ignatieff earlier, is universal. Equality and difference are actually grounded in the ways in which people come to know and experience everyday life. That is to say, the occupational nature of communities is grounded in difference, and differences can be accommodated in everyday life. The key is for children and others to learn reciprocity, collaboration, and support in everyday occupations. It seems critical for people to develop self-confidence and a voice to be both different and a full participant in communities.

Rubin (13) maintains that a community's main function is to act as a go-between—between the individual and society. Rubin asserted that individuals relate to their larger societies through both geographic and nongeographic substructures, or communities. Prior to the establishment of modern communication technologies, communities were, of necessity, primarily geographic. But today, technology permits other kinds of communities to develop and serve the purposes of sharing traditions, values, and goals. Examples are professional societies, labor unions, or sports clubs that maintain themselves through a membership organization created through shared occupational interests. These communities meet face to face periodically, communicate through other means regularly with their members, establish ethical standards, and represent the interests of members to the state or internationally.

Rubin developed his beliefs of community from the writings of French sociologist Emile Durkheim (14) who believed that if the state were the only organized structure available to people, the individual would become detached and society would disintegrate. Durkheim wrote: "A nation can be maintained only if, between the State and the individual, there is [introduced] a whole series of secondary groups near enough to the individuals to attract them strongly in their *sphere of action* [emphasis added] and drag them in this way, into the general torrent of social life" (p. 28). Furthermore, people need communities to "serve as buffers between the individual and the larger society" (p. 60).

From Durkheim's work, Rubin (13) identified five structural characteristics for a community to mediate between an individual and society. Each characteristic makes it possible to experience shared occupations: size, focus, stability, social structure, and participation (Table 7-1).

The implication is that positive experiences of shared occupation are founded on discovering just the right size of community, whether it be a geographic or a common interest community. Rubin advocates that a central focus will generate a sense of connectedness through what people are doing. He highlights the interconnect-

TABLE 7-1   *Rubin's Structural Characteristics of Communities*

Characteristic	Features
Size	Size must be intermediate—small enough to provide a sense of community and large enough to enable members to feel they are part of a larger social structure.
Focus	Must address some of the important central problems of social life to help members feel connected to the larger society.
Relative stability	Should have a history and core nucleus of members.
Concrete social structure	People must be able to interact and identify with each other.
Participative and congenial social interactions	Interactions must be primary and secondary and allow for social structure.

Source: Adapted from Rubin, I. (1983). Function and structure of community: Conceptual and theoretical analysis. In R. L. W. L. Lyon (Ed.), *New perspectives on the American community* (pp. 54–61). Homewood, IL: Dorsey Press.

edness of communities, or the glue that keeps communities together, as that sense of shared focus, purpose, mission, or project. One might suppose that communities that fish together, that dance or generate art together, that protect the environment together, or that worship together are all communities with the shared focus that makes belonging to that community worthwhile. As Rubin notes, communities succeed when they are relatively stable (13). He uses the example of having a shared history (stability over time) or a core nucleus of members (stability of persons).

As a sign of community success, one might also include stability of occupations, wherein the community retains its focus on particular projects or actions over a sufficient time, and with sufficient attention to completion of occupations so that members experience the shared satisfaction of work, play, or expression well done. Rubin's characteristics of communities also include the need for both structure and participation (13). In other words, a framework of habits, customs, policies, or regulations makes it possible for people to participate with congeniality as they go about their shared occupations. One might extrapolate from this that Rubin would include both structure and participation as characteristics of the occupational nature of communities. Individuals and groups participate together in occupations that express a common sense of focus over time with a core of people sustaining a group that is neither too large nor too small.

Interdependence is a fundamental experience in shared occupations. Condeluci describes interdependence as the expression and satisfaction of being and doing with others (6). Mutual dependence, sometimes referred to as codependence, may negatively draw people into collusion in harmful occupations. Examples are communities of people who are occupied interdependently in violence, or codependent families caught up in alcohol, drug, gambling, or other addictions. Positive interdependence, however, generates mutual aid and reciprocal giving. As Brown notes, interdependence is founded on mutual respect, acknowledgment, accommodation, and cooperation that both connect people and provide them with the independence to develop their communities (15). Interdependence engenders a spirit of social inclusion, mutual aid, and a moral commitment and responsibility to recognize and support difference. A common example is the sense of belonging and connectedness generated when communities grow, prepare, and eat food together. Religious communities have long recognized the power of breaking bread or breaking a fast with others when there is a sense of purpose and focus. Health and social programs have a long history of involving people in shared occupations to sustain community farms or community mental health programs (16–18). Intentional communities may support "independent living" by people with a disability, or activism against poverty, drugs, or crime (19, 20). Community schools may seek to create a culture of inclusion so that students with diverse intellectual or physical abilities can all benefit from educational programs.

History-making and documentation are occupations that seem necessary for community continuity. Those who participate in recording historical events they have shared together, or who write stories about their home communities, create public tools for generating connectedness and a sense of belonging. The making of written histories, visual documentaries, films, plaques, cemetery tombstones, logos, plaid tartans, uniforms, or ceremonial clothing are history-generating, shared occupations. These are occupations that often spark a sense of recognition and reconnection with communities. Such occupations express community values, customs, rules, sanctions, and a community identity. When we visit a cemetery, we are instantly reminded of the times when we participated together in occupations such as building a house, celebrating an anniversary, or playing games (Figure 7-1). When we read stories about the development of a community project, the rebuilding of a town after a fire, or the genealogy of a clan, we remember doing something in particular times and places and with particular people. Historical as well as organizational documentation is fundamental, not only for sentimental reasons, but also in the organization of empowered communities (21).

Individual identity is intertwined with the occupational nature of communities. Ironically, the Internet and communication technologies have enabled occupations that create virtual communities at the same time that people around the world are experiencing an erosion of connectedness and moral responsibility in their daily occupations. Many have noted this, such as American sociologist Amatai Etzioni who has advocated what he refers to as *communitarian practices.* Like other communitarian advocates, Etzioni proposed that we more carefully balance individual rights with a community member's responsibilities to the greater good (22). Communities develop a sense of commitment and emotional support in times of need as members generate shared beliefs, traditions, and goals through shared occupations. Feeling safe and supported by a group engenders feelings of loyalty and attachment. McMillan and Chavis (23) describe four ways in which members generate a psychological **sense of community:** by creating a sense of belonging, by fulfilling member needs, by providing influence, and by offering shared connections.

The occupations that foster individual identity also give rise to shared identity (24). Communities support or limit individual development of identity or selfhood. Neither is separate from the other as identity emerges in two fundamental directions, each creating tension with the other (25–27). The first direction is to satisfy individual and shared needs for power, autonomy, status, and excitement. The sec-

FIGURE 7-1   The concept of community cooperation and interdependence is clearly exemplified in collective efforts to build physical structure—either for the community-at-large or for individuals. In this photo, the practice of barn raising is shown. In rural areas, it is not uncommon for neighbors to collectively assist with harvesting or building barns, especially when a family or individual suffers misfortune.
(Photograph © by Dennis L. Hughes, 6/20/02. Courtesy of Dennis L. Hughes.)

ond is to satisfy individual and shared needs for love, intimacy, acceptance, respect, belonging, connectedness, and interdependence. Bakan (28) describes these two directions as agency and communion. *Agency* refers to mastery, self-assertion, and the capacity of individuals to reason and exert power through thought, language, and action. *Communion* refers to joining with others to become part of a larger whole. Considered together, agency and communion are both necessary to and are the results of participation in the shared occupations of communities. Shared occupations are a platform for individual experiences of power, autonomy, status, and excitement, as well as for the development of communal experiences of love, intimacy, respect, and connectedness. Individual and community identity are intertwined. As Page and Czuba (29) highlight, "the individual and community are fundamentally connected" (p. 3) in a multidimensional journey in which people learn either to dominate and disempower others or to share power by empowering everyone.

The collective efficacy of a community appears to generate cohesion among neighborhood residents combined with shared expectations for informal social control of public space. Collective efficacy is a concept that combines the efficient use of community resources to achieve what a community defines is important. Collective efficacy builds on the beliefs people have about themselves and the actions they take to address those beliefs. Included in this concept are information and knowledge, skills to do what people need and want done, and the ability to learn and apply new information and skills to develop their communities. Consistent with the experiences of

BOX 7-1 The Broken Window Hypothesis

One theory of violence and crime in cities is called the *broken window hypothesis* (109). This theory suggests that when conditions called *structural disorder* occur in neighborhoods, crime rises (Figure 7-2). Structural disorder results when neighborhoods are not maintained. People become fearful because crime is perceived as common on the streets. Structural disorder in neighborhoods is said to be caused by poverty and mixed land use, an example of which is when residential dwellings are combined with businesses or places of manufacturing. Structural disorder in one neighborhood prompts residents to migrate to other neighborhoods. The community that is abandoned experiences lower investment, economic decline, and higher rates of robbery as the most prevalent crime. It is important to note that structural disorder does not directly promote crime, although the two are related. Both structural disorder and crime are closely associated with poverty.

FIGURE 7-2 The broken window hypothesis suggests that when structural disorder occurs in a neighborhood, a rise in crime results.
(S. Meltzer, Photolink/Getty Images.)

shared occupations already noted, collective efficacy emerges in supportive conditions that foster mutual respect, commitment, informational integration, mediation, compromise, and social cooperation (30, 31). Conditions that do not foster these qualities result in scenarios that have led to the broken window hypothesis (Box 7-1).

HOW AND WHY DID GROUP LIVING IN COMMUNITIES DEVELOP? EVOLUTIONARY HIGHLIGHTS IN DEVELOPING THE OCCUPATIONAL NATURE OF COMMUNITIES

Language to Generate and Transmit Ideas About Occupations

Humans came to live in groups specifically because we are social and occupational beings who are genetically predisposed to exist and act together (32–34). Mutuality and reciprocity appear to be an evolutionary necessity (35). Although the biological basis for humans living in groups is a complex topic, the field of neuroscience has provided some useful theories regarding why and how group living occurred. A key event in group living was the incredible increase in human brain size over thousands of years. Brain size has been closely related to the development of language.

One theory proposes that language evolved as a functional necessity for group living. Interestingly, this theory directly relates language development to group occupations. It seems that language development correlates with the greater amount of time humans spend in social grooming. From observation of primates, it seems that social grooming, a basic occupation of self-care and care of others, enables social relationships to be established. Social grooming requires individuals to be in close, physical proximity to each other for purposes other than procreation. Social and physical proximity enable the development of social relationships, initially for mutual support. Mutual support is necessary to protect one's standing in the larger social group. As social groups develop, social grooming extends to other shared occupations such as food gathering and play within groups, and posturing or fighting with other social groups. In other words, the interaction of shared occupations requires language, and language fosters more shared occupation.

A more widely accepted theory suggests that language was a consequence of group hunting or protection, which required that individuals be able to direct others to the location of threats or prey. Pinker and Bloom (36) suggest that language evolved in humans for two reasons. First, early humans cooperated in their endeavors, especially those related to protection and support. Second, they had a need to share knowledge about the local environment and their ways of doing things with their family and group members in order to sustain the group over time. As humans evolved beyond hunting and gathering to the development of agricultural communities, great benefit resulted from dividing labor. For example, cooperation in the **division of labor** enabled such innovations as the construction of irrigation systems. Communities gain stability and a sense of belonging over time by transmitting customs, rules, and beliefs from one generation to the next. This requires the use of language, which evolved to a point during the history of humankind where written symbols could be used to provide an enduring record.

Compared to other species, *Homo sapiens* is not large, fast, or strong. Humans, however, have used intellectual capacities to compete with other species and the forces of nature. A key part of this intelligence and survival has been the development and use of language. Communities are possible because of the ability to communicate, and civilizations have evolved as ideas were transmitted through oral, written, or other expressions of language from one community to another and from one generation to the next. Conversely, communities require face-to-face contacts for transmitting innovation, as in the American West Coast fishery, even within what is usually considered a homogeneous occupational group of fishers (37).

Ideas, like genes, replicate over time through successive generations. However, ideas also replicate immediately through communication between people. A **meme** refers to an idea, belief, or other bit of information that is replicated through transmission to others immediately or over time (38). **Memetics** is the science that studies the process and impact of idea generation and adoption (39). As with the science of genetics, the science of memetics has recognized that memes have benefited from

BOX 7-2   Memes: The Genes of Language

A central feature of group living is the development and spread of innovations or new ideas. Computer technologies have produced the Internet and created instant communication that assists in diffusing or spreading new ideas. This is an important development for human language and human occupation, because the sending and receiving of novel ideas sparks occupations that prompt community growth. During the 1970s, the concept of *memes* emerged to describe the evolution of cultural ideas. Memes and memetics, the study of memes, were first described by Richard Dawkins in *The Selfish Gene* (38). The term refers to ideas that are imitated, extended, or otherwise spread through human cultures and across generations. Dawkins argued that human beings are different from other social animals in that they can replicate in ways other than through genes. Because of the ability to think symbolically, humans are able to communicate ideas through stories, music, and concepts. Like genes, memes evolve, are replicated, and refined over time as they are passed along through generations of communication.

The concept of memes, as an important aspect of human evolution, has gained significant scientific support. Memes appear to be particularly important in the emergence of occupations that express culture through creative thought. Heylighen (40) points out that memes are countergenetic. That is, they serve to propagate themselves under conditions that are directly contrary to genetic means of replication. He uses the contrasting examples of celibate priests and suicide bombers as illustrations of this paradox. In both cases, there is no genetic transmission of the species. However, in each case, the goal of replicating or spreading powerful ideas is accomplished.

the contrasting forces of cooperation and competition (40). Moreover, idea generation is closely linked to human occupations, because ideas typically refer to beliefs and knowledge that influence ways of living (Box 7-2). The digital revolution is an interesting case in point. The idea that information can be harnessed electronically has enabled humans to create new industries that drastically changed the manner in which people transmit or gain information (such as through the Internet), pursue leisure (such as through electronic gaming), and perform other daily occupations from shopping to writing letters or balancing bank statements, to building cars.

The development of language also resulted in something more important than the ability to communicate. It enabled the problem-solving ability and creativity associated with intelligence (41, p. 70). As William Calvin observed, the superior intellect accompanying a larger brain not only enabled humans to develop language and symbolic thought, it also enabled the capacity for music, poetry, and humor (41). Early humans were sufficiently advanced that they were able to make and use tools, throw spears, and communicate in a primitive fashion. At some point during the human evolutionary process, for reasons that remain unclear, the human brain increased in volume as well as in problem-solving and creative ability.

Ian Tattersall suggests that the Cro-Magnon humans, who inhabited Northern Europe 40,000 years ago, were significantly more advanced in the complexity of language, occupations, and social relationships than the Neanderthals (42). Tattersall proposes that their inferior tools and poorer problem-solving ability made the Neanderthal highly vulnerable to environmental change. In contrast, the Cro-Magnons, with their larger brains, were able to begin shaping their world rather than becoming victimized by it. Apparently Neanderthal burial sites are devoid of symbolic objects, whereas Cro-Magnon graves provide evidence of a deeply spiritual way of life (42). The ability to think, to communicate, to solve problems, to share experiences and emotions, and, importantly, to anticipate the future has enabled humans to develop increasingly complex social groups with increasingly complex variations in everyday occupations. Thus, language has played a huge part in fostering the shared occupations that are fundamental to group living in communities.

Biological Forces Prompting Group Living in Communities

Sociobiology has been the traditional field generating much of the theory and research on biological evolution as a basis of group living, although many disciplines are now joining this quest. In summary, it appears that humans have taken advantage of several evolutionary strategies to survive and flourish. These include adapting to an ecological niche and finding ways to cooperate in groups to achieve survival advantage. A central process in species evolution is genetic trial and error, which enables a species to adapt to the requirements of a given environment. At the cellular level, trials take the form of successive stages of replication, which can produce advancement quickly because cells divide and multiply rapidly. Cellular changes or adaptations that work, survive. Those that fail fade into extinction. Surviving cells then replicate, only to be replaced by cells with characteristics more suited to survival. For this reason, genes are said to be selfish based on their insistence on the survival only of cells with strong survival traits. Accumulated changes occurring over generations usually result in greater chances of survival according to the environmental conditions in which the cell must exist and reproduce. It is important to note that evolutionary changes occur at multiple levels in systems. That is, they occur at three main levels: cells, organs, and the characteristics of multicellular organisms such as humans and other animals.

Three concepts that are fundamental to an understanding of the past, present, and future evolution of social animals and, thus, of communities are **ecological niche, competition,** and **cooperation.** *Ecological niche* refers to the environments or environmental conditions to which a particular species can successfully adapt. Species evolve with genetic characteristics that give them the best chance for long-term survival. For humans, it appears that the development of group living in occupational communities has been key to human evolution and survival. *Competition,* in biological terms, refers to the rivalry or struggle between or within species to secure the resources necessary for survival. Humans' symbiotic development of language and survival occupations appears to have been critical in the competition for food and shelter resources with other species and other humans. *Cooperation,* also known technically as the group or **Allee effect,** occurs when members of a species work as a group to ensure reproduction and survival of the species (43). Cooperation is rare in animals because it runs counter to the genetic tendency to be selfish, that is, for genes to compete for evolutionary survival at all cost. Thus, little cooperative organization is seen in most species of insects, fish, lizards, birds, or mammals except for occasional demonstrations of cooperation among parents and offspring. Where cooperation does exist, it never reaches the level of complexity in daily occupations that is achieved by human societies.

Biological Cooperation and Altruism as Foundations for Shared Occupations

Both language and biological traits of problem solving and creativity have made it possible for humans to develop cooperation and altruism in shared occupations. The willingness of an organism to cooperate with another for survival requires **altruism** according to Trivers (44). These two biological traits are actually the building blocks for shared occupations discussed earlier under the question *What makes communities inherently social and occupational?* In biology, altruism means the active donation of resources to one or more individuals at cost to the donor. This definition is strictly resource based and has no moral connotation. It goes beyond the sharing that occurs among parents and offspring (known as kin selection) to a reciprocal sharing of resources among members of a group who are not related. Beyond humans and other primates, examples of reciprocal altruism have been found only in a few species of animals such as vampire bats, dolphins, and elephants, and in some species of monkeys and apes.

Certain conditions must exist in order for altruistic cooperation to succeed biologically. The biological tendency to compete for advantage and survival results in attempts by some group members to take advantage of the efforts of the group. This is known as the **free rider problem.** Biological cooperation succeeds in nature only when there are biological penalties (being eaten or poisoned) or social sanctions against those who cheat or take advantage of the circumstances by not doing their share. The expression "gaming the system" means cheating, or taking advantage of a group's lack of effective safeguards against cheaters. Nonhuman species, such as elephants or wolves, exert social sanctions by ostracizing members who bully the group or by attacking and killing same or other species that interfere with mating or parenting of the young.

Because every group will have rule breakers, effective cooperation requires precautions, often in the form of systems for the detection of cheating and exploitation, and mechanisms to confirm group identification. Systems of social consent or trust develop as a result of long term group-living. In such systems, members are able to recognize each other as individuals, recall the history of cooperation by each member, and keep track of help given and help received. Reciprocal altruism can occur in the absence of close genetic relationships, but only if those who receive aid do so with the understanding that they will reciprocate (44). Moore took the idea of reciprocity to the practical level of everyday occupations in an analysis of the need to synchronize human activity cycles for group cooperation (45).

FIGURE 7-3 The ability to hold a pencil or writing tool is an example of an exaptation. (Keith Brofsky/Getty Images.)

Adaptation and Exaptation in Shared Occupations

Language and biological evolution underpin theories such as game theory, as well as concepts such as adaptation and exaptation. The word **adaptation** is formed by the combination of the Latin words *ad + aptus*, which together mean "toward a particular fit." The adaptation described here refers to the fit between biological organisms and the demands of their environments. Rather than adapting, some species have experienced **exaptations,** a term proposed by Gould and Vrba (46). Exaptations refer to evolved traits that are functional. They have emerged not as the result of genetic changes, but rather as opportunistic consequences of such changes. Gould and Vrba cite as an example the human hand and its ability to write (Figure 7-3). They note that humans did not evolve fingers to hold pencils and pens. However, a side effect or consequence of manual dexterity, which was evolved for reasons other than writing, enabled the ability to write. It may be useful to view exaptations as extensions of evolutionary adaptations. The invention of many tools and their corresponding occupations are examples of exaptations rather than adaptations. Imagine the disadvantage posed to communities in the modern world if members could not read or write or use banks and accounting systems. Exaptations have thus led to many occupations that are vital to group living in communities.

Game Theory and Shared Occupations

Because cooperation is a central feature of group living, researchers have long been interested in understanding the conditions under which cooperation evolves. One interpretation comes out of game theory. **Game theory** is the mathematical study of games and strategy, and it represents one of the most important 20th-century developments in the social sciences. The most significant early work in this area was done in the 1940s by John von Neumann and Oskar Morgenstern (47). The purpose of game theory is to determine the most likely strategy to be used by each player from a given set of rules and to find the best strategy. Game theory tries to understand the strategy of a game rather than its elements of chance. Its purpose is to understand how decisions are made between individuals or groups, based on a belief that players in any competitive situation have preferences and multiple options, and that they pursue their individual interests logically and to the best of their ability.

Game theory proposes that competing strategies create balance that furthers the survival of the population. This is known as an evolutionary stable strategy. Game theory also suggests that social animals learn that cooperation is in their best interest. Game theory emphasizes the importance of communication and symbolic reasoning and suggests that the evolution of these capabilities in humans has helped create the conditions that enabled cooperation to become a viable strategy in evolution. Game theory provides evidence that the communication of ideas in modern society may be equally important to the transmission of genes (48). The evolution of community occupations requires reciprocal altruism in the form of cooperation that was made possible by the development of language. Because cooperative strategies place a group at risk for free riders, rules and sanctions are necessary to ensure conformity and maintain the group while also teaching behavioral expectations to younger group members. Box 7-3 describes an exercise called **Prisoner's Dilemma,** which is used to study cooperation. Consider the occupational choices presented. One choice will restrict occupations in prison, the other will release the person to engage in a wider range of occupations.

HOW AND WHY DO OCCUPATIONS DETERMINE A COMMUNITY'S POTENTIAL TO FLOUNDER OR FLOURISH?

Let us now turn to the question of how and why occupations determine a community's potential to flounder or flourish. A flourishing community appears to offer positive experiences of interdependent participation in occupations (49, 50). Occupations that characterize community life are documented through historical records, logos, films, and other media. Moreover, expressions of individual agency (power, excitement) are balanced with communal expressions of mutual respect, love, accommodation, and connectedness (51, 52). Individual identity and empowerment develop through individual and shared occupations in a supportive community context (53–55).

BOX 7-3 Game Theory: The Prisoner's Dilemma

In the social sciences, game theory has focused mostly on non-zero-sum games, particularly those where payoffs are such that players are better off if they select strategies of cooperation rather than competition. The classic model of this situation is called *Prisoner's Dilemma* (110). The Prisoner's Dilemma game and its variations are used to illustrate and understand economic, social, and political conflict and the coordination that is required for social groups to achieve desired outcomes. Game theory has been used as a means of demonstrating how cooperative strategies may explain the evolution of social groups and communities. This theory of cooperation contradicts evolutionary theories as explained by genetics. Whereas game theory considers cooperation, evolutionary theories consider competition as a "zero-sum" process. That is to say, competition results in winners and losers, in contrast to cooperation in which everyone can be a winner or everyone can be a loser. Game theory proposes that people select strategies of cooperation with varying results.

The name of the Prisoner's Dilemma game is derived from the following situation typically used to exemplify it:

> Suppose that the police have arrested two people who they know have committed an armed robbery together. Unfortunately, they lack enough admissible evidence to get a jury to convict. They do, however, have enough evidence to send each prisoner away for two years for theft of the getaway car. The chief inspector now makes the following offer to each prisoner: If you will confess to the robbery, implicating your partner, and she does not also confess, then you'll go free and she'll get 10 years. If you both confess, you'll each get 5 years. If neither of you confess, then you'll each get 2 years for the auto theft.

Most people think that the outcome of the Prisoner's Dilemma will be that the two prisoners cooperate with each other and each refuses to confess in order to secure the best outcome for both (2 years in prison). In contrast, the expected outcome of the Prisoner's Dilemma in game theory is that neither cooperates with the partner to refuse confession. Rather they both strategize to cooperate with the chief inspector to confess and implicate the partner, thinking that the other partner will not confess. Each believes that a confession and implication of the partner will result in personal freedom while the partner faces 10 years. In other words, under pressure of imprisonment, cooperation with the partner disappears, and cooperation with authority and self-interest prevail. Each partner's shift in cooperation from their partner to the chief inspector results in an outcome where both confess, both implicate the other partner, and both receive 5 years, rather than the 2 years they would have received if they had retained solidarity with the partner and neither had confessed.

Throughout this section, there is an underlying theme that occupations occur within community organization and structure. Positive occupational experiences are made possible by organizing and building communities with explicit aims to promote health, wellness, quality of life, and justice (11, 21, 56). However, the everyday world of occupations is problematic if policies and other regulations do not support these goals. State representatives are challenged to create sufficient social support for health and quality of life without undermining social freedoms (57). If the primary focus of education, health, employment, and other institutions defines efficiency and accountability only from the perspective of professions, management, and business, person-centered goals for quality of life are undermined. In this section we consider a range of occupations and structural features that are instrumental to a community's potential to flounder or flourish (58).

Participation in Occupations

Participation and partnership are two central, interconnected features of flourishing communities. A fundamental principle in community development is that community members are active participants and partners in all actions, particularly in decision making (49, 59–73). Participation is a people-centered approach through which people not only take on a community identity, they also generate their own empowerment to shape the community to their interests and needs (61, 64). As disadvantaged community members participate, rather than accepting their dependence, they generate a common vision and awareness of the radical changes needed to create a more inclusive community structure and organization (65, 66). An important feature in these community occupations is their generation of optimism and hope (67).

Participatory research has grown particularly since the 1970s as a means of involving oppressed or disadvantaged people in their own empowerment through participation in occupations that change their daily lives as well as their communities (66, 68–72). Scott MacAulay (73) offers an interesting comparison between two powerful community economic development traditions in Nova Scotia on Canada's East Coast. He analyzes similarities and differences in citizen participation in the Antigonish Movement (from 1939, continuing today as an inspiration for community initiatives) and the Family of community development corporations (starting in the early 1970s), which includes New Dawn Enterprises Limited, the oldest community development corporation in Canada. These are examples of changing community occupations by engaging in strategic occupations that promote participation, education, and decision making. As MacAulay says (73):

> The innovation of the Antigonish Movement was its combination of a commitment to economic democracy through consumer co-operatives with a program of adult education that was to be brought directly to workers and primary producers. (p. 113)

Whereas,

> the Family of community development corporations is a strategic effort by a small group of people in the community. They volunteer their expertise and scarce time to work on behalf of the whole community. (p. 115)

Participation by citizens and partnership with government officials sparked a variety of volunteer and community-oriented occupations that had as their aim social change as well as economic development. Quoting Jim Lotz, a local commentator on community economic development, MacAulay considers that these participatory initiatives offer lessons for the world:

> The Antigonish Movement flowered here, and the community economic ventures that started with New Dawn have created a history of local achievement through which both local residents and government officials have learned much about working together in mutually beneficial ways. That history, in fact, is a rich and marketable resource. (74, p. 253)

In discussing "continuities and discontinuities" between these movements, MacAulay (73) points to differences in participation and partnership in educational and decision-making occupations. The Antigonish Movement was based on community cooperatives and study clubs that promoted reflective self-awareness and active participation in economic, educational, and social occupations. In contrast, the Family of community development corporations was managed by a core group of volunteers who took a business approach with a focus on policy and economic occupations.

Occupations That Express Cultural Rituals and Rules

Williams (75) proposes that rules or expectations for successful group living have evolved over time. Groups need to ensure health and survival, as well as adequate biological reproduction. However, groups and communities only flourish when there is a means to socialize children into the group as productive members. Also needed is a means of communicating skills and values to all group members. Of major importance for communities to flourish is a system of sanctions or authority mechanisms to ensure that group members comply with expectations or abide by rules (21, 76). This is a delicate matter of balance. On the one hand, communities need to regulate compliance with everyday occupations that create community cohesion (driving on the same side of the road, sanctions against violent occupations, etc.). On the other hand, communities need regulations that protect individuals and groups so they can be different yet equal and also express different ways of knowing and doing (11).

As the oldest, continuous communities on earth, Australia's aboriginal communities have been studied extensively for clues regarding societal development. Australian aboriginal settlement dates back more than 50,000 years, and the tools and symbols used in the occupations of this culture are reminiscent of those used by early Europeans. Their language and occupations appear to have been used to define the cultural rituals and rules of their communities. In addition, the everyday occupations of sharing living quarters appear to be closely tied to the biological and social survival of communities. Lévi-Strauss, one of the early anthropologists who studied Australian aboriginal people, points out that taboos against incest are made possible through designations of kinship that provide guidance for alliances and residential arrangements (77). These people resisted agricultural occupations, possibly because subsistence was provided through plentiful seas and the natural animals and plants of the Australian bush. They also relied on a loosely organized tribal elder system for the occupations of group decision making, rather than developing more formalized institutional systems (77).

We can learn from Australian and other aboriginal groups about the making of successful communities (78, 79). Rituals and rules that encourage voluntary cooperation in the division of labor are extremely important. Also critical is the huge range of decision-making and management occupations that make social governance systems work. Primary resource communities rely on the occupations of farmers, fishers, and wood workers. In contrast, industrial and technical communities rely on the occupations of plant workers, scientists, teachers, health professionals, and many others. Collectively, communities need occupations that attend to the cultural rituals and rules required for that community to flourish. Communities need diversity and ongoing negotiation. Parents, teachers, and child care workers help to socialize children into groups but also to give voice to children's and others' differences. Those employed in the legislative, law enforcement, judicial, and correctional systems need to listen to diverse voices as they develop systems of rules and sanctions for living in communities.

Occupations That Offer Artistic Expression

Artistic expression has occupied humans virtually since the dawn of our species (Box 7-4). Communities that flourish appear to support occupations that offer artistic expression. These include the pursuit of literature, music, dance, and forms of visual art that enrich the experience of life and contribute to the "soul" of a culture. In the minds of many, occupations that offer artistic expression are a distinguishing feature of thriving versus merely surviving communities. Philosophy, religion, home design, community planning, and the creative use of everyday

---

BOX 7-4   Evidence of Artistic Expression by Prehistoric Humans

Approximately 20,000 years ago, humans in Europe lived primarily as hunters. It is likely that questions about the nature of life were becoming common to these people who sought to understand the world about them. Early explanations of existence gave rise to ideas about magic and mythology. The greatest evidence of such ideas is found in prehistoric cave paintings. These mainly depict animals, which, in the cave dweller's primary occupation as hunters, they believed were their source of life.

FIGURE 7-4   Prehistoric cave paintings provide clues to early humans' thinking about magic and mythology.
(Albert J. Copley/Getty Images.)

materials are all expressions that occur through what people think and do each day. Humans understand that life is finite. Within that sense of previous time and opportunity, communities seem to flourish when members are at liberty, individually and collectively, to explore a sense of self, relationships with and perceptions of other beings, creation, purpose, and place within the universe. Like participation and cultural expression, artistry thrives when community organization and structures balance both freedom and compliance with agreed social sanctions.

Occupations That Sustain Communities

A key concept in modern community development is **sustainability** (80). The current world emphasis on sustainability gained prominence in a United Nations conference called the Earth Summit held in Rio de Janeiro, Brazil, in 1992 and in Johannesburg, South Africa in 2002. However, the idea of conserving natural resources dates back more than 2,000 years. The United Nations defines a sustainable society as one that meets the needs of the present without sacrificing the ability of future generations to meet their own needs (81).

According to the model principles for sustainable communities proposed by the Ontario Roundtable on Environment and Economy (Table 7-2), sustainable communities take responsibilities for themselves. They do not compromise the sustainability

TABLE 7-2 *Model Principles for Sustainable Communities*

A sustainable community is one that

1. Recognizes that growth occurs within some limits and is ultimately limited by the carrying capacity of the environment
2. Values cultural diversity
3. Has respect for other life forms and supports biodiversity
4. Has shared values among the members of the community (promoted through sustainability education)
5. Employs ecological decision making (e.g., integration of environmental criteria into all municipal government, business, and personal decision-making processes)
6. Makes decisions and plans in a balanced, open, and flexible manner that includes the perspectives from the social, health, economic, and environmental sectors of the community
7. Makes best use of local efforts and resources (nurtures solutions at the local level)
8. Uses renewable and reliable sources of energy
9. Minimizes harm to the natural environment
10. Fosters activities that use materials in continuous cycles

And, as a result, a sustainable community

11. Does not compromise the sustainability of other communities (a geographic perspective)
12. Does not compromise the sustainability of future generations by its activities (a temporal perspective)

Source: Ontario Roundtable on Environment and Economy, 1994 (82, pp. 43–47).

of other communities or future generations. The occupations related to community sustainability include those that organize, use, and protect energy; those that mine yet also study natural resources; those that tend rather than exploit the natural environment; and those that address humans' needs for food, shelter, goods, enjoyment, and biological reproduction. Human occupations that are consistent with community sustainability involve the production, purchasing, and selection of energy and environmentally friendly goods. Reusing, renovating, and recycling are occupations that now take considerable time in many homes and businesses. Sustainability occupations are driven by values for cultural diversity, that is, respect for other life forms including plants and animals.

Sociopolitical occupations of community sustainability control public and private decision making on policies and regulations (65). A prosperous economy is of little use to a local community if its people are not employed in paid occupations, or if the available paid occupations undermine community sustainability. When the only paid occupations are in factories that pollute the air or water of a community, community members find their occupations and their ideas about a sustainable planet in conflict. An economically vibrant community will not thrive for long if it does so at the expense of people's health or without safeguarding the environment.

The dilemma is that many businesses and occupations that generate economic wealth to sustain communities will not move to places where workers are only interested in an easy lifestyle (83). A debate continues between those who view natural resources as finite and likely to diminish as population growth continues, and those who believe that human enterprise and ingenuity will create solutions to problems through technology and resourcefulness (84). Inherent in this debate are difficult occupational choices for individuals and groups to make if they want sustainable, flourishing communities.

Group living in communities is what enables individuals to work together in occupations that enable communities to flourish. New partnerships are springing up that involve participants in occupations as individuals, as members of community environmental groups, as industry and business partners, as representatives of universities and schools, or as representatives of local and national governments.

The Healthy Communities Movement is an example of advocacy for sustainable, healthy communities (Box 7-5). Shared occupations are focused on health, with a common purpose of creating stable, ongoing community structures as well as positive experiences of participation in health-producing behaviors. Community empowerment is both a means and a result of a strategy to involve a total community in health promotion occupations (53, 85–87).

Of particular note is the importance of creating a health-enhancing built environment to encourage health-promoting occupations. Needed is interdependence—between built form and overall quality of life, as measured by health, safety, welfare, transportation, and land development. Frank and Engelke (56) analyze literature on transportation and land use planning to illustrate the impact on physical activity of the built environment. They conclude that "land development patterns define the arrangement of activities and impact the proximity between trip origins and destinations" (p. 210).

BOX 7-5   Group Advocacy for Community Improvement

The Healthy Communities Movement

The Healthy Communities Movement was started by Trevor Hancock and Len Duhl in 1986 in Toronto, Canada, as part of a World Health Organization initiative (111). Its purpose was to assemble health institutions, businesses, nonprofit organizations, community groups, and individuals to address community well-being using a systems perspective. This approach views communities as environments that enable the well-being of their inhabitants. Healthy communities provide the jobs, educational systems, and public safety and health services necessary to support satisfying lifestyles. A key part of a healthy community is the involvement of the entire community in problem-solving occupations. Participation in group problem solving is viewed as a group occupation necessary for the community to flourish.

Interestingly, the historical roots of this initiative go back to the Healthy Towns Movement in mid-19th-century Britain. Hundreds of communities across the globe are now making efforts that started almost two centuries ago to improve the health of the working poor in growing industrial cities. A Healthy Towns commission looked into the causes of health and saw a direct correlation between poor health and the conditions within towns and cities. The Healthy Towns movement spread beyond Britain and led to major improvements in public health, building, and sanitation, such as the creation of improved water supplies.

The growth of the current worldwide Healthy Communities Movement has gathered energy from social sentiments that favor local solutions over the bureaucracy required for action at the national level. Concerns about community issues, such as the rise in violence, crime, poverty, and abused and neglected children, have created a sense that communities are disconnected and threatened. These concerns have been used to spearhead community approaches that promote health by tending to a community's root problems.

Most supporters of the Healthy Communities Movement look for solutions beyond improving the physical health of communities. At its core, this movement requires power sharing among individuals and groups in an effort to improve the quality of life for all. Their efforts are aimed at the development of social capital and the development or rejuvenation of community spirit. To foster change, groups become learning communities that seek to modify strategies rather than just attain goals. The idea is that community change will not last unless shared approaches to decision making and responsibility, including power sharing, become an established part of community life.

Magic, Religion, and Science

Magic, religion, and *science* are terms that describe collective thinking aimed at understanding the world and the events that happen in it. These "occupations of understanding" each have creeds, codes, and cultures. That is, they represent certain beliefs, they establish doctrines or expectations for behavior based on those beliefs, and they evolve practices that encourage or enforce the principles of the belief system. Throughout the ages, humans have wanted to know about natural phenomena that occur and are beyond their control (such as death, lightning, or earthquakes). The occupations of magic and religion, have been intertwined over the centuries, since they each deal with nonmaterial aspects of life. Humans have developed ideas and actions of magic, witchcraft, or religion as explanations for accidents, chance occurrences, or events that happen in nature (88).

Cultural groups, even those with complex civil structures, have typically developed occupations to divine the meaning of natural or supernatural events. Examples of occupations involved in divination are tarot card reading, palm or tea leaf reading, and the reading of astrological charts. Rituals have either linked humans to gods and goddesses or granted a select group the occupational status of divine representation. Our daily lives in North America and elsewhere commonly reflect vestiges of concern with the supernatural. Many people wear amulets, or good luck charms, and their occupations are shaped by superstitions, such as avoiding being under a ladder or throwing salt over one's shoulder if it is spilled. Organized religion provides a practical occupation for drawing people together in action toward mutual goals (Figure 7-5) (89). Whether this involves traditional or new forms of religious or spiritual expression, religious or spiritual occupations foster mutuality, interdependence, and reciprocity within a particular community.

Philosophers over the ages, beginning with Aristotle, began to counter supernatural explanations of occurrences with a preference for experimentation and logic (90). The scientific revolution that started in the middle ages has not changed beliefs in magic or other supernatural forces for many people because they continue to ponder as yet unanswered questions (90). Nevertheless, a new wave of scientific investigation includes empirical work as well as the insights and diverse ways of knowing generated through cooperative, participatory, interpretive, and critical inquiries (91, 92).

The importance of magic, religion, and science in communities is apparent in the occupations attached to them. In addition, communities that seem to flourish also value and preserve buildings, artifacts, symbols, traditions, routines, and rituals. The occupations that express these interests are visible in the horoscopes, worship rituals, and accepted research methods of investigation employed within a community. It seems that flourishing communities tolerate diverse occupations that express diverse ideas about magic, religion, and science. Conflict and violence appear to erupt where some magic, religion, or scientific occupations are confined or even punished while others are celebrated. Unequal sanctioning of these important occupations seems to divide rather than unite communities.

FIGURE 7-5   Weddings as community rituals. Throughout the world, weddings serve as a common and visible reminder of the importance of public ceremonies and rituals in fostering shared beliefs and traditions. Typically, weddings involve symbols, rituals, superstitions, and elements of religion. In this photo, friends and neighbors enjoy a traditional Jewish dance following the wedding ceremony.
(Buccina Studios/Getty Images.)

Volunteer Occupations

Volunteer occupations appear to build cooperation and enhance the social and possibly the economic strength of communities. Volunteer occupations are those in which people give time, resources, effort, skills, and abilities to serve other people without formal expectation of recognition or reward (93). Ellis and Noyes (94) define volunteerism as those ". . . acts taken in recognition of a need, with an attitude of social responsibility. . . . To volunteer is to go beyond one's basic obligations" (p. 4).

Through a tremendous range of volunteer occupations, people help others in almost all aspects of life. Volunteers help to construct homes, provide health services, care for elderly citizens, look after children, attend to children and adolescents in the classroom or library, welcome community newcomers, judge projects at science fairs or Special Olympics, clean and maintain public areas, and tutor and mentor learners of all ages. Retired workers, persons without employment, and others may also volunteer to support public or nonprofit agencies by publishing newsletters or preparing correspondence.

There are many benefits to volunteerism, both to communities and organizations, as well as to the volunteers themselves (95). Benefits to communities include developing informal support networks that provide assistance otherwise not available and providing meaningful roles for retired individuals and others seeking opportunities to serve their communities. While businesses are oriented to private interests and governments are oriented to public interests, volunteers focus on the interests of social groups within the society—including disadvantaged groups whose members are poor or living with a disability (96).

Wuthnow (97) noted that "Voluntarism symbolises the antithesis of impersonality, bureaucracy, materialism, utilitarianism, and many of the other dominant cultural trends we worry about in our society" (p. 305). Benefits of volunteerism to individuals include developing a sense of self-satisfaction, learning new skills, developing rewarding social relationships, enhancing career opportunities, and providing affirmation and a sense of completion through doing something that others say is important. Coles (98) suggests that the most successful volunteers are those who like interacting with others, who do not view volunteering as a sacrifice, and who realize that volunteering is a practical occupation that conveys reciprocal benefits.

Work and Employment: Occupations That Generate Economic Capital

Work is the most publicly recognized occupation. In fact, the most typical answer to the question "What do you do?" is for people to describe their paid work, even though they are actually occupied in parenting, maintaining a home, studying, caregiving, sports, games, or other occupations. Most writing about occupation in communities is about work and employment—about occupational classification and the division of labor, occupational health and safety on the job, occupational satisfaction with career choices, occupational training and retraining or retooling, occupational transitions as people change jobs or retire, and so on.

It is clear throughout this chapter that the occupations of work and employment are only part of the occupational nature of communities. Work and employment are not even the full source of community economic development. Look at the bartering and self-sufficiency occupations that create an informal, underground economy.

Being employed in work occupations has obvious financial benefits for individuals, their families, and their communities. The income gained through employment provides the means to purchase goods that meet basic survival needs such as housing, food, and clothing. The economic profits of paid work also provide people with financial independence and the opportunity to make choices in their lives. The quality of employment in one's working life also has consequences for financial independence in retirement.

Beyond meeting material needs and desires, employment has many nonfinancial benefits that enable communities as well as individuals to flourish. Having a job provides individuals with a sense of identity and contributes to the "common good." Employment provides individuals with opportunities to form social associations that foster community connectedness outside the family. Paid work involves people in regular physical, intellectual, and social interactions that offer communities the resources of their knowledge, skills, and capacities. Employment also imposes a routine or time structure to the day and week and allows nonwork time to be defined and used as leisure.

BOX 7-6   The Concept of Mass-Society

The concept of mass-society underpins interest in fostering the idea of social capital, including the idea that successful communities develop trust and cooperation. A mass-society is viewed as one in which industry and bureaucracy have eroded traditional social ties. The concept of mass-society refers to communities and societies that have deteriorated to the point where there is weak kinship, impersonal neighborhoods, and a feeling by individuals that they are isolated and alienated.

The concept of mass-society grew out of the work of Emile Durkheim, (14), Ferdinand Tonnies (112), and Max Weber (113) . The major argument is that the scale of modern life has increased in size as a result of industrialization. The result has been an increasing rate of change, an increasing gap between social differences, and weakening moral values. Modern communities lack the solidarity required to clearly define and uphold social sanctions. In a mass-society, people are known more by their jobs than through kinship, and personal communication has gradually been replaced by mass media. Advocates of the concept of mass-society argue that there may be some benefits to changes taking place in communities. However, geographic mobility, mass communications, and tolerance for social diversity in modern communities have eroded traditional values. Furthermore, individual rights and freedom of choice are achieved at the expense of cultural heritage. In such communities, individuals have too many choices and very few boundaries to define what is important to the community. Although individuals have many rights, responsibilities, and freedoms, they also feel isolated, powerless, and materialistic.

Occupations That Generate Social Capital

The concept of social capital was proposed to counter the emphasis on economic capital as an indicator of a community's well-being. **Social capital** is defined as the set of informal values or norms shared among members of a group that permits cooperation among them (99). Social capital is not a static phenomenon; it is actively built and destroyed through human actions and processes. Drawing together the ideas of Putnam (100) and Coleman (101), social capital has been described as (1) obligations, expectations, and trustworthiness of structure; (2) information channels or networks; and (3) norms and effective sanctions. The idea of social capital has grown out of the concept of mass-society (Box 7-6). In a world with weakening kinship, impersonal neighborhoods, and feelings of isolation and alienation, social capital is viewed as an antidote to mass society.

The idea of social capital as a result of or indeed a form of occupation has received less attention. Volunteerism, civic participation, social and political involvement, and community engagement are the occupations through which trustworthy structures, networks, and norms are founded and facilitated within communities.

Occupations that generate social capital facilitate the interdependence, communal experiences, and individual identity within a community context that are fundamental to flourishing communities. The presence of occupations that generate social capital, in effect, is a barometer of cooperation and community success. Cooperation, as has been noted, is a fundamental requirement for the evolution of humans living in groups, and cooperation remains essential if societies are to flourish. Cooperation in the occupations of social capital makes it possible to develop efficiencies and accountability for creating community life beyond economic wealth. It seems reasonable to assume that flourishing communities generate both social and economic capital, neither one being sufficient for humans without the other.

Occupation in Communities That Flounder

This chapter has emphasized the positive occupational nature of communities. The underside is that the lack of certain occupations or occupational experiences undermines communities. Communities that flounder, in essence, are without the occupations, the experiences of shared occupation, and the organization and built environment through which communities flourish. Lacking are experiences of interdependence, shared history, and possibilities for individual identity to grow within a supportive, interconnected, respectful communal environment. Lacking also are occupations that enable a community to express a diversity of routines, rules, artistry, magic, religion, and science. Volunteer and paid occupations build only economic capital rather without social capital. Lack of cooperation undermines the trust, effective communication, and systems required to govern group living. Lack of organizational and physical environmental support makes it impossible to participate in some community occupations. Without supportive organization and structures, communities limit citizens from occupations. A concrete example is communities that limit people from walking to work to promote health when there are no safe walkways. Floundering communities seem likely to limit people from engaging in diverse cultural or religious occupations when there are punitive sanctions.

Moreover, it seems that communities flounder if some members are deprived of occupation or they are somehow isolated and alienated from the occupations that they need or want to do. Occupational deprivation is the inability of people to engage in daily occupations that they define as meaningful for reasons beyond their control (102–104) (see also Chapter 10). Communities also flounder when a major discrepancy exists between groups that have nothing much to do and groups that are overburdened by too much to do. Such a gap is particularly dangerous to communities if those without something to do live in poverty and crime, while those with too much to do have garnered a large proportion of available economic resources. These occupational discrepancies are symptoms of occupational injustice—injustices that go beyond limitations of rights, responsibilities, and freedoms. Occupational injustices occur when some groups in society are deprived of occupations, alienated from their true occupational selves or restricted and possibly exploited in their occupations (105) (see also Chapter 11).

The poverty inflicted by unemployment has many material and nonmaterial effects that limit occupational choices, social participation, and social networks for those in communities. Moreover, violence is caused by multiple factors, including the disintegration of family life, poverty, social influences such as the availability of weapons and antisocial peer influence, and substance abuse or mental illness (106–108). Floundering communities seem to lose the struggle to address painful occupations resulting from child abuse and neglect, adolescent delinquency, adult criminality, senior abuse, or other persistent social violence.

CHAPTER SUMMARY

Three questions have been addressed in considering the occupational nature of communities: (1) What makes communities inherently social and occupational? (2) How and why did group living in communities develop? (3) How and why do occupations determine a community's potential to flounder or flourish? The premise was that occupations are a central feature of successful communities since occupations are essentially social and occur in a social context. Literature and examples have illustrated experiences of shared occupations, biological forces shaping occupations, and various occupations that appear to be necessary for communities to flourish. It was noted that, conversely, communities that lack the conditions and occupations that promote quality of life seem more likely to flounder. It seems that communities need occupations that generate social as well as economic capital, with a supportive organization and built environment. Individuals need community supports for occupational experiences of positive interdependence, respect, connectedness, and resource sharing. The occupational nature of communities is thus central in determining whether individuals and communities will flourish or flounder. This means that communities have the power to use and support occupations to generate both social and economic benefits in areas such as education, parenting, health, employment, retirement, transportation, land use planning, decision making, and policy development. Occupations, it seems, are the foundation for economically productive and healthy communities where quality of life is paramount.

Acknowledgment

We are grateful to Loretta de Rozario, Ph.D., and Susan Pettifor, M.A., for their early contributions to the conception of this chapter.

REFERENCES

1. Poplin, D. (1979). In Poplin, D. (Ed.), Theories of community. In *Communities: A survey of theories and methods of research* (pp. 63–107). 2nd ed., New York: McMillan.
2. MacLeod, A. (1999). *No great mischief.* Toronto, Ontario: MacLennan and Stewart.
3. do Rozario L. (1998). From ageing to sageing: Eldering and the art of being as occupation. *Journal of Occupational Science: Australia, 5*(3), 119–126.

4. Lamoureux, H., Mayer, R., & Panet-Raymond, J. (1989). *Community action.* Montreal: Black Rose Books.
5. Rousseau, C. (1993). Community empowerment: The alternative resources movement in Quebec. *Community Mental Health Journal, 29,* 535–546.
6. Condeluci, A. (1991). *Interdependence: The route to community.* Orlando, Fl: Paul M. Deutsch, Co.
7. Jordan, J. (1991). The meaning of mutuality. In J. Jordan, A. G. Kaplan, J. B. Miller, I. P. Stiver, & I. L. Surrey (Eds.), *Women's growth in connection: Writings from the Stone Center* (pp. 81–96). New York: Guilford.
8. Ignatieff, M. (1995). *Blood and belonging.* London: Farrar, Straus, & Giroux.
9. Ignatieff, M. (1984). *The needs of strangers: An essay on privacy, solidarity and the politics of being human.* New York: Penguin Group.
10. Ignatieff, M. (2000). *The rights revolution.* Toronto, Ontario: House of Anansi.
11. Belenky, M. F., Bond, L. A., & Weinstock S. (1997). *A tradition that has no name: Nurturing the development of people, families, and communities.* New York: Basic Books.
12. Belensky, M. F., Clinchy, B. M., Goldberger, N. R., & Tarule, J. M. (1986). *Women's ways of knowing: The development of self, voice and mind.* New York: Basic Books.
13. Rubin, I. (1983). Function and structure of community: Conceptual and theoretical analysis. In R. L. W. L. Lyon (Ed.), *New perspectives on the American community* (pp. 54–61). Homewood, IL: Dorsey Press.
14. Durkheim, E. (1964). *The division of labor in society.* New York: The Free Press.
15. Brown, K. (1990). Connected independence: A paradox of rural health? *Journal of Rural Community Psychology, 11,* 51–64.
16. Pentland, W., Krupa, T., Lynch, S., & Clark, C. (1992). Community integration for persons with disabilities: Working together to make it happen. *Canadian Journal of Occupational Therapy, 59,* 127–130.
17. Townsend, E. (1997). Inclusiveness: A community dimension of spirituality. *Canadian Journal of Occupational Therapy, 64*(3), 146–155.
18. Townsend, E., Birch, D., Langille, L., & Langley, J. (2000). Participatory research in a mental health clubhouse. *Occupational Therapy Journal of Research, 20,* 18–44.
19. Lord, J. (1987). *Toward independence and community: A qualitative study of independent living centres in Canada.* Canada: Secretary of State.
20. Oakley, P. (1998). Community development in the Third World in the 1990s. Review article. *Community Development Journal, 33*(4), 365–376.
21. Maton, K. I., & Salem, D. A. (1995). Organizational characteristics of empowering community settings: A multiple case study approach. *American Journal of Community Psychology, 23*(5), 631–656.
22. Etzioni, A. (1993). *The spirit of community: Rights, responsibilities, and the communitarian agenda.* New York: Crown.
23. McMillan, D.W., Chavis, D. M. Sense of community: A definition and theory. *Journal of Community Psychology, 14*(1), 6–23.
24. Pretty, G. (1990). Relating psychological sense of community to social climate characteristics. *Journal of Community Psychology, 22,* 346–358.
25. Hogan, R. (1983). A socioanalytic theory of personality. In M. M. Page (Ed.), *Nebraska symposium on motivation* (pp. 55–90). Lincoln: University of Nebraska Press.
26. Adler, A. (1927). *The practice and theory of individual psychology.* New York: Harcourt Brace.

27. Kegan, R. (1982). *The evolving self: Problem and process in human development.* Cambridge, MA: Harvard University Press.

28. Bakan, D. (1966). *The duality of human existence: Isolation and communion in Western man.* Boston: Beacon Press.

29. Page, N., & Czuba, C. (1999). Empowerment: What is it? *Journal of Extension, 37*(5) published on www at www.joe.org.

30. Bandura, A. (2000). Exercise of human agency through collective efficacy. *Current Directions in Psychological Science, 9,* 75–78.

31. Peterson, E., Mitchell, T., Thompson, L., & Burr, R. (2000). Collective efficacy and aspects of shared mental models as predictors of performance over time in work groups. *Group Processes and Intergroup Relations, 3*(3), 296–316.

32. Clark, F. (1997). Reflections on the human as an occupational being: Biological need, tempo and temporality. *Journal of Occupational Science: Australia, 4*(3), 86–92.

33. Wilcock, A. A. (1998). Reflections on doing, being and becoming. *Canadian Journal of Occupational Therapy, 65*(5), 248–256.

34. Wilcock, A. A. (1998). *An occupational perspective of health.* Thorofare, NJ: Slack.

35. Kropotkin, P. (1989). *Mutual aid: A factor of evolution.* Montreal: Black Rose Books.

36. Pinker, S., & Bloom, P. (1990). Natural language and natural selection. Behavioral and Brain Sciences, *13,* 707–784.

37. Smith, C. L., & Hanna, S. S. (1993). Occupation and community as determinants of fishing behaviours. *Human Organization, 52*(3), 299–303.

38. Dawkins, R. (1989). *The selfish gene* (2nd ed.). Oxford: Oxford University Press.

39. Aunger, R. (Ed.). (2000). *Darwinizing culture: The status of memetics as a science.* Oxford: Oxford University Press.

40. Heylighen, F. (1992). Selfish memes and the evolution of cooperation. *Journal of Ideas, 2*(4), 77–84.

41. Calvin, W. H. (1986). *The river that flows uphill: A journey from the big bang to the big brain.* San Francisco: Sierra Club Books.

42. Tattersall, I. (1998). *Becoming human: Evolution and human uniqueness.* New York: Harcourt Brace.

43. Allee, W. C. (1934). *Animal aggregations: A study in general sociology.* Chicago: University of Chicago Press.

44. Trivers, R. L. (1971). The evolution of reciprocal altruism. *Quarterly Review of Biology, 46,* 35–57.

45. Moore, A. (1995). The band community: Synchronizing human activity cycles for group cooperation. In R. Z F. Clark (Ed.), *Occupational science: The emerging discipline* (pp. 95–106). Philadelphia: F. A. Davis.

46. Gould, S. J., & Vrba, E. S. (1982). Exaptation—A missing term in the science of form. *Paleobiology, 8,* 4–15.

47. von Neumann, J. M., & Morgenstern, O. (1944). *The theory of games and economic behavior.* Princeton, NJ: Princeton University Press.

48. Smith, J. M. (1982). *Evolution and the theory of games.* Cambridge: Cambridge University Press.

49. Boyce, W. (1993). Evaluating participation in community programs: An empowerment paradigm. *Canadian Journal of Program Evaluation, 8,* 89–102.

50. Castelloe, P., & Watson, T. (1999). Participatory education as a community practice method: A case example from a comprehensive Head Start program. *Journal of Community Practice, 6*(1), 71–89.

51. Gould, R. (1989). Power and social structure in community elites. *Social Forces, 68*(2), 531–552.

52. Ross, L., & Coleman, M. (2000). Urban community action planning inspires teenagers to transform their community and their identity. *Journal of Community Practice, 7*(2), 29–45.

53. Braithwaite, R. L., & Lythcott, N. (1989). Community empowerment as a strategy for health promotion for black and other minority populations. *Journal of the American Medical Association, 261,* 282–283.

54. Dossa, P. A. (1992). Ethnography as narrative discourse: Community integration of people with developmental disabilities. *Rehabilitation Research, 15,* 1–14.

55. Florin, P., & Wandersman, A. (1990). An introduction to citizen participation, voluntary organizations, and community development: Insights for empowerment through research. *American Journal of Community Psychology, 18,* 41–54.

56. Frank, L. D., & Engelke, P. O. (2001). The built environment and human activity patterns: Exploring the impacts of urban form on public health. *Journal of Planning Literature, 16*(2), 202–218.

57. Hunsley, T. (1991). Canada's social future: Mutual aid, or sauve qui peut? *Canada Journal of Public Health, 82,* 222–228.

58. Stein, J. G. (2001). *The cult of efficiency.* Toronto, Ontario: House of Anansi.

59. Aryeetey, E. B. D. (1998). Consultative processes in community development in Northern Ghana. *Community Development Journal, 33*(4), 301–313.

60. Campbell, M., Copeland, B., & Tate, B. (1998). Taking the standpoint of people with disabilities in research: Experiences with participation. *Canadian Journal of Rehabilitation, 12*(2), 95–104.

61. Korten, D. (1984). People-centred development: Toward a framework. In D. Korten & R. Klauss (Eds.), *People-centred development: Contributions toward theory and planning frameworks.* West Hartford, CT: Kumarian.

62. Krogh, K. (1998). A conceptual framework of community partnerships: perspectives of people with disabilities on power, beliefs and values. *Canadian Journal of Rehabilitation, 12*(2), 123–134.

63. Zimmerman, M. A, & Rappaport, J. (1988). Citizen participation, perceived control, and psychological empowerment. *American Journal of Community Psychology, 16,* 725–750.

64. Wallerstein, N., & Berstein, E. (1994). Introduction to community empowerment, participatory education, and health. *Health Education Quarterly, 21,* 141–148.

65. Mulenga, D. C. (1994). Participatory research for a radical community development. *Australian Journal of Adult and Community Education, 34,* 253–261.

66. Stewart, R., & Bhagwanjee, A. (1999). Promoting group empowerment and self-reliance through participatory research: A case study of people with physical disability. *Disability and Rehabilitation, 21*(7), 338–345.

67. Kuyek, J. N. (1990). *Fighting for hope: Organizing to realize our dreams.* Montreal: Black Rose Books.

68. Davis, S. M., & Reid, R. (1999). Practicing participatory research in American Indian communities. *American Journal of Clinical Nutrition, 69*(4 Suppl), 755S–759S.

69. Diaz, M., & Simmons, R. (1999). When is research participatory? Reflections on a reproductive health project in Brazil. *Journal of Women's Health, 8*(2), 175–184.

70. Freire, P. (1970). *Pedagogy of the oppressed: The letters to Guinea-Bissau.* New York: Continuum Books.

71. Freire, P. (1976). *Education: The practice of freedom.* London: Writers and Readers.

72. Freire, P. (1985). *The politics of education: Culture, power and liberation* (trans. D. Macedo.). South Hadley, MA: Bergin & Garvey Publishers.

73. MacAulay, S. (2001). The community economic development tradition in Eastern Nova Scotia, Canada: Ideological continuities and discontinuities between the Antigonish Movement and the Family of community development corporations. *Community Development Journal, 36*(2), 111–121.

74. Lotz, J. (1998). Marginality, liminality, and local development. In G. A. MacIntyre (Ed.), *Perspectives on community: A community economic development roundtable.* Cape Breton, NS: University College of Cape Breton.

75. Williams, R., Swan, P., Reser, J., & Miller, B. (1992). Australian aborigine communities: Changing oppressive social environments. In D. Thomas & A. Veno (Eds.), *Psychology and social change.* Palmerston North, NZ: Dunmore Press.

76. Davies, L., & Shragge, E. E. (1990). *Bureaucracy and community.* Montreal: Black Rose Books.

77. Lévi-Strauss, C. (1969). *The elementary structures of kinship.* Boston: Beacon Press.

78. Macaulay, A. C., Delormier, T., McComber, A. M., Cross, E. J., Potvin, L. P., Paradis, G., et al. (1998). Participatory research with native community of Kahnawake creates innovative code of research ethics. *Canadian Journal of Public Health, 89*(2), 105–108.

79. Simpson, L. R. (1998). Aboriginal peoples and the environment. *Canadian Journal of Native Education, 22*(2), 223–337.

80. Scandrett, E. (1999). Sustainable development in communities. *Adults Learning England, 10*(5), 12–14.

81. United Nations. (1992). *Report of the United Nations conference on environment and development* (Report A/CONF.151/26, Vol. I). New York: Author.

82. Hancock, T. (1993). Health, human development and the community ecosystem: three ecological models. *Health promotion international, 8*(1), 41–47.

83. Kemmis, D. (1990). *Community and the politics of place.* Norman: University of Oklahoma Press.

84. Bailey, R. (Ed.). *Earth report 2000: Revisiting the true state of the planet.* New York: McGraw-Hill.

85. Flynn, B. C., Ray, D. W., & Rider, M. S. (1994). Empowering communities: Action research through healthy cities. *Health Education Quarterly, 21,* 395–405.

86. Labonte, R. (1989). Community empowerment: The need for political analysis. *Canadian Journal of Public Health, 80,* 87–88.

87. Mildenberger, V., & Rosenfeld, E. (1992). Strengthening community health services: An exercise in knowledge development. *Health Promotion, 31,* 7–14.

88. Kieckhefer, R. (2000). *Magic in the Middle Ages* (2nd ed.). Cambridge: Cambridge University Press.

89. Staral, J. M. (2000). Building on mutual goals: The intersection of community practice and church-based organizing. *Journal of Community Practice, 7*(3), 85–95.

90. Shapin, S. (1996). *The scientific revolution.* Chicago: University of Chicago Press.

91. Depoy, P., & Gitlin, L. (1998). *Introduction to research: Multiple strategies for health and human services.* New York: Mosby-Year Book.

92. Jackson, W. (1999). *Methods: Doing social research.* Scarborough, Ontario: Prentice Hall/Allyn Bacon Canada.

93. Rebeiro, K. L., & Allen, J. (1998). Voluntarism as occupation. *Canadian Journal of Occupational Therapy, 65*(5), 279–285.

94. Ellis, S. J., & Noyes, K. J. (1990). *By the people: A history of Americans as volunteers* (rev ed.). San Francisco: Jossey Bass.

95. Fischer, L. R., & Schaffer, K. B. (1993). *Older volunteers.* Newbury Park, CA: Sage Publications.

96. Najam, A. (1996). Understanding the third sector: Revisiting the prince, the merchant, and the citizen. *Nonprofit Management and Leadership, 7*(2), 203–219.

97. Wuthnow, R. (1991). *Acts of compassion: Caring for others and helping ourselves.* Princeton, NJ: Princeton University Press.

98. Coles, R. (1993). *The call of service: A witness to idealism.* Boston: Houghton-Mifflin.

99. Fukuyama, F. (1995). *Trust, the social virtues and creation of prosperity.* New York: The Free Press.

100. Putnam, R. D. (2000). *Bowling alone: The collapse and revival of American community.* New York: Simon & Schuster.

101. Coleman, J. S. (1988). Social capital in the creation of human capital. *American Journal of Sociology, 94*(Supplement), S95–S120.

102. Whiteford, G. (1995). A concrete void: Occupational deprivation and the special needs inmate. *Journal of Occupational Science, 2*(2), 80–81.

103. Whiteford, G. (1997). Occupational deprivation and incarceration. *Journal of Occupational Science: Australia, 4*(3), 126–130.

104. Whiteford, G. (2000). Occupational deprivation: Global challenge in the new millennium. *British Journal of Occupational Therapy, 64*(5), 200–210.

105. Wilcock, A., & Townsend, E. (2000). Occupational justice: Occupational terminology interactive dialogue. *Journal of Occupational Science, 7*(2), 84–86.

106. Levine, F. J., & Rosich, K. J. (1996). *Social causes of violence: Crafting a science agenda.* Washington, DC: American Sociological Association.

107. Rae-Grant, N., McConville, B. J., Fleck, S., Kennedy, J. S., Vaughan, W. T., Steiner, H., et al. (1999). Violent behavior in children and youth: Preventive intervention from a psychiatric perspective. *Journal of the American Academy of Child and Adolescent Psychiatry, 38*(3), 235–241.

108. Reiss, A. J., Jr., & Roth, J. A. (Eds.). (1993). *Understanding and preventing violence.* Washington, DC: National Academy Press.

109. Wilson, J. Q., & Kelling, G. L. (1982, March). Broken windows: The police and neighborhood safety. *The Atlantic Monthly,* pp. 29–38.

110. Axelrod, R. (1984). *The evolution of cooperation.* New York: Basic Books.

111. Duhl, L. J. (1991). *Social entrepreneurship of change.* New York: Pace University Press.

112. Tonnies, F. (1887/1957). *Community and society (Gemeinschaft und Gesellschaft).* Lansing: Michigan State University Press.

113. Weber, M. (1921/1968). *Economy and society.* New York: Bedminster Press.

CHAPTER 8

Occupations and Places

Toby Ballou Hamilton

KEY WORDS

Affordance
Archetypal places
Archetype
Avatar
Community
Displacement
Environmental press
Habitus
Life-world

Places
Semiotics
Sense of place
Social geography
Socially constructed meaning
Tele-immersion
Temporal
Virtual places

CHAPTER PROFILE

In recent times, the study of geography has gone well beyond a consideration of the physical features of the planet to consider the interaction of places, cultures, and living things. This chapter focuses on how the cultural and physical features of places influence the occupations that take place there. Topics to be explored include the idea of places with universal meaning and purpose (archetypal places), the various dimensions or characteristics that are used to describe locations and how these influence occupations, how places create meaning, and how movement between places influences lifestyles from a temporal perspective. Other topics considered include the concepts of home and community and the creation of virtual places through modern technology. The chapter concludes with a discussion of the

www.prenhall.com/christiansen
The Internet provides an exciting means for interacting with this textbook and for enhancing your understanding of humans' experiences with occupations and the organization of occupations in society. Use the address above to access the free, interactive companion web site created specifically to accompany this book. Here you will find an array of self-study material designed to help you gain a richer understanding of the concepts presented in this chapter.

contribution of places to well-being, followed by brief discussions of the consequences of displacement and homelessness.

INTRODUCTION

When people engage in everyday pursuits that capture their time and attention, they must do so in places. The places in which people find themselves strongly influence what they do and the meaning of their time spent there. In fact, the contribution of place is an important and necessary element of occupation. This is because all occupational situations have three components: places, people (with their attributes, thoughts, feelings, and memories), and the occupations in which the people are engaged. Thus, the link between person, place, and occupation is so strong that one cannot consider occupations without considering that they involve people in places.

In this chapter, the term **place** is used to refer to physical surroundings or environments that are either natural or produced through human labor (built). To a great extent, places influence how people work, play, and care for others and themselves. This located or *where* dimension also partly influences the *what*, the *why*, the *how*, and the *how well* of occupations.

Each day, individuals must meet basic human needs, such as eating, grooming, and sleeping, to support their survival and quality of life. Daily life revolves around the places associated with meeting fundamental needs. When surroundings include places that meet these needs, the results benefit individuals as well as their social groups. However, when places do not provide for full satisfaction of basic needs, people's engagement in everyday occupations becomes difficult and can have negative consequences that extend beyond the immediate family or living group.

Places influence the occupations that are engaged within them. These influences can be subtle clues based on traditions and social expectations, or they can be more obvious, based on the physical characteristics of a place. Groups of people often establish relationships with places, so that their collective values and personalities are translated into a type of cultural landscape. When people have known and occupied a place that carries such a special relationship, the symbolic meaning that is conveyed is called a **sense of place.**

Similarly, places have a spatial dimension, in that they represent distances from other places. In daily life, distance equates with travel, which requires time. People gain familiarity with regions, cities, and neighborhoods because of their proximity. This familiarity contributes to safety and security, which forms the basis for the ideas of shelter and territoriality.

This chapter will also explore aspects of place and the relationships between places, people, and their occupations. Many of the ideas presented in this chapter are fundamental to the study of social and cultural geography, sociology, and psychology.

UNDERSTANDING PLACE

The word *place* has many meanings, revealing the fact that the meanings of places are "socially constructed." That is, places are given different meanings by different people for different purposes, often as the result of shared experiences. Thus, meanings are attributed to places largely as a result of what happens in them and how people interpret those experiences over time. This multidimensional nature of place is conveyed well by Harvey, (1, p. 4), who notes that many terms, such as *region, territory, location,* and *neighborhood,* are used to describe general qualities of places, as well as terms for particular kinds of places, such as *city, village,* and *state.* We also use words such as *home, turf, community,* and *nation* to evoke particular meanings. In addition, there are designations for places that specify the kinds of occupational pursuits that take place within them, such as *school, shopping center, football stadium, factory, amusement park, kitchen,* and *bedroom.*

Places as Archetypes

The first experienced environment for all humans is the uterus and the experiences of the physical properties of the womb can influence behavior for a lifetime. The rhythmic sounds of amniotic fluid created by the mother's movement and the muted sensory impressions of vision, hearing, and touch serve to stimulate growth and development of the fetus yet provide protection and security. The small dimensions of the womb help explain why swaddling, or tight wrapping in blankets, calms newborn babies. The desire to re-create the pleasure of infantile security and comfort remains in adulthood. Most people enjoy the physical expression of love created by embracing and hugging.

When problems and challenges arise for individuals and groups, it is not unusual for them to seek places of quiet and relaxation in order to inspire the courage, creativity, and resourcefulness necessary for solving problems. The implicit message behind this adaptive strategy is one of seeking protection and support to meet threats and challenges. All humans possess the basic needs for security and protection.

Just as nature has provided the womb to serve as the primeval shelter, humankind has learned to construct places that serve a fundamental requirement of meeting basic needs. Spivak (2) has identified 13 types of places that evoke and support behaviors that meet basic needs. He called these **archetypal places.** An **archetype** is any object that is deeply rooted in human history and serves as a symbol or model for other objects. Hence, Spivak proposed that archetypal places represent the basic settings necessary to sustain human existence. According to Spivak, archetypal places meet humankind's needs for shelter, territory, and the routes that link places for sleeping, mating, grooming, feeding, excreting, playing, competing, working, storing possessions, and meeting with others to fulfill spiritual, educational, and communication needs (2). Spivak's list of archetypal places provides an excellent universal approach for classifying places by type.

Although archetypal places are found universally, their forms differ by region and custom and their use varies by age and life stage. As "containers of culture" (2, p. 46), archetypal places necessarily vary from one place to another. The differences in forms and use reflect the geographic, climatic, and natural resources of the regions in which people live. The meanings associated with archetypal places also differ by culture and across the life span according to the behaviors associated with age and stages of development. For example, the meaning of places for preparing and eating food differ as one matures from child to adult. Similar changes influence the perception and use of sleeping areas.

It is interesting to note the correspondence between archetypal places and the everyday occupations of life. Archetypal places are necessarily associated with the occupations that secure our survival and quality of life. Just as certain places evoke particular occupations, occupations dictate design features of the built environments. People usually store, prepare, and clean up from preparing meals in the kitchen. The bedroom is the archetypal sleeping room and often the place for the occupation of sexual expression. We tend to do personal care tasks, such as grooming, hygiene, and dressing, in the bathroom and bedroom. Although such personal care occupations are usually performed as habitual routines, a change in place can offer either a refreshing change from routine or disrupt important and essential habits and routines that support daily life. Generally, unexpected and permanent changes of place represent stressful situations because of their importance in supporting the routine occupations of personal care, work, and leisure.

Dimensions of Place

Every place consists of different aspects or layers, each influenced by the other (3). The most obvious aspect of place concerns its physical attributes and location as well as the objects and furnishings associated with it. People can experience physical space through their senses because of properties such as temperature, lighting, color, and noise. Many places have natural attributes or characteristics, such as proximity to mountains, water, trees, or open spaces that make them unique, undesirable, or appealing. In addition to their location, the distance between places is also an important dimension. This is because distances influence daily routines.

Distances are based on natural geography as well as human planning. London and New York are separated by 3,488 nautical miles of the North Atlantic Ocean—a geographical reality that cannot be changed. Yet, the distance from any office to the nearest staircase or toilet facilities is a function of architectural design. Some built places provide locations for sharing commonsense knowledge and contesting social norms; others enable quiet, solitude, and privacy by providing distance or shelter from noise and large numbers of people.

Architects and designers are aware that the design of places and objects provide **affordances** that signify their use. The word **affordance** was originally invented by the perceptual psychologist J. J. Gibson (4) to refer to the actionable properties between the world and a person (or animal). To Gibson, affordances represented a relationship that was part of nature. Affordances do not have to be visible, known, or desirable and may yet remain undiscovered.

The relationship between person and place can be used to influence behaviors. Thus, subtle cues in the design of spaces can facilitate access and movement within a place (Figure 8-1). Similarly, designs may facilitate privacy or social interaction. Objects help to define a place's meaning and shape its physical characteristics. Examples include memorial objects such as gravestones at cemeteries, ancient artifacts displayed at museums, and works of art at galleries.

FIGURE 8-1   This campus architectural design has created an affordance for sitting and study. (Ryan McVay/Getty Images)

A second and perhaps more important aspect of place relates to its **socially constructed meaning.** Through experiences, places become associated with events and action that give them both individual and collective meaning. Thrift (5) has identified that the social nature of places provides structure for daily routines and life paths by providing both opportunities and constraints that influence economic and social life. Places provide an arena for social gatherings that are necessary for the development of language, culture, and values and the education to convey them to others. As places become associated with purposes and events over time, they acquire symbolic meanings that influence what goes on within them. These meanings then contribute to a shared identity associated with places through direct experience or stories told over time. The wonders of the world represent places with significant meanings associated with their actual and mythical histories, passed on through generations in a manner that makes them larger than life. On a smaller scale, each region and town has places that convey special meaning to the persons living in that area. These meanings develop over time through shared understanding of the people associated with them. Thus, places hold socially constructed meaning.

Place and Meaning

The meaning attributed to a place is influenced by its familiarity, which is in turn influenced largely by the amount of time a person spends there. People who are familiar with places and locations are *insiders*. The insider's view commonly holds these familiar places to be safe, secure, and nonthreatening (6). Humans are territorial, and safety and security are important dimensions of territoriality. Territoriality makes spaces and places instruments of power, inclusion, and exclusion (7). Places have meaning in direct proportion to the degree of "insideness" that people feel toward them, which is directly related to the time people spend there.

In his book, *The Experience of Place*, Tony Hiss (8), writes: "The places where we spend our time affect the people we are and can become. Whatever we experience in a place is both a serious environmental issue and a deeply personal one" (p. xi). This personal or experienced part of places has been called a *sense of place* (9, 10). Sociologist David Hummon (11) relates sense of place with feelings of community related to satisfaction, attachment, and identity. People clearly have feelings and thoughts about environments that include a subjective assessment of their level of comfort with being there. Taken together, these thoughts, feelings and evaluations create a sense of meaning associated with place (11). Recent research supports the idea that meanings associated with place are laden with value and highly dependent on the environment, experience with others, and a person's sense of self or identity (12).

A discussion of the meanings of places would not be complete without mention of semiotics. The term **semiotics** refers to the study of anything in social life that stands for something else (13). This can include words, signs, nonverbal behaviors, gestures, objects, and even the design of buildings. Clearly, the understanding of how people derive a sense of place by embodying it with personal meaning involves semiotics. The collective attributes of a place, its location, its objects, its memories, and the feelings it evokes are signs that stand for something else. The meanings apparent when a group of people sings a national anthem while gazing at a collective symbol such as a flag in a place that evokes feelings of national pride provide another example of the influence of such "signs of meaning." Clearly, the study of semiotics provides a key dimension for understanding occupations in places.

Time and Place

Not only are many places archetypal, the routes that link them are also an archetype (2). When people commute to work or school or run errands, they are simply connecting archetypal places. Daily occupations link archetypal places into patterns. Just as a piece of cloth consists of vertical and horizontal strands woven together as warp and weft, so too are daily occupations woven into patterns that are influenced by locations and distances.

In a larger sense, the idea of life as a journey is an archetype (14) that has been frequently reflected in the motifs of the world's mythology and folktales (15, 16). The journeys of cultural heroes follow a particular pattern regardless of the time and cultures that produced them (15). Hundreds of myths and folktales tell of journeys to other worlds, including the upper and lower worlds (15, 16).

For example, the ancient Greeks explained the cycle of seasonal change by the story of Demeter and her daughter, Persephone. After Hades, ruler of the underworld, seized Perspehone, Demeter allowed crops to fail. To restore order to the world, Persephone spent part of the year with her mother and part of the year with

Hades. Winter occurred when Persphone was in the underworld with Hades, and her return to earth explained spring and summer.

There is a temporality of place that influences the duration and timing of everyday events. Places often display a rhythm of occupations that is influenced by their geographic location and purpose (17). A farm is an excellent example of a place where daily and seasonal rhythms influence the occupations that are done there. The rising sun brings early morning chores, and the seasons dictate the planting and harvesting of crops. Archaeologists have determined that the position of the sun during the day and during the year influenced the location of various work tasks among the indigenous peoples who inhabited the cave-like pueblos in the southwestern United States (18). The movement of occupations was an example of seasonal adaptation related to the changes in temperature and light as the sun moved through daily and yearly cycles.

Clearly, places are also associated with rituals that mark life events. The cathedral, which towered above other structures in the medieval villages of Europe, was a commanding reminder of religion and the social power of the church. As such, it greatly influenced daily life through the tolling of its bells, its location as a place for regular worship and social meeting, and as a place for baptisms, weddings, funerals, and other ceremonies that signified important points along the life course of villagers.

The locations of places in neighborhoods can also create informal rituals. In many small towns in North America on Saturday nights, young people gather or cruise Main Street in order to see and be seen by others. Here, place and time acting together create a social ritual. Similarly, if a bakery is located between the workplace and home, a person may develop a personal ritual of stopping on the way home to buy bread or pastry. Families may develop personal rituals surrounding locations within the home. These rituals may be related to gatherings around certain parts of the house, such as the fireplace or stove, or relate to locations such as summer cottages or other favorite locations for regular family reunions or weekend getaways. Many people develop rituals around neighborhood itineraries where they take their daily strolls to exercise or walk the dog (Figure 8-2).

Movement from Place to Place as Occupation

Transportation provides human access to other people and places. Similarly, lack of transportation options can limit access to occupational engagement, including work, school, and various social activities. This lack of access can undermine wellbeing by limiting earning potential and social participation. As urban areas grow, the importance of transportation increases.

In the industrialized world, the growth of urban areas has changed daily life. Many people no longer live and work in their homes or in the same neighborhood. Instead, they commute between home and work, often traveling long distances in cars or public transportation. Commuting has a negative effect on the traveler's psychological state by increasing stress and contributing to insomnia (19). Lengthy commuting times also adversely impact family and social life by reducing the time available for socialization (20). For example, on a typical weekday, the average Canadian commuter spends 48 minutes going to and from work. Significant proportions of workers spend an hour or more each day in travel (21).

FIGURE 8-2 Occupational rituals are often linked to time and place. Many people have a set time and route for walking their dogs.
(Steve Cole/Getty Images)

The stress of commuting varies by mode of transport as well as the nature of the commute. Traveling on a busy multilane road is not as pleasant an experience as driving along a tree-lined residential street. Some scenic neighborhoods offer drivers many of the visual experiences that make walking or cycling in greenways appealing. Attractive scenery changes the perception of time associated with a commute and reduces stress. Drivers perceive the time spent driving on a suburban arterial road to be 23% more than the actual time elapsed. In contrast, the perceived time spent driving along a traditional tree-lined residential street is experienced as 16% less than the actual time (22).

The cost of transportation is also a consideration, especially for economically disadvantaged people, that can limit access to shopping, education, and recreation. In some parts of the world, money for work-related commuting is given first priority for poor families, often leaving inadequate resources for transportation for other purposes. In many urban environments, the working poor reside in the inner city, with little opportunity to visit suburban areas, which often have limited access by public transportation. This characteristic of place and transportation can have economic consequences that result in pervasive threats to quality of life (Figure 8-3) (23).

OCCUPATIONS AS EXPERIENCES IN PLACES

A term frequently used in sociology to communicate daily experiences is **life-world.** A life-world can be defined as the routine patterns and interactions of everyday life.

FIGURE 8-3　Movement from place to place is often a key element of participation in necessary and chosen daily endeavors. The significance of available public transportation to quality of life is often overlooked.
(John A. Rizzo/Getty Images)

The concept of life-world is experience-based and emphasizes the meanings that people give to the spaces they occupy. Because it is familiar, routine, and recurring, the life-world is seldom given conscious thought. This contributes to its enduring nature, creating a sense of secure, continuous reality as life is lived on a daily basis (24).

When people are interacting with other people or objects within their life-worlds, their experiences can be described as embodied. Within the embodied experience, individuals employ their own characteristics, dispositions, and attributes to shape and interpret the places they occupy. Pierre Bourdieu, a world renowned sociologist, uses the term **habitus** to describe the unconscious patterns of doing, thinking, speaking, and perceiving that people exhibit in these circumstances. These characteristics are basic to the creation of shared meaning within places (25).

In the life-world, a person's doing, thinking, speaking, and perceiving most often take place in the context of daily occupations, which occur in places. Thus, occupations always occur within a context of place and time. Since ancient times, people all over the world have engaged in production, personal care, and recreational occupations and they have needed shelter for sleep. In a more restricted sense, occupation happens in a particular place that has observable physical properties that happen within the rhythms of natural, cultural, and personal routines.

Because of the dynamic nature of people, their occupations, and the places in which occupations are done, no element can be understood in isolation. So enmeshed are the person, the place, and the performance of occupation, their respective influences must be considered. In short, a complete understanding of occupations can only occur with careful consideration of the settings and people who are engaging in them. In the sections to follow, these influences are described in greater detail.

HOW PLACES INFLUENCE OCCUPATION

Places invite certain types of occupations and prohibit or restrict others (3). When people go into a store, they look at items and may purchase some of them, but most people would not steal anything. People invite others to talk while eating lunch but expect silence while visiting the cinema. Given the outdoor setting of a playground, children find it easy to run and play but difficult to complete lessons. The elements and rules inherent to a place may combine and build on each other (3). When students enter a classroom, they typically sit in chairs that are placed to face the front of the room where they expect the instructor to stand. Only under special circumstances that alter the rules of the classroom space would students or faculty rearrange the seating.

These behaviors are a consequence of social expectations associated with places. Some customs and rules of social behavior are learned and generalized from one place to another. People learn to be quiet and reverent in spiritual places. Obvious spiritual places, such as mosques, churches, synagogues, temples, cathedrals, or other houses of worship, commonly elicit such behaviors. Behaviors in spiritual places known only to insiders will be less obvious to visitors, and inappropriate behaviors in these places will elicit sanctions by those more familiar with customs.

The traditions associated with behavioral expectations in places have been called **environmental press** and were theorized by psychologist Henry Murray in the 1930s (26). More recent work on behavioral influences has recognized that press is a phenomenon associated with social experiences and the presence (imagined or real) of other people within places. Kurt Lewin's field theory (27) and Latane's social impact theory (28) form the basis for more recent research confirming the influence of social expectations on behavior within settings or places. Their frameworks support the basic proposition advanced here—namely, that occupations are influenced by the nature of the individuals and the settings in which people find themselves.

Physical Influences

The physical characteristics of places also influence the performance of occupations—how frequently, efficiently, or effectively people are able to achieve their purposes there. This is due to psychological factors, emotional factors, and simple design and logistical issues related to the requirements of given tasks, the abilities of people, and the environments in which they perform their occupations. The science of human factors, or *ergonomics,* has evolved as a means of determining how the psychological, physical, and social characteristics of people and environments influence task performance in work settings. A goal of ergonomics is to improve the fit between people and their working conditions while improving safety, productivity, comfort, and efficiency (29). To accomplish these goals, human factors engineers must take the various aspects of place into account. Human factors specialists recognize that psychological issues, particularly those related to the perception and meaning of places to their inhabitants, are an important influence on task performance and safety in the home and workplace.

Just as the person brings abilities and capacities and desires mastery and competence in a setting, the place makes occupational performance demands on the individual that can change within the same setting during the course of a day. The demands that a place makes on everyday occupations can vary according to difficulty, complexity, familiarity, intricacy, speed, effort, integration, exertion, responsiveness, timing, span, and scope.

For example, consider the demands that school places on children. During breaks, the physical aspects of the outdoors and the playground equipment challenge children by offering opportunities for swinging, climbing, running, or playing competitive or cooperative games. Back in the classroom, they must interact in socially appropriate ways with others to complete projects, wait in line, eat lunch or snacks, sit in their seats, and participate in class discussions. Rules regulate their behaviors whenever they move in the classrooms and halls, work or play alone or with others, and even determine when they can meet biological needs to eat or drink. Teachers expect students to be prepared for class, use unstructured school time to meet educational objectives, avoid disruption of others' work, and independently complete assignments and projects at school and at home.

Schools are good examples of places where exploration and experience lead to enhanced abilities. This may explain why school experiences often hold such special meaning for people. In addressing this point, Platt (30) writes:

> Places capture experience and store it symbolically. Its collective meanings are extractable and readable by its later inhabitants. This symbolic housing of meaning and memory gives place temporal depth. But not only do places of experience store meaning about the past; they also are platforms for visions and plans about the future. Places of experience provision us with identity to venture forth out of this place into less certain or orderly spaces. Places of experience provide categories for managing new adventures and new cycles of old adventures. Places of experience connect the past to the future, memory to expectation, in an invigorating way. Places of experience give us a sense of continuity and energy. (p. 112)

Geographical Variations in Occupation

Part of the continuity of place is related to the traditions and customs that are practiced there. People in different places often do things differently, based on experience and teachings passed down through generations. Often, these ways of living are influenced by the natural resources and physical characteristics of the places. A comparison of child care practices serves as a useful example to illustrate the diversity and similarity of occupations as they vary by geographic places.

Universal child care occupations include carrying, bathing, diapering, and feeding babies as well as comforting them when crying and getting them to sleep. Parents protect their infants from weather and the invisible world that consists of either evil spirits or germs, depending on the culture's beliefs (31). Parents find methods of meeting their children's needs by using the physical features of a place and the materials at hand.

A place's climate and available materials influence how mothers carry their babies. Babies may be carried either close or far away from the parent's body, and the infants may be free to move or be tightly swaddled into virtual immobility.

Babies among the tribal peoples in various regions of the globe are carried in slings, hammocks, leather pouches, nets, or baskets supported by the mother's back, neck, hip, or forehead. For example, mothers in the Amazon rain forests carry their babies from a strap over the mother's forehead so her hands are free to gather food. The manner of transporting the infant determines how much of the world the baby can see and hear. Infants carried in a horizontal sleeping position see and hear very little, while babies carried upright on the parent's back or hip experience a great deal more of life. In places in which the infant is strapped to the mother's body as she goes about her daily work, the infant not only has rich sensory experiences but also "serves as a witness" to the work occupations in that place (31, p. 17).

In some cultures, bathing is a part of the personal care routine carried out to remove dirt and germs from the baby's body. People bathe babies in sinks, conventional bathtubs, or small child-sized tubs. In tribal societies, bathing fulfills the need to cleanse the infant both literally and ritually. Tribal mothers in South America, Africa, Indonesia, and Oceania fill their mouths with water, warm it, and spray the water over the infant for a literal "spit bath." The baby may then be covered with oils, spices, herbs, juices, paints, powders, pastes, or even dung for protection from the elements, disease, and vectors. Tribal babies in Australia, Africa, and India may be cleansed by being held in the smoke of a fire fueled by plant materials and animal dung. This practice is both ritual and practical, giving the benefits of fragrance, antisepsis, and healing (31).

Lullabies are a universal phenomenon (31) that underscores the problems that all parents sometimes have in getting their babies to sleep. Lulled to sleep by songs, gentle pats, or cradled in the arms of family members, tribal babies sleep on mats, in hammocks, or in suspended wooden cradles. Cradle designs vary by nomadic or sedentary lifestyle and are made of animal skin, wool, or plant materials like bark, wood, reed, palm, or cotton. Pygmy fathers yodel their children to sleep. Turareg babies sleep in a cradle of reeds suspended from a cord or hung on a camel. In Tibet, Sherpa babies are placed in a basket swing with high sides. Inuit mothers in Siberia spontaneously make up lullabies for their babies (31).

Mothers in Western industrialized nations have discovered that the characteristics of cars and common household appliances can help babies sleep. For example, the vibration, warmth, and constant noise of riding in a car or lying on top of a clothes dryer have served to lull many babies to sleep. To tribal mothers, such parenting acts may represent incomprehensible acts of desperation. But they work. The point to be gained is that in each example, the characteristics and resources of a place are used to support the necessary occupations of daily life.

PLACES AS ENVIRONMENTS FOR LEARNING AND PLAY

Every time a child interacts with a place, an intense encounter in development occurs. With each increase in balance, posture, and muscular control the child is more able to move, leading to new places to explore and novel sensory experiences to relish. In turn, new places stimulate the child's increased ability to move and explore. With increased mobility, the child ventures further from the security of a parent, but can return to emotionally "refuel" with frequent forays back to the parent (32). As the distance and time between child and parent increases, so does the memory of a reassuring hug and a special object that gives comfort. With these memories come feelings of security for independence in exploring, so that the child returns with new sensory experiences that spur the development of senses, muscles, brain, and language. With an expanding repertoire of experience in various places, children gain confidence in their ability to master challenges in place, and the resulting feelings of competence lead to further exploration. In short, children grow, learn, and develop in response to their experiences in place. However, it is the "just right" amount of challenge that promotes growth. Challenges that require too much or too little competence can cause the child to draw closer to safety for a while. Given the opportunity to safely move indoors and outdoors and fully experience the place, children quickly learn concepts such as hot and cold, wet and dry, big and little, and heavy and light. These sensory experiences are the basis for language and thought that in turn underlie speaking, reading, and writing.

Play in Neighborhoods

Researchers who studied the physical features of four California neighborhoods found that place dictated the play patterns of 11- and 12-year-olds (33). The neighborhood, defined by the distance from home to school, comprised the children's "social universe" (33, p. 320). In each neighborhood, constraints on children's play patterns included the terrain; the number of and access to other children; ages of the children; the relationship of major streets to designated play areas; and availability of undeveloped, unstructured play space. Children living in hilly, sparsely populated neighborhoods spent more time planning social interaction than other children. Children who lived in flat neighborhoods with many children spent more time in spontaneous social interactions. In neighborhoods with a higher density of children, friendships tended to be more casual, less structured, and inclusive of a variety of children of different ages.

The importance of this research lies in the fact that the children in all four neighborhoods adapted to the assets and constraints that the physical place of their neighborhoods presented. The children's "energy, imagination, and perseverance make it possible for them to define an acceptable play environment" (33, p. 320) despite the physical limitations of the places in which they lived and played.

Home

What people think of as *home* is a single place that allows them to meet their archetypal needs for shelter, storage, and territory to enable the tasks and occupations of sleeping, mating, grooming, feeding, and excreting (2). Home is itself an archetypal place that ideally offers the security to meet those needs, the opportunity to interact with loved ones, and the freedom to be ourselves. The ideal of such a place as home permeates a society's culture. Dorothy's desire to return home with the magic phrase "There's no place like home" was the basis of the L. Frank Baum's series of books about Oz (34). Because of his intense desire to return to his home planet, the most quotable line in Steven Spielberg's movie *E. T., The Extraterrestrial* (35) is "E.T. phone home." Advertisers use the archetype of the idealized home to promote products designed to enrich home as place, express our feelings of love and caring, and promote our desire to return home. Many holidays evoke idealized images of home that are reinforced by art, books, magazines, movies, theater, and advertisements.

However, not all such ideal images of home are actually realized. Domestic violence, child and elder abuse, and homelessness represent violations of the idea of home as an archetypal place. Instead of meeting basic needs in an environment of safety and caring, domestic violence and abuse are crimes that disrupt the privacy of homes and alter its archetypal meaning as place of safety, nurturance, and love.

HOW OCCUPATIONS INFLUENCE PLACES

Places can be classified according to certain fundamental occupations necessary for daily life. These archetypal places present important influences of everyday occupations on places. Examples of occupation influencing place can be seen in homes. People who enjoy preparing elaborate meals and entertaining often select homes that feature well-equipped gourmet kitchens. On the other hand, others may meet their cooking needs with a single-burner stove and microwave oven. Expecting parents often redecorate the baby's room and continue to change its design according to the growing child's interests and hobbies. Families with adult children who have long since left the home often convert the extra living space into home offices, craft rooms, or storage areas. From these examples, one can see that people modify places to meet individual occupational needs.

Place as Community

When people consider places that encourage them to engage in public places as part of the life of a **community,** they usually think of two aspects of place. First are the naturally occurring geographic features, such as mountains or ocean beaches. The second aspect is the constructed or built place, such as entertainment centers, hiking paths, museums, performing arts stages, and parks. When companies search for a new site in which to locate or relocate a business, they consider the geographical location and available resources and people as well as the entertainment, cultural, and educational aspects of place.

However, people can consider community life on a smaller scale. Older persons living in their homes often face challenges in personal care and homemaking occupations. These challenges result not only from age-related changes in their physical capacities, but also from the physical characteristics of the places in which they live. Both the demands of daily occupations and physical features of place influence the ability of older persons to function independently at home. Occupations requiring bending, reaching, carrying, and lifting pose the most difficulties for older persons (36). Such limitations influence the lifestyles of seniors both in the home and in the community.

In one study, investigators found that older persons reported more frequent shopping trips to food stores because they experienced difficulty in lifting and carrying their purchases. They also found that meal preparation was affected when weak grasp made it difficult to open refrigerator and cabinet doors or operate sink faucets (36). As an alternative to meal preparation, seniors in many countries eat meals at a community center or have meals delivered to their homes. Despite the limitations sometimes imposed by aging as shown in this study, another study has shown that a lifetime of familiarity with the physical place of one's home can facilitate continued function despite limitations or impairments associated with aging (37).

Graham Rowles, a social geographer, found that one's house, community, and the habits of neighbors helped the residents of a small Appalachian town to overcome the losses caused by normal aging and poor health (37). Residents made simple modifications such as moving furniture to aid mobility and enlarging windows to increase visibility of outdoors and their neighbors. Some timed their necessary everyday occupations to occur at the same time that certain neighbors walked by their windows. They created elaborate systems of checking on each other through regular patterns of community activity and extensive telephone communication. By skillful use of the features of the place in which they lived, these older adults mitigated the mismatches in person and place that could have led to the need to move to safer, more structured places, such as their children's homes or nursing homes.

For about four decades, people in the United States and in other countries have witnessed a trend to move people with physical disabilities, mental illnesses, or developmental disabilities out of large institutions into independent living places or group residences in community settings. The premise underlying this movement is that if people live and work in more normalized settings, the experiences and opportunities available for them will be more typical, and their lifestyles will be enhanced. Unfortunately, the residences occupied by persons with disabilities in community settings have retained a character more like institutions than homes (38). These characteristics of place have, in turn, influenced the lifestyles and behavior of their occupants.

In a study of the relationship of architecture and the behavior of residents in 20 group homes for adults with developmental disabilities, researchers found that residents living in home-like places behaved more normally and engaged in more typical occupations than residents living in places that were more institution-like. The residents of home-like buildings were more likely to do household chores independently, help with meal preparation, and pursue individual leisure interests. Residents of less home-like places were observed to be less active and more disengaged. The study found that design features and furniture of the dining room were the best predictors of resident behavior. The most influential dining room factor was the number of seats at the dining room table. Settings with dining seating exceeding 12 places at a table tended to be associated with more institution-like characteristics generally and the observation of less normalized behaviors among residents. The researchers found that the physical arrangements of the group homes also affected the behavior of staff, so that all three factors influenced the behavior of residents.

Loss of Place (Displacement)

Changes in place can interfere with the performance of even the most routine occupations. Anyone who travels becomes familiar with the frustration of having to change the personal care routines of hygiene, grooming, and dressing. A forgotten toothbrush, the maintenance of clothes, and the inability to easily locate clothing and grooming items from luggage or travel bags create significant disruption that influences the performance of these routines at the moment and also changes the **temporal** pattern of everyday occupations. Mealtimes must be adjusted to the schedules of restaurants, and diets must accommodate to the vagaries of available menu items and the accommodations of waitstaff and cooks. Added to this, one must accommodate the difficulties of local travel in an unfamiliar environment. Changes in routines and location can also upset biological rhythms, making sleep more difficult. Because these consequences are expected even in first class travel, it should be easy to appreciate how changes in place can have undesired consequences for people who must move involuntarily. Involuntary displacement from the living environment can occur as the result of hospitalization, progressive aging, or illness that requires supervision or care in attended settings, disasters that necessitate displacement such as fires or floods, and economic situations, such as unemployment or chronic poverty. Because of its growing prevalence in North America, homelessness presents an excellent case study of the consequences of **displacement.**

Homelessness violates the concept of home as a secure, permanent, private place where one meets a variety of archetypal needs. Homelessness is an outcome of complex societal issues for those who may experience domestic violence, mental illness, addiction disorders, low wages, lack of affordable housing, decline in public assistance, and poverty. Families with children comprise the fastest growing segment of the homeless population, accounting for 40% (39).

Homelessness disrupts the most basic everyday occupations. Without a single place that meets the most basic needs, the everyday occupations of people who are homeless center around efforts to find sufficient food, clothing, and shelter to survive on a day-to-day basis. The inability to meet such basic needs in one place fragments sleeping, eating, and grooming activities, resulting in a daily routine of traveling to several places in order to meet basic needs.

People who are homeless have more health problems than the general population, experience social problems that may be exacerbated by their lack of shelter, and are more likely to become involved in criminal activity than the general public (40). Health consequences of homelessness occur because people in these circumstances are exposed to more infectious and communicable diseases and experience more stressors, thus resulting in lowered resistance (41). These circumstances also place homeless people at greater risk for drug addiction, suicide, and other mental health problems (42, 43, 44). At the same time, homeless people are often displaced from stable housing because of unemployment, low income, and family difficulties such as spousal or child abuse (45). Of young people on the streets, it is estimated that 70% have experienced physical and sexual abuse (46).

Evidence suggests that people who are homeless may be involved in criminal activity more than youths in the general population (40). Some observers speculate that because of their lack of access to private spaces, the crimes of homeless people are more visible and therefore more apparent. Statistics indicate that the criminal behavior involves crimes against property, such as theft and fraud, prostitution, and minor infractions, such as failure to pay fines, and loitering (46). These victimless crimes seem to arise more out of the circumstances of homelessness than serious criminal intent (40). Taken together, the effects of homelessness would seem to underscore the important role that a stable and consistent shelter plays in everyday existence, and the consequences of diminished social support that result when living environments are disrupted or substandard.

The concept of not knowing where the next meal will come from or where one will sleep for the night is foreign to many people. The struggle to meet the most basic needs taxes the person–environment interaction in ways that are hard to imagine. A person may be able to sleep in a shelter for the night, but must stay alert to safeguard possessions because of the lack of secure storage of belongings. Staple foodstuffs may be available from food banks and pantries but go unused without the utensils and means of preparing food. A given shelter may offer only one meal a day, necessitating travel between several shelters to eat more than once a day. The place where one gets a meal may be some distance from the place where one sleeps. Although people who are homeless are sometimes eligible for government assistance, no one can receive mail without a permanent address. Meeting archetypal needs through such fragmented occupational performance strains the person–environment interaction when the search for means of survival dominates daily routine (Figure 8-4). The routes that link the places that partially meet archetypal needs provide the only patterns of daily occupation.

Virtual Places

It cannot be doubted that computer technology and the Internet have profoundly changed the lifestyles of many people. Using a computer to interact, shop, discover, learn, play games, and even do paid work has become commonplace. As computers have become more advanced, improved processing speeds and data memory have enabled the creation of digital experiences that hold great potential for changing the way life is lived for millions of people throughout the world. The Internet and digital communications create the sense that physical distances are no longer a barrier to social interactions. The ability to instantly engage in everyday occupations across vast distances and to visit **virtual places** can reconfigure the time, place, and pattern of everyday experiences.

Occupations that once required travel to another physical place can now be conducted without leaving the room. Instead of going to a store, we can browse, shop, and purchase goods and services from our computers. We can electronically send and receive mail instantaneously, whereas people used to compose and write a letter on paper, mail it from the nearest post office or letter collection box, and hope our

FIGURE 8-4 In the United States, one prevalent symbol of homelessness is a grocery cart filled with personal belongings. (Jack Star/Getty Images)

correspondent would receive our letter in a few days. Instead of going to a university campus, students can enroll in and complete courses emanating from a digital campus.

Because it is digital, every web site can be construed as a virtual place. As technology has matured, web experiences have become more sophisticated. Using broadband connections capable of transmitting or streaming huge amounts of digital images and sound, computers can display images of real-time events from across the globe.

The term *virtual reality* refers to any simulation of a real or imaginary environment in which it is possible for a user to interact with objects and people within that environment. Immersion refers to the sense that users are interacting within an environment represented digitally (47).

The digital representation of environments, or immersive virtual places, is becoming more sophisticated as the environments are rendered in three-dimensional form. Here, the user can move within the virtual environment and experience visual, auditory, and tactile sensations through devices known as haptic interfaces (Figure 8-5). As these technologies mature, the potential for re-creating places and simulating real-world experiences using virtual reality is perhaps inestimable. The term **avatar** refers to a representation of the self that can be used in virtual environments. Avatars can be similar to the self or can be imagined representations. In effect, the use of imagined avatars in virtual places enables people to gain experiences and to experiment with identities that transcend those possible in the physical world.

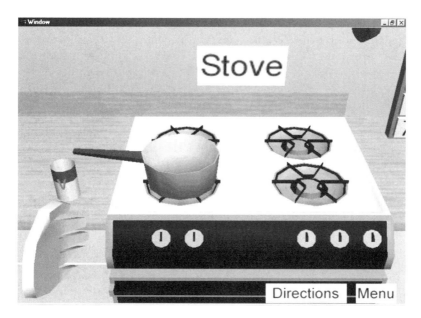

FIGURE 8-5   Virtual environments can vary from entire buildings to specific rooms. This virtual kitchen enables the user to perform many tasks necessary for food preparation, including opening cans, running water, and heating food on an electric range.
(Courtesy of the University of Texas Medical Branch and the Transitional Learning Center of Galveston)

More recently, scientists interested in interactive virtual reality technology used over distances have used the term **tele-immersion** to describe networked applications of virtual reality that enable immersive three-dimensional interactions from multiple sites (47). The immediate goal of current research on tele-immersion is to create work environments that facilitate scientific collaborations in networked-based virtual reality. The potential significance of this and other technological developments on cultures, people, and daily occupations is difficult to estimate.

PLACE, OCCUPATIONS, AND WELL-BEING

Research on the relationship between place, occupations, and well-being has crossed many disciplines and focused on a variety of variables. Much of the current research in **social geography** and cultural geography has occurred in naturalistic settings through ethnographic approaches. *Ethnography* refers to studies in which an investigator observes behaviors and places to provide a written description of a social group focusing on cultural characteristics based on concrete experiences (48). Ecological psychology research has been concerned with specific environmental, physical, and social characteristics and their influence on task performance, perception, or emotions. Studies have repeatedly shown that place influences the type, frequency, duration, and style of behavior, and that it can have both positive and negative influences on lifestyle and well-being.

For example, an ethnographic study conducted at six low-rise apartment communities supported the premise that having natural settings in the view from the window contributes substantially to residents' satisfaction with their neighborhood and with various aspects of their sense of well-being (49). Another study of students' favorite places found that natural settings were prevalent among these and that these settings had perceived characteristics that facilitated relaxation and personal restoration (50). Finally, a study of the effects of physical environment on the behavior of preschool children showed that ceiling height and wall color in classrooms can influence cooperative behaviors (51).

While physical characteristics of environments have an influence on performance and emotions, the most important characteristics of places that influence occupations are their social dimensions and the meanings associated with those dimensions. A study by psychologist Ellen Langer illustrated this (52). In her research, volunteer men aged 75 to 80 years old were asked to either assume or recall their state of mind at age 55. The men were divided into two groups. Men in the experimental group were asked to be the person they were 20 years ago. Men in this group were asked to live as if it was actually 1959, and the men and researchers used the present tense to refer to that year. Researchers suggested that the men might even feel as well as they did in 1959. Men in the other group also focused on conditions 20 years earlier, but their temporal context was the present. That is, they discussed life as it was in 1959 using the past tense.

Before and after a separate 5-day country retreat, researchers measured the men's physical strength, taste, hearing, vision, gait, perception cognition, values, and behavior. Researchers photographed the men's faces and videotaped their gait and posture. At the retreat, researchers videotaped the men eating meals to record how much food and with how much vigor they ate and their independence in serving themselves and cleaning up after meals.

The men in both groups engaged in the same daily routines with the only difference being the focus on 1959 as if it were the present (experimental group) or past (control group). The experimental group experienced news, music, movies, magazines, television, and sports as if it was 1959 and the other group used media to reminisce about 1959.

The results showed changes in both groups. Both groups showed improvements in hearing and hand strength and all looked younger as judged by the facial photos. Their memories improved. They ate heartily and gained a little weight, were less dependent on others, and were more involved in serving and cleaning up from meals. In fact, all of the men in both groups were functioning independently from the first days of the retreat, despite the fact that they had all been dependent on the help of others before the retreat.

The differences between the two groups that were apparent in 5 days included gains for the experimental group and losses for the reminiscence group. The experimental group showed changes in their physical condition, including improvements in cognitive skill (IQ and problem solving), vision, flexibility, and overall fitness. The control group showed improvement only in the measures for friendliness and emotional expressiveness.

The study showed that when researchers changed the time context, this dramatically altered the men's experience of where they were. By controlling that aspect alone, researchers found that the men in the experimental group had reversed what had always been considered "irreversible" measures of the aging process (52, p. 112). The interaction of the men and place was altered by time-improved measures of health, perceived well-being, and everyday occupations of the experimental group. Perhaps in the process of depicting an earlier time in their lives, men in the experimental group lived out the everyday occupations of a time when they were presumably healthier.

In another study of place, occupation, and well-being (53), investigators examined whether the perceived supportiveness of an environment in connection with an individual's personal projects was related to psychological well-being. Well-being was defined as a person's overall satisfaction with life and the presence of depression as measured by psychological scales. Personal projects referred to the goal-directed pursuits that were currently being undertaken by the study's participants. The researchers were also interested in determining those specific characteristics of personal projects and everyday places that were associated with the level of perceived supportiveness of the environment. The investigators were interested in getting a detailed understanding of how places supported the goal-directed occupational pursuits of the individuals being studied.

Approximately one-third of the participants' personal projects were connected to a specifiable place, which most often referred to home, the workplace, or sports facilities. The results showed that perceived supportiveness of the environment in connection with personal projects predicted life satisfaction but was not indicative of depression. Highly supportive environments were associated with projects that were accomplishable, socially supported, and difficult to complete successfully. Those study participants who showed evidence of depression tended to have projects that were more abstract, more stressful, and more self-related. Each aspect of the environment was perceived to have supportive functions. Informal action by friends and associates was perceived to support personal projects more often than more formal structures in a setting.

Clearly, the health and well-being of people depend to a great extent on the places in which they work, rest, sleep, play, and care for themselves and others. Although it is important for places to have natural and physical resources, it is the influence of place on social interaction and the social dimensions of places that seem most to impact the quality of life and overall well-being.

CHAPTER SUMMARY

This chapter has provided an overview of the relationship between places and everyday occupations. The multiple dimensions of places were identified, including their physical and geographic dimensions, and their socially constructed meanings. Archetypal places were identified as those that fulfill basic needs in everyday life, many of which serve as focal points for specific daily occupations. The reciprocal influences of occupations on places and places on occupations were described, and geographic differences in occupation by place were illustrated. The importance of the time–space dimension related to the location of places and the distances between them was described. Technological developments and the creation of virtual places were identified as a significant development for the new millennium. The chapter concluded with descriptions of research showing how dimensions of place can influence health and well-being.

REFERENCES

1. Harvey, D. W. (1993). From space to place and back again: Reflections on the condition of post-modernity. In J. Bird et al. (Eds.), *Mapping the futures: Local cultures, global change.* London: Routledge.
2. Spivak, M. (1973, October). Archetypal places. *The Architectural Forum,* pp. 44–49.
3. Barker, R. G. (1963). On the nature of the environment. *Journal of Social Issues, 19,* 17–38.
4. Gibson, J. J. (1979). *The ecological approach to vision perception.* Boston: Houghlin-Mifflin.
5. Thrift, N. (1985). Flies and germs: A geography of knowledge. In D. Gregory & J. Urry (Eds.), *Social relations and spatial structures.* Basingstoke: Macmillan.
6. Ralph, E. (1976). *Place and placelessness.* London: Pion.
7. Sack, R. (1992). *Place, modernity and the consumer's world.* Baltimore: Johns Hopkins University Press.
8. Hiss, T. (1996). *The experience of place.* New York: Vintage Books.
9. Hummon, D. (1990). *Commonplaces: Community ideology and identity in American culture.* Albany: State University of New York Press.
10. Steele, F. (1981). *The sense of place.* Boston: CBI Publishing.
11. Hummon, D. (1992). Community attachment: Local sentiment and a sense of place. In S. Altman (Ed.), *Place attachment.* (pp. 253–278). New York: Plenum.
12. Gustafson, P. (2001). Meanings of place: Everyday experiences and theoretical conceptualizations. *Journal of Environmental Psychology, 21*(1), 5–16.
13. Danesi, M. (1994). *Messages and meanings: An introduction to semiotics.* Toronto: Canadian Scholars Press.
14. Stevens, A. (1990). *On Jung.* London: Penguin.
15. Campbell, J. (1973). *The hero with a thousand faces.* Princeton, NJ: Princeton University Press.
16. MacDonald, M. R. (1982). *The storyteller's sourcebook: A subject, title and motif index to folklore collections for children.* Detroit: Neal-Schuman Publishers.
17. Knowles, R. L. (1992). Rhythms of perception. *Places,* 8(2), 72–81.
18. Calvin, W. H. (1986). *The river that flows uphill: A journey from the big bang to the big brain.* San Francisco: Sierra Club Books.
19. James, L., & Nahl, D. (2000). *Road rage and aggressive driving: Steering clear of highway warfare.* Amherst, NY: Prometheus Books.
20. Federation, E. (1984). *Improvement of living and working conditions.* Dublin, Ireland: European Foundation for the Improvement of Living and Working Conditions.
21. Marshall, K. (1994). *Getting there* (Report 75-001E). Ottawa: Statistics Canada.
22. Kulash, W. (1990). Traditional neighbourhood development: Will the traffic work? In *Eleventh Annual Pedestrian Conference* (pp. 4-1–4-2). Bellevue, WA.
23. World Bank (IRBD).(1986). *Urban transport.* (Report PB86-194321).Washington, DC: Author.
24. Ley, D. (1983). *A social geography of the city.* New York: Harper and Row.
25. Bourdieu, P. (1990). *In other words: Essays towards a reflexive sociology.* Stanford, CA: Stanford University Press.

26. Murray, H. A., Barrett, W. G., & Hamburger, E. (1938). *Explorations in personality.* New York: Oxford University Press.
27. Lewin, K. (1997). *Field theory in social science.* Washington, DC: American Psychological Association.
28. Latane, B. (1981). The psychology of social impact. *American Psychologist, 36,* 343–356.
29. Wickens, C. D., Gordon, S. E., & Liu, Y. (Eds.). (1998). *An introduction to human factors engineering.* New York: Addison-Wesley.
30. Platt, K. (1996). Places of experience and the experience of place. In L. Rouner (Ed.), *The longing for home* (pp. 112–127). Notre Dame, IN: University of Notre Dame Press.
31. Fontanel, C. (1998). *Babies celebrated.* New York: Harry Abrams.
32. Mahler, M. (2000). *Psychological birth of the human infant: Symbiosis and individuation* (reprint ed.; original ed. published 1975). New York: Basic Books.
33. Berg., M, & Medrich, E. A. (1980). Children in four neighborhoods: The physical environment and its effect on play and play patterns. *Environment and Behavior, 12,* 320–348.
34. Carpenter, J. L. (1991). *Frank Baum: Royal historian of Oz.* Minneapolis: Lerner Publications Co.
35. Spielberg, S. (Producer & Director), & Kennedy, K. (Producer) (1982). *E. T. The Extra-Terrestrial* [Motion Picture], United States: Universal City Studios.
36. Czaja, S. J., Weber, R. A., & Nair, S. N. (1993). A human factor analysis of ADL activities: A capability demand approach. *Journal of Gerontology, 48,* 44–48.
37. Rowles, G. (1999). Beyond performance: Being in place as a component of occupational therapy. *American Journal of Occupational Therapy, 45*(3), 265–271.
38. Robinson, T. (1999). Stigma and architecture. In G. S. Steinfeld (Ed.), *Enabling environments: Measuring the impact of environment on disability and rehabilitation* (pp. 251–270). Norwell, MA: Kluwer Academic/Plenum Publishers.
39. Shinn, M., & Weitzman, B. (1998). Predictors of homelessness among families in New York City. *American Journal of Public Health, 88,* 1651–1657.
40. Fischer, P. J. (1992). Criminal behavior and victimization among homeless people. In R. I. Jaheil (Ed.), *Homelessness: A prevention-oriented approach.* Baltimore: The Johns Hopkins University Press.
41. Steiner, L. P., Looney, S. W., Hall, L. R., & Wright, K. M. (1995). Quality of life and functional status among homeless men attending a day shelter in Louisville, Kentucky. *Journal of the Kentucky Medical Association, 93*(5), 188–195.
42. Rosenbeck, C. (1998). Homelessness, health service use and related costs. *Medical Care, 36*(8), 1256–1264.
43. Weinbreb, L., Goldberg, R., & Perloff, J. (1998). Health characteristics and medical service use patterns of sheltered homeless and low income housed mothers. *Journal of General Internal Medicine, 13,* 389–397.
44. Gelberg, L., Linn, L. S., & Leake, B. (1998). Mental health, alcohol and drug use, and criminal history among homeless adults. *American Journal of Psychiatry, 145*(2), 191–196.
45. Williams, J. C. (1998). Domestic violence and poverty: The narratives of homeless women. *Frontiers, 19*(2), 143–165.
46. Davey, T. L. (1998). Homeless children and stress: An empirical study. *Journal of Social Distress and the Homeless, 7*(1), 29–41.
47. Lanier J. (2001). Virtually there. *Scientific American, 284*(4), 64–65.
48. Marshall G. (Ed). (1994). *The concise Oxford dictionary of sociology.* Oxford: Oxford University Press.

49. Kaplan R. (2001). The nature of the view from home. *Psychologial Benefits, 33*(4), 507–542.

50. Korpela K. M., Hartig, T., Kaiser, F. G., & Fuhrer, U. (2001). Restorative experience and self regulation in favorite places. *Environment and Behavior, 33*(4), 572–589.

51. Read M. A., Sugawara, A. I., & Brandt, J. A. (1999). Impact of space and color in the physical environment on preschool cooperative behavior. *Environment and Behavior, 31*(3), 413–428.

52. Langer E. (1989). *Mindfulness.* Reading, MA: Addison-Wesley.

53. Wallenius M. (1999). Personal projects in everyday places: Perceived supportiveness of the environment and psychological well-being. *Journal of Environmental Psychology, 19*(2), 131–143.

CHAPTER 9

Occupations as a Means for Individual and Group Participation in Life

Janice Miller Polgar and Jennifer E. Landry

KEY WORDS

Community animation

Occupational deprivation

Occupational participation

Rhythm

Sense of accomplishment

CHAPTER PROFILE

Occupations can be viewed as the means through which human beings relate to themselves, to others, and to the world at large. Occupations enable people to meet the requirements for living by achieving individual and group goals. In this chapter, we review and examine these relationships from the standpoint of required as well as chosen occupations. We also consider various issues related to the opportunities, challenges, and consequences resulting from daily occupations.

INTRODUCTION

Participation in occupation defines who we are, either as individuals or as members of our communities. Occupation is as essential to the health of humans as breathing (1). Without everyday occupations, our lives would be devoid of meaning and purpose. These are very strong statements about the importance of occupation, and this chapter will provide a basis for these assertions.

www.prenhall.com/christiansen

The Internet provides an exciting means for interacting with this textbook and for enhancing your understanding of humans' experiences with occupations and the organization of occupations in society. Use the address above to access the free, interactive companion web site created specifically to accompany this book. Here you will find an array of self-study material designed to help you gain a richer understanding of the concepts presented in this chapter.

As suggested in the chapter profile, here we examine the historical and current concepts of participation in relation to occupation, as well as the importance of participation in occupations in our daily lives, both as individuals and as members of a community. Later, we consider the occupations of Samantha, a case example, to illustrate and highlight some principles and characteristics of occupations as ways and means of living.

A large body of literature exists on human activity. What this chapter offers is a discussion of how people engage in everyday life from the perspective of occupational scientists. It addresses questions such as *What does it mean to individuals when they participate in occupations? and What does it mean to communities when their members engage in shared occupations?*

Thus, in this chapter, we frame our discussion of occupation from the standpoint of the individual and from the standpoint of the community. Daily life is filled with predictable and unexpected challenges and benefits, often associated with what we do. When circumstances limit or restrict our occupational pursuits, we experience consequences, which are sometimes adverse. On the other hand, when our intentions and plans work out as we expect or want, we derive benefits or pleasures from these outcomes.

In reviewing these topics, historical and current beliefs regarding participation in occupation will be explored. A discussion of individual participation in occupation will be followed by an example of participation in occupations that involve a community. Readers are invited to contemplate a broader perspective of participation, one that is grounded in the notion that humans actively seek and need to participate in occupation. Further, this notion is extended to community participation, to include occupational engagement that meets the needs and goals expressed by groups and communities, as discussed in Chapter 7.

FUNDAMENTAL IDEAS OF PARTICIPATION IN OCCUPATION

The term *occupation* refers to actually doing something, whether the doing is physical, cognitive, psychological, social, or spiritual. In this chapter, we refer to both participation in occupation and to **occupational participation.** Each of these terms emphasizes the importance of the relationship between participation and occupation. It is not sufficient to understand that a person or community is doing something. Rather, it is the exploration of what they are doing, why they are doing it, and what it brings to their lives, individually or collectively, that adds to our understanding of human behavior. A distinction needs to be made between occupations that the individual or group *wants* to do versus those that they *need* to do. Occupation can be an expression of self-determination when participation is based on choice. On the other hand, there are some occupations that we participate in out of necessity, out of a sense of duty, or because we do not have other options.

The broad concept of "doing" in occupational participation is fundamental to an understanding of what occupation is to the everyday life of individuals and to communities. Occupations, as discussed throughout the book, are not merely technical acts or even tasks performed physically. Participation in occupations, then, engages the whole person—their body, mind, and soul—either on an individual basis or as a member of a group.

Most often, when we think of doing something, we envision being physically active as in getting dressed, participating in a sports activity, or engaging in manual labor. However, occupations that are not physically active also engage an individual, so that a person may be cognitively doing something when he is reading an absorbing book or listening to a lecture. Similarly, a person may participate in occupations spiritually when he or she is engaged in meditation or contemplative thoughts (2, 3). The point here is that a person does not have to be physically active to participate in an occupation. Csikszentmihalyi (4), when discussing his concept of flow, indicates that the active use of the mind is imperative if the person is to participate in an occupation. He argues that when the mind is free to wander, thoughts are chaotic and boredom results. The person does not feel productive or involved.

The process of living is predicated on doing or participating in various occupations (5). All those things that occupy individuals—what people *do*—are viewed as the essential processes and products of daily life. Consistent with the idea that the journey is as important as the destination, participation in occupations may be conceptualized as both the means and the ends of everyday living. Participating in occupations, or doing and the experience of doing, is critical to the well-being and health both of individuals and communities. In addition to personal reasons, human beings participate in occupations individually and collectively to meet social needs and expectations.

As social beings, humans are typically members of multiple groups at any one point in time, and across the life span. We are members of families, peer groups, neighborhoods, clubs, and organizations, and each group we belong to also participates in occupations within some setting or another. The basic principles of ecology recognize the interconnectedness of all living organisms and their environments and the dynamic nature of life (6):

> In the context of all of these group memberships, we interact with a moveable feast of richly diverse communities. Each of these interactions, whether with our families, social groups or physical environment, is ecological in that there is an opportunity for exchange of ideas or energy. As a result, we and the environment are transformed, even in a small way. Ecological exchange yields both constraints and enhancements to personal and population health. (7)

From an ecological perspective, participation in daily living through occupation is a process whereby people interact with their environments in a way that sustains well-being for individuals, communities, and the environment. Healthy communities sustain and are sustained by healthy environments. The health of a community depends on maintaining a balance between the aspirations, needs, capabilities, and goals of individuals and entire communities within the context of their environment (7).

BELIEFS ABOUT OCCUPATIONAL PARTICIPATION

The health-related value of participation in physical occupations has been recognized since ancient times. The Persians, Chinese, and Greeks all emphasized physical training and the need for activity. Aristotle believed that physical development of the body must occur prior to development of the intellect. Activity and work were considered to promote greater intellectual capacity, be diversional, and have physical benefits. Aristotle believed that the highest good was to live a life filled with occupations that require the exercise of our reason or intelligence. A good life will be one in which such occupations are performed well (8). During medieval times, however, interest in and emphasis on the benefits of physical activity waned (9).

Attention returned to participation in occupations in the latter part of the 18th century. Again activity, predominantly physical activity, was thought to be important for the maintenance of health as well as a balance and satisfaction with life. Physical exercise and manual labor were considered to be conducive to good morale and discipline (10), thus introducing behavioral and spiritual dimensions to the beliefs concerning occupational participation.

The effects of occupational participation were described more broadly in the early part of the last century. A lack of adaptation to the demands of the environment was linked to illness (11). Work helped to alleviate problems by creating pleasure and satisfaction through achievement and the completion of a task. Further, achievement and task completion promoted a sense of competency and pride in one's work. Doing was considered the only way to achieve a balance in life and a wholesome lifestyle. These historical ideas form the foundation for what we currently believe to be the consequences or effects of participation in occupation.

Today, the idea of participation has led to new and exciting changes for individuals and societies. Sports and health enthusiasts point to participation as the key to health, wellness, and other concepts related to quality of life. Consumers are invited to provide feedback to corporations to shape product design and utility. As urban areas grow increasingly larger, communities strive for activities, such as local festivals, that foster participation and a sense of belonging among their residents. These brief examples illustrate our current focus on participation.

Yet, as we suggested earlier, participation itself is insufficient. It is the dynamic relationship between participation and occupation that is of interest. Recent ideas (12) about occupational participation relate to consequences in the daily life of individuals and their communities, the developmental changes of this participation, and the importance of the interaction with the environment.

Meaning in Life

Occupation is believed to give *meaning to life,* providing the individual values occupation. A great deal is written about meaningful occupation, but the meaning of this concept is often elusive because significance is frequently unique and personal to the individual. Meaningful occupation gives individuals a sense of purpose and a goal in their lives. Victor Frankl (13) describes life in a German concentration camp where the internees were systematically stripped of their sense of being valued persons. Many of these people retained a sense of survival by surreptitiously participating in some occupation that was meaningful to them. Frankl, for example, reconstructed a manuscript that had been destroyed during his imprisonment, using whatever bits of paper he could find. In this way, he managed to retain his sense of being a valued human with a future, despite the attempts of the guards to dehumanize him.

Sense of Accomplishment

Completion of a project, whether by an individual or a community, brings closure and a **sense of accomplishment.** When a goal is reached, such as the completion of an educational level or the successful end to a community development project, participants can reflect on their accomplishment with pride and know that they were responsible for the outcome. In contrast, when a goal is not satisfactorily achieved, the participants may feel a sense of frustration or lack of confidence in their efforts or the outcome. Some participants are undeterred by lack of success and continue their efforts. In contrast, others will not risk a second attempt at a failed goal. The difference between those who persist and those who do not is thought to be based on many psychological factors, including optimism and efficacy (14, 15). Further, environmental factors contribute to whether a person will persist at a goal or not. Children at risk, who have an advocate or someone who believes in them in their social environment, are more resilient than those who do not (16).

People derive their *identity* from occupation (17). It is something that helps define the individual. Commonly, when people are asked about what they do, they respond by describing their job, naming their profession or their hobbies, depending on the circumstances. A typical example of such identity is the titles that many workers are given. These titles serve to describe the holder's place within an organization and to recognize the contribution and value they add to their community.

Determinant of Health

Participation in occupation is an important *determinant of health* (18). The experience of doing and reflection on participation are critical to well-being on both an individual and a community level. Many reports indicate that individuals who participate regularly in physical activity, and other meaningful occupation, and who have a strong social network have high satisfaction with life and a strong sense of well-being (19, 20) (Figure 9-1). Individuals who have a chronic illness describe themselves as healthy if they are able to participate in occupations important to them (21). When they are unable to participate in these occupations, they feel that they are removed from the world and are unhealthy. There is some evidence that participation in occupations is the means by which individuals who have experienced a life-threatening illness regain their sense of being healthy and capable (22). They shift their identity from being a patient to being a person *living with* the illness (23).

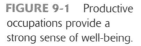

FIGURE 9-1   Productive occupations provide a strong sense of well-being.

Rhythm in Life

Rhythm in life is established through occupational participation. Most of us follow a daily routine that is a mix of self-care, work, rest, and leisure occupations. Additionally, some occupations are completed only on a weekly or monthly basis, such as bill paying or going to group meetings or lessons. The seasons of the year, both natural and socially determined, give another form of **rhythm** to occupational participation.

Over time, occupational participation develops and changes. The infant and young child are concerned with development of motor, cognitive, and social skills, mainly through play (24). As the child enters school, the balance between play and work, as expressed through school occupations, changes so that more time is spent in work (25). In adulthood, this balance further tips in favor of work-related occupations, including those in which the person participates outside of paid employment, such as volunteer occupations (26). On retirement, most people find themselves with more leisure time.

How we participate in occupation also has a developmental perspective. Children usually receive care from adults. In the elderly, this situation may reverse. When we first participate in an occupation we most likely assume a role as a learner and perhaps find someone who will act as our mentor. A young football player who is guided by a senior player or coach provides an example of this early role. With development in this occupation, we may become the mentor or coach, guiding those who are less experienced. An interesting body of literature explores the transition from a novice to an expert in various occupations (27). Chapter 5 describes our current understanding of the developmental aspects of occupation.

Choice and Control

The presence or absence of *choice and control* in occupational participation is important on both the individual and community levels. Here we are describing the degree to which participants are able to make choices or exert control over what they will do and how they will do it. When choice and control are available, participants may derive a sense of self-determination and empowerment (28). However, choice and control also entail risk. For example, individuals in control of their finances are at risk of needing money for necessities if they spend lavishly when their pay is first received.

Choice and control are limited in some circumstances. For example, students often do not have control over their curriculum, particularly in earlier grades. Some students with disabilities have expressed their resentment toward school officials who restrict curricular choices, thus limiting subsequent career opportunities. Other consequences of limited or lack of control within an occupation are lowered self-esteem, or self-efficacy, and decreased sense of independence and motivation to participate in occupation (29, 30).

Imbalance in Occupational Participation

The concept of balance in participation in occupation, and across the life span was mentioned earlier. The effects of an *imbalance in occupational participation* are interesting to consider. Such an imbalance may result from personal choice, external influences, or a person's abilities. Perhaps the most obvious cause is personal choice when people choose to focus time and energy in a particular area (e.g., work). External influences include peers who pressure an individual to participate in certain occupations, persons who have power over another such as an employer or educator, an environment that restricts occupational choice (e.g., an institution, including the government), or societal or cultural influences on a person or community to conform, perform, or achieve in a certain manner. Finally, a person's abilities may determine the occupational participation. For example, those persons with physical limitations may not be able to participate in occupations to the degree they desire.

Environment

Related to the elements of choice and control is the belief that the *environment* shapes and is shaped by a person's participation in occupations. If the environment affords opportunities for participation in many occupations, the individual or community then has the choice to determine the nature of that participation. A young child, entering a room that holds many interesting toys, will participate in a variety of gross and fine motor occupations using the available objects. In contrast, an uninviting or restrictive environment limits opportunities for occupational participation, self-expression, development, and other positive outcomes. Again, Frankl's work (13) illustrates the effect on both the individual and the community when the environment is extremely restrictive. In the setting of the concentration camp, people sought a variety of means of self-preservation, some cooperative, others guided only by self-interest. Cooperative behavior was demonstrated by sharing food, whereas rushing to the middle of a crowd to avoid the blows of a guard is an example of actions taken in self-interest.

Just as the environment exerts an influence on the individual or community, so too, do these influence the environment. Various social movements provide excellent examples of how communities can affect policy changes to improve the lifestyles of their citizens. Native people in Canada and the United States spoke out on the conditions under which they lived when forced to attend federal schools where their culture was denied. Within these communities, a strong sense of heritage is resurging. We see the resulting pride in their culture, through native healing practices, teaching of cultural traditions and language, and native forms of law enforcement (31). The aging of the population in Western countries and the strong political voice of older persons have resulted in greater responsiveness to the physical, psychological, and social needs of seniors.

Technology

Technology is a specific aspect of the environment that has had a major influence on participation in occupations in the past decade. The rapid development of technology facilitates participation in occupations while also creating challenges for some individuals. Technology makes tasks more efficient and eliminates some of their physical and cognitive demands. However, in some situations, improved efficiency creates demands for greater productivity, potentially creating stress for an individual or collective. Further, when a person relies on technology for physical and cognitive skills and does not exercise these skills in other ways, the capacity to use them may be diminished.

This paradox of technology is amply illustrated by considering the myriad of communication methods available, such as conventional mail, voice mail, e-mail, fax, Internet, and cellular phones. All of these devices make staying in touch with others much simpler. At the same time, however, they create an expectation that a person or group will be available at any time and be able to respond to any request immediately. Thus, new technology saves time in one area, but may create demands and consumption in other areas (32).

Technological devices may require fewer physical and cognitive demands for task completion than are required by the task in their absence. When an individual has limited cognitive or physical capacity, technological devices can compensate for these limits. Devices can also complete simple tasks quicker, freeing the individual for other, more complex tasks. In the case of cognitive demands, however, individuals may come to rely on the technical device to do a task and be unable to complete it independently in the absence of the technology. Consider the university students who are unable to complete long division without the aid of a calculator.

Technology also results in fewer physical demands for the completion of a given task. Devices can be a useful asset for individuals with physical disabilities because they enable them to participate more fully in a variety of occupations. Wheelchairs make mobility easier for individuals unable to walk independently (easier, that is, until faced with an inaccessible building). Communication devices provide voices for those with articulation problems. Computer access devices enable students and employees to complete work with relative independence. Finally, electronic aids to daily living enable persons with very limited physical abilities to access the stereo, answer the telephone or door, or switch on lights. All of these devices can be used effectively to enable persons with disabilities to participate more fully in their community (33).

However, when the use of devices replaces physical activity, undesirable results may occur. With limited access to technology, adults and children expend energy when completing tasks such as homemaking or playing active games. However, our current technology minimizes the physical demands for many tasks, requiring persons to meet physical health or fitness needs in other ways. A person who does not meet physical health needs in other ways may become sedentary, which can lead to health problems (34).

Sanctioned Occupations

We discuss a final, general concept, *sanctioned occupations*, before examining participation in occupations from the individual and then community perspectives. Within a community or society, certain occupations are considered acceptable, or desirable, while others are not. The former may be labeled *socially sanctioned* and the latter *socially unsanctioned* or *deviant*. An important caveat to consider here is that different perspectives, values, or beliefs will define unsanctioned occupations for the individual or community; that is, what one person considers deviant may be seen as acceptable by another. Incest and murder are obvious examples of deviant occupations. Less obvious examples include living on the streets, choices of music or dress, smoking in public, communal lifestyles, or drinking and driving. Of interest here are the effects participation in these occupations has on the individual or community.

What are some of the results of participation in occupations that are not socially sanctioned or supported on a larger scale? Such occupations may be criminal such as gang activity, but they may also be religious in nature or those of fringe communities or of stigmatized groups. A person or community may be marginalized from the mainstream of society, which may limit access to adequate housing, health care, or employment. Consider a person who lives on the street. Without a home address, social support and employment are not readily available. Others may experience discomfort when approached by a person who lives on the street because the latter's lifestyle is not understood. These people live on the fringe of society, and may not have access to full participation in their community occupations (35).

The challenge here is to identify the needs that are being met by the person who chooses the nonsanctioned occupation rather than participation in occupations more readily accepted by the larger community. Further, a balance must be struck between tolerating those occupations that, while not socially acceptable, are harmless, versus finding ways to redirect the efforts of communities whose activities do cause harm to its members or members of other groups, such as gang wars in the inner cities.

Stigma may be attached to certain persons or communities when others do not accept their lifestyle or behaviors. Stigma refers to "an attribute that is deeply discrediting" (36, p. 3). In other words, some aspect of a person or community reduces the value or worth of that individual in the eyes of others. One example is seen in the treatment of persons with disabilities. A physical disability can have no effect on intellectual skills. However, stigma may cause people to assume that those with physical disabilities also have cognitive limitations. As a result, a person's actual abilities are not recognized. Instead, one attribute has a negative influence on others' perceptions about an entire person.

Segregation is another aspect to consider. Here, the experiences of Native Americans, First Nation peoples in Canada, and aboriginal peoples in Australia illustrate how communities of people whose activities or lifestyles are not understood by the mainstream of society are not accepted by and are segregated from the larger society. As a result, their occupations, beliefs, and values are less likely to be understood by others, resulting in further segregation. Moreover, their traditional lifestyles may be discouraged. In some instances, these communities are also geographically isolated from others, which limits their inhabitants' opportunities to earn a living or gain an education.

Restriction of personal freedom is another possible result of participation in unsanctioned activities or membership in a group whose behavior is not sanctioned. Incarceration, for example, in prison or another form of institution, limits the choice and control a person has over participation in occupations. A person's participation in socially unsanctioned behavior or some characteristic of the individual may lead to incarceration. Incarceration or institutionalization based on a person's sex, culture, religious affiliation, or abilities may also occur. In these situations, a person's choice of occupation and environment and freedom of movement are severely limited. Daily routines such as eating, bathing, or exercising may be determined by the rules of the institution and, in some cases, participation in such occupations may be denied completely. Whether persons find themselves in such a situation because society feels they deserve punishment or are undesirable, detrimental effects on their development and occupational participation result. In some situations where opportunities for participation in occupations are severely restricted, cognitive, affective, and physical development or skill maintenance are significantly impaired. (See Chapter 10 for further elaboration on the consequences of being deprived of occupational opportunities.)

INDIVIDUAL PARTICIPATION IN OCCUPATION

In this section, to further illustrate the dynamic influence of occupations on lives, we draw on the information about Samantha presented in Box 9-1. Sam participates in many different occupations that contribute in different ways to her health, her sense of identity, and her development. She has regular involvement in strenuous physical activity. In addition, the physical occupations that she enjoys involve structure, rules, and roles that help develop skills needed to socialize with others and assume different roles (e.g., leader or group member). Not only does she enjoy physical occupations, she also participates in creative pursuits and more quiet occupations such as crafts, reading, and computer games.

Sam has some responsibilities in the home, such as caring for her fish, which are preparing her to be more independent and to assume more responsibility when she gets a dog. Examination of her life roles indicates that she is a daughter, sister, friend, student, and athlete. A child of this age is constantly learning who she is, what her

BOX 9-1 Portrait of Sam

Samantha, or Sam as she is known to friends and family, is a precocious 9-year-old who loves animals and sports. She readily identifies herself as a tomboy and is proud of this label, telling all that she owns no dresses. In soccer, she likes to challenge her opponent for the ball and does not fear being hit with it. Her favorite positions in hockey are defense and goaltender (Figure 9-2). She displays no fear when going after the puck. Although she likes to play these sports, she does not show much interest in watching them, either on television or live.

Since she was 7, Sam has asked for a dog. Her parents require her to wait until she is 12 so that she is old enough to assume some of the responsibility for its care. In the meantime, she has two cats and an aquarium of fish, the fish being her responsibility.

Sam is an enthusiastic participant in school, with physical education and mathe-

FIGURE 9-2   Hockey promotes physical, cognitive and social development.
(Photograph courtesy of Jan Miller Polgar)

matics being her favorite subjects. Although she likes to write stories, and these are creative, she does struggle to put her ideas on paper and, in particular, to spell correctly. She is learning to create a draft of her work so that she can correct any errors before she completes the finished project. Recently, she says that she likes to read. Another organized occupation in which she participates is a church group for young girls.

She is the older of two children; her brother is 2 years younger. Usually, they enjoy playing together, and with neighbors and friends, particularly participating in road hockey, soccer, and bike riding. They also like to participate in creative play and crafts and watch TV and movies.

skills are, her strengths and areas needing improvement, likes and dislikes, and how to cooperate with others, socialize, and become independent. Participation in occupation fosters development in these areas, as we shall see in the following discussion.

Let's consider Sam's participation in occupations and how it illustrates the concepts discussed earlier as they relate to an individual. Because Sam is a child, her experiences with participation in occupation may not reflect that of an adult, so we will also draw examples from the lives of adults and seniors for a richer discussion of these concepts.

FIGURE 9-3   Regular physical activity is beneficial to our well-being.
(Photograph courtesy of Jan Miller Polgar)

Sam's involvement in a variety of occupations contributes to her *health and well-being,* physically, psychologically, and socially. In childhood, as at other ages, a certain level of *physical activity,* which is determined individually, assists with the development of strength, endurance, and flexibility, and with achievement and maintenance of a desirable weight. For a child, physical activity helps to develop coordination, both for large and small movements.

Regular physical activity decreases the risk of cardiovascular diseases. Once a concern primarily for adults, the recent advances in technology that make computer games, the Internet, movies and multichannel television available mean that children now lead a much more sedentary lifestyle, such that cardiovascular risk factors are appearing with greater regularity (37).

In adults, regular physical activity has weak links to the prevention of certain diseases such as some cancers and diabetes mellitus (Figure 9-3). Within limits, physical activity is beneficial for individuals with various forms of arthritis. For example, many individuals with arthritis experience greater freedom of movement when participating in a regular aquatics program. In postmenopausal women, there is some evidence that resistive physical exercise limits bone density loss (38).

Seniors who are more physically active tend to have a greater capacity to maintain their functional independence than those with more restricted lifestyles. Participation in strength training and other types of exercise minimizes the risk of falls in seniors. Falls are a major factor in loss of independence in daily activities for this group (38). Further, seniors and others whose ability to participate in occupations is restricted indicate that satisfactory participation in chosen occupations is necessary for well-being and feeling healthy (19, 35, 36).

Health and well-being also have a *psychological side.* When Sam is successful and satisfied with her performance in her occupations, she gains greater self-confidence or self-efficacy. As she gains self-confidence, she will accept increasing demands and challenges on her abilities, resulting in the acquisition of more advanced skills and knowledge (18). She feels a sense of accomplishment when she scores goals in soccer or successfully completes a school project.

Other people also have an influence on the self-confidence of a person. When their performance is valued by society, individuals feel they are worthy. Such messages further enhance a feeling of personal control (i.e., feelings of being responsible for one's actions and life). In contrast, individuals may derive a sense of worthlessness when they perceive that what they do is given little value. Many studies indicate that participation in meaningful occupations promotes a sense of well-being and increased satisfaction with life (41). Following treatment for a life-threatening illness, people have reported that reengaging in occupations that hold meaning for them provides them with a sense of satisfaction with their accomplishments (22, 23).

Participation in her chosen occupations also assists Sam's *cognitive development*. At this age, Sam is still developing cognitive skills, although certain cognitive strengths are already apparent. She is beginning to think in abstract terms and to independently test and refine problem-solving abilities. At this stage, when greater volume and independence in school work are required, Sam must develop strategies that will minimize the effect of some of her less developed abilities to ensure that she is successful academically.

Older adults help us understand further how participation in occupations influences cognitive abilities. Seniors have identified the benefits of occupations, recognizing that active participation enables them to remain mentally alert. Many seniors may participate in leisure occupations such as golf or card games that not only provide social contact but a cognitive challenge as well. Occupations that are perceived as challenging and stimulating engage the individual, thus holding her attention, so that the cognitive benefits can be realized. Csikszentmihalyi (4) articulates this idea with his notion of flow. When an occupation has an optimal level of challenge for the participant's skill, the individual will maintain her attention to it and derive a maximal benefit. Crossword puzzles are a good example of a challenging occupation with cognitive benefits.

As indicated earlier, participation in occupations promotes the individual's *sense of identity*. Participation in occupations helps define who Sam is and how she views herself. Because she excels at sports and is not interested in things typically considered feminine, she calls herself a tomboy. She likes to determine her own path and has always resisted following the crowd. Additionally, her involvement in occupations at school, church, and home further helps her define who she is as a person and how she should or will perform in certain roles.

When considering the psychological aspects of health, a comment should be made on links between occupation and psychological issues, specifically, between physical activity and depression (37). Physical activity appears to reduce feelings of depression and anxiety and have a positive effect on an individual's mood. There is some evidence that participation in physical activity may reduce the chances of developing depression although the research is not yet conclusive.

Participation in occupations provides the means for gaining *meaning from life*. Participation in valued occupations gives individuals a sense of meaning and value in their lives. This spiritual aspect is the essence of an individual. It helps define the core of our being (42). It captures who we are and helps us derive purpose and direction. Sam is probably on the verge of having sufficient insight to express the meaning participation in chosen occupations has to her. Consideration of what persons with chronic or life-threatening illness describe as the importance of doing helps to illustrate this point. Such individuals indicate that a return to previously enjoyed occupations means that they are living, not dying (22). Regardless of the presence of a chronic illness, doing sends the message that they are healthy and capable (43).

The previous section discussed the reciprocal influence between the person and the environment. Sam participates in many *social environments*, including home, school, church, and community. In these environments, she learns and expresses her roles in society, the rules of the society, and how to interact with others in cooperative or competitive ways. Play is one occupation where children learn about roles, rules, and interactions with others and their society.

Culture is another aspect of the environment that influences Sam's participation in occupation. She lives in a culture where girls and women are considered to have access to the same opportunities as do men and boys. Thus, she is able to go to school, participate in hockey, and will be able to choose any career for which she has the skills and capacity. Women's roles are more rigidly defined outside North America. In certain cultures where women and girls are not considered equal to men and boys, Sam would not be able to go to school, play sports, or earn her own living. A more subtle influence of culture is reflected in the current value placed on participation in physical activity. Sam excels in sports and gains self-confidence because sports are valued in her society.

These illustrations demonstrate that participation in occupations defines who we are, gives meaning to our lives, and helps develop or maintain our skills and abilities. We now turn our attention to community participation in occupations.

COMMUNITY PARTICIPATION IN OCCUPATION

To a large extent, what we do defines who we are as people, and who we are as people generally defines what we do on a daily basis. This statement holds true for groups of people or communities, as well as for individuals. Chapter 7 notes that a group or community may be defined in many different ways. Regarding participation, communities are groups of people acting collectively in a desired or needed occupation. In this section we explore what it means to participate in occupations as a member of a community.

Community participation in occupation shares many similarities with individual participation. The "Running for Charity" vignette presented in Box 9-2 is provided to illuminate these connections and to provide a point of departure for reflecting on the challenges and opportunities afforded by community participation in occupations. Readers are also encouraged to consider other examples of community participation beyond volunteering, such as participation in paid occupations, occupations for enjoyment, occupations with a spiritual focus, and so forth.

BOX 9-2　A Bridge Between Individual and Community Participation in Occupation

Running for Charity

Participation in the occupation of "marathoning for charity" (fund-raising and training to run a marathon) involves one's whole being for the runner, but ultimately is about community participation. A personal story from one of the authors, Jennifer E. Landry, illustrates this:

For a number of years, I have had what I considered a very personal goal of running a marathon. Although others would support me by asking how my training was going, by encouraging me when my confidence wavered, and sometimes by accompanying me on those long runs, I would ultimately be the one training and running on race day. Running has been a part of my life, on and off, for the last decade or so. I set goals for myself and work toward them. I find participation in this occupation challenging, meaningful, and satisfying. I also enjoy the social aspect and camaraderie of being part of a diverse group of people who identify themselves as "runners." We like to think and tell all who will listen, that we are a "breed apart."

One sunny afternoon, as I waited in line to order my lunch, a poster caught my eye. In bold black letters it stated "Joints in Motion Marathon Training Team. Need a reason to join? We've got four million." I was intrigued. The Arthritis Society's Training Team is a North American program designed to raise money to support research for the cure and prevention of arthritis, as well as to support team members in meeting their goal of participating in a half- or full marathon in honor of someone with arthritis.

A few weeks before spotting the "Joints in Motion" advertisement, I had run a half-marathon that contributed all proceeds to Rose Cherry's Home in Ontario, Canada. Rose Cherry's Home provides pediatric hospice care and respite services to families with a child with a life-limiting or life-threatening illness. I was pleased that I was contributing to a good cause. During the race, there also was a sense that everyone was in this together, as demonstrated through words, gestures, and deeds. The runners, the race organizers, the onlookers, and of course the volunteers were all participants in that early morning road race. The absence of any of these groups within the road race community would have left a gap; their presence made the occupation what it was. In that sense, we were all "running" the race, participating in occupation as a community.

The Joints in Motion Training Team seemed like an incredible opportunity to contribute even more. It was a chance to meet the very personal goal of running a marathon, but just as significantly, it was an opportunity to participate in a community of people committed to fund-raising and training for a marathon. I joined the team. My involvement on the team enabled me to enhance my own health and well-being, as well as to contribute to funding much needed research and programs for people living with arthritis. Participation in this context bridged the individual and the community.

CHALLENGES AND OPPORTUNITIES

For individuals who participate together in occupations on a community level (such as the Joints in Motion Training Team from Box 9-2), the challenges and opportunities go beyond those experienced through individual participation. In shared community endeavors, the potential to reap benefits is realized on a personal and large scale, contributing to social, political, economic, and physical fabric of their group or community.

For instance on the level of the individual, much has been written about the physical, cognitive, and psychological effects of regular participation in aerobic exercise, such as running. It is easy to list some of these effects, such as increased cardiovascular fitness, increased life expectancy, lower incidence of morbidity, heightened mental alertness and motivation levels, and mood stabilization. We can picture the physical, cognitive, and psychological preparation that is involved in training to run a 42-kilometer (26-mile) race. Training for and running a marathon involves one's whole being and, as such, it is also a spiritual endeavor. From a spiritual standpoint, participation in long-distance running is an "expression of will, drive, and motivation" and demands dedication, commitment, determination, personal control, and sacrifice (12, p. 43).

Running can be, and for some individuals is, a very solitary occupation. When considering community participation, we ask what are additional consequences when people participate in occupations as a collective by choice or necessity? What happens when a community takes on a collective project?

Community Health and Quality of Life

The Joints in Motion Training Team encompasses a number of stakeholders, including each local chapter and the national offices of the Arthritis Society, people living with arthritis, the fund-raising coaches, the runners, the trainers, the volunteers, the sponsors, and the race organizers. Each individual within the group is working to promote the development of a healthier community by advancing community awareness, by raising much needed funds to support arthritis research and programs for people living with arthritis, and by promoting a healthy lifestyle that includes exercise.

Promoting community health involves people collaborating to design and develop their community in a way that will enable optimal health for all (7). Examples include occupations such as responsible child-rearing, participating in a resource management program that emphasizes a reduction in consumption and waste, or engaging in ethical business practices, enable community members to contribute to the sustainability of the social and physical environments.

Sense of Community

As illustrated in the Joints in Motion vignette, the events leading up to and including race day give each individual involved a real sense of community spirit or of "all being in this together." The race organizers are relying on the sponsors, on the volunteers, and on the participants to each do their parts. For the runners, there is the feeling of support from the organizers, volunteers, and the other runners. For the charitable organization involved, in this case the Arthritis Society, there is the potential to broaden connections with the community, to network, and to build a team of individuals committed to working together to improve the daily lives of individuals living with arthritis.

Participating in occupations as a collective endeavor builds a sense of connectedness, and cultivates feelings of cohesiveness, belonging, and group solidarity among members. Through collaboration and mutual support, working together for a common cause or toward a common end helps alleviate feelings of alienation and/or loneliness, while fostering a sense of community spirit. Achieved through mutual participation in common occupations, group solidarity connects people with others in their environment and serves as a source of social interaction. The sense of community developed through participation in occupations also encourages commitment to the group and to the group's efforts. The result is a sense of a united front for group members, which serves to further connect and empower the community.

Empowerment

In addition to sharing a sense of connection in working together to achieve a desired goal, the training team in Box 9-2 consists of a group of people who are confident that their collective efforts will make a difference. The people involved support the notion that people can make their community a better place by championing the research and programs of the Arthritis Society and by supporting each of the runners in their journey toward completing a half- or full marathon.

An empowered community feels it has choice and control over its actions and direction. By organizing and participating in occupations directed toward a common goal or end, communities construct a united front that capitalizes on the strength of numbers and the stronger collective voice. Participation in community decision making and successful occupational ventures engenders a sense of contribution and value within the community. This feeling is fortified with a sense of ownership and responsibility.

Empowerment through collective participation and "making a difference" in the community provides individual members and the community with a powerful source of motivation, drive, initiative, and commitment to the project and the community itself. McMurray notes that "empowered communities strive for access, equity, and self-determination using all sectors of their environment to achieve health and well-being" (7, p. 4). Involving members in occupations at the community level helps build understanding of the issues the community faces and creates the confidence to confront, question, and work to change the status quo. As Gilman stated, "The crucial building blocks in any community empowerment effort are bringing people together and building their sense of possibility through concrete action" (44, p. 16).

Trust and Respect

Involvement in a variety of occupations, together or in parallel, facilitates the growth of respect and appreciation for the different ways in which people participate in the occupations of daily life. At the community level, members learn to appreciate and use local knowledge, expertise, and skills. Consider a group of retired, skilled laborers that organizes to provide low-cost services such as plumbing or electric work to other seniors on limited incomes. Further yet, consider the young adults of aboriginal background who work with community support workers to plan and conduct programs aimed at improving life opportunities for adolescents on native reserves. Community trust and respect allow self-expression in the performance of a common occupation. When respect for an alternate method of performing an occupation is not present, the minority members lose their sense of worth and contribution to the community.

The Joints in Motion Training Team brings together a fairly diverse cross section of individuals who are committed to raising funds for programs and much needed research through participation in the marathon event in one capacity or another. Each individual brings unique experiences, goals, perspectives, and backgrounds to the community. Each individual has a different reason for participating in this occupation and a different "way" or approach to participation. Some members of the team embrace the community aspect of participation more than others by making every effort to involve others in their efforts, whereas others choose a more individualized approach to the common goal. For the runners, group runs and social activities tend to be attended by a "core group" of people who can be counted on to show up to everything, whereas other runners choose to run alone or limit their involvement to the essentials. The team is constructed to support individual differences and to embrace self-expression while participating as a community. Fitting the varied lifestyles of the team members to the project enables participation.

Shared Meaning and Purpose

Previous discussion has demonstrated that participation in "running for charity" provides a source of shared meaning and purpose for team members. Although the meaning of participation may vary between individuals, there are also shared meanings among members of a community. Shared meanings provide common communication, as well as a means to collectively interpret a situation, understand the past, and look to the future (45).

While recognizing individual variations, a group of individuals who participate in yoga classes at a local facility make meaning together through the shared experience of yoga. The desire for wellness, a belief in the connection between the mind, body, and spirit, and a commitment to collective meditation motivate participation by the members of this community.

In the exchange of experiences and perspectives, members of the community realize that their needs and issues are not unique to themselves, but rather represent a communal need, issue, or problem (46). By identifying and focusing on common issues, community members declare a shared purpose and work together when acting on a particular goal. By providing a forum for collective action, participation in occupations enables individuals with shared needs to come together and actively pursue the identification of their needs, to make decisions, and to establish mechanisms to meet the distinctive needs of the community.

Organizing Behavior and Generating Resources

Shared community occupations provide a means of organizing group behavior and generating resources, or the products of occupations. As a means of organizing time, resources, and the human and nonhuman environment, occupation orchestrates daily life (12). Collective participation allows the members of a community to fulfill certain functions and meet the needs necessary for daily life that they would be unable to achieve individually. Members participate in parts of a larger whole, and they achieve their goals through organized, common efforts toward a desired outcome. It is the established infrastructure, as well as the support and commitment of each of the stakeholders, that enables a program such as the Joints in Motion Training Team to exist. While possible, it is doubtful that participants would individually be able to achieve the goals outlined by the program.

In addition, participation in occupations establishes rhythm in life, be it the daily routines of a community or the larger cultural time markers such as holidays or occupations associated with different seasons of the year, or at different stages of development. Like individuals, communities go through different stages of development characterized by different occupations or by an emphasis on certain occupations. For some stakeholders involved in the arthritis run, the completion of the event marks the end of their formal involvement, but their participation has resulted in changed relationships with members of that community. Within the span of 8 months, a shared occupation is born, evolves, and is completed. Team members may continue to be involved in different ways or continue to forge relationships based on new objectives or other occupations. Clearly, shared occupations, such as running a marathon to support a charity, provide the means for contributing to the social and economic fabric of a community.

Imbalance/Overkill

Participation can be problematic for communities if daily life is highly focused on a limited number of occupations, or if the community is unreceptive to change or development. Consider "single-industry" towns such as coal mining communities. As the focus of community life, mining defines and orchestrates much of the daily round of occupations. Decisions to close down the mine for economic and environmental reasons can shake a community to its core. It is important to balance traditional ways of living with the recognition of the need for constructive change and for sustainable community development.

There may come a time in the future when the community no longer supports the idea of the Joints in Motion program. Like most fund-raising ideas, the program's popularity may wane. The larger community may decide that one charitable organization has been receiving a lot of support and that it is time to advance another worthy cause. The public may tire of hearing about the occupation of "running for charity."

Loss of Productivity/Disillusionment

While participation as a collective enables groups of people to fulfill certain functions and meet needs that they would be unable to achieve individually, communities can also be challenged by poor leadership, disorganization, and inefficiency, resulting in a loss of productivity.

When members do not share the goals of community leaders, a sense of disillusionment and dissociation from the larger body may result. People may feel that their efforts are not valued. Members may choose to undermine the leadership if they feel their views are not being heard and their needs are not being addressed. Being part of a collective means that individual goals and needs may be sacrificed for the benefit of the larger body. When members feel that all are working toward the same goal and that all have the opportunity to express themselves, the community moves forward. When this situation is not present, the leadership of the members may block the work of others to the detriment of the collective occupation.

A change in leadership or strategic direction may make a charitable organization less responsive to a certain segment of the shareholders, thereby restricting or reducing their participation in fund-raising. Mismanagement of the money raised can lead to disillusionment on a community participation level and is an example of how a charitable organization can lose the support of sponsors, volunteers, and others.

Inequity of Representation

Within any community, the potential exists for a few strong voices to take over and determine community priorities and direct courses of action and prescribe, conscribe, or restrict participation, while other voices go unheard. Organizers of a charitable sports event may limit participation to elite athletes to obtain a higher profile. Consider how this practice would influence participation for the average individual.

Consider a further example. In some political communities, methods are established to ensure equity of representation, although the criteria for determining this equity may not recognize all the possible collectives who require a voice. In other situations, there is little or no attempt to represent the majority voice. The will of the leaders determines the course of the collective.

Occupational Deprivation

When faced with circumstances that limit participation, or when freedom of choice in daily living is restricted, the drive for communities to participate in meaningful occupations is so strong that groups will go out of their way to do something that engages them. Having a source of identity and purpose in familiar occupations is so strong that people will risk personal injury to maintain them. Csikszentmihalyi asserts that communities need to provide occupational opportunities "that present a diversity of meaningful outlets for a variety of skills" (47, p. 39). Consider underground religious movements during the past century, or ethnic groups who strive to retain their language in the face of overwhelming pressure to assimilate into a dominant culture. The power of participation in occupations for the community is evident in these examples.

Source of Conflict

Participation in occupations with competing motivations or interests to other groups is a potential source of conflict. A quick review of many of the current trouble spots in the world presents many examples of competing interests resulting in conflict. The extent of the effects of the conflict depends on the magnitude of the commitment or beliefs of the communities involved and, consequently, the ease of resolution. The point here is that occupational participation involves shared meaning and purpose, and when communities come into contact, conflict may arise if these beliefs are in competition. Referring back to the charity run vignette, there are a number of agencies and groups competing for donations through participation in fund-raising activities. Hypothetically, while sharing some aspects of meaning and purpose, different charities may come into conflict if support for one overwhelms the resources of another, or if one charity is believed to be using unfair tactics.

COMMUNITY ANIMATION

The last section of this discussion of community participation draws together many of the opportunities and challenges discussed above. It provides a starting point for readers to consider their participation in community events. The word *animation* comes from the Latin *animare*, which is translated as "to move into action." The goal of **community animation** is to help build community spirit through participation in occupations that develop, mobilize, and sustain the community. Interested readers are encouraged to refer to Gilman's article (44) for a more detailed discussion of the concept of community animation.

As illustrated by Box 9-2, by participating in specific projects, community members identify resources, create networks of friends and acquaintances, and build confidence in their ability to find solutions to some of the challenges they face. Bercuvitz, a community animator, speaks of creating "an umbrella under which people can do small things, but feel connected to each other" (44, p. 20). Participation in collective doing and interconnected occupations provides members with a sense of purpose, with a source of motivation and drive, with an outlet for creativity, and with an appreciation of their ability to share in shaping their communities and their daily lives.

CHAPTER SUMMARY

The vignettes and concepts presented in this chapter support the idea that occupations are the fabric of life. Participation in occupations enables people to shape their identity, meet instrumental goals and needs, develop skills or resources, and generally create meaning in life. When participation is restricted, individuals and communities find ways to continue old or develop new occupations in order to reap the benefit that participation brings to them. Continued study of occupational participation will bring a greater understanding of why we do what we do, whether individually or in groups and helps us identify ways to promote a healthy balance of participation for individuals and communities.

REFERENCES

1. Yerxa, E. J., Clark, F. A., Frank, G., Jackson, J., Parham, D., Pierce, D., et al. (1989). An introduction to occupational science, A foundation for occupational therapy in the 21st century. In J. A. Johnson (Ed.), *Occupational science, The foundation for new models of practice*. New York: Haworth Press.
2. Howard, B., & Howard, J. R. (1999). Occupation as spiritual activity. *American Journal of Occupational Therapy, 51*(3), 181–185.
3. Christiansen, C. (1997). Nationally speaking. Acknowledging a spiritual dimension in occupational therapy practice. *American Journal of Occupational Therapy, 51*(3), 169–172.
4. Csikszentmihalyi, M. (1990). *Flow—The psychology of optimal experience*. New York: Harper and Row.
5. Bateson, M. C. (1996). Enfolded activity and the concept of occupation. In R. Zemke & F. Clark (Eds.), *Occupational science: The evolving discipline*. Philadelphia: F. A. Davis.
6. McFarlane, J. (1996). Ecological connections. In E. Anderson & J. McFarlane (Eds.), *Community as partner* (pp. 82–121). Philadelphia: Lippincott.
7. McMurray, A. (1999). *Community health and wellness. A socioecological approach*. Toronto: Mosby.
8. Biffle, C. (Ed.). (1991). *A guided tour of selections from Aristotle's Nichomachean ethics*. Palo Alto, CA: Mayfield Publishing.
9. Hollister, C. W. (1998). *Medieval Europe: A short history* (8th ed.). New York: McGraw-Hill.
10. Braudel, F. (1995). *A history of civilizations*. London, Penguin.
11. Meyer, A. (1922/1997). The philosophy of occupation therapy. *The American Journal of Occupational Therapy, 31*(10): 639–642.
12. Canadian Association of Occupational Therapists. *Enabling occupation: An occupational therapy perspective*. Ottawa, ON: Canadian Association of Occupational Therapists.
13. Frankl, V. (1984). *Man's search for meaning* (rev. ed.). New York: Washington Square Press.
14. Seligman, M. E. P., Abramson, L. Y., Semmel, A., & von Bayer, C. (1998). *Learned optimism*. New York: Pocketbooks.
15. Bandura, A. (2000). Exercise of human agency through collective efficacy. *Current Directions in Psychological Science, 9*, 75–78.
16. Patterson, J., & Blum, R. W. (1996). Risk and resilience among children and youth with disabilities. *Archives of Pediatric & Adolescent Medicine, 150*, 692–698.
17. Christiansen, C. H. (1999). Defining lives: Occupation as identity: An essay on competence, coherence, and the creation of meaning—The 1999 Eleanor Clarke Slagle lecture. *American Journal of Occupational Therapy, 53*(6), 547–558.
18. Gauvin, L., & Spence, J. C. (1996). Physical activity and psychological well-being: Knowledge base, current issues and caveats. *Nutrition Review, 54*(4), S53–S65.
19. Morgan, K., & Bath, P. (1998). Customary physical activity and psychological well being: A longitudinal study. *Age & Ageing, 27*(S3), 35–40.
20. Laliberte, D. (1993). *An exploration of the meaning seniors attach to activity*. London, ON: The University of Western Ontario.
21. Charmaz, K. (1994). Identity dilemmas of chronically ill men. *Sociological Quarterly, 35*(2), 269–288.
22. Vrkljan, B., & Polgar, J. (2001). Meaning of occupational engagement in life-threatening illness: A qualitative pilot project. *Canadian Journal of Occupational Therapy, 68*(4), 237–246.

23. Kagawa-Slinger, M. (1993). Redefining health: Living with cancer. *Social Science and Medicine, 37*(3), 295–304.

24. Parham, L. D. (1996). Perspectives on play. In R. Zemke & F. Clark (Eds.), *Occupational science: The emerging discipline* (pp. 71–88). Philadelphia: F. A. Davis.

25. Reilly, M. (1974). *Play as exploratory learning*. Beverly Hills, CA: Sage.

26. Frederick, J. A. (1995, December 6). *As time goes by: Time use of Canadians* (Report No. 89-544-XPE). Ottawa: Statistics Canada.

27. Bransford, J., Brown, A. L., & Cocking, R. R. (Eds.). (2000). *How people learn: Brain, mind, experience and school* (expanded ed.). Washington, DC: National Academy Press.

28. Rodin, J., & Langer, E. J. (1977). Long term effects of a control-relevant intervention with the institutionalized aged. *Journal of Personality and Social Psychology, 35*, 897–902.

29. Gage, M., & Polatajko, H. J. (1996). Enhancing occupational performance through an understanding of perceived self-efficacy. In R. P. Fleming-Cottrell (Ed.), *Perspectives on purposeful activity: Foundation and future of occupational therapy* (pp. 367–371). Bethesda, MD: American Occupational Therapy Association.

30. Bandura, A. (1982). Self efficacy mechanism in human agency. *American Psychologist, 37*, 122–147.

31. Josephy, A. M., Jr., Nagel, J., & Johnson, T. (Eds.). (1999). *Red power: The American Indian's fight for freedom* (2nd ed.). Lincoln: University of Nebraska Press.

32. Goodland, R., Daly, H. E., & El Serafy, S. (Eds.). (1996). *Population, technology and lifestyle: The transition to sustainability*. Washington, DC: Island Press.

33. Scherer, M. J. (2000). *Living in the state of stuck: How assistive technology impacts the lives of people with disabilities* (3rd ed.). Cambridge, MA: Brookline Books.

34. Williams, P. (2001). Physical fitness and activity as separate heart disease risk factors: A meta-analysis. *Medicine and Science in Sports and Exercise, 33*, 754–761.

35. Liebow, E. (1995). *Tell them who I am: The lives of homeless women*. New York: Viking Penguin.

36. Goffman, I. (1963). *Stigma: Notes on the management of a spoiled identity*. Englewood Cliffs, NJ: Prentice Hall.

37. Centers for Disease Control. (1999). *Physical activity and health: Report of the surgeon general*. Atlanta, GA: Author.

38. Maki, B. (1997). Gait changes in older adults: Predictors of falls or indicators of fear? *Journal of the American Geriatrics Society, 45*(3), 313–320.

39. Christiansen, C. H., Backman, C., Little, B. R., & Nguyen, A. (1999). Occupations and well-being: A study of personal projects. *American Journal of Occupational Therapy, 53*(1), 91–100.

40. Schroeder, J., Nau, K., Osness, W., & Potteiger, J. A. (1998). A comparison of life-satisfaction, functional ability, physical characteristics, and activity level among older adults in various living situations. *Journal of Aging and Physical Activity, 6*, 640–649.

41. Emmons, R. A. (1996). Striving and feeling: Personal goals and subjective well-being. In P. M. Gollwitzer (Ed.), *The psychology of action: Linking cognition and motivation to behavior* (pp. 313–337). New York: Guilford Press.

42. Christiansen, C., Clark, F., Kielhofner, G., Rogers, J., & Nelson, D. (1995). Position paper: Occupation. *American Journal of Occupational Therapy, 49*(10), 1015–1018.

43. Charmaz, C. (1991). *Good days, bad days: The self in chronic illness and time.* New Brunswick, NJ: Rutgers University Press.

44. Gilman, R. (1992). Community animation: An interview with Jeff Bercuvitz. In context, 1992, 33: 16–20.

45. Bruner, J. (1990). *Acts of meaning.* Cambridge, MA: Harvard University Press.

46. Townsend, E. (1997). Inclusiveness: A community dimension of spirituality. *Canadian Journal of Occupational Therapy, 64*(3), 146–155.

47. Csikszentmihalyi, M. (1993). Activity & happiness: Torward a science of occupation. *Occupational Science: Australia 1*(1), 38–42.

CHAPTER 10

When People Cannot Participate: Occupational Deprivation

Gail Whiteford

KEY WORDS

Disability
Dislocation
Displacement
Incarceration
Occupational deprivation

Occupational disruption
Overemployment
Refugeeism
Sex-role stereotyping

CHAPTER PROFILE

This chapter focuses on what happens when people are unable to participate in occupations for reasons outside their immediate control. The concept of occupational deprivation is defined, contrasted with occupational disruption, and illustrated through examples that are highly relevant in the context of modern society. These examples include geographic isolation, employment conditions, incarceration, gender stereotypes, refugeeism, and disability. Implications of occupational deprivation for individuals, communities, and societies are briefly discussed.

INTRODUCTION

In previous chapters, we have seen how occupations, or the doings of everyday life, provide a means for providing structure, identity, and meaning in people's lives. As a way of understanding their experiences over time, people tell stories about themselves and their lives through accounts of what they have done, are doing, or what they are going to do in the future. A person's sense of self and his or her relationship with the world at large is very much influenced by participation in occupations chosen and performed during each stage of life. In turn, those occupations are shaped by the values, culture, regulations, and economics of the societies in which people live.

What happens, then, when people are unable to do the things they want and need to do for extended periods of time? What consequences does this have for people individually, in families, in communities, and even in countries? In this chapter we consider some of the factors and conditions that may prevent people from living out their occupational lives to the fullest extent. In so doing, we introduce the concept of occupational deprivation and provide some examples of deprived conditions and their causes.

The three major objectives for this chapter are as follows:

1. To define occupational deprivation and distinguish it from occupational disruption.
2. To illustrate occupational deprivation through five globally recognizable examples: geographic isolation, extreme conditions of employment, incarceration, sex-role stereotyping, and refugeeism.
3. To identify environmental features that produce occupational deprivation for people with special needs, impairments, and disabilities.

The three main sections of this chapter address these three objectives. The opening section offers a definition of occupational deprivation. The second section provides examples of occupational deprivation. Included in this section is the example of extreme conditions of employment which have created a growing gap between people who experience considerable stress because they are doing too much and those who experience boredom, anxiety or more severe consequences because they are doing too little. Discussed in the third section is the occupational deprivation created by disability and its consequent limitations to activity and social participation.

DEFINING OCCUPATIONAL DEPRIVATION

Occupational deprivation as a concept is relatively new, but it has stimulated interest internationally. A pioneer in articulating the theoretical concept of occupational deprivation is Ann Wilcock (1) who suggested that not all people are afforded equal opportunities to participate in occupations of choice or in occupations having individual or cultural meaning. Using Wilcock's premise and research with prison inmates, occupational deprivation is defined here as "a state of prolonged preclusion from engagement in occupations of necessity and/or meaning due to factors which stand outside of the control of the individual" (2, p. 201).

The factors that produce occupational deprivation may be social, economic, environmental, geographic, historic, cultural, or political in nature, as discussed in the next section. It is important to emphasize that occupational deprivation occurs when someone or something *external* to the individual is creating conditions that lead to deprivation.

A related but different concept is **occupational disruption** (2). Occupational disruption may appear to be similar to occupational deprivation but it refers to a different, common experience in most people's lives. The most important distinctions are, first, that occupational disruption is temporary or transient. Second, that disruption results from factors that are internal or individual, such as illness, moving to a new town, or changing jobs. In contrast, occupational deprivation is prolonged, and external or environmental forces, such as prolonged isolation, confinement, or war, cause the deprivation.

Consider an example of occupational disruption that occurs frequently during ski season. You fall on the slope during a ski trip and break your leg. With your leg in a plaster cast for 8 weeks, your occupations are disrupted. During this time, going for a jog will be impossible, as will some of your other pursuits, such as swimming or dancing. Your normal pattern of occupational engagement is disrupted. However, when your leg has healed, you expect to return to your usual occupations (perhaps you will not choose skiing!).

Occupational disruption may also result from internal or individual circumstances. Examples might include grieving the loss of a loved one or electing to work a night shift. The most important things to remember about occupational disruption are that (a) it constitutes a temporary state and (b) given supportive conditions, this temporary state can be resolved (2, p. 201).

Indeed, sometimes after a period of occupational disruption people return to an enhanced level of occupational functioning. Their attitude toward certain occupations may change or they may establish different priorities. This may result from their having spent time reflecting on the importance of certain occupations missing from their life during the disruption. Women, for example, after becoming a parent and getting through the occupational disruption associated with caring for a new infant, often report that they value and use their leisure time more highly than they did previously. Similarly, students who have experienced occupational disruption while preparing for and undertaking examinations may experience a renewed sense of pleasure in a range of restorative occupations when examinations are finished.

FIVE ILLUSTRATIONS OF OCCUPATIONAL DEPRIVATION

In this section, examples of occupational deprivation are presented. Five illustrations of occupational deprivation were selected for their global relevance: geographic isolation, unsatisfactory conditions of employment (unemployment, underemployment, and overemployment), incarceration, sex-role stereotyping, and refugeeism.

Geographic isolation results from the conditions of location that place some people at great physical distance from others or that separate them by terrain or climatic conditions creating difficult navigational access. By way of contrast, people who live in large urban centers may have employment conditions that make them vulnerable to occupational deprivation resulting from time pressures and demands of everyday living. Economic and cultural forces cause these. The remaining illustrations of occupational deprivation from this section (incarceration, barriers

FIGURE 10-1   Occupational deprivation can be caused by restricted access to people, events, and places. Remote, isolated geographic locations can result in occupational deprivation. (Russell Illig/Getty Images)

created by social stereotypes, and refugeeism), result from social, cultural, or political circumstances. As these concepts are presented, readers may be able to consider other examples of occupational deprivation drawn from their own experiences and sociocultural contexts.

Geographic Isolation

Since the earliest times, one of the most powerful constraints on people's opportunities to engage in occupations, particularly those of a social nature, has been geographic isolation (Figure 10-1). It is hard to go bowling or meet friends in a café if you tend a lighthouse on a remote coastal peninsula and your nearest neighbor is a 2-hour drive away! Whereas some people actively choose to live in remote locations and accept the occupational deprivation that goes with it as a lifestyle choice, the impact of geographic isolation on some groups has very serious, long-term negative consequences.

What are the negative effects of geographic isolation and why do they come about? One of the most important dimensions of occupations is that they locate us within the social world. Not being able to engage in occupations with other people results in diminished opportunities for social interaction, a primary source of feedback about who we are and how others perceive us. Feedback from others is where we gain recognition for our efforts, and this feedback directly shapes our self-image and sense of self (3). Consider the following poignant account of geographical isolation as told by Australian aboriginal author Ruby Langford. Here she recounts her experiences living in a camp in outback Queensland:

> The day came to pack up, we looked along the fence, the heat haze above the wires
> and said "well that's done, lets go to town". . . this town was a Mecca of civilisation
> to me, look—here was a dress shop, I went right in. I needed a new dress. Halfway
> in the shop I saw myself in the shop mirror, close up. Here was a pregnant woman
> with blistered hands like a man's, her face peeling like flaky pastry and black . . .
> I stared at myself for a long time and then I bought a sleeveless cotton dress and
> went outside. I hadn't been to town for so long I was so lonely for another woman
> to talk to, so every woman who passed I said hello, hello, just to get them to talk
> to me. (4, p. 93)

Ruby's story is a poignant account of being desperate for interaction with other
women whom she rarely encountered during her time in the outback. She is driven
to seek feedback of any kind—even "Hello!" Although Ruby brings a touch of humor to this story, she does manage to highlight how being deprived of opportunities
to do relatively normal, social things due to the tyranny of distance can lead to a
sense of social isolation and the development of maladaptive coping strategies. Although not directly related to her story, problems such as alcohol abuse, petrol sniff-
ing, domestic violence, and suicide tend to be more prevalent in rural and isolated
communities (5). These problems are, without question, complex and multidimensional. Yet they do point to potentially adverse effects of the occupational deprivation brought about by prolonged geographic distance from others.

Another source of occupational deprivation related to geographic isolation is
the lack of resources and opportunities in some of the central desert communities
in Australia. The remote communities, inhabited largely by aboriginal people who
live west of Alice Springs, are, generally speaking, places in which there is little or
nothing to do. Such geographic isolation is particularly problematic for the young
people. In his inquiry into these communities, Paul Toohey described them as being places where

> life is sedentary and aimless . . . they are artificial hubs constructed from the imagi-
> nations of . . . people who hoped that people, who had only 30 years before lived in
> small wandering groups, could live happily next to a bore, church, generator and a
> store. It hasn't worked. The petrol sniffing is epidemic and proves that life in these
> desert communities holds little meaning for the teenage generation. In their tradi-
> tional nomadic society, they had a great deal of autonomy. They have that same in-
> dependence now that they live in big stationary groups with the result that they are
> bored stiff, so they sniff (petrol). (6, p. 3)

This is an extreme example, and one that has many layers of complexity including
the intersection of history, politics, race relations, and economics. The point about
occupational deprivation is that there seems to be a link between being geographically isolated, being unable to participate in occupations that are meaningful and rewarding (particularly those that are socially oriented), and health. This is because,
as Wilcock (1) has pointed out, humans are inherently occupational by nature and
being unable to "do" much for long periods of time is ultimately detrimental. It will
be interesting to see how access to technologies such as the Internet will influence
the sense of geographic isolation over time. The reality remains that, for many people currently living in remote communities, such technology is still inaccessible.

Problem Conditions of Employment

Another category of occupational deprivation relates to paid employment. Employment can create difficulties with occupational engagement when its availability or demands are not commensurate with need. The most common and visible type of employment problem is unemployment. Unemployment is probably one of the most challenging and complex problems of our time. In Western societies in particular, the occupation of paid employment has assumed a central position in identity construction. One need only think back to the last social gathering where inevitably someone asked the question "What do you do?" and most often the response would be linked to paid employment (e.g., "I am a town planner" or "I'm a teacher"). Generally, people highlight their employment above other occupational pursuits, even when employment is not the occupation of most interest or importance to them. Accordingly, one rarely hears people respond with non-work-related roles, such as "I am a parent" or "I am a church volunteer." For most people in Western countries, paid employment is the occupation that most significantly influences social acceptance and social status. Declaring oneself to be a ski instructor will be met with a different response than one might receive from declaring oneself to be a graphic artist or a cardiologist. People's perceptions of us, at least initially, are strongly influenced by our primary occupations of paid employment. Such perceptions are shaped by social and cultural value systems.

Given that one's vocation tends to influence social perceptions, what happens when people are deprived of the occupation of paid employment for long periods of time? What is the impact on sense of self or on general well-being? From research on long-term unemployed people, the effects are becoming understood. Most significantly, unemployment seems to have a negative impact on both physical (1, 7–9) as well as mental health (10–13). Platt (14) suggests that a link exists between unemployment and rates of self-harm and suicide. Psychologically and emotionally, unemployed people report that they are less confident, with lower self-esteem and diminished efficacy beliefs, than are employed people. At a skills level, it appears that the longer people remain unemployed, the more difficult it is to obtain employment due to diminished skills and work related behaviors. In short, unemployment incurs a huge price for people as individuals and for society at large (15). Thus, unemployment can be viewed as a primary contributor to occupational deprivation for multitudes of people worldwide.

Unemployment is viewed here as one form of occupational deprivation. To fully understand it, however, we need to consider the factors that influence employment participation rates and have an appreciation for the forces that preclude full employment for whole populations. To begin to understand these issues, we must recognize that declining workforce participation is a global phenomenon historically linked to rapid advances in technology, prevailing economic systems, and shifting demographics (16).

If we consider technology first, differing perspectives are needed for a rounded discussion. Considered simply, the rapid rise in technological advances may be seen as having released people from a whole range of backbreaking and monotonous, repetitive jobs. Paradoxically, although technological development may be viewed as representing progress for humankind, it can also be seen as the root cause of diminished employment opportunities for legions of semiskilled and unskilled workers. Jones (16) cites Drucker in describing the blue-collar working class as the fastest class to rise and fall that society has witnessed in its evolution. Indeed machinery, robotics, and computer-driven systems have replaced the blue-collar workforce in sectors as diverse as the manufacturing sector (especially the automotive industry), the agrarian sector, and the tertiary service sector. The impact of technology on the labor market has been unquestionably negative from an employment perspective, an outcome that economic forecasters were slow to predict and one for which there are few contemporary solutions (15). The financial viability of many industries has depended on their ability to embrace technology-reducing strategies in order to reduce the costs associated with large numbers of workers. Computerization, as well as downsizing of workers and outsourcing of services (corporate strategies that became buzz words during the 1990s), has inevitably resulted in fewer full-time employment opportunities for many people. Jones summarizes:

> At a time when technology provides a unique capacity to break down hierarchies and promote individual autonomy, citizens feel confused, marginalised and frustrated, and fear encourages desperation. Voters complain of a leadership vacuum and a sense of being disenfranchised. (16, p. 132)

Let us consider a second influence on employment: prevailing global and national economic forces. Generally speaking, the financial viability of an industry depends to a large extent on the type of political and economic context in which it is located. Most First World, liberal democracies have capitalist economies based on the twin principles of competition and free-market trade. It has been argued that capitalist systems have commodified the labor force; that drives for increased productivity and a demand for the best (most profitable) bottom line have ultimately required substantive levels of unemployment. As Farnworth (17) suggests, "unemployment is, in part, a consequence of the goals of capitalism" (p. 22). Governments in many countries appear to have recognized the social costs associated with unemployment. Typical government responses to this problem have been to introduce a variety of federally funded programs ranging from work for the dole schemes, to job creation programs, to mandatory retraining (18). However, these approaches have not been without unwanted consequences. The problem is that such employment assistance programs cannot help but have an impact on the labor force as a whole, such is the complexity of modern economies. Additionally, care has to be taken to ensure that the individual and human rights of unemployed people are protected. Many people believe that well-intentioned government unemployment programs can degenerate into a form of dehumanizing "slave labor." Nevertheless such programs exist, and full-time employment may never be available in future societies for all people. Lobo suggests pessimistically, but perhaps realistically, that

> Many young people without jobs or underemployed live in deprivation, impermanence and temporary relationships in new ways. Emergent lifestyles include . . . welfare claimant careers, extended full-time education, and single parenthood. (19, p. 32)

A third factor that compounds occupational deprivation through unemployment is the pattern of shifting demographics of nations around the globe. Fundamentally, as a result of people living longer, healthier lives, the world has an increasing number of countries with aging populations. People are remaining in the workforce longer and, as a consequence, less turnover in available jobs is seen. One approach toward dealing with this, implementing mandatory retirement ages, has been questioned on equity grounds in many places. The potential consequences of these demographic shifts on participation rates in the labor force, and on the ability of young people to enter the workforce, are now being questioned. Concern exists about the possible psychological consequences of current trends that are leading to fewer work opportunities and constraints on full-time employment, because the identities of many people are associated primarily with their occupations of paid employment.

Neither futurists nor science fiction novelists are optimistic in their predictions of employment patterns in the coming decades. Consider this extract from Marge Piercy's account (20) of a future in which the world is no longer divided by national borders but by multinational zones. In Piercy's future world, people are either citizens/ employees of a huge multinational corporation that controls all facets of their lives, or they live in the "Glop," a vast underworld of unemployed and unskilled people who have no access to education or reliable technology. Surviving, for those in the Glop is the central occupation:

> Day workers and gang ninos and the unemployed lived in the Glop—the great majority of people on the continent. Most of the remainder were citizens of the enclaves . . . parts of the Glop were under domes, but the system had not been completed before governments stopped functioning . . . every quadrant was managed by the remains of the old UN, the eco-police, that had authority over earth, water, and air outside domes and wraps. Otherwise, the Multis ruled the enclaves, the free towns defended themselves as best they could and the Glop rotted under the poisonous sky, ruled by feuding gangs and overlords. (20, pp. 45–46)

With this dramatic construction of a possible future, it is worth reflecting on some of the themes highlighted in Piercy's description of how the world could be. To what extent, for example, do we already have a global situation in which some people are being pressured to do more and more, while others are drifting further from not only opportunities for paid employment, but from other meaningful occupations? Indications are that this may already be happening in some countries. Due to the technological advances that many First World countries are experiencing, whole communities of people previously involved in industries, such as automobile manufacturing and mining, have been occupationally deprived by mass unemployment. Other industries, such as fishing and logging, have similarly left legions of people without work, without even the hope of work, in the wake of diminished natural resources and the absence of management for sustainability. In some communities it has become common for families to experience third-generation unemployment.

Simultaneously, the demands of employed people have changed dramatically in the last two decades, leading to overemployment for some. People are routinely being asked to work longer, unpaid hours, increase margins of productivity, and accept less annual leave than previously (21). The stress associated with greater work-related demands in increasingly competitive work environments is that people are constantly faced with the possibility of redundancy or downsizing. It is harder and harder for these people to live occupational lives that have a balance of work and leisure. Beder describes the situation, rather grimly as one in which:

> Millions of people are being encouraged and coerced to work long hours, devoting their lives to making or doing things that will not enrich their lives or make them happier . . . they are so busy doing this that they have little time to spend with their family and friends, to develop other aspects of themselves, or to participate in their communities as full citizens. And the best brains of a generation are engaged in persuading them to go on doing this without question. (22, p. 3)

As Beder suggests, those caught up in the busy-ness of overemployment are materially rich but time poor. They do more and more (at work), though arguably, contribute less and less to their immediate communities. Overemployed people are chronically stressed because they are doing too much. The corollary is that increasing numbers of people are chronically stressed because they are doing too little. There is a strange inversion occurring: Some people are materially rich but time poor, whereas others are materially poor but time rich.

It seems that, as Piercy (20) suggests, a new two-class system of overemployed people versus unemployed or underemployed people is emerging. The economic conditions that surround this phenomenon are complex, but are easier to understand when the global distribution of wealth is examined. Huge differences in wealth exist between technologically developing and technologically advanced countries. In fact, it is estimated that U.S. $60 million is transferred every day from the world's poorest countries to repay the debts they owe to the richest (23).

What needs to be done to prevent the world from realizing Piercy's frightening depiction? This complex situation requires complex, multifaceted approaches. Education, global economic reforms, and sustainable environmental practices are all part of the solution. Recommendations toward solutions often involve controversial political and philosophical differences related to equity and the redistribution of wealth. As a result, solutions will not be easily attained.

In summary, employment patterns have changed dramatically during the last three decades, leaving large numbers of people at risk of occupational deprivation due to unemployment, underemployment, or overemployment. **Overemployment** is a new situation in which smaller numbers of people are working increasingly long hours and have little or no discretionary time. They experience occupational imbalance and a form of occupational deprivation that results when a single occupation dominates a life devoid of the rich tapestry of occupations available to us. There is a strange two-class inversion contrasting one group of people who are materially rich but time poor (overemployed) with another group of people who are materially poor but time rich (unemployed or underemployed). Occupational deprivation for both classes appears to be one of the most pressing global issues for the 21st century.

Incarceration

Prisons and detention centers in First World nations continue to grow at an alarming rate. **Incarceration** has long been viewed in Western countries as a deprivation of liberty (Figure 10-2). The philosophic argument is that persons forfeit their right to freedom and are removed from society if they have committed acts defined as crimes. The rationale for such punishment is that through removal from society, convicts are unable to repeat the acts that constituted the original crime, and they

FIGURE 10-2   Social sanctions, such as imprisonment, create occupational deprivation as a type of punishment.
(Photograph courtesy of Francois Po Plessis)

are denied the freedom to engage in any other occupations at their discretion (24). From an occupational perspective, incarceration deliberately withdraws opportunities to participate in occupations. Thus, through legal sanctions, societies determine that some people will be occupationally deprived through imprisonment.

Inside the institutional environment of prisons, inmates experience another level of occupational deprivation (to a greater or lesser extent, dependent on a number of factors). Prisons are institutions, and institutional life always imposes restrictions on occupational choice. One added feature to institutional life in prisons is security. Keeping inmates and prison staff safe restricts the types of occupations available and the timing of occupations. In many high-security units, tool use is restricted due to the risk of self-harm and the threat of injury to others. Total restriction of tool use, however, can compound problems associated with occupational deprivation (25). Another added feature of institutional life in many prisons is geographic isolation. Arguably the protection of communities is increased when prisons are in geographically isolated places, but this isolation curtails any normative interaction with the "outside." Institutional policies, types of settings, and the severity of crimes all influence the extent to which inmates can interact through visits with the outside world and significant others.

What are the consequences of occupational deprivation during imprisonment? The term **stir crazy** is sometimes used to describe the negative effect of being deprived of opportunities for normal occupational engagement. One of the potential psychological consequences is disorientation and potential psychosis brought on by a combination of isolation, temporal dislocation, and inactivity (24, 26). Through everyday doing, we locate ourselves in time. The occupations of daily life form a temporal structure that provides predictable routines. For example, we prepare breakfast at the beginning of the day and may take the trash out at night. Our occupations are also very much influenced by the social and cultural expectations that accompany the meanings associated with different days of the week. Thus, we may tend to do different things on Friday, Saturday, and Sunday than we do on other days of the week. We experience Monday as being different from Friday. These important, yet subtle, distinctions of routine and meaning situate us in time and help to orient us to the external world, providing us with a rhythm and tempo to our daily lives. In prison, there is little differentiation between hours, days, weeks, and months. One day is much the same as the next, punctuated by normal variations (sleeping in on a holiday, for instance). Incarceration also deprives inmates of the opportunity to participate in special occasions and the occupations that accompany them, such as shopping for family birthdays. Such deprivation of occupational engagement, experienced as living in an apparently endless, featureless sea of time, can be extremely detrimental to mental health. Psychosis and increased suicide attempts are major mental health risks of imprisonment (27), as are depression and increased aggression (28). Rioting in prisons has even been interpreted as a response to diminished occupational opportunities (29).

Changes in correctional policy over the years in some countries reflect the sentiment that dehumanized prison environments and unnecessary incarceration are ultimately counterproductive to the long-term interests of societies. Studies supporting this point of view have been equivocal. This has made it easier for critics of correctional reform to assert that the purpose of incarceration is punishment, not rehabilitation. Winston Churchill observed that "The mood and temper of the public in regard to the treatment of crime and criminals is one of the most unfailing tests of the civilization of any country" (30). Yet, educational programs and other humane efforts that may be conducive to preventing recidivism are not universally adopted.

Harsh conditions during incarceration can lead to prison unrest and violence and have not clearly demonstrated their value as a compelling deterrent to crime (31). An occupational perspective on prison life appears necessary both to understand the consequences of incarceration and to reduce the recidivism of repeat offenders who are unprepared to contribute to society outside prison. An understanding of occupational deprivation and the contrasting concept of occupational enrichment are critical in planning for the community and occupational reintegration of those who have been incarcerated.

In summary, incarceration leads to a condition of occupational deprivation that varies across inmates. When occupational restrictions are too severe, the effects are highly detrimental, ranging from boredom to psychosis, suicide, and rioting. Occupational deprivation actually militates against inmates' future abilities to reintegrate successfully into communities. With rates of incarceration growing internationally, this form of occupational deprivation is of immediate concern.

FIGURE 10-3   Some cultures have defined expectations for the occupations of women. These sex-role stereotypes are sometimes slow to change. (Copyright by Hava Gurevich, July 1987, Antiparos, Greece)

Sex-Role Stereotyping: Gendered Constructions of Occupational Deprivation for Women

Geographic isolation and incarceration are fairly obvious sources of occupational deprivation, but being of a particular gender is not. **Sex-role stereotyping** refers to the social judgments made about what men and women typically should and should not do. An historical examination of sex-role stereotyping in different cultural contexts shows that women have been deprived from engagement in a vast array of occupations otherwise available to men. Wilcock began to explore the impact of sex-role stereotyping on women when she wrote that "women, too, have generally suffered occupational deprivation for hundreds of years" (1, p.147).

One of the most apparent reasons for women experiencing occupational deprivation is religious and cultural sanction (32). Historically, many religions have prescribed which occupations are acceptable for women to engage in and which are not (Figure 10-3). Prohibited occupations for women have been as diverse as manual labor of certain types, creative pursuits (such as playing music or painting), building, hunting, drinking alcohol, or socializing. Whereas some occupations have been forbidden because of religious law, other occupations have been historically viewed as unacceptable for women because of prevailing social and cultural belief systems. The right to vote, play certain sports, socialize in a public bar, fly an airplane, or work in a mine are all occupations that have been denied to women in some cultural contexts until recent times, when some countries have opened these opportunities to women (32).

The biological argument for depriving women of the opportunity to engage in some occupations has been and, in some situations, continues to be reproduction and fertility cycles. Health risks associated with reproduction may also contribute to diminished levels of occupational engagement and performance (33). Following childbirth, the raising of an infant is most likely to be the occupational responsibility of the mother. Despite the postmodern context in which we live, child rearing is still regarded by most societies as the occupational domain of women. Primeau (34) points to research undertaken in the United States indicating that even in households where both partners are employed in paid work, women still assume the majority of responsibility for child-care-related tasks. A "second shift" of household and child-rearing-related tasks appears to deprive employed women of opportunities (in the form of free time) to participate in leisure occupations (35).

Economically, the work of women is of central importance in most countries. In their examination of the workloads of women in sub-Saharan Africa, Barrett and Brown (33) point out that women are the major contributors to agricultural production. They cite several studies that point to differences in time spent in agricultural occupations between men and women. For example, among the Beti people of Cameroon, men spend 7.3 hours per day in agricultural occupations while women spend 10.6 hours. When such workloads are coupled with child rearing and other domestic duties, it is evident that women may be occupationally deprived because they have very little discretionary time.

Three main ideas have been presented to highlight the occupational deprivation experienced by women because of inherent, historical sex stereotyping. First, women, as a subgroup of society, are vulnerable to sustained states of occupational deprivation through both the overt exclusions of some religions and the influence of cultural and social values that deny certain occupational behaviors. Second, biological imperatives, particularly women's reproductive cycles and responsibilities, influence women's occupational participation rates, most notably in leisure occupations. Third, discrepancies in divisions of labor in both technologically developing and technologically advanced countries deprive women of opportunities to participate in leisure and discretionary occupations.

Refugeeism: Displacement and Dislocation of Refugees

It is difficult for someone who has not been a refugee to imagine what it is like to be deprived of participation in lifelong valued occupations. Many refugees are escaping from situations in which they have been victims of violence or persecution, such that they have often undergone a level of trauma from which they never fully recover (Box 10-1). Often added to the trauma is a period of sustained deprivation from opportunities to participate in a whole range of familiar occupations that would ordinarily provide structure, meaning, and coherence on a daily basis. **Refugeeism** is a large and complex problem internationally. Here, we will briefly consider some factors that contribute to the occupational deprivation of refugees.

When refugees escape the situation from which they have fled or been ejected, the first experience of **displacement** is one of transitory living in which most occupations differ, whether in form or location, from those that were habitual. Refugees may live in numerous temporary facilities, including camps, for periods sometimes extending to years. Their fate is often uncertain, as numerous bureaucratic processes unfold to determine their ultimate destination and fate. In these temporary and transitional facilities, it is very difficult for refugees to engage in the occupations of meaning that characterized their lives in their home country. Lack of facilities, space, artifacts, and tools, and **dislocation** from a normative sociocultural context creates great difficulties for doing the things that previously imbued life with purpose and meaning. Even the basic occupations associated with self-care and maintenance may assume a radically different form in the environment of a refugee camp. Food preparation, for example, may afford little opportunity for family involvement given the large numbers of people in a camp. Too much time, too little to do, a lack of objects and tools, and the effects of trauma all contribute to a state of occupational deprivation in the short term for refugees.

BOX 10-1   What Is Refugeeism?

According to the 1951 Convention Relating to the Status of Refugees, a refugee is a person who "owing to a well-founded fear of being persecuted for reasons of race, religion, nationality, membership in a particular social group, or political opinion, is outside the country of his nationality, and is unable to or, owing to such fear, is unwilling to avail himself of the protection of that country." Refugeeism pertains to attitudes that restrict appropriate aid to refugees for various social, political, and cultural reasons. For example, restrictive immigration policies may be implemented within a climate of hostility and fear toward refugees, asylum seekers, and migrants (Figure 10-4). Refugees and migrants may be unfairly blamed for the social and economic ills of society, including rising crime and unemployment. Such reactions contribute to an increase in racism, violence, and unwarranted fear and prejudice against refugees, asylum seekers, and migrants.

FIGURE 10-4   War and internal political strife within nations can deprive people of the safety and support of community. A column of Hutu refugees escape from Burundi into Tanzania with cooking pots, food, and a few chickens.
(Copyright Martha Rial/*Pittsburgh Post-Gazette,* 2002. All rights reserved. Reprinted with permission.)

Upon resettlement in a host country, some conditions change for refugees. They may, however, continue to face occupational deprivation due to cultural, social, and economic isolation. Language, for instance, is a huge barrier for many newly arrived refugees in their new home country. Insufficient language skills limit educational opportunities and diminish refugees' opportunities to engage in occupations of paid employment. Sharing a language creates opportunities for interaction and the development of understanding of the occupations of a sociocultural milieu. Not sharing a language with local residents isolates and deprives people from interaction and the development of occupational opportunities.

Differences in cultural and religious orientations can compound occupational deprivation when a host country isolates refugees, expresses indifference toward them, or responds with outward hostility to the beliefs and specific practices of refugee groups. Understandably, national and ethnic communities then form where values and belief systems can be shared rather than challenged, compounding refugees' isolation from mainstream society.

A case example of this is the settlement of Hmong refugees in America. Faderman (36) has chronicled detailed accounts of the lives of Hmong people adjusting to life in the United States. Faderman points out that "what may have been legal and socially acceptable in the Hmong village is often criminal or taboo here" (p. 11), a situation compounding the disengagement from occupations of meaning. The environment of urban America itself, so radically different from that of the traditional Hmong, is a place where doing anything different is challenging. A Hmong elder provides a narrative account of the agony and confusion of trying to do things in the United States:

> Life in America is very tough for me because I'm old. I'm sixty-five now and can't do anything . . . I am very frustrated, I thought that by coming to America I would find a new life. I did, but its harder than in Laos. You see, everything in America is confusing. They have red lights, yellow lights, green lights. I have just barely learned what these mean . . . this is hard enough. But imagine, whenever you wish to go somewhere you have to wait for someone . . . It has been very hard for me, like I said, if I would have had a choice, I would have remained back in Laos. Or if I could, I'd go back now. It's much nicer and peaceful back home. Here everything feels too lonely. Everything is too much. I always find myself lost in this world. (p. 101)

Social isolation, coupled with the economic pressures, means that many refugees face limitations to their full participation in occupations of meaning and necessity in the context of a new, dominant culture. Not all refugees experience such isolation, but common issues do exist that need to be understood and addressed, particularly since national and ethnic tensions will likely continue if not increase the dislocation of people from their communities of origin. Refugees typically experience occupational deprivation because they are dislocated physically and socially from familiar environments. Their linguistic, economic, and cultural isolation in host countries is understandable, but compounds the occupational deprivation that characterizes refugee life.

▬▬ DISABILITY AND OCCUPATIONAL DEPRIVATION

Occupational deprivation refers to situations and conditions that exist outside people, depriving them of important occupational opportunities beyond their immediate control. Geographic isolation illustrates how the physical environment can lead to occupational deprivation. Refugeeism offers a prime example of how political situations can lead to occupational deprivation. Cultural forces that create sex-role stereotyping and the social and economic factors that bring about wide-scale unemployment, underemployment, or overemployment have also been considered with reference to occupational deprivation.

Occupational deprivation may also arise from social and cultural practices related to individual characteristics. Some conditions that exist within individuals constitute barriers to occupation because "someone or something external to the individual is doing the depriving" (2, p. 201). Of concern here are conditions that have a physical causation and those that are psychological, emotional, or cognitive in nature. Occupational deprivation is not inherent in limited physical, psychological, emotional, or cognitive abilities. The point needs to be emphasized that deprivation from occupations of meaning or cultural significance is made worse by someone or something external to the individual, the human and nonhuman environment.

Being born with or acquiring a chronic illness or a **disability** is a reality that many people are faced with around the world. Being blind, having cerebral palsy, contracting multiple sclerosis, developing schizophrenia, becoming depressed, or sustaining a head injury are only some of the examples of situations that represent a personal challenge to people trying to live full and rewarding occupational lives. In the past, disabling conditions, whether these were physical, psychological, emotional, or cognitive, were often synonymous with social isolation and severely restricted occupational opportunities. Even aging precluded engagement in certain occupations. The central question is whether various types of disabilities in themselves are barriers to participation in occupations or whether human and physical environments are the real impediments. We need to ask how social attitudes have precluded participation in occupations by people with disabilities. How have social attitudes constrained people with various types of disabilities from self-expression through action?

Narrative accounts of life with a physical disability point to the attitudes of other people as one of the biggest barriers to participation in the world around them. Stereotyped perceptions, limited expectations, and subtle marginalization all serve to constrain people who have chronic physical illness or physical disability from accessing and fully engaging in occupations of meaning and choice. Attitudes of the physical able-bodied population may have changed in recent times due to better education and increased opportunities for interaction (e.g., through mainstream schooling). Yet, it still seems that many able-bodied people have definite views on what people with disabilities should and should not do. People with disabilities have reflected on the difficulties they have had in "breaking out" of society's stereotyped perceptions. Some prevailing attitudes may have changed, but they tell people with able bodies that there is still a long way to go before people with disabilities can participate fully in leisure and work occupations as diverse as flying a plane, dating, dancing, or being a competitive athlete.

The nonhuman, that is, the physical or built, environment can either enable or inhibit occupational engagement for people with some form of physical limitation. People with physical disabilities have chronicled their frustrations with physical environments that, on a daily basis, prevent them from doing what they want and need to do. They may not use the language of occupation, but they are referring to their everyday experiences of occupational deprivation. A perspective often reflected by people with so-called "disabilities" is that it is not they as individuals who have the disability; rather, it is the shortcomings of the physical environment that disable them. As Gerhart suggests, "often, a change in the environment can foster independence far more readily than a change in the individual" (37, p. 139).

How, then, can environments enable or constrain opportunities for occupational engagement? For a start, the conceptualization of a physical environment determines who can participate. Free-flowing space with unrestricted access should be the ultimate aim of public places so that everyone can participate, regardless of whether they are elderly persons with walkers, toddlers, or persons using electric wheelchairs. Ensuring that things like signage, switches, doors, parking, seating, and ramps are user friendly to a range of people (not just the able-bodied), facilitates engagement in the occupations we enjoy in public places. Occupations such as shopping, having a picnic, listening to an outdoor concert, or browsing in the botanical gardens should be possible for all people if the physical environment has been conceptualized and accordingly designed to be barrier free.

Assistive technology is another facet of the physical environment that can be introduced to enable occupation. A wide range of technology is available to assist people with the instrumental aspects of occupational performance such as opening a door, switching on a computer, or holding a fork. The use and availability of such technology within the environment can facilitate opportunities for all people to engage in occupations that are meaningful. Technology can actually transform occupational opportunities. An example of technology creating opportunities for social occupations is Internet "chat rooms." The Internet, with its chat rooms, bulletin boards, and interactive programs, has created a new range of social occupations that are particularly popular with persons with physical disabilities who may otherwise be socially isolated.

What occupational deprivation is experienced by persons with disabilities that arise from a psychological disorder, a cognitive difficulty, or a mental illness? Such conditions may impair occupational performance, but they need not be in themselves barriers to occupational engagement and satisfaction, if the human environment is supportive. The conceptualization and construction of the physical, nonhuman environment is important, but the social environment is what really enables or constrains occupational opportunities for people with nonphysical impairments and disabilities. In the not so distant past, people with mental illnesses and intellectual disabilities were often subjected to alienating and marginalizing treatments including heavy medication and surgery. In addition, opportunities to be involved in the everyday occupational world of so-called "normal"' people were denied them through the process of physical isolation brought about by institutionalization.

The extent to which society has changed its understanding of and tolerance of nonphysical impairments is still a matter of some debate. From the excellent book *I Always Wanted to Be a Tap Dancer* (a collection of stories by women with disabilities about their lives), one narrator's comments on her experiences with disability are compelling. In the following excerpt, Meg reflects on her experiences of having manic depression, the attitudes of others toward the disorder, and their perceptions of the "doing" dimension of her life:

> Having once had a mental illness, everything you do in the future becomes suspect. I sat through a committee meeting where the issue of mature age people returning to study was being debated. One committee member spoke scathingly about "fruit-cakes" who come to study as therapy . . . I never really decided to make the choice to be open about my experiences, they are part of me and my qualifications just as much as my university qualifications and my employment experience. When I applied for my position . . . I was asked why did I start the Manic Depressive self help group . . . so I told them. I am grateful for the tolerance and understanding that has been extended to me in my job. But why should I be grateful? . . . I do my job well, yet I am always conscious of needing to prove that I am as good as anyone else or that I have to make up for the years I lost to illness, and most importantly, never appearing to be mad or high or nervous in any way. (38, p. 112)

From this account it is clear that the attitudes and beliefs of others still exert a strong influence on the daily occupations of the lives of people with mental illness. From Meg's story it is evident that because of her history of mental illness, all her actions became "suspect." Accordingly, going about everyday activities for people having been so affected is complicated by needing to appear "OK," including how happy or sad she can be in her interactions with others.

From accounts such as the one just presented, it is clear that facilitating greater occupational opportunity for people dealing with such conditions is a shared responsibility. Through increased community education and by enacting pragmatic strategies in the workplace, we can move to a point in the future wherein the occupational potential of people with mental illness or cognitive or emotional disorders can be more fully realized. The challenge is to heighten awareness in communities that it is the attitudinal barriers that most often restrict people with nonphysical disabilities from participation in occupations, particularly outside the home. Principles such as *reasonable accommodation* can go a long way toward enabling people to be involved in numerous everyday occupations, but particularly in paid employment. *Reasonable accommodation* refers to the modification of a physical, social, or emotional environment to enhance the occupational performance of individuals or groups. For example, reasonable accommodations are made when work environments allocate specific tasks rather than the whole of occupations to persons with diminished concentration due to a cognitive impairment or the effects of antidepressant medication.

In this section, the occupational deprivation produced by conditions in the physical, social, and emotional environments has been explored. Special attention was given to the deprivation experienced by persons with disability, highlighting the observation that constraints to occupational engagement in disability are imposed by the human and nonhuman environment and are not inherent in the disability itself. Recent advances in technology, education, and attitudinal shifts have all helped to reduce the occupational deprivation of people with disabilities. We are now exposed to exciting images of people in wheelchairs hang gliding and people in nursing homes lifting weights. Such images have the power to improve awareness that all people, regardless of age and status, have a fundamental human need to live meaningful occupational lives—to create and recreate themselves through what they do.

CHAPTER SUMMARY

We have introduced the concept of occupational deprivation, describing it as a condition in the environment in which individuals, for reasons beyond their control, are unable to participate or engage in occupations necessary for their spiritual, mental, physical, or economic well-being for extended periods.

Examples of conditions that illustrate occupational deprivation were provided, including geographic isolation, unsatisfactory conditions of employment (unemployment, underemployment, and overemployment), incarceration, sex-role stereotyping, and, refugeeism. Occupational deprivation was contrasted with occupational disruption, which is described as a temporary condition that can be resolved through supportive efforts that may be initiated by the individual affected.

The special case of occupational deprivation that occurs for people with special needs, who have permanent acquired or congenital disabilities, was also described. In this instance, deprivation is often a consequence of social conditions, such as attitudes and policies that lead to environmental designs that fail to make them accessible for the diversity of physical, mental, and cognitive abilities that exist within a population. Improved awareness of the importance of occupations in daily lives will lead to a more widespread appreciation of the effects of occupational disruption and deprivation when these occur.

REFERENCES

1. Wilcock, A. A. (1998). *An occupational perspective of health*. Thorofare, NJ: Slack.
2. Whiteford, G. (2000). Occupational deprivation: Global challenge in the new millennium. *British Journal of Occupational Therapy, 63*(5), 200–204.
3. Mead, G. H. (1934). *Mind, self and society*. Chicago: University of Chicago Press.
4. Langford, R. (1988). *Don't take your love to town*. Ringwood, VIC: Penguin.
5. AIHW (Australian Institute of Health and Welfare). (1992). Health in rural and remote Australia (Report No. AIHW Cat. No. PHE 6). Canberra: Australian Institute of Health and Welfare.
6. Toohey, P. (2000, August 5–6). Another generation stolen by the fumes. *The Australian,* p. 3.
7. Cook, D. G., Cummins, R. O., Bartley, M. J., & Shaper, A. G. (1982). Health of unemployed middle aged men in Great Britain. *Lancet*, pp. 1290–1294.
8. Beale, N., & Nethercott, S. (1985). Job loss and family morbidity. A study of factory closure. *Journal of the Royal College of General Practitioners, 280,* 510–514.
9. Government of Australia. (1992). Enough to make you sick: How income and environment affect health (Report No. 1). Canberra: Ministry of Health.

10. Colledge, M., & Bartholemew, R. (1980). *A study of the long term unemployed.* London: Manpower Services Commission.
11. Jackson, P. R., & Warr, P. B. (1984). Unemployment and psychological ill health: The moderating role of duration and age. *Psychological Medicine, 14*(1), 605–614.
12. Warr, P. (1987). *Work, unemployment and mental health.* Oxford: Oxford University Press.
13. Smith, R. (1987). *Unemployment and health: A disaster and a challenge.* Oxford: Oxford University Press.
14. Platt, S. (1984). Unemployment and suicidal behaviour: A review of the literature. *Social Science Medicine, 19,* 93–115.
15. Toulmin, S. (1995). Occupation, employment and human welfare. *Journal of Occupational Science: Australia, 2*(2), 48–58.
16. Jones, B. (1998). Redefining work: Setting directions for the future. *Journal of Occupational Science, 5*(3), 127–132.
17. Farnworth, L. (1995). An exploration of skill as an issue in unemployment and employment. *Journal of Occupational Science, 2*(1), 22–29.
18. Botsman, P., & Latham, M. (2000). *The enabling state.* Sydney, Australia: Pluto Press.
19. Lobo, F. (1998). Social transformation and the changing work–leisure relationship in the late 1990's. *Journal of Occupational Science, 5*(3), 147–154.
20. Piercy, M. (1991). *Body of glass.* London: Penguin.
21. Bittman, M., & Rice, J. (1999). Are working hours becoming more unsociable? *Australian Social Policy Research Centre Newsletter, 74*(1–4).
22. Beder, S. (2000). *Selling the work ethic.* Carlton, Australia: Scribe.
23. Roodman, D. M. (2001). *Still waiting for the jubilee: Pragmatic solutions for the Third World debt crisis* (Worldwatch Paper 155). Washington, DC: Worldwatch Institute.
24. Molineux, M., & Whiteford, G. (1999). Prisons: From occupational deprivation to occupational enrichment. *Journal of Occupational Science, 6*(3), 124–130.
25. Whiteford, G. (1995). A concrete void: Occupational deprivation and the special needs inmate. *Journal of Occupational Science, 2*(2), 80–81.
26. Whiteford, G. (1997). Occupational deprivation and incarceration. *Journal of Occupational Science: Australia, 4*(3), 126–130.
27. Liebling, A. (1993). Suicides in young prisoners: A summary. *Death Studies, 17*(5), 381–409.
28. Zamble, E. (1992). Behaviour and adaptation in long term prison inmates: Descriptive longitudinal results. *Criminal Justice and Behaviour, 19*(4), 409–425.
29. Useem, B. (1985). Disorganization and the New Mexico Prison riot of 1980. *American Sociological Review, 50*(5), 677–688.
30. Churchill, W. S. (1910). Statement of the Rt. Hon Winston. S. Churchill, Secretary of state for the Home Department. In *Hansard Column. London: The Stationery Office,* British Government.
31. Andrews, D. A., Zinger, I., Hoge, R. D., Bonta, J., Gendreau, P., & Cullen, F. T. (1990). Does correctional treatment work? A clinically relevant and psychologically informed meta-analysis. *Criminology, 28,* 369–404.
32. Rowbotham, S. (1996). *Hidden from history: 300 years of women's oppression and the fight against it.* Sydney, Australia: Pluto Press.
33. Barrett, H., & Brown, A. (1993). Workloads of rural African women: The impact of economic adjustment in sub-Saharan Africa. *Journal of Occupational Science, 1*(2), 3–12.
34. Primeau, L. (1996). Work vs nonwork: The case of household work. In R. Zempke & F. Clark (Eds.), *Occupational science: The evolving discipline.* Philadelphia: F. A. Davis.
35. Zuzanek, J., & Mannell, R. (1993). Gender variations in the weekly rhythms of daily behaviour and experiences. *Journal of Occupational Science, 1*(1), 25–37.

36. Faderman, L. (1998). *I begin my life all over again: The Hmong and the American immigrant experience.* Boston: Beacon Press.
37. Gerhart, K. (1998). Consequences for Personal Independence. In M. A. McColl & J. E. Bickenbach (Eds.). *Introduction to Disability.* London: W. B. Saunders. p. 139.
38. Smith, R. (1989). Meg's story. In A. Lawrence (Ed.), *I always wanted to be a tap dancer.* Parramatta, NSW: New South Wales Womens' Advisory Council.

SUGGESTED READINGS

Australian Government. (1992, September). *Enough to make you sick: How income and environment affect health* (Australian National Health Strategy Research Paper No.1). Canberra: Author.

Australian Institute of Health and Welfare. (1998). *Health in rural and remote Australia* (AIHW Cat. No. PHE 6). Canberra: Author.

Barrett, H., & Brown, A. (1993). Workloads of rural African women: The impact of economic adjustment in sub-Saharan Africa. *Journal of Occupational Science, 1*(2), 3–12.

Beale, N., & Nethercott, S. (1985). Job loss and family morbidity: A study of factory closure. *Journal of the Royal College of General Practitioners, 280,* 510–514.

Beder, S. (2000). *Selling the work ethic.* Carlton, Australia: Scribe.

Bittman, M., & Rice, J. (1999). Are working hours becoming more unsociable? *Australian Social Policy Research Centre Newsletter, 74,* 1–5.

Botsman, P., & Latham. M. (2000). *The enabling state.* Annandale, NSW: Pluto Press.

Colledge, M., & Bartholemew, R. (1980). *A study of the long term unemployed.* London: Manpower Services Commission.

Cook, D. G., Cummins, R. O., Bartley, M. J., & Shaper, A. G. (1982). Health of unemployed middle aged men in Great Britain. *Lancet,* pp. 1290–1294.

Farnworth, L. (1995). An exploration of skill as an issue in unemployment and employment. *Journal of Occcupational Science, 2*(1), 22–29.

Gerhart, K. (1998). Consequences for personal independence. In M. A. McColl & J. E Bickenbach (Eds.), *Introduction to disability.* London: W. B. Saunders.

Jackson, P. R., & Warr, P. B. (1984). Unemployment and psychological ill health: The moderating role of duration and age. *Psychological Medicine, 14*(1), 605–614.

Jones, B. (1998). Redefining work: Setting directions for the future. *Journal of Occupational Science, 5*(3), 127–132.

Langford, R. (1988). *Don't take your love to town.* Ringwood, VIC: Penguin.

Liebling, A. (1993). Suicides in young prisoners: A summary. *Death Studies, 17*(5), 381–409.

Ljubica, T. (1996). Violets. In R. Zarkovic (Ed.), *Sjecam se: I remember. Writings by Bosnian women.* San Fransisco: Aunt Lute.

Lobo, F. (1998). Social transformation and the changing work–leisure relationship in the late 1990's. *Journal of Occupational Science, 5*(3), 147–154.

Molineux, M., & Whiteford, G. (1999). Prisons: From occupational deprivation to occupational enrichment. *Journal of Occupational Science, 6*(3), 124–130.

Piercy, M. (1991). *Body of glass.* London: Penguin.

Platt, S. (1984). Unemployment and suicidal behaviour: A review of the literature. *Social Science Medicine, 19,* 93–115.

Primeau, L. (1996). Work vs nonwork: The case of household work. In R. Zempke & F. Clark (Eds.), *Occupational science: The evolving discipline.* Philadelphia: F. A. Davis.

Smith, M. (1989). Meg's story. In A. Lawrence (Ed.), *I always wanted to be a tap dancer.* Parramatta, NSW: New South Wales Womens' Advisory Council.

Smith, R. (1987). *Unemployment and health: A disaster and a challenge.* Oxford: Oxford University Press.

Toohey, P. (2000, August 5–6). Another generation stolen by the fumes. *The Australian,* p. 3.

Toulmin, S. (1995). Occupation, employment and human welfare. *Journal of Occupational Science, 2*(2), 48–58.

Useem, B. (1985). Disorganisation and the New Mexico Prison riot of 1980. *American Sociological Review, 50*(5), 677–688.

Whiteford, G. (1995). A concrete void: Occupational deprivation and the special needs inmate. *Journal of Occupational Science, 2*(2), 80–81.

Whiteford, G. (1997). Occupational deprivation and incarceration. *Journal of Occupational Science, 4*(3), 126–130.

Whiteford. (2000). Occupational deprivation: Global challenge in the new millennium. *British Journal of Occupational Therapy, 63*(5): 200–204.

Wilcock, A. (1998). *An occupational perspective of health.* Thorofare, NJ: Slack.

Zamble, E. (1992). Behaviour and adaptation in long term prison inmates: Descriptive longitudinal results. *Criminal Justice and Behaviour, 19*(4), 409–425.

Zuzanek, J., & Mannell, R. (1993). Gender variations in the weekly rhythms of daily behaviour and experiences. *Journal of Occupational Science, 1*(1), 25–37.

CHAPTER 11

Occupational Justice

Elizabeth Townsend and Ann Wilcock

KEY WORDS

Empowerment
Enablement
Justice of difference
Meaningful occupations
Occupational alienation
Occupational deprivation

Occupational imbalance
Occupational justice
Occupationally just world
Rights, responsibilities, and liberties
Theory of occupational justice

CHAPTER PROFILE

This chapter unites the concept of justice with the broad view of occupation presented throughout this book. Starting from the premise that humans are occupational beings and that just societies are guided by ethical, moral, and civic principles, we introduce principles of occupational justice that focus on humans' occupational needs, strengths, and potential. Explored are situations in which humans are deprived of individually meaningful occupation, and situations in which inequality results between those who have too much to do versus those who have too little to do. Presented as a framework for considering these experiences is an exploratory theory of occupational justice. Included in this theory are ideas, reasoning, beliefs, principles, and distinctions between occupational and social justice.

www.prenhall.com/christiansen
The Internet provides an exciting means for interacting with this textbook and for enhancing your understanding of humans' experiences with occupations and the organization of occupations in society. Use the address above to access the free, interactive companion web site created specifically to accompany this book. Here you will find an array of self-study material designed to help you gain a richer understanding of the concepts presented in this chapter.

INTRODUCTION

Occupational justice arose as an intriguing topic for consideration in the mid-1990s. The authors drew together shared interests in occupation and justice and began to ask the questions posed in this chapter (1–6).[1] Contemplation of occupational justice grew out of research on the occupational foundations of human existence (Wilcock), and on the principles of empowerment and justice that implicitly inform practices that strive to be client centered (Townsend). The concept of social justice did not appear to address sufficiently occupational injustices. We lacked a language and concept to raise concerns about the unfairness of some people flourishing in what they do, while other people are leading unhealthy, empty, or dangerous lives.[2] Occupational justice was first described as complementary to social justice "Whilst social justice addresses the social relations and social conditions of life, occupational justice addresses what people *do* in their relationships and conditions for living" (p. 84).

Motivating this exploration is a utopian vision of an **occupationally just world.** At this exploratory stage, an occupationally just world is envisioned as one that is governed in such a way as to enable individuals to flourish by doing what they decide is most meaningful and useful to themselves and to their families, communities, and nations (8). Many questions are prompted by such a vision. One could ask what if people do not want to do something meaningful or useful? How can individuals decide what is meaningful or useful when they do not fully appreciate how families, communities, or nations work? Isn't justice about society, not about individuals? Likely the chapter will raise as many questions as it answers.

Whereas the first publication about occupational justice introduced the terminology (7), this chapter provides an orientation to issues and literature for an investigation of occupational justice. We first discuss definitions of occupational justice and social justice, then propose an exploratory theory of occupational justice. Stories of occupational injustice and questions for continuing a dialogue on this topic complete the chapter.

DEFINING OCCUPATIONAL JUSTICE: EARLY CONSIDERATIONS

What is occupational justice? Occupational justice juxtaposes particular concepts of occupation and justice. The concept of occupation is grounded in a belief that humans are occupational beings. Humans participate as interdependent, active agents in culturally defined occupations that determine their health and quality of life. From this perspective, humans' occupations are more than what the marketplace defines as work. The concept of justice is focused on **rights, responsibilities, and liberties** of **enablement** related to individual, diverse occupational needs, strengths, and potential.

Why consider occupational justice? As the exploration in this chapter reveals, occupational justice offers a new lens for looking at and acting on local and world struggles from an *occupational* perspective. Occupational justice seems to diverge from social justice through an interest in individual as well as group differences, through a concern for enablement of diversity contrasted with the distribution of equal rights and goods, and through a focus on the relationships between occupation, health, and quality of life.

Workshop Participants' Views[3]

We began to explore occupational justice collaboratively by inviting definitions from colleagues who share our concerns for individuals and groups who seem to experience injustices that limit their occupational potential. Participants at an Occupational Justice Workshop in Canberra, Australia, in April 1999 generated the definitions that follow.

One group suggested that occupational justice could be defined as "enabling equal opportunity for meaningful and diverse occupations through redefining the way resources are shared. . . a social revolution, changing cultural values, redistribution of money, access to environments that promote occupational development, requiring the transformation of systems such as prisons where some people lack access to meaningful occupations" (9).

Another group considered occupational justice in relation to health. Beyond the reduction of illness and disability, health was associated with "meaningful occupation in accordance with the World Health Organization's 1986 statement that health is the ability and opportunity to live, work, and play in safe, supportive communities, not just the absence of disease" (10).

Bringing attention to the participatory and cultural nature of occupations, occupational justice was described as "the opportunity and resources (personal, environmental, societal) for individuals and communities to select and engage in a range of purposeful occupations that are culturally and personally meaningful—key words being 'active', 'participation', 'empowerment', 'choice', 'opportunity', 'equity in living' (11).

The notion of rights was raised by another group. They proposed that "occupational justice means that there is equal distribution of the right to have satisfying, meaningful occupations that are specific to individual needs, and that nourish development of the mind, body, and spirit of individuals and communities. . . including facilitation and empowerment so that individuals and communities adapt to changing occupational roles" (12).

Rights were linked to responsibility in defining acceptable or unacceptable occupations in relation to social and ethical standards of a community. One group pointed to the importance of "defining whether occupations such as gun recreation, drug dealing, or prostitution, for instance, infringe on the rights and responsibility of others. . . but who takes the responsibility? . . . what are the policy implications?" (13). Attempting to recognize the interconnectedness of individuals and communities, this group proposed that occupational justice occurs "when individuals are able and empowered to participate in occupations of their own choice *as an act of sharing* [the group's emphasis] in and contributing to the community" (13).

Workshop participants referred frequently to issues of power. They talked about power directly with reference to equality, participation, and **empowerment.** They also referred indirectly to the use of power to transform systems, and to define culturally based rights, responsibilities, and opportunities for people to live, work, and play. Issues of power were linked with concepts such as health, wellness, quality of life, **meaningful occupation,** and occupational potential. These are contentious concepts, yet it seems important to link occupational justice with culturally defined ideas about health, quality of life, and meaningful occupation.

SOCIAL JUSTICE

Workshop participants' interests in occupational justice started from their interest in human occupation, empowerment, and the implications of these interests on justice. Justice is generally accepted to be an ideal vision of society expressed through ethical, moral, and civic principles (14–19). Justice has been debated since the earliest humans recognized the need for principles to adjudicate disputes over food, land, women, men, children, and their possessions (14). Definitions of justice have developed over time to adjudicate the sharing of resources and land. Other definitions have outlined expectations for acceptable and unacceptable behavior among families, communities, nations, and, more recently, global communities.

Consider children's play in light of North American ideas about social justice. Social justice would guide an equal, same application of rules for each child to use a playground or to become leader of the game regardless of social class, race, ability, disability, or other characteristic. In his 1971 *A Theory of Justice,* the American philosopher John Rawls highlighted individual rights, responsibilities, and liberties as moral principles of justice (17). Rawls might be concerned with the individual right and liberty of each child to use the same playground, and he might emphasize the responsibility of each child and family to look after the playground.

In contrast, Jürgen Habermas, a German philosopher, might have raised questions about the liberty and freedom of all children to play without interference. Habermas proposed an ideal speech situation in which everyone can express opinions without restriction, and disputes are settled through argumentation rather than violence (19), an ideal that Armstrong contends has not yet been achieved in reality (20). In a socially just community, children and their families might experience an ideal speech situation in which children and parents are free to speak their true opinions about the playground. A mediator might assist everyone to voice similar or dissenting opinions about the management of the playground without fear of violence or other retribution from dominant families. Tara Smith has explored justice as a personal virtue of respect and fair treatment of others (21). This perspective reminds us that justice on the playground seems to require that, for justice to work in everyday life, individual children and families need to exercise respect and fairness in their dealings with each other.

Looking beyond the playground itself, one might examine the policies and other texts used to govern possibilities for children's play. Governance is regulated by many types of texts, including written policies, procedures, and laws and extending to the texts of films, media advertising, web sites, and cultural materials that convey a message about social expectations (22, 23). When people experience justice or injustice, they are not fully aware of the invisible decisions about policy, professions, health, economics, social welfare, education, transportation, and industry that determine possibilities for participating or not in various occupations or the function of the state in regulating what they do (24).

In the example of play, families are not always fully aware of the policies, market forces, cultural biases, and so on that determine where, when, with whom, and how play can take place beyond the home, such as in a playground. Only those who make a conscious effort to learn would know how broad economics determine the pricing of games or sports that may or may not be affordable and accessible for play by children from different backgrounds. Not readily visible are power conflicts and tensions between competing interests, or over competing visions of what facilities people want for play in their communities. Many of the beliefs, values, and assumptions about children, playgrounds, and communities are either unknown or taken for granted. In the everyday world, disputes about who can play, where, and what with are typically settled through local mediation, such as community meetings, to resolve differences between the individuals or groups involved. Parents may select individual policies about access to playgrounds, yet there is an invisible, interconnected set of policies that advances some children and limits other children. Interconnected, for instance, are welfare policies that determine whether the monthly check can cover transportation to playgrounds that may be a distance from home. Also interconnected to playground opportunities are prenatal and neonatal policies that control spending on public health children's programs and on nutritional subsidies that would increase the likelihood of low-income children being healthy enough to play.

Adult international sports show how political dimensions of social justice have public as well as private ramifications. Governments, agencies, businesses, or organizations regulate what a population can and cannot do beyond the interpersonal decisions one makes in private life. Adult international sports funding and regulations are powerful determinants over which athletes will be supported for competition. Public policy and laws play a large part in determining athletes' empowerment not only to participate in sports but also to travel, accept certain kinds of financial sponsorship, make choices about the use of performance-enhancing drugs, and visit countries on scholarships and visas. The public regulation of justice in sports sets the stage for the interpersonal experience of justice (or injustice) during competition, although this ruling apparatus is invisible and unconscious in everyday experience. It is true that individual motivation and energy make a difference, but the organization of society is a powerful force in determining whether or not there will be unfair advantage, mistreatment, exclusion from opportunity, and domination by some adults while others are disempowered to act (25). A socially just society is enacted through everyday life if and when people insist on respect, fairness, equitable opportunity, and shared responsibility in their social relationships (26).

Iris Morton Young has argued that power is a central feature in defining justice. To illustrate her point, she contrasts distributive justice from a **justice of difference** (27). Her distinction is between a focus on *possession* in distributive justice and a focus on *opportunity* in a justice of difference. She defines opportunity as a concept of *enablement,* and she seeks a justice that *enables* individuals to play, work, and live without exploitation or violence in the everyday world. Enablement is contrasted with possession as a concept of *having.* Public interests in *having* are congruent with public support for equal distribution of rights, responsibilities, liberties, and goods. For instance, distributive justice supports equal access for everyone to the same health services (28–36). Young's concept of a justice of difference is congruent with writers who argue that empowerment, not just access to services, is closely linked with health and quality of life (37, 38).

Distributive justice, in Young's view, addresses principles of allocation in which biological or social differences cannot be taken into account. In particular, she raises concerns of justice and injustice that are rooted in unequal power relations wherein some are empowered to direct their lives while others remain exploited, marginalized, disempowered, culturally subordinated, or abused. To illustrate these features of injustice, she points to the everyday experiences of persons with disabilities, persons of color, women, and others. Highlighted are the alienating experiences of members of small cultural groups struggling for a voice in a dominant cultural context, even if some individuals from these groups gain power.

One might apply Young's thinking to children's play and adult international sports by considering how differences related to gender, ethnicity, or disability require different opportunities and resources. A justice of difference would consider what forms of enablement are needed to create opportunities for individual children with disabilities or from various ethnic groups. Differences in ability are already taken into account in the Para-Olympics that enable diverse forms of participation. The resources needed for different groups to ski or play basketball are not equal to those for able-bodied athletes.

AN EXPLORATORY THEORY OF OCCUPATIONAL JUSTICE

Definitive declarations about occupational justice are presumptuous at this early stage of inquiry. Instead, let us contemplate four linked components of an exploratory **theory of occupational justice:** ideas, reasoning, a set of beliefs and principles, and distinctions between occupational and social justice (Figure 11-1).

FIGURE 11-1   An exploratory theory of occupational justice.

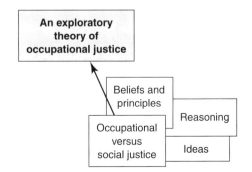

At some future point, people will ask about the history of ideas behind occupational justice. There is never a clear starting point for complex concepts such as this, although there is some historical sequence. In formulating a concept of occupational justice, ideas about humans as occupational beings led Wilcock to propose an occupational perspective of justice (5, 6, 39). Concurrently, ideas about the democratic, collaborative underpinnings of client-centered practice, focused on enabling meaningful occupation, led Townsend to propose that the everyday practice of justice involves enabling empowerment through occupation (1–3). The relationship between occupation and justice was an interest in common when the authors met in 1997.

Critique and reflection on intersecting ideas led to the development of reasoning summarized in the three interconnected pillars of occupational determinants, occupational forms, and outcomes of occupational injustices. As ideas and reasoning advanced, it became clear to the authors that interests in occupational justice were based on certain beliefs and principles. With an emerging outline of beliefs and principles came a growing awareness of features that seem to distinguish occupational justice as complementary to, but different from, social justice.

The four components described next appear to be necessary, although they are not likely at this exploratory stage to be sufficient to capture fully the concept of occupational justice. As well, the positioning of components in our exploratory theory of occupational justice in Figure 11-1 is arbitrary. Rather, components are nested to display the foundation of current thinking that informs the concept of occupational justice.

Intersecting Ideas About Occupational Justice

Intersecting ideas that gave rise to an exploratory theory of occupational justice are illustrated in Figure 11-2. The concept of occupational justice rests on the idea that individuals are different and have different needs. Different needs are expressed through the occupations that comprise daily life, since humans are autonomous, occupational beings. Humans need and want to be occupied for purposes of health, quality of life, and the sustenance of families and communities. Humans' drive to participate in occupations derives from many needs. Although occupational classifications vary greatly, there is a common recognition that the range of purposes for occupation may encompass looking after the self or others, enjoying life, or doing something that feels or is acknowledged by others to be productive (40).

Humans are also social beings whose lives are embedded in social values, rules, constraints, cultures, and communities (41). In real life, humans are interdependent with each other in diverse contexts. A major challenge in the survival of the human race is to reconcile differences in social values, rules, constraints, cultures, and communities. Enablement appears to be a concept for recognizing difference and diversity (27). Enablement is aimed at drawing out different, individual occupational needs, strengths, and potential. To reconcile ideas that humans are simultaneously occupational and social beings and that individual differences require a

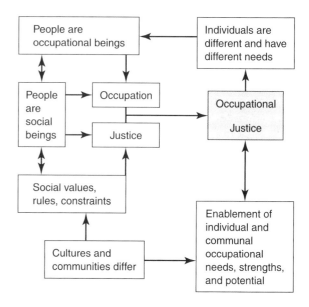

FIGURE 11-2 An exploratory theory of occupational justice: intersecting ideas.

justice based on enablement, we propose the juxtaposition of occupation and justice to form the concept of occupational justice.

Occupational Determinants, Forms, and Outcomes of Occupational Injustices

Ideas about occupational justice have been expanded through reasoning to test the viability of this concept. The three pillars of reasoning in Figure 11-3 list structural occupational determinants that shape occupational forms that, in turn, shape possible outcomes of occupational injustices.

The pillar on the left of Figure 11-3 identifies major underlying determinants of occupational justice as the type of economy, national and international policies, and cultural values. The economic structure determines which occupations are economically rewarded and which occupations are private or of social rather than economic value. Policies such as wages, job descriptions, pensions, health benefits, and environmental protection determine the ways in which certain occupations are conducted. Farming and fishing, for instance, are highly regulated to bring consistency to the economic market and, in some instances, to protect the environment. Cultural values determine what work will be given the highest and lowest wages. Moreover, cultural values are translated into decisions about what rituals and routines will be followed in a particular community or nation. Such values also define who will be included in occupations based on gender, race, age, or other distinction. In essence, occupational determinants regulate through economics, law, policy, or culture what people do and how they are rewarded. Hence, the particular structure of these determinants sets out the possibilities and limits of occupational justice or occupational injustice.

Underlying occupational determinants		Socially determined occupational forms		Possible outcomes of occupational injustices
Type of economy: Nomadic Agrarian Industrial Postindustrial Capitalist Socialist **National/International Policies:** War or peace Materialism Capital growth Sustainable ecology Multinational support Community development **Cultural values:** Social justice Work ethic Individualism Community Religious practices Gender	**Occupational Justice or Injustice Leading to**	**Opportunity/ restrictions** Examples include: Corporate management Division of labor Dole/social services Education Employment Environmental management Health services Industry Job creation schemes Legislation Media Farming/fisheries Parenting supports Professions Play/recreation Sports/fitness Technology in daily life Transportation	**Occupational Justice or Injustice Leading to**	Occupational deprivation (isolation/overcrowding) Occupational alienation (loss of meaning and purpose) Occupational imbalance (boredom/burnout) **Dis-ease Individual/familial:** Anxiety stages Decreased fitness Depression Eating disorders Fatigue Immune system disorders Metabolic disturbance Sleep disturbance **Dis-ease Family/community/ National/International:** Civic disturbance Ethics breakdown Social disintegration

FIGURE 11-3   An exploratory theory of occupational justice: occupational determinants, forms, and outcomes of occupational injustice.

The structure of occupational determinants, in turn, governs socially determined occupational forms, such as the types of technology used in daily life, the division of labor, and employment practices, including social services and job creation schemes listed in the middle pillar of Figure 11-3. Outside the labor market, opportunity or restrictions are determined by economic practices, policies, and cultural values that shape budgets, education, fitness, health services, legislation, management of the environment, media, parenting, play, recreation, and sports. Depending on how they are organized, socially determined occupational forms can prevent or increase occupational injustices.

Occupational injustices are experienced through the occupations of daily life as ongoing, unresolved stress to individuals, communities, and environments. Occupational injustices are thus socially structured, socially formed conditions that give rise to stressful occupational experiences. In Figure 11-3, the pillar on the right lists three occupational injustices that may result from or lead to "Dis-Ease." Dis-Ease is experienced individually, in families, in communities, nationally, or internationally. People develop real, physical symptoms that can range from individual fatigue and immune system disorders, to international civic disturbance and social disintegration of health, education, and other services.

It is difficult to predict what types of occupational injustices will come to light over time. Discussions of occupational justice have suggested that occupational exploitation, occupational marginalization, and occupational segregation are also issues for consideration under occupational justice. The three outcomes of occupational injustices highlighted in Figure 11-3 are **occupational deprivation, occupational alienation,** and **occupational imbalance.**

An example of occupational deprivation occurs when children are deprived of opportunities and resources to play because of poverty, childhood disability, or economic and social forces that lure them into child labor. Such children fail to fully develop their physical and mental talents, and they fail to learn about themselves and others in the world (42). When adults are isolated in prison, refugee camps, or institutions with a limited range of occupations that are unconnected to the real world, they become mentally depressed and physically frail, and they are unable to participate in the cultural occupations that bind families and communities (43). Injustice results when societies tolerate occupational deprivation for some while others in their own or other communities have full reign to play, go to school, remain active while in institutions, or participate fully in family and community. The sociology of occupations and current classifications of occupations exclude many of the occupations that comprise and are necessary for daily life (44–46). One might argue that these occupational classifications were developed in order to define the work required for the public and private sector economies, not to define everything people do. The impact of having no complementary or alternate classification means that societies are not sufficiently aware to support other important occupations, such as children's play or adolescents' need to experience adventure (47). An unequal lack of occupational development because of isolation or confinement at any age is both a matter of human development and a matter of justice.

Occupational alienation is the outcome when people experience daily life as meaningless or purposeless. Take the example of those with chronic illness (48). There is increasing interest worldwide in using health resources to repair, heal, and replace body parts (kidneys, knees, hearts, joints, stem cells). There is an injustice in such practices when societies expend so many financial and social resources on fixing the body and mind of a select few people that there are insufficient resources to enable these same and other people to do something in life that is important to them (29, 30). We may value life enough to expend resources on its preservation through medical and surgical interventions, but if people are alienated from themselves and others because of limited occupational opportunities, why are we preserving life? Occupational alienation can also be a concern for those involved in paid work occupations. Beyond their economic value, some occupations may enrich people mentally and spiritually, whereas other occupations are experienced by some or all people as boring or lacking in meaning (49). Participation in occupations is a major force in shaping identity, so lack of positive experiences in occupation can distort identity formation (50). Repetitive, mind-numbing occupations may suit some people, whereas for others they generate a sense of occupational alienation. These are usually occupations that are highly standardized, rigidly repetitive, and without opportunities for individual choice, control, decision making, or creativity (51). To be regimented, confined, and possibly exploited in daily occupations at work or elsewhere becomes a matter of justice when some people are privileged while others are alienated (52).

A third occupational injustice is occupational imbalance. Occupational imbalance is a temporal concept since it refers to allocation of time use for particular purposes and is based on the reasoning that human health and well-being require a variation in labor, work, and leisure occupations (53). Within individuals, an occupational imbalance may occur when a person has no time for occupations other than paid work, or conversely when family and parenting responsibilities present such a burden that a person lives in poverty, unable to develop skills or time for paid work (54, 55). Within societies, an occupational imbalance is seen when some people are overoccupied and others are underoccupied. Within the marketplace, this is called overemployment versus underemployment or unemployment. Occupational imbalance is unjust when work is so separate from other occupations that some people do almost nothing but work, while other people have little or no work. Although individual motivation, ability, and other personal factors may explain occupational imbalance in part, the hierarchical classification of occupations drives a labor market in which those with particular skills and knowledge are paid well and have lots of work, while others are unable to find paid work at all. The result is a growing occupational imbalance in which some people are overoccupied, or occupationally overburdened, and others are underoccupied, or occupational deprived (56).

Beliefs and Principles About Occupational Justice

A third component of an exploratory theory of occupational justice is beliefs and principles. Four beliefs and four principles are introduced next (Table 11-1). The beliefs in this theory of occupational justice are based on ideas, values, and assumptions

TABLE 11-1 *An Exploratory Theory of Occupational Justice: Beliefs and Principles*

Beliefs

- Humans are occupational beings
- Humans participate in occupations as autonomous agents
- Occupational participation is interdependent and contextual
- Occupational participation is a determinant of health and quality of life

Principles

- Empowerment through occupation
- Inclusive classification of occupations
- Enablement of occupational potential
- Diversity, inclusion, and shared advantage in occupational participation

about humans as autonomous, yet interdependent occupational beings whose occupations determine health and quality of life.

Beliefs

Humans Are Occupational Beings   Occupational justice is conceptually grounded in the belief that humans are occupational beings. Humans need and want to be occupied in various ways and for various purposes (41). In an early description of occupational science, Johnson and Yerxa (57) stated that individuals are most true to their humanity when engaged in occupation. Their belief that occupation is central to virtually everything human was derived from more than just their own and colleagues' values. They reference, for example, research on human curiosity (58), the behavior of East African primates (59), and adaptation in daily living (60).

Quoting from Karl Marx (61), Wilcock (5) refers to occupation as "man's species nature" (p. 19). In her initial publication of a theory of the human need for occupation, historical and contemporary research are used to illustrate occupation's three major functions in species survival. These are to (1) provide for immediate bodily needs for sustenance, self-care, shelter, and safety; (2) develop skills, social structures, and technology aimed at superiority over predators and the environment; and (3) exercise and develop personal capacities enabling the organism to be maintained and to flourish (5, p. 20). Furthermore, she asserted that the human development of an "occupational brain encompasses, integrates and tries to balance the social, selfish, physical, emotional, intellectual and spiritual nature of people" (6, p. 71). Drawing from her study of a history of ideas about occupation, Wilcock (4) concluded that "occupation is so central to the study of origins and development of humans in society that much of the evolution of the human species, from pre-*Homo sapiens,* is traced by studying occupations, such as tool usage, food production, creativity, and domestic and communal activities" (p. 72).

A rapidly expanding literature on occupational science is illuminating what occupation and lack of occupation mean to humans, although many disciplines are interested in participation, activity, involvement, and community action. What is new in exploring occupational justice is the broad understanding that these interests can be united through the concept of occupation. Also new is the assertion of occupational scientists that, at our core, humans are occupational beings.

In her stock-taking of occupational science accumulated insights, Hocking (62) offered a framework for research to advance our understanding of human occupation. The three areas of occupational focus she suggested were (1) essential elements of occupation, (2) occupational processes unfolding through time, and (3) relationship of occupational to other phenomena (p. 59). On the matter of the need for occupation, Blair (63) highlighted the importance of various occupations for people who are undergoing life transitions. Change is a process of separation from familiar occupations and experimentation with new occupations. In the gap between the familiar and the new, Blair notes that it is easy to experience occupational alienation since there is no firm grounding in a known occupational context. Change may be personally or culturally transformative since occupation is fundamentally embedded in the rituals and meaning structures of a community (64). Vrkljan and Polgar (65) explored the meaning of occupational engagement when people experience life-threatening illness. An expectation of death prods people to look at what is most essential in their life. This pilot study suggests that engagement in occupations that are familiar or important is extremely meaningful for those who are still able to reflect on their life.

Time, habits, and routines are strong interests in occupational science. There is growing evidence of humans' need to create temporal order in what we do everyday, everyday week, and throughout life. Natural seasons, weather, and rotation of the moon around the sun impose a temporal order on daily occupations. Humans interact with that environment and create cultural rituals and other patterns of behavior. In Chapter 4, Harvey and Pentland consider what people do in looking at occupational time use. Walker (66) has examined shift work from an occupational perspective. She redefines the struggles of shift work as a process of occupational adaptation. Her recognition that humans are occupational beings provides a framework to capture the changes in occupational routines and habits required to manage a life of shift work. Clark (67, 68) has also explored occupational habits and routines by synthesizing the growing literature on this topic. She reports that time is a major force in organizing occupations.

Space, like time, is both imposed on daily occupations and created by humans' need to create order in the physical space that we inhabit. Hamilton (Chapter 8) emphasizes humans' need to be occupied in a diversity of spaces and places that shape what we do over the course of a lifetime. Those who have experienced prolonged confinement describe going *stir crazy* without enough space to be occupied without choice about the places for their occupations.

Community, identity, and occupation are closely related. In a study of urban community action planning, Ross and Coleman (69) involved teenagers in occupations for the purpose of developing their communities and their identities. It seems that individual humans have a need for occupation in part for growth of mind, body, and spirit for development of the self as well as for engagement with other individuals in groups and communities (see Chapter 6). Occupations are "enfolded," blurring distinctions between what is considered to be work, leisure, parenting, and more (70). In old age, humans use occupation as a means of connecting with others to avoid loneliness and loss of meaning (71). In her ethnography of 20 elderly individuals with disabilities, Jackson (71) identified a human need for occupation in the adaptive strategies used to deal with loss. Elderly health care advocates took up new occupations or let others go in their need for risk and challenge, and they ordered their time and routines by considering what they wanted and needed to do each day.

Humans Participate in Occupations as Autonomous Agents   In our need for occupation, humans are individual, autonomous, active agents (persons) with differing capacities to choose and participate in occupations (72). This belief rests on the concept of personhood and rational will (73). Kant and others recognized that human agency, the will and drive to act, lies in individuals. Hence, individuals are active agents who hold the power to allocate resources as a means toward a visionary or *ideal* goal such as justice (33). The idea of personhood has given rise to belief in the equal worth of individuals regardless of difference, a point debated in public services such as health care (29). Individual persons experience that "occupational participation is important because it undergirds much of our temporal sphere of existence" (74, p. 144).

Individuals' will and drive to participate in occupations is actually a biological, not a theoretical, idea. Individuals posses the biological power to act and to reflect on, assess, and make decisions about participation in occupations. The spirit informs choices to seek meaning and purpose in the range of occupations that constitute daily life. Human needs and power to participate in occupation differ greatly because human bodies and minds are individually unique (75).

The active, autonomous power of humans to act is an important point. If all active agents are worthy, one is prompted to ask whether participation in all occupations is also worthy, regardless of the results people accomplish through their occupations. The question is whether those who lack particular physical, intellectual, or emotional capacities deserve less material wealth, or fewer opportunities to work, enjoy life, and live with others in families or communities (76).

Occupational Participation Is Interdependent and Contextual   Although humans are autonomous occupational beings, participation in occupations is interdependent and contextual. Occupations do not occur in a vacuum, rather interdependent participation occurs. Because occupations are more than an abstraction of the mind, occupations occur in real-life contexts grounded in real time and real places, using real equipment, materials, and supplies with real people. Furthermore, occupations occur in a context of invisible occupational determinants and forms that determine possibilities and limits for occupational participation.

Beyond biological traits that determine autonomous interest, ability, and will, occupational participation involves interaction with other humans in a physical, social, cultural, and institutional context. An interplay is seen between nurture and nature, and an interplay between individual autonomy and individual interdependence in doing things with others. Humans are both a biological entity and a product of society. Whereas Kant explored the autonomous self, Giddens (22) and Habermas (19) are examples of modern philosophers who present the self and society as interwoven and interdependent—the self being shaped by society, and society being shaped by the concerted will of the many selves who comprise a society. Conceptions of social and occupational justice hinge on debates about the responsibility of the state to mediate on matters that are beyond individual control (77).

Socially defined occupational determinants and occupational forms such as health services have been put in place to respond to particular ideas about health and the use of economic resources for health. It is these forms that shape what humans decide about the real places, methods, and tools that humans recognize as the technology of daily life. The interdependence and contextual nature of occupations may not be visible and immediate, but we are nonetheless dependent on what others have done before or are doing around us. Even when humans engage in solitary occupations, such as reading a book, there is an interdependence with the author who wrote it, and the publisher and workers who produced it. The chair or bed used to read is most likely built by someone other than the reader. Although some people do make their own furniture, it is highly likely that others have fashioned the tools used to exert the self-sufficiency required of reading. We design our communities and societies, then, to offer opportunities for people to play sports, or to attend school, or to build cars. Conversely, the presence of sports facilities encourages sports, and the presence of an automotive factory in a community determines that many people will look for paid occupations in the automotive industry.

Occupational Participation Is a Determinant of Health and Quality of Life   A belief that humans are occupational beings who participate as autonomous yet interdependent agents in a context prompts the question *Why do humans participate in occupations? An Occupational Perspective of Health* (4) presents a history of ideas and evidence that participation in a broad range of occupations is a determinant of health. This is true when health is defined as the ability and opportunity to live, work, and play in safe, supportive communities as outlined in the Ottawa Charter for Health Promotion, a Canadian and World Health Organization definitive statement about health (78).

The terms *leisure-rich* or *leisure-poor* convey the belief that wellness is about more than the absence of disease (54). Time is a major health issue because humans have a biological need for temporality in the regulation of sleep as well as mental health (67, 79, 80). Gendered differences in time use point to gendered differences in occupations and health status and quality of life (81). "Activity" is known so widely to enhance health that communities are being urged to use urban planning and public transportation as tools to encourage more physical activity within the built environment as a strategy for health promotion (82). Moreover, we know that humans need to feel useful, and that we fail to flourish and remain healthy when we feel that there is nothing useful to do (64).

Health can be promoted through occupation. However, occupation does not always promote health. Participation in some occupations may be degrading or debilitating, a point argued in Braverman's classic analysis of 20th-century work (83). The concept of occupational risk actually provides a framework for exploring the chronicity of illness, such as the persistent mental illness experienced by people who use community mental health services and who are often unemployed (84). The impacts of occupational participation on families, communities, and the world are just beginning to be understood, but it is clear that communities struggles to survive when a community industry leaves or the community's natural environment is destroyed.

Principles

The principles in this theory outline rights, responsibilities, and freedoms of enablement. They derive from a recognition that individuals have occupational needs, strengths, and potentials that affect our health and quality of life.

Empowerment Through Occupation   The concept of occupational justice is based on a principle described here as "empowerment through occupation." This principle takes a stand in favor of equality in power sharing. Power sharing refers to power exerted and accepted through horizontal collaboration and partnership (77). The contrast with collaborative power sharing is hierarchical, authoritative control of power whether this is done with benevolence or cruelty (85). Hierarchical, authoritative behavior both reflects and perpetuates hierarchical structures. A more equitable distribution of power would reduce the hierarchical dominance of some while generating the empowerment of everyone (86–88).

Empowerment has many meanings that refer to taking on power (3). Some use this as a term to describe the growth of individual or group feelings of power. To feel empowered is to generate feelings of personal drive, motivation, purpose, confidence, identity, and even joy (89, 90). Others describe empowerment with reference to everyday behavior. To act empowered is to behave assertively, to be decisive, or to be reflective and confident about the actions of oneself or a group, family, or community (91, 92). To organize empowering structures, one brings an empowerment lens to policies, procedures, laws, media images, language, or funding priorities (93, 94).

To bring an empowerment lens is to ask questions about power. One might ask, for instance, *Who has power and whose interests are served or not served?* One would also ask, *Who has control and privilege, who is expected to comply, and what are the consequences for not complying?* The principle of empowerment through occupation emphasizes that the structure and organization of society determine possibilities for feeling or acting empowered in everyday occupations.

The reasoning that links empowerment with injustice (see Figure 11-3) is that occupational determinants, such as economic practices, policies and laws, and cultural forces are also determinants of empowerment. In turn, occupational determinants shape socially determined occupational forms. Examples of occupational forms are the division of labor, managerial regulation of services, professions, or wars that shape possibilities for empowerment to choose and participate in various occupations (95, 96). Disempowerment leaves people powerless and alienated to shape what they do with their lives (90, 92, 97).

People experience empowerment or disempowerment in everyday actions and feelings. Empowerment through occupation might be experienced, therefore, as occupational enrichment, meaningful occupation, or occupational balance. Disempowerment through occupation would be experienced as occupational injustices, examples being the three highlighted in this chapter: occupational deprivation, occupational alienation, or occupational imbalance.

The principle of empowerment through occupation is congruent with Iris Morton Young's analysis of power. Her critique of distributive social justice is that the concept does not address domination and oppression experienced in everyday life by women, immigrants, and persons with disabilities (27). Her concerns with power are in "five faces of oppression": exploitation, marginalization, powerlessness, cultural imperialism, and violence. Restated as occupational injustice, some women, immigrants, and persons with disabilities are exploited, marginalized, or rendered powerless by requiring them to participate in occupations that exploit their talents for someone else's gain. Others participate in occupations that keep them on the economic margins because of low pay. Still others remain powerless to face threats of job loss, poverty, or violence if they do not comply with participation in certain occupations. They are held subject to public policies, laws, and finances that distribute and regulate their lack of rights (38, 98).

Inclusive Classification of Occupations   If one accepts that occupational justice involves the empowerment of everyone through a diverse array of occupations, one accepts that a cornerstone of occupational justice is a more inclusive classification of occupations. From an occupational justice perspective, the principle of an inclusive classification of occupations "concerns the definition of the occupations themselves" (27, p. 23). To challenge the definition of the occupations themselves, one might ask whether intellectual or management occupations should receive greater monetary rewards and social status than physical labor. Occupational injustices appear to arise in the separation of work from other occupations and in the hierarchical definitions of occupations. Therefore, one might ask how some occupations historically became paid work while other occupations were considered private and unpaid. When occupations are classified hierarchically, inequalities in status and wages perpetuate a social class structure between the haves and the have nots. From an occupational perspective, one would question the definitions of occupations that are included or left out of the hierarchical classifications of work. What part do hierarchical occupational classifications play in creating a world where some people have too much to do while others are underemployed or unemployed?

Some people may seek greater occupational enrichment, meaning, or balance beyond as well as through their work. When they look to occupations outside work, these tend to be dismissed as unproductive, frivolous, or a backdrop to what is really important—paid work (99). Those who succeed at paid work generate greater income and greater influence in the organization of society. Conversely, those who are occupationally deprived become disempowered, particularly where they are deprived of work. There is a fundamental injustice in the discrepancies of pay, privilege, and status allocated to occupations. Those who are interested in social justice have already raised concerns about gender, racial, and other segregation in the division of labor. Added here is a critique of the actual definitions of occupations. The concern is with the hierarchical advantages in status and wages accorded to intellectual and managerial occupations over occupations for creativity, environmental sustainability, or community building.

Enablement of Occupational Potential   The principle of enablement of occupational potential builds on the previous ones, and particularly on the idea of individual difference. Enablement refers to approaches and conditions that might be developed to support all people individually and collectively in developing their occupational potential. Enablement of occupational potential is interconnected with the principles of empowerment through occupation and an inclusive classification of occupations. Enablement would focus on the empowerment of those who are currently disempowered or occupationally deprived, and would involve all people as participants in the decision making as well as the performance of occupations related to their lives. An inclusive classification of occupations would highlight the worth of a greater array of occupations and would equalize the social and economic rewards of participating in a balanced occupational life.

Enablement approaches would emphasize collaborative interpersonal forms of helping, combined with the development of enabling policies, laws, and economic practices (100). An example of enablement could be the facilitation of children with various talents to participate in a school play. Without enablement, assertive and vocal children might do well, but those who lack occupational development because of poverty, disability, cultural attitudes, or other reasons would become increasingly disadvantaged. Enablement approaches could also involve encouragement or the explicit education of new computer users to participate in office occupations. Enablement might mean listening, coaching, mediating, or negotiating with employers or landlords to create supportive work or housing conditions that enable people to build on their strengths.

The development of enablement conditions would involve writing policies that attend to the empowerment of all participants or stakeholders in a particular issue. An example might be policies that involve professionals, managers, and the public in making budget decisions concerning playgrounds. The aim would not necessarily be to develop the most efficient playground measured in terms of successful sports teams or resource management. Rather the aim would be to develop the most participatory and inclusive playground operated within a defined budget. Enabling legislation would be written with broad stakeholder input to ensure that playground and community buildings are physically and attitudinally accessible for parents with children, for persons of diverse cultural backgrounds, for older people, and for people who use mobility aids. Or enabling legislation could require health services to focus on health promotion equally with acute health services. Enabling economic practices would reorganize accounting systems to calculate social production as well as economic production. Evaluation of the effectiveness of enablement would focus on participation, based on an *empowerment paradigm* (101). An advocate for occupational justice might envision all citizens participating to empower themselves and others to draw out their full potential as humans.

An important point to inject in a discussion of enablement is the matter of choice. Basic to the idea of occupational justice is an assumption that humans ought to have some choice about what to do with their lives. Choice is also the means by which humans decide what occupations are priority, and more to the point, what occupations they consider to be most useful and meaningful to them. Those living in poverty may face survival choices of sending their children out to work at a young age if they want to eat (102). Choices for others may be culturally defined within acceptable traditions and rituals. In its fullest, unconstrained sense, "choice is a luxury of an affluent society, comfortable and secure in its economic future. . . . Talk about choice grows out of the comfortable silence" (103, p. 199). Occupational justice would foster a "culture of choice" knowing the constraints on choice. Let us not overlook, though, the possibilities for choice if one recognizes that humans are occupational beings who make physical and occupational choices as autonomous individuals. In the most restrictive or exploitive situations, people make bodily choices to deliberately work slowly or to make mistakes that delay the production of goods. As expressions of limited but real choice, humans risk tremendous pain, injury, and losses to escape violence in order to live a simple but safer life in exile. The language of choice fits with the language of occupational justice and enablement because it reminds humans that withdrawal of participation in occupations is the ultimate choice, even in the most restrictive of conditions. Occupational justice emphasizes choice in accepting opportunities and resources that support the enablement of individuals to expand their choices. This is particularly true where unequal choices are available to different individuals or groups because they have different abilities or different circumstances.

Diversity, Inclusion, and Shared Advantage in Occupational Participation   Three related principles are explored together. Diversity follows on the principle of enablement. Occupational justice depends on recognition of the occupational needs and potentials of individuals who are also members of social groups. The first description of this concept stated that "occupational justice implies that societies value different occupational capacities and different occupational meanings. Rather than sameness, occupational equity and fairness demand respect for differences which arise in different, individual capacities, and different meanings derived from both personal and cultural meanings" (7, p. 84). This recognition of difference is a fundamental challenge to what Janice Gross Stein (103) calls the "cult of efficiency" that favors standardization.

Inclusion and shared advantage are linked principles within the concept of occupational justice. An occupationally just community or nation would be socially inclusive—that is, in an occupationally just society no one would be denied participation in occupations that he or she needed or wanted to do to build their individual lives or their communities. The corollary to social inclusion is shared advantage. Everyone in an occupationally just community or nation would share the social and economic advantages of that community or nation. Privilege would be equalized, not only as a social principle, but through the use of an inclusive classification of occupations that would flatten the hierarchical system of privileges that go with some work and leisure occupations but not with others.

The combined principles of diversity, inclusion, and shared advantage are difficult to consider. One is left wondering if more equal recognition of the worth of all occupations means that everyone would have a similar income or even a guaranteed income? The clearest implication is that these combined principles oppose social exclusion and differential privileges that create different classes of people. A recognizable example would be the social exclusion of people of lower socioeconomic status from the occupations associated with healthy eating. This principle would, for instance, lead to questions about the occupational differences of those with and without financial resources. While families with financial resources have many occupational choices for purchasing a variety of foods or eating at restaurants, hungry children and hungry mothers are economically deprived of the occupation of shopping at will and of cooking the proteins, vegetables, fruits, and other foods that are required for good physical and mental health (104).

The combined principles of diversity, social inclusion, and shared advantage would guide an occupationally just society to watch out for individuals or groups who are excluded from choosing and participating in the typical occupations of that society. One might consider as an example that an occupationally just community

TABLE 11-2   *An Exploratory Theory of Occupational Justice: Distinctions Between Occupational and Social Justice*

Occupational Justice

- Humans are occupational beings
- Interests in health and quality of life
- Different opportunities and resources
- Enablement
- Individual differences

Social Justice

- Humans are social beings
- Interests in social relations
- Same opportunities and resources
- Possession
- Group differences

would try to minimize the exclusion of diverse immigrants from certain kinds of employment, or the exclusion of persons with mental illnesses from the occupations of political office.

DISTINCTIONS BETWEEN OCCUPATIONAL AND SOCIAL JUSTICE

Complementary features as well as distinctions between occupational and social justice are becoming clearer as ideas, reasoning, beliefs, and principles are articulated. As summarized in Table 11-2, occupational justice seems to be more than a subcategory of social justice.

Social justice is a concept that recognizes humans as social beings who engage in social relations (22, 105, 106). The advocacy in this concept favors equitable (same) access to opportunities and resources in order to reduce group differences related to characteristics such as age, ability, culture, gender, social class, and sexual orientation.

Occupational justice, in contrast, is a concept to guide humans as occupational beings who need and want to participate in occupations in order to develop and thrive. The advocacy in this concept favors enablement of different access to opportunities and resources in order to acknowledge individual differences resulting from human biology and human interaction with their natural and human environment.

USING STORIES TO CONSIDER AN EXPLORATORY THEORY OF OCCUPATIONAL JUSTICE

After discussing occupational justice, four groups of participants in an Occupational Justice Workshop in Brisbane, Australia, in April 2001 offered stories of what they perceived to be occupational *in*justices. Their stories describe individual circumstances from which general features of occupational justice or injustice were derived using the language of occupation. Here are examples of insights that emerged as workshop participants applied ideas, reasoning, beliefs, and principles that they perceived were congruent with occupational justice. They were drawing on their own ideas and experiences as occupational therapists.

Story 1: Deprived of a Valued Occupation

I work with a woman who has dementia, about 70 years of age, who is living on a rural property. I was asked to see her because she has significant memory loss, and there is significant conflict and tension between my client and her husband. Her husband trains horses and they have their own training track for 10 horses. She, however, owns the "racing colors." This refers to the registered banners needed to enter a horse in a race. To add to the situation, both have children from previous marriages, and this causes conflict. The issues for her are that she is unable to participate in an occupation she values because she forgets where the racing colors are. Over and over, she and her husband end up in violent conflicts. The local health authority is questioning whether the woman needs institutional care for her own and her husband's safety.

It seems to me that there are two key occupational injustice issues from the point of view of the woman. First, she is experiencing occupational deprivation because she is unable to participate in her valued occupation of racing. This deprivation is undermining her mental wellness beyond the impact of her dementia. When she is denied access to tend her horses, she is resisting occupational deprivation and her husband's attempts to control this occupation. Second, her occupational deprivation is closely related to what seems like an occupational protectionism related to her husband's zealous attempts to protect her safety. His occupational fulfilment in maintaining their life of horse training is disrupted by his attempts to protect her from harm around the horses. He is unaware that her sense of occupational deprivation is likely contributing to her increasing resistance. She probably needs to find a safe, constant place for the racing colors, such as in a locked glass cabinet, where she and he can both see that they are safe. Then she needs to find someone who will become a buddy in working around the horses, watching for her safety, but affording her opportunities to work with the horses in simple ways that do not rely on her memory (107).

Story 2: Isolated from a Desired Occupational Community

I work in a forensic, mental health program in a prison. Recently one of the detainees escaped while on an escorted visit in the community. Managers responded by canceling all leave due to community pressure and fear. Issues related to occupation are that those in prison are expressing needs and wishes to experience community life and to ensure that they prepare themselves to return to community life.

From the point of view of the detainees, I think that the occupational justice issues are about occupational isolation in prison. There is also an issue of occupational privilege whereby the needs for meaningful occupation of those outside prisons are privileged over the needs for meaningful occupation of those inside prisons. Privilege hinges on fear and perceptions of safety by those outside prisons. Communities are generalizing their fear of those in prison after an individual escapes. The safety of those outside prison is considered paramount to the extent that the community is willing to deny those inside prison who express needs to experience occupations in the community. The occupational isolation that results for those who are inside prisons may actually reduce their likelihood of participating in community-sanctioned occupations when they are released from prison (108).

Story 3: Alienated from a Cultural Community of Occupations

I know a woman who experienced a brain injury related to anoxia following routine surgery. She is a valued elder in her rural, aboriginal community. Now she is unable to remember and communicate well, and has great difficulty walking the 4 kilometers from her cabin to the nearest town where she has sold her crafts to support herself. The result is that she is now alienated from her cultural community as their elder, and alienated as an impoverished, disabled woman who was formerly a proud, financially self-sufficient leader. A local interpreter has volunteered to help me work with her.

Her situation is made worse by the normative expectations and standards of my own profession of occupational therapy and my culture. My standard assessment tools are culturally bound, and thus invalid, so my assessment of her lacks the formal data expected by health services before home support services can be approved. As well, she needs her caregiver to collect firewood, hunt for food, and take her to town, but these are not culturally expected duties in the standard list of approved caregiving services. Her rural life creates nonstandard needs. This is a woman who could continue to be financially self-sufficient and a proud community leader if support services were available to address her culturally specific and rural needs. Instead, our current system provides home support only to help her with bathing and cooking occupations. The impact on this woman is that she is both occupationally and financially deprived (109).

Story 4: Being Overoccupied While Others Are Underoccupied

One of the people with whom I work is a 10-year-old girl with cerebral palsy. She communicates through eye expressions and pointing. Her mother was occupationally overwhelmed with the work of tending to her daughter. The result for the mother was severe mental distress. The father is a shift worker and may too have felt occupationally overwhelmed. Whatever the case, the daughter's occupational and other needs were too much for the parents. They separated and now live a 3 hour drive apart. Because neither parent could manage the child, she was placed in a public hospital at age 4. Placement was to be temporary until adoption could be arranged, but she is still there. I have worked with her for 4 years. I was asked to enable the hospital workers to teach the child how to feed herself and manage toileting in preparation for her attending school. I was also asked by family and disability services to work with the school since the girl is entitled by law to an education.

Social justice would raise concerns about the equal burden of parenting for both men and women. As well, social justice would raise concerns that all children have equal access to an education. Here is a situation where social justice can be met, with ridiculous results. On the one hand, the mother is so overoccupied that she cannot look after her daughter. The parents' separation has left them both overoccupied in their own worlds. On the other hand, their daughter is underoccupied. She is brought to the classroom to sit for the day, without attention to her education other than her physical presence in an educational structure. We need the additional notion of occupational justice to consider how the parents might raise attention to their occupational overload without their relationship ending. We also need the notion of occupational justice to illuminate the importance of their daughter participating in educational occupations rather than just sitting in school. While there is no social discrimination, there is occupational discrimination. Opportunity and fulfillment of her educational needs are met in this situation by human and financial resources to make the school physically accessible, culturally inclusive to students with disabilities, and knowledgeable of the methods required to communicate with and teach individuals with special needs. Throughout this girl's life, her parents, her caregivers at the hospital, and now her teachers have been occupationally overemployed because there is a lack of resources to enable the girl to develop occupations that she will need for a fulfilling life (110).

Reflections on Stories

The four stories all implicitly recognize that humans are occupational beings, and they all express interests in justice in terms of health and quality of life. Workshop participants' interests in health and quality of life are likely linked to occupation because occupational therapists are interested in these issues. Whereas those with different interests might raise different occupational injustices. The stories focus on different needs for opportunities and resources and on the importance of enabling the diverse occupational potentials of individuals. None of these stories can be adjudicated sufficiently by considering rights, responsibilities, and liberties related to age, gender, or other characteristic. The woman with dementia required enablement through special home support to safely work with her horses and live at home. The adults in a correctional facility lacked opportunities to prepare for community living because one prisoner broke the trust of being on leave. The issue is not only financial or human resources to support prisoners in community preparation but rather a philosophy of group punishment that overrides a philosophy of occupational enablement. The aboriginal woman lacked opportunities to earn money through culturally based crafts. Neither the aboriginal community nor state services were in a position to offer transportation or a helper for her to resume her income-generating occupations. Finally, the child lacked sufficient opportunities and resources to actually participate in learning after some resources had been expended to get her to the classroom. Moreover, her parents lacked personalized resources to support them in caring for her, having located resources for such care only in state institutions.

Lack of enablement approaches for the empowerment of these and other similarly challenged individuals extends beyond a social justice concern for equal rights. The examples point to the limitations of social justice to address issues of difference. From a social justice perspective, these people may all have had equal rights to access existing home support services. The prisoners were equally treated within a particular punishment philosophy of correctional services. Some might say that the problem here is still one of social justice—and that what is needed is more financial and human resources, not another concept of justice. But how can social justice address their different resource needs without breaking the principle of equality? Needed are enablement approaches. Social justice might define equal access to services, but social justice cannot speak to the specialized resources needed to enable some people to accomplish what they need or want to do. Equal access to a society's resources for health and quality of life would fall under the rubric of social justice. But equal access to the same resources is not sufficient, as clearly illustrated by the girl who can access education to sit in a classroom where the resources are insufficient for her to actually learn. In other words, a justice that addresses equality of access to opportunity and resources is not sufficient when what is needed is recognition of difference.

Furthermore, the stories illuminate the overvaluing of some occupations and undervaluing of others, a point not addressed under social justice. Social justice addresses equality of payment for equal work. Calls for social justice have produced changes in occupational classifications to reduce gender, race, and other discrimination in the workplace. But social justice does not address the moral and civic questions of the growing discrepancy between salaries for the highest and lowest paid occupations. Nor does social justice address vast differences in status and salary accorded, for example, to the problem-solving (mental) occupations of professionals and managers versus the skilled physical labor of boat builders. We may argue about the "importance" of some occupations to society over others. But the ethical, moral, and civic principles of social justice cannot fully adjudicate questions about whose decisions prevail on the "importance" and "value" of different occupations. The concerns raised as examples of occupational injustice illuminate, in particular, the need for a new formulation of justice to address differences in ability, differences in the division of labor, and differences in the value of occupations in both private and public realms of society.

Those who are interested in occupational justice are encouraged to continue this exploration through a dialogue for raising awareness. An exploratory theory of occupational justice presents the authors' analysis of ideas, reasoning, beliefs, and principles. Through a dialogue around questions, such as those suggested in Table 11-3, others will consider whether occupational justice is a viable concept on its own, or whether the concerns for justice raised here are actually within the realm of social justice. If occupational justice is a viable concept, the next steps will be to consider appropriate activism to bring occupational justice to greater public attention.

TABLE 11-3 *Occupational Justice: A Dialogue for Raising Awareness*

Are all occupations worthwhile?

Are occupations an economic or social issue? Should all occupations be paid in order to achieve occupational justice? Are income averaging and guaranteed minimum income occupational justice policies? Should people be paid to enjoy themselves? Should manual occupations (such as cleaning) and nonmanual occupations (such as research) be accorded equal prestige and pay? Do any criteria or conditions justify occupational privilege of prestige or pay?

What rights, responsibilities, and freedoms should govern the enablement of occupational potential?

Should society be responsible for enabling individuals to achieve their occupational potential? What if the enablement of some to do what they want, such as driving a car, disables others who cannot do what they want, such as exercise outside because of car exhaust fumes and smog? What priorities should be given to using economic resources for enablement? How should enablement of community and family occupations be balanced with enablement of economic occupations?

How can a society deal with the concepts of diversity, social inclusion, and shared advantage?

Why are there different economic rewards for being a chef in a restaurant and cooking meals for a large family? Both engage in similar occupations of food purchasing, preparation, and presentation, but one is paid and the other is not. Why is this? What if the person cooking for a large family is living in poverty associated with lack of education rather than lack of hard work? Would occupational justice be done if the family was paid to cook nutritious, economical meals to ensure healthy occupational development of the children and any grandparents who live there? What if social inclusion undermines the occupational potential of some people; for instance, should children with a disability be included or segregated in schools if the aim is enablement of their occupational potential?

Is occupational justice really different from social justice?

Are physically inaccessible buildings a matter of occupational injustice or social injustice? Does occupational injustice or social injustice occur when employers cannot or will not offer flexible hours and locations for people with disabilities?

CHAPTER SUMMARY

The discussion in this chapter has introduced occupational justice as a concept that is complementary to but different from social justice. Based on early workshop discussions on occupational justice and on the literature, the authors proposed an exploratory theory of occupational justice. The foundations of this theory are ideas, reasoning, beliefs, and principles that lead to distinctions between occupational and social justice. Occupational justice seems to diverge from social justice through an interest in individual as well as group differences, through a concern for enablement of diversity contrasted with the distribution of equal rights and goods, and through its focus on the relationships between health, quality of life, and meaningful occupation. Readers are left to contemplate occupational justice as a new formulation of justice that would define the rights, responsibilities, and civic principles of an occupationally just world.

Acknowledgments

Our appreciation is extended for research assistance to Tammy Coles, a student occupational therapist at Dalhousie University. Appreciation is also extended to participants in occupational justice workshops and presentations whose challenging discussions helped to refine the ideas presented in the chapter.

REFERENCES

1. Townsend, E. (1993). Muriel Driver Memorial Lecture: Occupational therapy's social vision. *Canadian Journal of Occupational Therapy, 60*, 174–184.
2. Townsend, E. (1996). Enabling empowerment: Using simulations versus real occupations. *Canadian Journal of Occupational Therapy, 63*, 113–128.
3. Townsend, E. (1998). *Good intentions overruled: A critique of empowerment in the routine organization of mental health services.* Toronto, ON: University of Toronto Press.
4. Wilcock, A. A. (1998). *An occupational perspective of health.* Thorofare, NJ: Slack.
5. Wilcock, A. (1993). A theory of the human need for occupation. *Journal of Occupational Science: Australia, 1*(1), 17–24.
6. Wilcock, A. (1995). The occupational brain: A theory of human nature. *Journal of Occupational Science: Australia, 2*(1), 68–73.
7. Wilcock, A., & Townsend, E. (2000). Occupational justice: Occupational terminology interactive dialogue. *Journal of Occupational Science, 7*(2), 84–86.
8. Wilcock, A. (2001). Occupational utopias: Back to the future. *Journal of Occupational Science, 1*(1), 5–12.
9. Starbuck, R. A., Whitehead, B. J., Holdsworth, C. R., Gray, M. I., Frontin, G. R., Preston-Stanley, S., & Maxwell, P. (1999). Unpublished. Occupational justice workshop. Notes from *Australian Association of Occupational Therapists Conference,* Canberra, Australia.
10. Browning, J. M., Trevan-Hawke, J., Wilson, L. H., Jensen, H., West, K., Fisher, A., Denham, H., & McLennan, M. (1999). Unpublished. *Occupational justice workshop.* Notes from Australian Association of Occupational Therapists Conference, Canberra, Australia.
11. Grainger, C. (1999). Unpublished. Occupational science workshop. Notes from *Australian Association of Occupational Therapists Conference,* Canberra, Australia.
12. Crombie, S., French, G., & Wright-St. Clair, V. (1999). Unpublished. Notes from Occupational Justice Workshop.
13. Howard, L., Gamble, J., Bye, R., Arblaster, K., Dean, P., & Casley, L. (1999). Unpublished. Occupational Justice Workshop. Notes from Australian Association of Occupational Therapists Conference; Canberra, Australia; 1999.
14. Adelson, H. L. (1995). The origins of a concept of social justice. In K. D. Irani, M. Silver, (Eds.), *Social justice in the ancient world* (pp. 25–38). Westport, CT: Greenwood Press.

15. Habermas, J. (1995). *The philosophical discourse of modernity: Twelve lectures* (Trans. F. Lawrence). Cambridge, MA: MIT Press.
16. Pitkin, H. F. (1981). Justice: On relating public and private. *Political Theory, 9,* 327–352.
17. Rawls, J. (1971). *A theory of justice.* Cambridge, MA: Belknap Press of Harvard University Press.
18. Irani, K. D. (1995). The idea of social justice in the ancient world. In K. D. Irani & M. Silver (Eds.). *Social justice in the ancient world.* Westport: Greenwood Press, pp. 3–8.
19. Habermas, J. (1990). *Moral consciousness and communicative action* (Trans. Christian Lenhardt and Sherry Weber Nicholsen). Cambridge, MA: MIT Press.
20. Armstrong, H. (2000). Reflections on the difficulty of creating and sustaining equitable communicative forums. *Canadian Journal for Studies in Adult Education, 14,* 67–85.
21. Smith, T. (1999). Justice as a personal virtue. *Social Theory and Practice, 25,* 361–384.
22. Giddens, A. (1991). *Modernity and self-identity: Self and society in the late modern age.* Stanford, CA: Stanford University Press.
23. Smith, D. E. (1990). *Texts, facts, and femininity: Exploring the relations of ruling.* New York: Routledge.
24. Gough, I. (1979). *Political economy of the welfare state.* London: Macmillan Press.
25. Callan, E. (2000). Liberal legitimacy, justice, and civic education. *Ethics, 111,* 141–155.
26. Marshall, G., Swift, A., & Roberts, S. (1997). Social justice. *In Against the odds? Social class and social justice in industrial societies* (pp. 7–20). Oxford: Clarendon Press.
27. Young, I. M. (1990). *Justice and the politics of difference.* Princeton, NJ: Princeton University Press.
28. Cookson, R., & Dolan, P. (2000). Principles of justice in health care rationing. *Journal of Medical Ethics, 26*(5), 323–329.
29. Daniels, N., Kennedy, B. P., & Kawachi, I. (1999). Why justice is good for our health: The social determinants of health inequalities. *Daedalus, 128*(4), 215–251.
30. Emanuel, E. J. (2000). Justice and managed care: Four principles for the just allocation of health care resources. *Hastings Center Report, 30*(3), 8–16.
31. Jennings, B. (1990). Democracy and justice in health policy. *Hastings Center Report, 8* (1): pp. 22–23.
32. Maynard, A. (1999). Inequalities in health: An introductory editorial. *Health Economics, 8,* 281–282.
33. McGary, H. (1999). Distrust, social justice, and health care. *Mount Sinai Journal of Medicine, 66*(4), 236–240.
34. Moskop, J. C. (1983). Rawlsian justice and a human right to health care. *Journal of Medicine and Philosophy, 8,* 329–338.
35. Christiansen, C., Clark, F., Kielhofner, G., Rogers, J., & Nelson, D. (1995). Position paper: Occupation. *American Journal of Occupational Therapy, 49*(10), 1015–1018.
36. Veatch, R. M. (1990). Justice in health care: The contribution of Edmund Pellegrino. *Journal of Medicine and Philosophy, 15,* 269–287.
37. McKnight, J. L. (1989). Health and empowerment. *Canadian Journal of Public Health, 76,* (suppl 1), 37–38.
38. Labonte, R. (1989). Community empowerment: The need for political analysis. *Canadian Journal of Public Health, 80,* 87–88.
39. Wilcock, A. (1998). *An occupational perspective of health.* Thorofare, NJ: Slack.
40. Christiansen, C. H. (1994). Classification and study in occupation: A review and discussion of taxonomies. *Journal of Occupational Science: Australia, 1*(3), 3–21.
41. Doyal, L., & Gough, I. (1991). *A theory of human need.* London: Macmillan.

42. McIntyre, L., Connor, S. K., & Warren, J. (2000). Child hunger in Canada: Results of the 1994 National Longitudinal Survey of Children and Youth. *Canadian Medical Association Journal, 163*(8), 961–965.

43. Whiteford, G. (2000). Occupational deprivation: Global challenge in the new millennium. *British Journal of Occupational Therapy, 64*(5), 200–210.

44. Cormack, R. M. (1971). A review of classification. *Journal of the Royal Statistical Society, 34*(3), 321–367.

45. Simpson, L. R. (1998). Aboriginal peoples and the environment. *Canadian Journal of Native Education, 22*(2), 223–237.

46. Krause, E. A. (1971). *The sociology of occupations.* Boston: Little, Brown.

47. Bergen, D. (1988). *Play as a medium for learning.* Portsmouth, NH: Heinemann.

48. Fieldhouse, J. (2000). Occupational science and community mental health: Using occupational risk factors as a framework for exploring chronicity. *British Journal of Occupational Therapy, 63*(5), 211–217.

49. Farnsworth, L. (1998). Doing, being, and boredom. *Journal of Occupational Science: Australia, 5*(3), 140–146.

50. Christiansen, C. (1999). Defining lives: Occupation as identity: An essay on competence, coherence and the creation of meaning. *American Journal of Occupational Therapy, 53*(6), 547–558.

51. Westwood, S. (1985). *All day, every day: Factory and family in the making of women's lives.* Chicago: University of Illinois Press.

52. Willis, P. (1977). *Learning to labor: How working class kids get working class jobs.* New York: Columbia University Press.

53. Gramm, W. S. (1987). Labor, work and leisure: Human well-being and the optimal allocation of time. *Journal of Economic Issues, 21,* 167–188.

54. Bernard, M. (1988). *Leisure-rich and Leisure-poor: Leisure lifestyles among young adults.* In *Leisure studies* (pp. 131–149). New York: Taylor & Francis.

55. Christiansen, C. (1996). Three perspectives on balance in occupation. In R. Zemke & F. Clark (Eds.), *Occupational science: The evolving discipline* (pp. 431–451). Philadelphia: F. A. Davis.

56. Sullivan, O. G. (2001). Cross national changes in time-use. *British Journal of Sociology, 52*(1), 331–348.

57. Johnson, J. A., & Yerxa, E. J. (1989). *Occupational science: The foundation for new models of practice.* New York: Haworth.

58. Berlyne, D. E. (1966). Curiosity and exploration. *Science, 153,* 25–33.

59. Goodall, J. (1996). Occupations of chimpanzee infants and mothers. In R. Zemke & F. Clark (Eds.), *Occupational science: The evolving discipline* (pp. 31–42). Philadelphia: F. A. Davis.

60. Montgomery, M. A. (1984). Resources of adaptation for daily living: A classification with therapeutic implications for occupational therapy. *Occupational Therapy in Health Care, 1,* 9–23.

61. Marx, K. (1843). Economic and philosophical manuscripts. In E. Fisher (Ed.), *Marx in his own words* (p. 31). London: Allen Lane, The Penguin Press.

62. Hocking, C. (2000). Occupational science: A stock take of accumulated insights. *Journal of Occupational Science, 7*(2), 58–67.

63. Blair, S. E. E. (2000). The centrality of occupation during life transitions. *British Journal of Occupational Therapy, 63*(5), 231–237.

64. do Rozario, L. (1994). Ritual, meaning and transcendence. The role of occupation in modern life. *Journal of Occupational Science: Australia, 1*(3), 46–53.

65. Vrkljan, J., & Polgar, J. (2001). The meaning of occupational participation in life-threatening illness. *Canadian Journal of Occupational Therapy, 68:* 237–246.

66. Walker, C. (2001). Occupational adaptation in action: Shift workers and their strategies. *Journal of Occupational Science, 8*(1), 17–24.

67. Clark, F. A. (1997). Reflections on the human as an occupational being: Biological need, tempo and temporality. *Journal of Occupational Science: Australia, 4*(3), 86–92.

68. Clark, F. A. (2000). The concepts of habit and routine: A preliminary theoretical synthesis. *Occupational Therapy Journal of Research, 20,* 123S–138S.

69. Ross, L., & Coleman, M. (2000). Urban community action planning inspires teenagers to transform their community and their identity. *Journal of Community Practice, 7*(2), 29–45.

70. Bateson, M. C. (1996). Enfolded activity and the concept of occupation. In R. Zemke & F. Clark (Eds.), *Occupational science: The evolving discipline.* Philadelphia: F. A. Davis.

71. Jackson, J. (1996). Living a meaningful existence in old age. In R. Zemke & F. Clark (Eds.), *Occupational science: The evolving discipline* (pp. 339–361). Philadelphia: F. A. Davis.

72. Sheldon, K. M., Ryan, R. M., & Reis, H. (1996). What makes for a good day? Competence and autonomy in the day and in the person. *Personality and Social Psychology Bulletin, 22,* 1270–1279.

73. Metz, T. (2000). Arbitrariness, justice, and respect. *Social Theory and Practice, 26,* 24–45.

74. Carlson, M. (1995). The self perpetuation of occupations. In *Occupational science: The emerging discipline* (pp. 143–158). Philadelphia: F. A. Davis.

75. Derber, C. (1979). *The pursuit of attention: Power and individualism in everyday life.* Boston: G. K. Hall.

76. Wilcock, A. A. (1998). Reflections on doing, being and becoming. *Canadian Journal of Occupational Therapy, 65*(5), 248–256.

77. Messick, D. M. (1991). Social dilemmas, shared resources, and social justice. In H. Steensma & R. Vermunt (Eds.), *Social justice in human relations, Vol. 2: Societal and psychological consequences of justice and injustice* (pp. 49–69). New York: Plenum Press.

78. World Health Organization. (1986). Ottawa Charter for Health Promotion. Geneva: Author.

79. Aronoff, M. S. (1991). *Sleep and its secrets: The river of crystal light.* Los Angeles: Insight Books.

80. Moore, A. (1995). The band community: Synchronizing human activity cycles for group cooperation. In R. Zemke & F. Clark (Eds.), *Occupational science: The emerging discipline* (pp. 95–106). Philadelphia: F. A. Davis.

81. Bird, C. E., & Fremont, A. M. (1991, June). Gender, time use, and health. *Journal of Health and Social Behavior, 32,* 114–129.

82. Frank, L. D., & Engelke, P. O. (2001). The built environment and human activity patterns: Exploring the impacts of urban form on public health. *Journal of Planning Literature, 16*(2), 202–218.

83. Braverman, H. (1975). *Labor and monology capital: The degradation of work in the 20th century.* New York: Monthly Review Press.

84. Fieldhouse, J. (2000). Occupational science and community mental health: Using occupational risk factors as a framework for exploring chronicity. *British Journal of Occupational Therapy, 63*(5), 211–217.

85. McQuarie, D., & Spaulding, M. (1989). The concept of power in Marxist theory: A critique and reformulation. *Critical Sociology, 16*(1), 3–26.

86. Byrne, C. (1999). A Process of dismantling professional boundaries: Nurses facilitating empowerment groups. *Issues in Mental Health Nursing, 19,* 55–71.

87. Illich, I., Zola, I. K., McNight, J., Caplan, J., & Shaiken, H. (1977). *Disabling professions.* London: Marion Boyers.

88. Zacharakis-Jutz, J. (1988). Post-Freirean adult education: A question of empowerment and power. *Adult Education Quarterly, 39,* 41–47.

89. Rappaport, J. (1985). The power of empowerment language. *Social Policy, 16*(2), 15–21.

90. Tandon, R. (1981). Participatory research in the empowerment of people. *Convergence, 14,* 20–27.

91. Stewart, R., & Bhagwanjee, A. (1999). Promoting group empowerment and self-reliance through participatory research: A case study of people with physical disability. *Disability and Rehabilitation 21*(7), 338–345.

92. Wallerstein, N., & Berstein, E. (1994). Introduction to community empowerment, participatory education, and health. *Health Education Quarterly, 21,* 141–148.

93. Maton, K. I., & Salem, D. A. (1995). Organizational characteristics of empowering community settings: A multiple case study approach. *American Journal of Community Psychology, 23*(5), 631–656.

94. Whitmore, E. (1991). Evaluation and empowerment: It's the process that counts. *Empowerment and Family Support, 2,* 1–7.

95. Lukes, S. (1986). *Power.* New York: New York University Press.

96. Smith, D. E. (1990). *The conceptual practices of power: A feminist sociology of knowledge.* Toronto, ON: University of Toronto Press.

97. Pizzi, M. (1992). Women, HIV infection, and AIDS: Tapestries of life, death, and empowerment. *American Journal of Occupational Therapy, 46,* 1021–1027.

98. Freire, P. (1985). *The politics of education: Culture, power and liberation* (Trans. D. Macedo). South Hadley, MA: Bergin & Garvey Publishers.

99. Primeau, L. A. (1995). Work versus non-work: The case of household work. In R. Zemke & F. Clark (Eds.), *Occupational science: The evolving discipline* (pp. 57–70). Philadelphia: F. A. Davis.

100. Townsend, E., & Landry, J. (2003). Enabling participation in occupations. In C. Christiansen & C. Baum (Eds.), *Occupational Therapy: Enabling function and well-being.* Thorofare, NJ: Slack.

101. Boyce, W. (1993). Evaluating participation in community programs: An empowerment paradigm. *Canadian Journal of Program Evaluation, 8,* 89–102.

102. Woodhead, M. (1999). Combating child labour: Listen to what the children say. *Childhood: A Global Journal of Child Research, 6*(1), 27–49.

103. Stein, J. G. (2001). *The cult of efficiency.* Toronto, ON: House of Anansi.

104. McIntyre, L., Travers, K. D., & Dayle, J. (1990). Children's feeding programs in Atlantic Canada: Reducing or reproducing inequities? *Canadian Journal of Public Health, 90,* 196–200.

105. Cooley, C. H. (1902). *Human nature and the social order.* New York: Charles Scribner's.

106. Rawls, J. (1975). A Kantian conception of equality. *Cambridge Review,* pp. 94–99.

107. Maxwell, P., Layton, J., & Isaacs-Young, J. Occupational Justice Workshop. In: Australian Association of Occupational Therapists Conference; 2001; Brisbane, Australia; 2001.

108. Schmid TH, A., Levack, D., Shiels, M., & Wallace, J. Occupational Justice Workshop. In: Australian Association of Occupational Therapists; 2001; Brisbane, Australia; 2001.

109. Crowe, J., Wex, M., Petherik, R., & Trevan-Hawke, J. Occupational Justice Workshop. In: Australian Association of Occupational Therapists Conference; 2001; Brisbane, Australia; 2001.
110. Young, J., Courtney, M., Lowe, R., & Maglaras, A. Occupational Justice Workshop. In: Australian Association of Occupational Therapists Conference; 2001; Brisbane, Australia; 2001.

Endnotes

[1] The authors have led workshops and given presentations on occupational justice in Canberra, Australia (1999), London, England (2000), Brisbane, Australia (2001), Calgary and Prince Edward Island, Canada (2001), and Los Angeles, United States (2002) and Stockholm, Sweden (2002). To date, more than 300 people have been directly involved in our exploration of this concept.

[2] Certainly declarations of *social* justice tend to generate controversies when societies set out principles for adjudicating rights, responsibilities, and liberties (17, 73). Therefore, the introduction of *occupational* justice will likely generate strong reactions. Some reactions may be to rejoice in the prospect of revisiting justice from an occupational perspective. Other reactions may be negative viewing the topic as *political ideology*. Be assured that the discussion is in fact small "p" political because it raises questions about power, but it does not take a stand with a large "P" Political Party. It is true that the discussion is about ideology, but we are considering small "i" ideology—a set of ideas, not large "I" Political Ideology.

[3] Workshops were scheduled to coincide with national occupational therapy conferences in Australian and Canada. Occupational justice and injustice are evolving concepts, having been proposed in the late 1990s. Not surprisingly, interest in occupational justice arose as a concern in two groups who are already exploring occupation. Leading this exploration are occupational scientists, who explore occupation as a field of academic interest, and occupational therapists, who use occupation as a medium of therapy with individuals, groups, agencies, or organizations, and who focus on outcomes of therapy related to a broad range of occupations that are contextually defined, including occupations to look after the self and others, occupations to enjoy life, and occupations to enhance social or economic productivity.

Glossary

Achievement motivation Psychological need to succeed or attain mastery.

Active participation Concept that views humans as active agents in their own development.

Activities A recognizable sequence of actions taken together in a particular context.

Activity An observable unit of behavior.

Adaptation Genetic changes in species necessary for survival within given environmental circumstances.

Affordance Any characteristic of a place or thing that enables or influences interactions with a living creature; an actionable property between the environment and individual.

Agency Capacity, condition or state of acting or exerting power; a transaction between a human and objects or people within his or her environment.

Allee effect A term used in sociobiology that is synonymous with cooperation.

Altruism A type of group cooperation characterized by active donation of resources to others at cost to the donor.

Archetypal places An approach to classifying places by the type of societal or individual function they serve; basic settings necessary to sustain human existence.

Archetype A typical, ideal or classical example, a universal symbol, or model.

Arousal A person's state of alertness or mental activation.

Assistive technology Any of a category of devices that permit active engagement or participation in necessary tasks or activities despite the presence of functional limitations or disabilities.

Attributions The explanations people give to the outcomes of their own behavior or that of others.

Automaticity A characteristic of behavior that is done automatically and repeatedly without direct or conscious attention or awareness.

Avatar A representation of the self that is used in virtual environments.

Behavioral area Groups of activities, which usually can be considered occupations.

Committed Occupations Occupations that are productive but typically unpaid, such as household work, meal preparation, shopping, childcare, eldercare, and home and vehicle maintenance.

Committed time Time spent in committed occupations.

Community A geographic or virtual connection between groups that engenders relationships based on proximity, interactions, or the development of shared values and experiences.

Community animation Processes that foster the building of community spirit.

Competence   A match between the demands or challenges of a task or occupation and the knowledge and/or skills of an individual who has chosen to pursue that endeavor.

Competition   The rivalry or struggle between and within species for survival.

Context   The circumstance, situation, or environment within which an occupation is performed.

Continuity theory   A perspective of the life course that views humans as developing continuously from birth until death.

Contracted occupations   Engagement in formal occupations such as work or education that are often governed by explicit contracts or expectations.

Contracted time   Time spent in contracted occupations.

Cooperation   Acting together to facilitate survival or other shared goals.

Disability   Social or cultural practices that create occupational deprivation for individuals because of their individual physical, psychological, cognitive or emotional characteristics.

Discretionary   Liberty or power of deciding, or of acting according to one's own judgment or as one thinks fit.

Dislocation   The displacement of something from its usual or customary location.

Displacement   Loss of place; movement from familiar places; involuntarily occupying a lodging other than one's customary home.

Division of labor   Specialization of occupations or roles within a society.

D-needs   Term given to unmet needs by Abraham Maslow in his theory of human motivation.

Drive theory   A view of motivation that identifies compensatory behaviors as predictable responses to needs (such as hunger, thirst, or pain).

Ecological niche   Environmental conditions that enable successful adaptation for a group.

Embedded occupations   Those occupations done concurrently with others (for example, talking on the telephone while watching children). Other terms for this concept are secondary activities and nested occupations.

Empowerment   A complex, participatory process aimed at achieving greater societal justice and equity through enabling groups with disadvantages to exercise power and influence.

Enablement   The positive form of the term *disablement;* creation of the opportunity to participate in life's tasks and occupations irrespective of physical or mental impairment or environmental challenges.

Environmental press   A term credited to U.S. psychologist Henry Murray to describe any environmental condition that works in combination with an individual's need, to influence behavior. In more current use, the term refers to any environmental characteristic that influences behavior.

Environmentalist viewpoint   View that human development is influenced exclusively by the environment, or through human experiences.

Epistemology   The study of knowledge.

Exaptation   Functional evolved traits that emerge not as genetic changes but as opportunistic consequences of genetic changes.

Five factor theory   A widely held view in psychology that personality can be described by five major factors, or groups of traits, including sociability, conformity, emotional stability, and intellect or openness to experience (also known as the "Big 5" or the five factor model).

Flow   Term given by U.S. psychologist Mihalyi Csikzentmihalyi to the experience of engagement that occurs when an individual is deeply interested in a task or occupation and his or her skills are at a level that matches or exceeds the challenges of the task.

Folk taxonomy A classification created through convention or popular discourse.

Free rider problem Situation created when members of a group take advantage of altruism without reciprocation, otherwise known as "gaming the system" (from sociobiology).

Free time Time available that is not consumed by necessary, contracted, and committed occupations.

Free time occupations Occupations done during free time.

Game theory An approach to understanding strategies of competition and cooperation that enhance the survivability of species.

Gendered Associated with being a male or female.

Habit A repetitive pattern of occupation or time use; a disposition to act in a certain way, without conscious attention.

Habitus Term credited to French sociologist Pierre Bourdieu to describe the unconscious patterns of doing, thinking, speaking, and perceiving that people exhibit in the personal or subjective worlds they occupy.

Homeostasis Term credited to U.S. physiologist Walter Cannon pertaining to the adaptive processes used by physiological systems to maintain a balance necessary for survival.

Human occupations Endeavors in which people participate that have personal meaning and are understood in the culture.

Incarceration The state of being confined.

Interactionist viewpoint A perspective that considers both environmental and individual factors as interacting to determine development.

Interdependence The reliance that people have on one another as a natural consequence of group living.

International Standard Classification of Occupations (ISCO) A hierarchical scheme or taxonomy of occupations developed in 1988 and adopted for use by several nations.

Justice of difference A specialized view of justice that more fully recognizes and accommodates diversity among humans.

Labor Physical exertion directed toward meeting the material wants of a community; the specific productive services rendered by a worker or artisan.

Leisure Freedom or opportunity to do something.

Leisure pursuits Occupations or activities that are freely chosen.

Life-world A phenomenological model of the world of the individual that sees behaviors in situations as the result of a person's culture, experiences, social relationships, beliefs, and attitudes.

Mastery Proficiency in dealing successfully with the challenges of living that occur at any point in time.

Maturationist viewpoint A developmental view characterized by the belief that heredity (genetic makeup) determines the life course.

Meaningful occupations Occupations that are chosen and performed to generate experiences of personal meaning and satisfaction in individuals, groups, or communities.

Meme An idea that gets replicated through transmission in a culture or group.

Memetics The science that studies the process and impact of idea generation and adoption.

Metacognition Higher order thinking representing the combination of types of thought processes considered together.

Methods of inquiry   Specific ways or techniques used to study phenomena.

Multiple determinicity   Being influenced by many factors.

Multiple patternicity   Having many patterns.

Multiple variation   The idea that growth and development show different patterns of change at different times.

Multivariate   Having many variables or characteristics that change.

Narrative   The personal story within which an individual constructs meaning through relating ongoing events.

Naturalistic paradigm   A qualitative approach to understanding phenomena which recognizes that a researcher's biases and values are part of the research process and emphasizes observation in naturalistic or "real world" settings and conditions.

Necessary occupations   Term credited to researcher Aas for describing those human endeavors aimed at meeting basic physiological and self-maintenance needs and class and therefore constituting necessary time.

Necessary time   Time spent doing necessary occupations.

Neural plasticity   The ability of the nervous system to change and adapt to environmental demands.

Obligatory   That which must be done.

Occupation   Engagement or participation in a recognizable life endeavor.

Occupational alienation   Experiences of meaningless or purposeless, a sense of isolation, powerlessness, frustration, loss of control, or estrangement from society or self that results from engagement in occupations that do not satisfy inner needs.

Occupational classification   Any systematic approach to describing or categorizing intentional human time use.

Occupational deprivation   A state of prolonged preclusion from engagement in occupations of necessity or meaning due to factors outside the control of an individual, such as through geographic isolation, incarceration, or disability.

Occupational disruption   A transient or temporary condition of being restricted from participation in necessary or meaningful occupations, such as that caused by illness, temporary relocation, or temporary unemployment.

Occupational habits   Recurring, largely automatic patterns of time use within the context of daily occupations.

Occupational imbalance   An individual or group experience in which health and quality of life are compromised because of being over-occupied or under-occupied.

Occupational justice   Term credited to Townsend (Canada) and Wilcock (Australia) referring to justice related to opportunities and resources required for occupational participation sufficient to satisfy personal needs and full citizenship.

Occupational participation   The engagement of the individual's mind, body, and soul in goal-directed pursuits.

Occupational performance   The task-oriented, completion or doing aspect of occupations, often, but not exclusively, involving observable movement.

Occupational routines   Recurring sequences of time use, such as the regimen repeated upon waking each day.

Occupational science   The study of human occupation; also known as *occupationology*.

Occupationally just world   A utopian vision of a world that is governed in such a way as to enable individuals to flourish by doing what they decide is most meaningful and useful to themselves and to their families, communities, and nations.

Occupationology The study of occupation (occupational science).

Occupations Things that people do to occupy life for intended purposes such as paid work, unpaid work, personal-care, care of others, leisure, recreation, or subsistence. Includes groups of activities and tasks of everyday life, named, organized, and given value and meaning by individuals and a culture. Categories used by researchers and governments to track human participation in the labor market and society.

Overemployment A form of occupational deprivation that occurs when people are over-occupied either in the paid workforce or in other aspects of daily life.

Paradigm A model or way of viewing the world or a given phenomenon.

Places The physical surroundings or environments that are natural or built in which people occupy themselves and create shared meaning.

Play Occupations selected for amusement, recreation, diversion, sport, or frolic.

Positivistic paradigm A view of the world based on the belief that phenomena can be best understood through observation and measurement.

Preformationist viewpoint An early historical view of human development, dating to the Middle Ages, that considered children as miniature adults.

Prisoner's dilemma A specific example of game theory used for teaching purposes.

Purposive view of motivation Emphasis on goal-directed or intentional action caused by anticipated benefit or a desire to avoid harm.

Qualitative research Methods for understanding phenomena that allow an investigator to experience events, identify themes on the basis of that experience, and formulate theories.

Reductionistic Reducing to parts; a way of explaining based on understanding the parts that make up a whole.

Refugeeism The state of being forced to evacuate one's home and community as the result of war, violence, natural disaster, famine, or fear of communicable disease.

Regulatory motivators Physiological influences on behavior that resist conscious control such as hunger, pain, and fatigue.

Rest The natural repose or relief from daily activity that is obtained by sleep or reduced physical activity.

Rhythm A regular and recurring pattern of living or occupational behavior.

Rights, responsibilities, and liberties Ideas and beliefs used to define the cultural norms, policies or laws in the governance of a society; foundations for theories of justice.

Role The part played by a person in society or life.

Routine A regular, predictable way of acting; a recurring pattern of occupational engagement or time use.

Self-actualization Term credited to Abraham Maslow referring to an intrinsic need to address "being needs," which he defined as autonomy, competence, and uniqueness as a person.

Self-determination theory Theory of motivation advanced by U.S. psychologists Edward Deci and Richard Ryan that emphasizes the development of identity and the importance of competence and autonomy in this process.

Semiotics The study of signs or structure or processes in the world that convey meaning directly and indirectly to an individual and thereby influence behavior.

Sense of accomplishment The state of feeling competent after completion of a goal.

Sense of community A psychological sense of belonging promoted by living in proximity to others and sharing experiences over time.

Sex-role stereotyping   Social jugements made about what men or women should and should not do.

Sense of place   A combination of characteristics that provide individual or collective meaning for a person or group attached to a setting or location.

Social capital   The set of informal values or norms shared by members of a group that permits cooperation among them and fosters interdependence. Social capital is a dynamic state that is influenced by obligations, expectations, trust, information channels, norms and sanctions within a group or community.

Social class   An advantage conferred on a group based on societal roles and privileges.

Social geography   The study of the people and cultural characteristics unique to a given region or place; the study of people in places.

Socially constructed meaning   The symbolic meaning of a place, object, or event based on shared experience.

Sociobiology   The study of group-living animals.

Stir crazy   A slang expression for being denied the opportunity for engagement in stimulating or meaningful occupations.

Suboccupation   A specialized form of work classified under a broader category. Also, a term referring to the nesting character of simultaneous occupations. (see also *embedded occupations*).

Sustainability   Use of natural resources in a manner that does not compromise the survival of future generations.

Symbolic interactionism   School of thought in psychology derived from the work of G. H. Mead. It views behavior as influenced by one's consideration of the image or thought of the self in relationship to others.

Tabula rasa   Concept credited to English philosopher John Locke in the 18th century, who viewed humans at birth as a blank slate

whose life course would be written by life's experiences.

Tasks   A means of accomplishing an activity.

Taxonomy   A classification used to distinguish between ideas, objects, events, or things based on their defined properties.

Tele-immersion   The creation of virtual environments that facilitate scientific collaboration over distances.

Temporal   Pertaining to time.

Theory of occupational justice   A theory to define beliefs, principles, and other features that distinguish occupational from social justice (see *occupational justice*).

Traits   Tendencies to behave or act in particular ways.

Underemployment   A form of occupational deprivation that occurs when people are underoccupied either in the paid workforce or in other aspects of daily life.

Unemployment   A form of occupational disruption (if short term) or occupational deprivation (if long term) caused by forces outside the individual, although individual responses to unemployment are important to consider.

Virtual places   Any nonphysical representation of a location, such as an electronic or digitally simulated environment created on the Internet.

Volition   Choice or will; intentionality.

Work   Labor or exertion; to make, construct, manufacture, form, fashion, or shape objects; to organize, plan, or evaluate services or processes of living or governing; committed occupations that are performed with or without financial reward.

Index

A

Ability requirements approach, 11
Achievement motivation, 129–130
Acquired drives, 126
Active participation, 100
Activities, 64, 70
Adaptation, 153
Affordance, 18, 176, 177
Alfred the Great, 20
Agency, 147
Agrarian Age, 21
Allee effect, 151
Altruism, 152
Ancient artifacts, 176
Anecdotes. *See* Vignettes
Antigonish Movement, 156–157
Archetypal places, 175–176
Archetype, 175
Aristotle, 13, 20, 162
Arousal, 124–125
Artistic expression, 158, 159
As You Like It (Shakespeare), 92–93
ASCO, 12
Assistive technology, 237
Attributions, 129
Australian Standard Classification
 of Occupations (ASCO), 12
Australia's aboriginal
 communities, 157
Authority constraints, 74
Automaticity, 6
Autonomous power of humans,
 255–256
Autonomy, 135
Availability of energy, 18
Availability of raw materials/
 finished goods/services, 18
Avatar, 190

B

B values, 134, 135
Babies, 184
Bargh, John, 6
Barn raising, 147
Basic duality, 31
Bathing, 184
Baum, L. Frank, 186
Behavioral areas, 65
Behavioral requirements
 approach, 11
Being (B) values, 134, 135
Bing, Robert K., 1
Biological clocks, 17
Biological cooperation, 152
Biological factors, 16–17
Biological penalties, 152
Birch, Margaret, 56
Blue-collar workforce, 227
Bourdieu, Pierre, 181
Brain size, 149, 150
Braverman, Harry, 54
Broken window hypothesis, 148
Bruner, Jerome, 137

C

Calvin, John, 21
Calvin, William, 150
Cannon, Walter, 123
Capability constraints, 74
Care of self, 15
Case studies, 37
Casual leisure, 13
Census databases, 39
Central desert communities
 (Australia), 225
Changing mastery, 107–108
Chat rooms, 237

Child care, 183
Children's rhymes, 48
Children's songs, 48
Choice, 260–261
Choice and control, 203
Christiansen, Charles, 1, 121, 141
Chronobiology, 17
Chronosystem, 102
Cicero, 20
Circadian desynchronization, 17
Circadian rhythms, 17, 41
Clans, 142–143
Codependence, 145
Cognitive development, 209
Cognitive style, 17
Coles, Tammy, 268
Collective efficacy, 147
Committed occupations, 66
Committed time, 66
Communion, 147
Communitarian practices, 146
Communities, 141–172
 active participation, 156
 adaptation/exaptation, 153
 artistic expression, 158, 159
 biological cooperation/
  altruism, 152
 biological forces, 151–152
 cultural rituals/rules, 157–158
 economic capital, 164
 floundering, 166–167
 flourishing, 154
 game theory, 154, 155
 go-between, as, 144
 interdependence, 145–146
 language, 148–151
 magic, religion, science, 162
 participation in occupation,
  210–217

Communities, *continued*
   place as community, 186–188
   Rubin's structural
      characteristics, 145
   social capital, 165–166
   sustainable, 158–161
   virtual, 143, 146
   volunteerism, 163–164
Community animation, 217
Community participation in
      occupation, 210–217
Commuting, 179–180
Competence, 135
Competition, 151
Constructed knowledge, 31
Continuity theory, 97
Contracted occupations, 66
Contracted time, 66
Cooperation, 151–152, 166
Coupling constraints, 74
Cro-Magnon humans, 151
Cultural rituals, 158
Culture, 210

D

D-needs, 127
Daily occupations, 64–65
Davis, J. A., 91
Dawkins, Richard, 150
DCD, 43
de Rozario, Loretta, 167
Deci, Edward, 134, 135
Definitions (glossary), 275–280
Demeter, 178
Demographic shifts on
      participation rates, 228
Deprivation. *See* Occupational
      deprivation
Descriptive questions, 35, 36
Descriptive studies, 36–37
Design and data collection
      methods, 35
Determinant of health, 201
Development. *See* Occupational
      development
Developmental coordination
      disorder (DCD), 43
Diary studies, 77
Dictionary of Occupational Titles, 11
Disabilities, 236–239
Disciplinary paradigms, 32
Disciplinary ways of knowing, 32

Displacement, 188–189
Distributive justice, 247–248
Diversity, 261
Divination, 162
Division of labor, 53, 54, 149
Division of Labor in Society, The
      (Durkheim), 53
Do What You Are, 99
Documentation, 146
Domestic violence, 186
Dreaming, 16
Drive theory, 126
Duhl, Len, 161
Durkheim, Emile, 53, 54, 144, 165

E

E.T., The Extraterrestrial, 186
Earth Summit, 158
Ecological models of adaptation, 23
Ecological niche, 151
Economic capital, 164
Electroenephalography, 124
Elias, Peter, 56
Embedded occupations, 4, 5
Embodied experience, 181
Employment, 164
Employment patterns, 226–229
Employment policies, 19
Empowerment, 213, 257–258
Enablement, 249, 259–260, 267
Enjoyment, 73
Environment, 203–204
Environmental factors, 17–19
Environmental press, 182
Environmentalism, 95
Epistemological positions, 31
Epistomologies, 32
Ergonomics, 182
Ethnographic studies, 37
Ethnography, 191
Etzioni, Amatai, 146
Exaptations, 153
Experience of Place, The (Hiss), 178
Experimental studies, 37
Explanatory questions, 35, 36
Exploratory theory of
      occupational justice, 248–262

F

Factors influencing what people
      do, 70–74
Fandom, 14

Farm, 179
Fatigue, 123
Field theory, 182
Finding out what people do, 75–77
Fishing, 14
Five factor theory, 130
Floundering communities, 166–167
Flourishing community, 154
Flow, 133
Folk taxonomies, 9
For whom, 73
Formal economy, 54
*Forms of Intellectual and Ethical
      Development in the College Years*
      (Perry), 31
Frankl, Victor, 200–201, 203
Free rider problem, 152
Free time, 66
Free time occupations, 66–67
Frieden, Betty, 9

G

Game theory, 154, 155
Gaming the system, 152
Gender
   epistemological perspectives, 31
   Japan, 58
   occupational development, 105
   sex-role stereotyping, 232–233
   work, 58–59
General ecological model, 102
General Social Surveys (GSS), 39
Genotype, 95
Geographic isolation, 224–225
Gesell, Arnold, 95
Gibson, J. J., 176
Glossary, 275–280
Goals, 127–129
Goffman, Erving, 67
Government statistics, 55–59
Great Depression, 21
Greek philosophers, 20
Greer, Germaine, 9
Gretzky, Wayne, 100
Grounded theory studies, 37
Group living. *See* Communities
GSS, 39

H

Habermas, Jürgen, 246
Habits, 4, 6
Habitus, 181

Hamilton, Toby Ballou, 173
Hancock, Trevor, 161
Haptic interfaces, 190
Harvey, Andrew S., 63
Havighurst, Robert J., 108
Health and happiness. *See* Well-being
Healthy communities movement, 160, 161
Healthy towns movement, 161
Heredity, 98–99
Hiss, Tony, 178
Historical Meanings of Work, The (Joyce), 33
History-making, 146
History of occupation, 19–22
Hmong refugees, 235
Hobbies, 14
Holland, John L., 14, 131, 132
Holland's theory of vocational choice, 131, 132
Home, 185–186
Homelessness, 188–189, 190
Homemaking, 9, 58–59
Homeostasis, 123
Homo Ludens (Huizinga), 12
Household and life maintenance, 15
Household time-allocation studies, 77
Huizinga, Johan, 12
Human brain, 149, 150
Human occupations, 9
Hummon, David, 178
Hunger, 125
Hunting and gathering societies, 19
Hutu refugees, 234

I

I Always Wanted to Be a Tap Dancer, 238
Idea generation, 150
Identity, 133–137
Ignatieff, Michael, 143
Imbalance in occupational participation, 203
Imbalance/overkill, 215
Imprisonment, 229–231
Incarceration, 229–231
Inclusion and shared advantage, 261

Industrial and technical communities, 158
Industrial Revolution, 21
Inequity of representation, 216
Information Age, 21
Insiders, 177
Interactionist view, 95–96
Interdependence, 145–146
Intergenerational occupation, 110
International Standard Classification of Occupations (ISCO), 12, 56
Internet
    chat rooms, 237
    virtual communities, 146
ISCO, 12, 56
ISCO-88, 56

J

Jarman, Jennifer, 47
Jefferson, Thomas, 29
Joints in Motion Training Team, 211
Just right challenge, 104
Justice. *See* Occupational justice

L

Landry, Jennifer E., 197, 211
Langford, Ruby, 224
Language, 148–151
Learned drive, 126
Learning, 99
Leisure, 13–15
Leisure-rich/leisure-poor, 257
Lewin, Kurt, 96, 182
Lewis, James, 99
Liberal arts hobbies, 14
Life as a journey, 178
Life projects, 69
Life stories, 137
Life-world, 180–181
Location, 72, 84
Locke, John, 95
Loss of place (displacement), 188–189
Loss of productivity/ disillusionment, 216
Lotz, Jim, 157
Lullabies, 184
Luther, Martin, 20

M

MacAulay, Scott, 156
MacLeod, Alistair, 142
Magic, 162
Main Street, 179
Male-female differences. *See* Gender
Market forces, 19
Marx, Karl, 254
Maslow, Abraham H., 126–127, 133–135
Maslow's theory of needs, 126–127
Mass-society, 165
Mastery, 107
Maturationists, 95
McAdams, Dan, 137
McClelland, David C., 130
Mead, George Herbert, 136
Mead, Margaret, 102
Meaning to life, 200–201
Meme, 149, 150
Memetics, 149
Memorial objects, 176
Mental illness, 238
Metacognition, 42
Methods of inquiry for study of occupation, 34–37
Mind in Society (Vygotsky), 103
Modes of understanding, 32
Morgenstern, Oskar, 154
Mother Goose Nursery Rhymes, 48
Motivation, 122–132
    achievement, 129–130
    five factor theory, 130
    goals, 127–129
    Holland's theory of vocational choice, 131, 132
    Maslow's theory of needs, 126–127
    personality, 130
    purposeful motivators, 125–126
    regulatory motivators, 123–125
Movement from place to place, 179–180
Multiple determinicity, 98
Multiple identities, 136
Multiple patternicity, 105–106
Multiple variation, 106–107
Multiplicity, 31
Murray, Henry, 182
Mutual dependence, 145

N

Narrative, 8
National census, 39
National Geographic, 42
National Occupational
  Classification (NOC), 11, 12
National Vocational Qualifications
  System (NVQS), 11, 12
Naturalistic paradigm, 33
Neanderthals, 151
Necessary occupations, 66
Necessary time, 66
Nested (embedded) occupations,
  4, 5
No Great Mischief (MacLeod), 142
NOC, 11, 12
NVQs, 11, 12

O

O*NET, 11
Observation, 76
Occupation
  defined, 2, 52
  historical overview, 19–22
Occupational alienation, 252
Occupational categories, 9
Occupational classification
  systems, 12
Occupational classifications, 9
Occupational deprivation,
  221–242
  defined, 222
  disabilities, 236–239
  employment patterns, 226–229
  geographic isolation, 224–225
  incarceration, 229–231
  occupational injustice, as, 252
  participation in occupation, 216
  refugeeism, 233–235
  sex-role stereotyping, 232–233
Occupational development,
  91–119
  active participation, 100
  ages/stages, 109–114
  changing mastery, 107–109
  continuity, 97
  defined, 96
  environment determinants,
    100–102
  environmentalist view, 95
  gender, 105

heredity, 98–99
interaction determinant,
  102–105
interactionist view, 95–96
learning/plasticity, 99–100
multiple determinicity, 98–105
multiple patternicity, 105–109
multiple variation, 106–107
occupational perspective on
  development, 93–96
person determinants, 98–100
preformationist view, 95
Occupational disruption, 223
Occupational form, 61
Occupational habits, 10
Occupational imbalance, 253
Occupational injustices, 251–253
Occupational justice, 243–273
  beliefs, 253–257
  choice, 260–261
  distributive justice, 247–248
  diversity, 261, 267
  early considerations, 244–246
  empowerment, 257–258
  enablement, 249, 259–260, 267
  exploratory theory, 248–262
  inclusion/shared advantage,
    261, 267
  inclusive classification of
    occupations, 259
  intersecting, 249–250
  occupational determinants, 251
  occupational forms, 251
  occupational injustices,
    251–253
  principles, 257–261
  social injustice, 246–248, 262
  stones, 262–266
  workshop participants' views,
    245–246
Occupational participation, 198.
  See also Participation in
  occupation
Occupational performance, 61
Occupational Perspective of Health,
  (Ann Wilcock), 257
Occupational rituals, 180
Occupational roles, 67–68
Occupational routines, 6
Occupational scaffolding, 51, 53
Occupational science, 34, 52

Occupational therapy, 49–53
Occupationally just world, 244
Occupationology, 34
OD = f (PoE), 96
Ontario Roundtable on
  Environment and Economy,
  158, 159
Ottawa Charter for Health
  Promotion, 257

P

Paid work, 11, 164
Pain, 124
Participation in occupation,
  197–220
  beliefs, 200–206
  choice and control, 203
  community animation, 217
  community participation,
    210–217
  determinant of health, 201
  empowerment, 213
  environment, 203–204
  imbalance, 203
  imbalance/overkill, 215
  individual participation, 206–210
  inequity of representation, 216
  loss of productivity/
    disillusionment, 216
  meaning in life, 200–201
  occupational deprivation, 216
  rhythm in life, 202
  sanctioned occupations, 205–206
  sense of accomplishment, 201
  sense of community, 212–213
  shared meaning and purpose,
    214–215
  source of conflict, 217
  technology, 204–205
  trust and respect, 214
Participatory research, 156
Pentland, Wendy, 63
Perry, William, 31
Persephone, 178–179
Person-environment, 23
Personal stories. *See* Vignettes
Personal well-being. *See* Well-being
Personality, 130
Personality type, 17
Pettifor, Susan, 167
Phenomenological studies, 37

Phenotype, 95, 96
Physical activity, 208
Physical characteristics of
    landscape, 17–18
Physical disabilities, 236–239
Physical status, 17
Physical zeitgebers, 71
Piaget, Jean, 12
Piercy, Marge, 228
Place, 173–196
    archetype, as, 175–176
    community, as, 186–188
    commuting, 179–180
    defined, 174
    dimensions of, 176–177
    displacement, 188–189
    geographic variations in
        occupation, 183–184
    home, 185–186
    influence of occupation,
        186–191
    influence on occupation,
        182–184
    life-world, 180–181
    meaning, 177–178
    movement from place to place,
        179–180
    physical influences on
        occupation, 182
    play, 184
    time, 178–179
    virtual, 189–191
    well-being, 191–193
Plasticity, 99
Plato, 13, 20
Play, 11–13, 185, 210
Polatajko, H. J., 29, 91
Polgar, Janice Miller, 197
Positive identities, 129
Positive interdependence, 145
Positive occupational
    experiences, 156
Positivistic paradigm, 33
Power, 258
Preformationist view, 94–95
Prehistoric cave paintings, 159
Presentation of Self in Everyday Life,
    The (Goffman), 67
Primary activities, 15
Primary activity, 71
Primary drives, 126

Primary resource
    communities, 158
Primeau, Loree, 51
Prisoner's dilemma, 154, 155
Prisons, 229–231
Procedural knowledge, 31
Productive time, 82
Psychological defense
    mechanisms, 134
Psychological factors, 17
Public transportation, 181
Purposeful motivators, 125–126
Purposive view of motivation, 125
Pye, Tracey, 60

Q

Qualitative designs, 35–36
Qualitative paradigm, 37
Qualitative research, 33
Quantitative designs, 35
Quantitative paradigm, 36–37
Quantitative research, 33
Questions of basic inquiry, 36
    how, 42–43
    what, 38–40
    when, 40–41
    where, 41–42
    who, 38
    why, 43–44

R

Rawls, John, 246
Reasonable accommodation, 238
Received knowledge, 31
Reciprocal altruism, 152
Reductionistic approach, 33
Refugee, 234
Refugeeism, 233–235
Regular physical activity, 208
Regulatory motivators, 123–125
Reinhold, K. L., 96
Relatedness, 135
Relativism, 31
Relativism subordinate, 31
Religion, 162
REM sleep, 15
Restriction of personal
    freedom, 206
Rhythm in life, 202
Rituals, 158
Roman philosophers, 20

Routines, 4, 6
Rowles, Graham, 187
Rubin, I., 144–145
Rubin's structural characteristics
    of communities, 145
Running for charity, 211
Ryan, Richard, 134

S

Sanctioned occupations, 205–206
Satisfaction, 73
Scaffolded play, 51
Scaffolding, 103
School, 183
Science, 162
Secondary activities, 15, 72, 83–87
Secondary drives, 126
Segregation, 206
Self, 135–137
Self-actualization, 134
Self-confidence, 208–209
Self-determination theory, 134–135
Self-efficacy, 129
Self-identity, 17
Self-report time log, 40
Selfish Gene, The (Dawkins), 150
Semiotics, 178
Sense of accomplishment, 201
Sense of community, 146, 212–213
Sense of identity, 209
Sense of place, 174. *See also* Place
Serious leisure, 13
Sex-role stereotyping, 232–233
Shared advantage, 261
Shared meaning and purpose,
    214–215
Shared occupations. *See*
    Communities
Sigerist, H. E., 49
Silence, 31
Single-industry towns, 215
Sleep, 15–16
Sleep disorders, 16
Smith, Tara, 246
Social advantage, 55
Social capital, 165–166
Social class, 55
Social contact, 72
Social determined occupational
    forms, 251
Social environments, 85–86, 210

Social expectations, 18
Social factors, 19
Social geography, 191
Social goal categories, 10
Social grooming, 149
Social impact, 182
Social inclusion, 261
Social isolation, 125
Social justice, 246–248, 262, 266
Social sciences, 53–55
Social zeitgebers, 71
Socially constructed meaning, 177
Socially unsanctioned behavior, 205, 206
Sociobiology, 151
Socrates, 20
Spiritual dimension of occupations, 8
Spit bath, 184
Springer, James, 99
Statistics Canada, 39
Stein, Janice Gross, 261
Stigma, 205–206
Stir crazy, 230
Stories. *See* Vignettes
Structural disorder, 148
Study designs, 37
Stylized questioning, 76
Subcultures, 18
Subjective knowledge, 31
Suboccupation, 50, 53
Supernatural, 162
Sustainable communities, 158–161
Symbolic interactionism, 136

T

Tabula rosa, 95
Talmud, 20
Tasks, 64
Tattersall, Ian, 151
Taxonomies, 9
Technology, 73, 86–87, 204–205

Tele-immersion, 191
Tension, 73
Terry Waite Taken on Trust, 38
Theory of Justice, A (Rawls), 246
Time, 72
Time-space diaries, 72
Time use across countries, 78–80
Time use across sub-populations, 81–83
Time-use diary, 77
Time use studies, 76
Tonnies, Ferdinand, 165
Toohey, Paul, 225
Townsend, Elizabeth, 1, 60, 141, 243
Traits, 130
Transportation, 180, 181
Trust and respect, 214

U

U.S. Census Bureau, 39
Unemployment, 226–227
Unsanctioned activities, 206

V

Van der Post, Sir Laurens, 63
VDTs, 19
Vicious cycle, 133
Victor ("wild boy" of Aveyron), 101
Video display terminals (VDTs), 19
Vignettes
  German concentration camp, 200–201
  Meg (mental illness), 238
  occupational justice, 262–266
  Ruby (camp-outback Queensland), 224–225
  running for charity, 211
  Sam (active participant), 207
  Victor ("wild boy" of Aveyron), 101

Virtual communities, 143, 146
Virtual kitchen, 191
Virtual places, 189–191
Virtual reality, 190, 191
Volunteer occupations, 163–164
von Neumann, John, 154
Vygotsky, Lev, 102, 103

W

Walby, Sylvia, 57
Walking the dog, 180
Ways of knowing, 30–34
Weber, Max, 165
Weddings, 163
Well-being
  occupations, 22–23
  physical activity, 208
  place, 191–193
  psychological aspects, 208–209
White, Robert, 129
Whiteford, Gail, 221
Why study what people do?, 74–75
Wilcock, Ann, 222, 225, 232, 243
With whom, 72, 85
Women. *See* Gender
Work, 164
Working (Terkel), 33
Works of art, 176
Works Progress Administration (WPA), 21

Y

Yerxa, Elizabeth, 34
Young, Iris Morton, 247–248, 258

Z

Zeitgebers, 71
Zone of proximal development, 103